AF780276

New Trends in Mathematical Modeling, Analysis and Optimization for Engineering and Mechanics

New Trends in Mathematical Modeling, Analysis and Optimization for Engineering and Mechanics

Guest Editors

Pedro Navas
Bo Li

MDPI

Basel • Beijing • Wuhan • Barcelona • Belgrade • Novi Sad • Cluj • Manchester

Guest Editors
Pedro Navas
Department of Continuum Mechanics and Theory of Structures
Universidad Politécnica de Madrid
Madrid
Spain

Bo Li
College of Engineering
Peking University
Beijing
China

Editorial Office
MDPI AG
Grosspeteranlage 5
4052 Basel, Switzerland

This is a reprint of the Special Issue, published open access by the journal *Mathematics* (ISSN 2227-7390), freely accessible at: https://www.mdpi.com/si/mathematics/Math_Modeling_Anal_Optim_Eng_Mech.

For citation purposes, cite each article independently as indicated on the article page online and as indicated below:

Lastname, A.A.; Lastname, B.B. Article Title. *Journal Name* **Year**, *Volume Number*, Page Range.

ISBN 978-3-7258-4705-1 (Hbk)
ISBN 978-3-7258-4706-8 (PDF)
https://doi.org/10.3390/books978-3-7258-4706-8

© 2025 by the authors. Articles in this book are Open Access and distributed under the Creative Commons Attribution (CC BY) license. The book as a whole is distributed by MDPI under the terms and conditions of the Creative Commons Attribution-NonCommercial-NoDerivs (CC BY-NC-ND) license (https://creativecommons.org/licenses/by-nc-nd/4.0/).

Contents

About the Editors

Pedro Navas

Pedro Navas is an Associate Professor at the Department of Continuum Mechanics, Civil Engineering School, Polytechnic University of Madrid (UPM), Spain, where he also serves as the Director of the Department of Continuum Mechanics and Theory of Structures. He obtained his Ph.D. from Universidad de Castilla-La Mancha (UCLM) in 2017. His research focuses on computational solid dynamics, mathematical modeling, and geotechnical engineering, with an emphasis on mesh-free methods for solving complex dynamic problems in civil engineering. His current project, "Meshfree Modeling of Dynamic Problems in Civil Engineering," involves advanced computational techniques, such as the Material Point Method (MPM), Optimal Transportation Meshfree (OTM), and Particle Finite Element Method (PFEM).

Bo Li

Bo Li is currently a tenured Associate Professor at the College of Engineering of Peking University (since 2022). Prior to this, he was a tenured Associate Professor (2020–2022) and, earlier, an Assistant Professor (2013–2020) in the Department of Mechanical and Aerospace Engineering at Case Western Reserve University (CWRU), USA. From 2009 to 2013, he worked as a Research Scientist at Caltech's Graduate Aerospace Laboratories and the Powell-Booth Computational Science Laboratory, following the completion of his Ph.D. in Aeronautics at Caltech in 2009. His research spans computational mechanics and materials science, with expertise in: (1) Dynamic material behavior under extreme conditions; (2) Multiphysics and multiscale material modeling; (3) Mesh-free methods and computational fracture mechanics; (4) Additive manufacturing; (5) High-performance CAE software development.

mathematics

MDPI

Article

On the Solution of Dynamic Stability Problem of Functionally Graded Viscoelastic Plates with Different Initial Conditions in Viscoelastic Media

Abdullah Sofiyev [1,2]

1 Department of Mathematics, Faculty of Humanities and Social Sciences, Istanbul Ticaret University, Beyoglu, Istanbul 34445, Turkey; aavey@ticaret.edu.tr
2 Scientific Research Centers for Composition Materials of UNEC, Azerbaijan State Economics University, 1001 Baku, Azerbaijan

Abstract: The widespread use of structural elements consisting of functionally graded (FG) materials in advanced technologies has led to extensive research. Due to the difficulties encountered during modeling and problem solving, the number of studies on the dynamic behavior of structural elements made of FG viscoelastic materials is quite limited compared to the number examining FG elastic materials. This study is one of the first attempts to solve the dynamical problem by the mathematical modeling of functionally graded viscoelastic plates (FG-VE-Ps) and viscoelastic media together with different initial conditions. FG-VE-Ps on viscoelastic foundations (VE-Fs) are assumed to be under compressive edge load in the longitudinal direction. The governing equations for FG-VE-Ps on VE-Fs are derived using Boltzmann and Volterra concepts. The problem is reduced to the solution of integro-differential equation system using the Galerkin method. Then, by performing Laplace transforms, new analytical expressions for the time-dependent deflection function and critical time at different initial conditions are found. The loss of stability of FG-VE-Ps on VE-Fs is modeled to cover three time-varying ranges: the first is the range in which the deflection function decreases; the second is the transition interval; the third is the increase range of deflection function, which leads to the loss of stability. The time corresponding to the sharp increase of the deflection function is defined as the critical time, and is determined both theoretically and numerically. The results are compared with the results obtained by various methods to confirm their accuracy. Finally, the effects of VE-Fs, VE material properties, and FG profiles on the critical time behavior of plates are studied numerically.

Keywords: dynamical problem; FG viscoelastic plates; viscoelastic foundation; buckling; critical time

MSC: 74Hxx; 74H55; 74K20; 74Dxx

1. Introduction

The widespread use of composite materials leads to the need to consider the viscoelastic properties specific to composites with polymers. General questions of the theory of viscoelasticity are considered in the fundamental works [1–3], including the constructions of hereditary relations between stresses and strains, the reciprocity of such relations, methods of analyzing the kernels of creep and relaxation, and methods for solving static and dynamical problems. The applied problems of the theory of viscoelasticity, including the construction of continuous and discrete models of homogeneous viscoelastic plates, are considered in [4–15].

A new class of advanced heterogeneous materials, which are called FGMs, have great potential in many areas of technology. The study of the behavior of FGM structural elements under various conditions is very important for the development of mechanical engineering and aircraft construction. The field of missile technology is also interested in intensive research of this class of problems [16,17]. In most studies, although FGMs are used as elastic materials, their time-dependent behavior should be modeled to fully reveal their potential. In recent years, there have been some remarkable initiatives for the creation and application of the viscoelasticity theory of FGMs [18,19]. Some attempts have been made to examine the static and dynamic behavior of FG-VE structural elements in the past few years [20–25].

An important problem in many branches of technology is to increase the reliability and extend the service life of composite structures that interact with viscoelastic foundations. Fundamental results in the theory of viscoelastic foundations are described in [26,27]. The review of the literature shows that there are mainly studies of the behavior of homogeneous viscoelastic structural elements on VE-Fs. Pouresmaeeli et al. [28] analyzed the vibration behavior of VE orthotropic nanoplates on VE-Fs. Karlicic et al. [29] studied the transverse vibration of a nonlocal VE-orthotropic multi-nanoplate system embedded in VE medium. Zhang et al. [30] presented a vibration analysis of VE single-walled carbon nanotubes resting on VE-Fs. Zamani et al. [31] examined the free vibration of thick VE-Ps on visco-Pasternak foundations (V-PFs) using higher-order theory. Zeighampour et al. [32] examined wave propagation in a VE thin nanoshell resting on V-PFs based on nonlocal strain gradient theory. Zenkour and Sobhy [33] studied the nonlocal piezo-hygrothermal analysis of the vibration characteristics of a piezoelectric Kelvin–Voigt VE nanoplate embedded in VE medium. Sophy and Zenkour [34] examined the modified couple stress model for the bending of normal deformable VE nanobeams resting on visco-Pasternak foundations. Sobhy and Radwan [35] studied the influence of a 2D magnetic field on the hygrothermal bending of sandwich CNT-reinforced microplates with VE core embedded in VE medium. Frahlia et al. [36] examined the vibration response of a functionally graded plate resting on a viscoelastic foundation. Alazwari and Zenkour [37] developed a quasi-3D refined theory for the linear vibration of functionally graded plates resting on visco-Winkler-Pasternak foundations.

The recent emergence of new-generation functionally graded viscoelastic materials and the introduction of their structural elements, which are often used in viscoelastic media, require the study of their dynamical problems. Zenkour et al. [38] presented a bending analysis of FG-VE beams resting on Pasternak elastic foundations. Shariyat and Alipor [39] analyzed the damping effect on the behavior of FG-VE-Ps on elastic foundations with variable thickness. Liu et al. [40] investigated the vibration of FG-VE magneto-electro porous nanobeams on V-PFs. Sofiyev et al. [41] examined the stability behavior of heterogeneous viscoelastic plates resting on two-parameter elastic foundations. Zenkour and El-Shahrany [42] presented the active control of a sandwich plate with reinforced magnetostrictive faces and a viscoelastic core resting on an elastic foundation. Li et al. [43] investigated the vibration behavior of a fiber-reinforced polymer composite plate with viscoelastic damping boundary conditions resting on a viscoelastic foundation. Yuan et al. [44] presented a magneto-hygro-thermal vibration analysis of viscoelastic nanobeams reinforced with carbon nanotubes resting on Kerr elastic foundations.

To the author's knowledge, the dynamic buckling and vibrational behavior of functionally graded viscoelastic plates on a viscoelastic foundation have not yet been analytically reported due to difficulties in modeling and problem solving. The novelty of the present work is the proposal of an analytical solution for the dynamical problem under various initial conditions of a functionally graded plate and soil having viscoelastic property in contact with each other. The rest of this paper is structured as follows: in Section 2, the basic relations and equations are derived after modelling of the material and soil properties; in Section 3, the solution of the problem under various initial conditions is presented by applying the Galerkin and Laplace methods; Section 4 consists of comparisons and an original numerical analysis; Section 5 summarizes conclusions.

2. Mathematical Modeling of the Problem

2.1. Basic Relationships

An FG-VE plate with length a, width b and thickness h on a VE-F and the coordinate system in the midplane is shown in Figure 1. It is subjected to compressive edge load, N, in the x direction and is resting on the VE-F. Displacement w is in the positive direction of the z axis, and is assumed to be quite small compared to the thickness. It is also assumed that the normal stresses acting on the midplane are negligible compared to other forces.

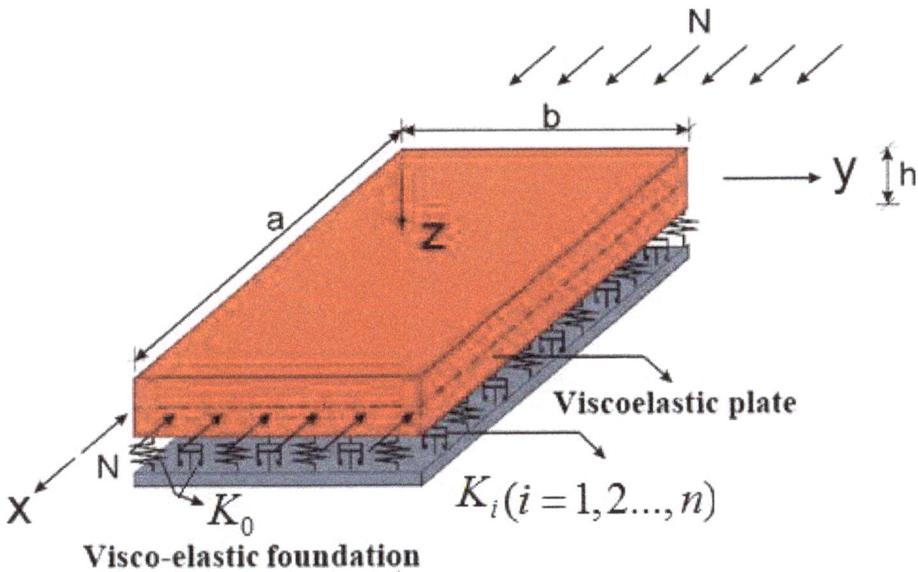

Figure 1. FG-VE plate subjected to compressive edge load N in the x direction, and resting on a VE-F.

The effective FGM properties change exponentially depending on the thickness coordinate [16]:

$$E^f = E^m e^{(\frac{z+0.5h}{h})\ln(\frac{E^c}{E^m})},\ \ \nu^f = \nu^m e^{(\frac{z+0.5h}{h})\ln(\frac{\nu^c}{\nu^m})},\ \ \rho^f = \rho^m e^{(\frac{z+0.5h}{h})\ln(\frac{\rho^c}{\rho^m})} \tag{1}$$

where the Young moduli of metal and ceramic surfaces of FGM are shown with E^m and E^c, Poisson ratios with ν^m and ν^c, and the densities with ρ^m and ρ^c.

The viscoelastic foundations are modelled as [27,35]:

$$K(w,t) = K_0 w + K_1\frac{\partial w}{\partial t} + \ldots + K_{n-1}\frac{\partial^{n-1} w}{\partial t^{n-1}} + K_n\frac{\partial^n w}{\partial t^n} \tag{2}$$

in which K_i, $(i = 0,1,\ldots,n)$ are constants for the VE-Fs and can be obtained from the experiments.

If the relaxation core of the integral operator is denoted as $R(t-\tau)$, the constitutive equations of FG-VE-Ps in the framework of the Boltzmann–Volterra principle are modeled as follows [1,5,41]:

$$\tau_{11} = \frac{E^f}{1-(\nu^f)^2}\left[\varepsilon_{11} + \nu^f\varepsilon_{22} - \int_0^t R(t-\tau)\left(\varepsilon_{11} + \nu^f\varepsilon_{22}\right)d\tau\right],$$
$$\tau_{22} = \frac{E^f}{1-(\nu^f)^2}\left[\varepsilon_{22} + \nu^f\varepsilon_{11} - \int_0^t R(t-\tau)\left(\varepsilon_{22} + \nu^f\varepsilon_{11}\right)d\tau\right], \quad (3)$$
$$\tau_{12} = \frac{E^f}{2(1+\nu^f)}\left[\gamma_{12} - \int_0^t R(t-\tau)\gamma_{12}d\tau\right]$$

The forces and moments are found from the following integrals [1]:

$$[(N_{11}, N_{12}, N_{22}), (M_{11}, M_{12}, M_{22})] = \int_{-h/2}^{h/2} (1, z)(\tau_{11}, \tau_{12}, \tau_{22})dz \quad (4)$$

The relationships between Airy stress function (F) and forces are formed as follows [1,23,24]:

$$(N_{11}, N_{12}, N_{22}) = (hF_{,yy}, -hF_{,xy}, hF_{,xx}) \quad (5)$$

2.2. Governing Equations

Using the relations of (3)–(5), the force and moment components are expressed by the functions of w and F, then these expressions and relation (2) are taken into account in the basic equations, the following system of integro-differential equations for dynamic stability and compatibility equations of FG-VE-Ps on VE-Fs is obtained:

$$L_{11}F(x,y,t) + (L_{12} + L_{13})w(x,y,t) - \int_0^t [L_{11}F(x,y,\tau) + L_{12}w(x,y,\tau)]R(t-\tau)d\tau = 0$$
$$L_{21}F(x,y,t) + L_{22}w(x,y,t) - \int_0^t [L_{21}F(x,y,\tau) + L_{22}w(x,y,\tau)]R(t-\tau)d\tau = 0 \quad (6)$$

where $L_{ij}(i = 1,2, j = 1,2,3)$ are expressed as:

$$L_{11} = hq_2\frac{\partial^4}{\partial x^4} + 2h(q_1 - q_5)\frac{\partial^4}{\partial x^2\partial y^2} + hq_2\frac{\partial^4}{\partial y^4}$$
$$L_{12} = -q_3\frac{\partial^4}{\partial x^4} - 2(q_4 + q_6)\frac{\partial^4}{\partial x^2\partial y^2} - q_4\frac{\partial^4}{\partial y^4}$$
$$L_{13} = -N\frac{\partial^2}{\partial x^2} - K_0 - K_1\frac{\partial}{\partial t} - K_2\frac{\partial^2}{\partial t^2} - \overline{\rho}^f\frac{\partial^2}{\partial t^2} \quad (7)$$
$$L_{21} = hp_1\frac{\partial^4}{\partial x^4} + h(2p_2 + p_5)\frac{\partial^4}{\partial x^2\partial y^2} + hp_1\frac{\partial^4}{\partial y^4}$$
$$L_{22} = -p_4\frac{\partial^4}{\partial x^4} - (2p_3 - p_6)\frac{\partial^4}{\partial x^2\partial y^2} - p_4\frac{\partial^4}{\partial y^4}$$

in which

$$q_1 = e_1^1p_1 + e_2^1p_2,\ q_2 = e_1^1p_2 + e_2^1p_1,\ q_3 = e_1^1p_3 + e_2^1p_4 + e_1^2,\ q_4 = e_1^1p_4 + e_2^1p_3 + e_2^2,\ q_5 = e_6^1p_5,\ q_6 = e_6^1p_6 + 2e_6^2,$$
$$p_1 = \frac{e_1^0}{\eta},\ p_2 = -\frac{e_2^0}{\eta},\ p_3 = \frac{e_2^0e_1^1 - e_1^1e_1^0}{\eta},\ p_4 = \frac{e_2^0e_1^1 - e_2^1e_1^0}{\eta},\ p_5 = \frac{1}{e_6^0}, p_6 = -\frac{2e_6^1}{e_6^0},\ \eta = (e_1^0)^2 - (e_2^0)^2, \quad (8)$$
$$e_1^k = \int_{-h/2}^{h/2}\frac{E^f}{1-(\nu^f)^2}z^kdz,\ e_2^k = \int_{-h/2}^{h/2}\frac{\nu^fE^f}{1-(\nu^f)^2}z^kdz,\ e_6^k = \int_{-h/2}^{h/2}\frac{E^f}{2(1+\nu^f)}z^kdz,\ k = 0,\ 1,\ 2.$$

It should be emphasized that in the viscoelastic foundation model, higher-order derivatives than the 2nd-order derivative have little effect on the behavior of the plate, so they can be neglected and those terms are not taken into account in the next steps. Therefore, $K(w,t) = K_0 w + K_1 \frac{\partial w}{\partial t} + K_2 \frac{\partial^2 w}{\partial t^2}$ is used in the basic equations instead of Equation (2).

3. Solution Procedure

Assuming that the edges of an FG-VE plate on a VE-F are simply supported, the solution of the basic equations is sought as follows [1,5,41]:

$$w = w_1(t)\sin(\overline{m}x)\cos(\overline{n}y), \;\; F = F_1(t)\sin(\overline{m}x)\cos(\overline{n}y) \tag{9}$$

where $w_1(t)$ and $F_1(t)$ are the functions depending on the time, $(\overline{m}, \overline{n}) = \left(\frac{m}{a}, \frac{n}{b}\right)\pi$, where m and n are the modes.

Substituting (9) into the set of Equation (6), performing the Galerkin procedure and removing $F_1(t)$ from the system, the following integro-differential equation is obtained:

$$\left(\overline{\rho}^f + K_2\right)\frac{d^2 w_1(t)}{dt^2} + K_1\frac{dw_1(t)}{dt} + \left[Q + K_0 - N\overline{m}^2\right]w_1(t) - Q\int\limits_0^t R(t-\tau)w_1(\tau)d\tau = 0 \tag{10}$$

where

$$\begin{aligned} Q &= q_3\overline{m}^4 + 2(q_4+q_6)\overline{m}^2\overline{n}^2 + q_3\overline{n}^4 - \frac{\left[q_2\overline{m}^4 + 2(q_1-q_5)\overline{m}^2\overline{n}^2 + q_2\overline{n}^4\right]}{p_1\overline{m}^4 + (2p_2+p_5)\overline{m}^2\overline{n}^2 + p_1\overline{n}^4}\left[p_4\overline{m}^4 + (2p_3-p_6)\overline{m}^2\overline{n}^2 + p_4\overline{n}^4\right] \\ \overline{\rho}^f &= \int\limits_{-h/2}^{h/2} \rho^f dz \end{aligned} \tag{11}$$

The following initial conditions (ICs) are taken into account:

$$w_1(0) \neq 0, \; w'_1(0) \neq 0, \;\; \text{at } t = 0 \tag{12}$$

By using the Laplace transform in Equation (10) for the ICs in (12), the following equation is obtained in the images:

$$W_1(s_1) = \frac{(1+s_1)\left[(s_1+\widetilde{K}_{11})w_{10} + w_{11}\right]}{s_1^3 + (1+\widetilde{K}_{11})s_1^2 + r_1(1-p^{VF})s_1 - r_1(p^{VF}-q^{VF})} \tag{13}$$

where $R(t-\tau) = \gamma\, e^{-\gamma(t-\tau)}$ $(0 < \gamma < 1)$, $W_1(s) = \int\limits_0^\infty w_1(t)e^{-st}dt$, $s = s_1\gamma$, in which $W_1(s)$ is the Laplace transformation of the original function $w_1(t)$, γ denotes the viscoelasticity parameter, s is the variable, and the following symbols are used [1]:

$$\begin{aligned} & w_{10} = \frac{w_1(0)}{\gamma}, \; w_{11} = \frac{w'_1(0)}{\gamma^2}, \; r_1 = \frac{r}{\gamma^2}, \; \widetilde{K}_{11} = \frac{\widetilde{K}_1}{\gamma}, \; p^{VF} = \frac{N}{N_{cr}^{VF}}, \; q^{VF} = \frac{K_0}{\overline{m}^2 N_{cr}^{VF}}, \\ & r = \frac{\overline{m}^2 N_{cr}^{VF}}{\overline{\rho}^f + K_2} = \left(\omega^{VF}\right)^2, \; \widetilde{K}_1 = \frac{K_1}{K_2+\overline{\rho}^f}, \; N_{cr}^{VF} = \frac{Q+K_0+\gamma K_1}{\overline{m}^2} \end{aligned} \tag{14}$$

Since $p^{VF} > q^{VF}$ and $r_1 >> 1$, one of the positive values that converts the denominator of Equation (13) to zero is indicated by u_0^{VF}, and the other two roots are easily found as follows:

$$u_{2,3} = -\frac{1+\widetilde{K}_{11}+u_0^{VF}}{2} \pm i\Lambda \tag{15}$$

where

$$u_0^{VF} = \frac{r_1(p^{VF}-q^{VF})}{r_1(1-p^{VF}) + u_0^{VF}(1+\widetilde{K}_{11}+u_0^{VF})}, \;\; \Lambda = \sqrt{r_2^{VF} - 0.25\left(1+\widetilde{K}_{11}-u_0^{VF}\right)^2} \tag{16}$$

in which

$$r_2^{VF} = \left(u_0^{VF}\right)^2 + r_1(1 - p^{VF}) \text{ and } r_2^{VF} - 0.25\left(1 + \widetilde{K}_{11} - u_0^{VF}\right)^2 > 0$$

When the following symbols are replaced in Equation (13),

$$B_1 = \frac{1 + \widetilde{K}_{11} + u_0^{VF}}{2},\ B_2 = \frac{1 + \widetilde{K}_{11} - u_0^{VF}}{2},\ B_3 = \widetilde{K}_{11}, A = \frac{1 + \widetilde{K}_{11} + 3u_0^{VF}}{2}, s_2 = s_1 + \frac{1 + \widetilde{K}_{11} + u_0^{VF}}{2} \quad (17)$$

after some mathematical operations, it takes the following standard form:

$$\begin{aligned} W_1(s_2) &= \frac{[A(B_2 - B_1) + A^2 - B_1B_2 + B_3]w_{10} + (A + B_2)w_{11}}{A^2 + \Lambda^2} \frac{1}{s_2 - A} \\ &+ \frac{[\Lambda^2 - A(B_2 - B_1) + B_1B_2 + B_3]w_{10} - (A + B_2)w_{11}}{A^2 + \Lambda^2} \frac{s_2}{s_2^2 + \Lambda^2} \\ &+ \frac{[A + (B_2 - B_1)]\Lambda^2 w_{10} + A(B_1B_2 - B_3)w_{10} - A(\Lambda^2 - AB_2)w_{11}}{A^2 + \Lambda^2} \frac{\Lambda}{s_2^2 + \Lambda^2} \frac{1}{\Lambda} \end{aligned} \quad (18)$$

By using the inverse Laplace transform, the original function of $W_1(s_2)$ from Equation (18) turns into the following form:

$$\overline{w}_1(t_1) = (d_1 + d_4)e^{u_0^{VF}t_1} + [(d_2 + d_5)\cos(\Lambda t_1) + (d_3 + d_6)\sin(\Lambda t_1)]e^{-\frac{1+\widetilde{K}_{11}+u_0^{VF}}{2}t_1} \quad (19)$$

where

$$\begin{aligned} d_1 &= \frac{[A(B_2 - B_1) + A^2 - B_1B_2 + B_3]w_{10}}{A^2 + \Lambda^2},\ d_2 = \frac{[\Lambda^2 - A(B_2 - B_1) + B_1B_2 + B_3]w_{10}}{A^2 + \Lambda^2}, \\ d_3 &= \frac{[A\Lambda^2 + \Lambda^2(B_2 - B_1) + A(B_1B_2 - B_3]w_{10}}{A^2 + \Lambda^2}\frac{1}{\Lambda},\ d_4 = \frac{A + B_2}{A^2 + \Lambda^2}w_{11}, \\ d_5 &= -\frac{A + B_2}{A^2 + \Lambda^2}w_{11},\ d_6 = \frac{\Lambda^2 - AB_2}{A^2 + \Lambda^2}\frac{w_{11}}{\Lambda} \end{aligned} \quad (20)$$

The loss of stability of FG-VE-Ps is a time-dependent process that develops over time. This process covers three ranges: the first is the range of decreasing the deflection function; the second is the transition interval; the third is the range of the deflection function, which leads to the loss of stability. The time corresponding to a sharp increase of the deflection function is defined as the critical time, and, in this study, it is determined both theoretically and numerically.

(a) In the particular case, as $w_1(0) \neq 0,\ w'_1(0) = 0$ or the first initial condition (FIC) and $r_2^{VF} >> 1$ are satisfied, $d_4 = d_5 = d_6 = 0,\ \ d_3 << d_2$, (19) is transformed as:

$$\overline{w}_{11}(t_1) = d_{11}e^{u_0^{VF}t_1} + d_{12}e^{-\frac{1+\widetilde{K}_{11}+u_0^{VF}}{2}t_1} \quad (21)$$

where

$$d_{11} = \frac{A(B_2 - B_1) + A^2 - B_1B_2 + B_3}{A^2 + \Lambda^2},\ d_{12} = \frac{\Lambda^2 - A(B_2 - B_1) + B_1B_2 + B_3}{A^2 + \Lambda^2},\ \overline{w}_{11}(t_1) = \frac{w_1(t_1)}{w_{10}} \quad (22)$$

The critical time of FG-VE-Ps on VE-Fs is found from the solution of $\overline{w'}_{11}(t_1) = 0$ as follows:

$$t_{11cr}^{VF} = \frac{2}{1 + \widetilde{K}_{11} + 3u_0^{VF}} \ln\left[\frac{1 + \widetilde{K}_{11} + u_0^{VF}}{2u_0^{VF}}\frac{d_{12}}{d_{11}}\right] \quad (23)$$

(b) In the particular case, as $w_1(0) = 0,\ w'_1(0) \neq 0$ or second initial conditions (SICs) and $r_2^{VF} >> 1$ are satisfied, $d_1 = d_2 = d_3 = 0,\ \ d_5 << d_6$, Equation (19) turns into the following form:

$$\overline{w}_{12}(t_1) = d_{14}e^{u_0^{VF}t_1} + d_{16}e^{-\frac{1+u_0^{VF}}{2}t_1} \tag{24}$$

where

$$d_{14} = \frac{A + B_2}{A^2 + \Lambda^2},\ d_{16} = \frac{\Lambda^2 - AB_2}{A^2 + \Lambda^2}\frac{1}{\Lambda},\ \overline{w}_{12}(t_1) = \frac{w_1(t_1)}{w_{11}} \tag{25}$$

The critical time of FG-VE-Ps on VE-Fs is defined as:

$$t_{12cr}^{VF} = \frac{2}{1 + \widetilde{K}_{11} + 3u_0^{VF}} ln\left[\frac{1 + \widetilde{K}_{11} + u_0^{VF}}{2u_0^{VF}}\frac{d_{16}}{d_{14}}\right] \tag{26}$$

In particular, at $N = 0$, Equation (19) is converted to the equation for the deflection function of the vibration of FG-VE-Ps on VE-Fs. Equations (23) and (26) are converted to the formulas for unconstrained FG-VE-Ps, with $K_i = 0\ \ (i = 0, 1, 2)$.

4. Numerical Analysis

To demonstrate the accuracy of the analytical expressions obtained in this study, our results are compared with the results of [4], which solves the free vibration problem of homogeneous isotropic VE shells without VE-Fs using the average method. In the current study, at $N = 0$, the first equation of the system (10) becomes the motion equation, and Equation (19) becomes the vibration equation of the FG-VE-Ps. The comparison is made for the following initial conditions: $w_1(0) \neq 0,\ w'_1(0) = 0$ or FIC. For comparison, the obtained Equation (26) for the vibration of homogenous isotropic VE shells is converted to the formula for the vibration of homogeneous isotropic VE-Ps (taking into account that $b = \pi R$). In our study, the influences of the compressive load and VE-Fs are ignored, and calculations are made by converting FGM into the homogeneous material ($V_c = 0$). The following data are used in the comparison:$a = 40h,\ \ b = 0.4a,\ \ E^m = 2.05098 \times 10^5(\text{Mpa}),\ \rho^m = 8.9 \times 10^3\ \text{kg/m}^3,\ \nu^m = 0.3262,\ n = 4, w_{10} = 10^{-3}$ and $\gamma = 0.05$. As can be seen from Figure 2, the results of our study are in harmony with the results of [4].

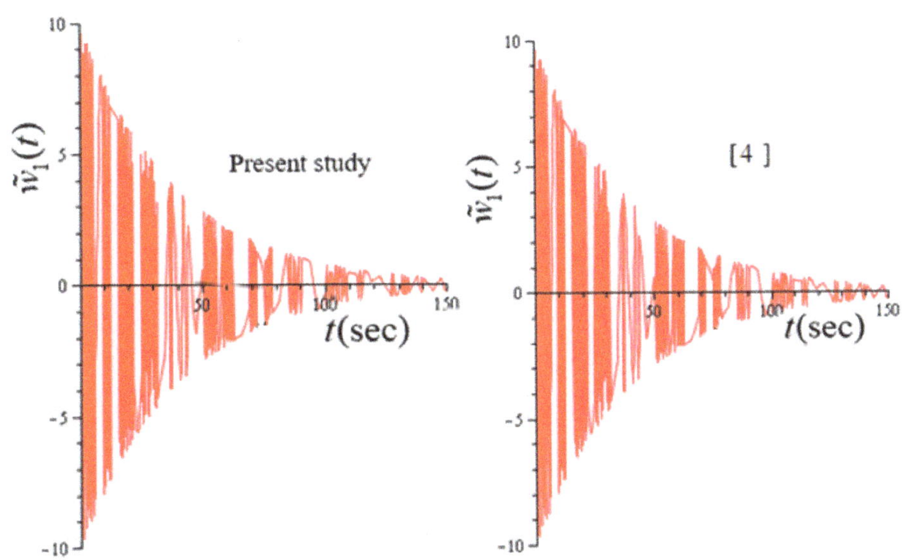

Figure 2. Comparison of our results for homogeneous isotropic VE-Ps with the results of [4].

In the next step, the specific numerical analyses are presented for the CTs of FG-VE-Ps resting on VE-Fs. The FGM consists of a mixture of silicon nitride (Si_3N_4) and Ni (Ni), and its properties are as follows [16]: $E^c = 3.22271 \times 10^5(\text{Mpa})$, $E^m = 2.05098 \times 10^5(\text{Mpa})$, $\nu^c = 0.24$, $\nu^m = 0.31$, $\rho^c = 2370\ \text{kg/m}^3$, $\rho^m = 8900\ \text{kg/m}^3$, where the above properties are calculated at room temperature, that is, for $T = 300$ K [16]. The viscoelastic parameter is $\gamma = 1/2$, and initial conditions are $w_1(0) \neq 0$, $w'_1(0) = 0$ and $w_1(0) = 0$, $w'_1(0) \neq 0$. In the tables and graphics created for the analysis, the width-to-length and the height-to-thickness ratios of VE plates, as well as the soil coefficients, are varied. The numbers of transverse and longitudinal modes corresponding to the critical times are obtained as $(m, n) = (1, 1)$ in all tables and graphs.

In Figures 3 and 4, the time-dependent change of $\overline{w}_1(t_1)$ is calculated numerically using the Maple program for Equation (19) to verify the accuracy of Equations (23) and (26), where the critical time values are obtained. In numerical calculations, the following data are used: $a = 50h$, $a = 2b$, $\gamma = 0.5$, $p^{VF} = 0.7$, $K_0 = 4.2 \times 10^7(\text{N/m}^3)$, $K_1 = 10\ (\text{N} \times \text{sec}/\text{m}^3)$ and $K_2 = 5\ (\text{N} \times \text{sec}^2/\text{m}^3)$ [1,3–5,27,33,41]. The units for the VE-Fs are also valid for the subsequent tables and figures. These calculations use FG-VE-Ps consisting of the mixture of materials presented above. The time-dependent variation of $\overline{w}_1(t_1)$ of FG-VE-Ps on VE-Fs according to Equation (19), and the critical time corresponding to the moment of increasing $\overline{w}_1(t_1)$ for the initial conditions $w_1(0) \neq 0$, $w'_1(0) = 0$ and $w_1(0) = 0$, $w'_1(0) \neq 0$, respectively, are presented in Figures 3 and 4. The moment when $\overline{w}_1(t_1)$ begins to increase is defined as the critical time. When the abovementioned data are used in Equations (23) and (26), the following values are obtained for the critical time: $t^{VF}_{11cr} = 3.6733$ and $t^{VF}_{12cr} = 1.755$, respectively. In Figures 3 and 4, the critical times corresponding to an increase in $\overline{w}_1(t_1)$ maintain the accuracy of the critical times obtained by Equations (23) and (26).

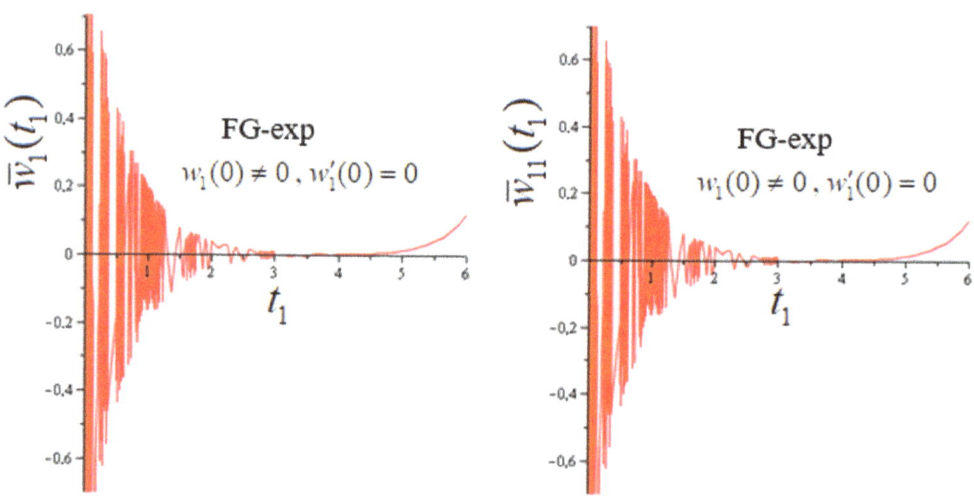

Figure 3. Variation of the deflection function of FG-VE-Ps on VE-Fs according to Equation (19) for the initial conditions $w_1(0) \neq 0$, $w'_1(0) = 0$.

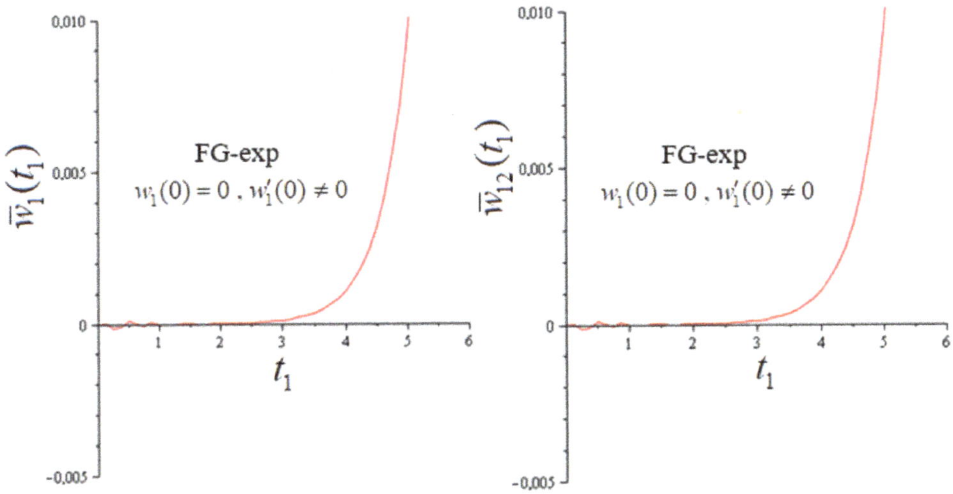

Figure 4. Variation of the deflection of FG-VE-Ps on VE-Fs according to Equation (19) for the initial conditions $w_1(0) = 0,\ w'_1(0) \neq 0$.

The changes of the critical times of FG-VE-Ps on VE-Fs depending on the viscoelasticity parameter γ with FIC and SIC are tabulated in Table 1. Additional data required for the numerical analysis are presented in Table 1. As can be seen, the critical time values decrease with and without VE-Fs with increasing γ. It is noted that the critical time has the largest value when $K_0 \neq 0$, while it has the smallest value when $K_2 = 0$. In addition, if the case of $K_i \neq 0 (i = 0, 1, 2)$ is compared with the case of $K_2 = 0$, although the critical time values increase, these values are less than those of unconstrained FG-VE-Ps for the small values of γ. The greatest influences of VE-Fs occur when $K_2 = 0$, and these effects are -16.4% and -15.22% for FIC and SIC, respectively, at $\gamma = 0.1$. When the VE-Fs' effects are compared to the critical times of FG-VE-Ps for the first and second initial conditions, the effect of the soil is great in the SIC for $K_0 \neq 0$ only, while the other effects are higher in the FCI. When the CTs of an FG-VE-P and Ni-VE-P are compared, the influence of the FG-exp. profile on the critical time parameter increases in both initial conditions due to the increase of γ in the groundless state. When $K_0 \neq 0$ and other VE-F coefficients are zero, although the influence of the FG-exp. profile decreases to the critical time, the increase continues due to the increase of γ. In both boundary conditions, the influence of the FG profile on the critical times for $K_0 \neq 0$ and $K_1 \neq 0$ varies irregularly depending on γ, while it is considerable. Compared with FG-VE-P and Si_3N_4-VE-P, the greatest effect of the FG profile occurs at $K_2 = 0$, and is approximately +18% for both initial conditions.

The changes of the critical times of FG-VE-Ps on VE-Fs depending on K_1 with FIC and SIC for different K_2 are tabulated in Figure 5. The data required for numerical analysis are: $a = 50h,\ a = 2b,\ p^{VF} = 0.7\ , \gamma = 0.5,\ K = 10^8 (\mathrm{N/m^3})$. In both initial conditions, the critical time values increase weakly with increasing K_1, while the critical time values decrease weakly as K_1 increases. In addition, it is observed that the influences of the VE-F on the critical time increase as K_1 and K_2 increase, the effect of the FG profile on the critical time increases weakly as K_1 increases, and this effect decreases with the increase of K_2.

The changes of critical times of FG-VE-Ps on VE-Fs (with various $K_i (i = 0, 1, 2)$) against a/h for FIC and SIC are shown in Figure 6. The critical times of FG-VE-Ps for various FIC and SIC decrease as a/h increases. The data for the numerical analysis are: $a/b = 2,\ p^{VF} = 0.7,\ \gamma = 0.5$ and $K_i (i = 0, 1, 2)$, as shown in Figure 6. With increasing a/h ratio, the influence of the VE-F (for $K_0 = 4.5 \times 10^7,\ K_1 = K_2 = 0$) on the values of the critical time increases, while the effect of the VE-F (for $K_0 = 4.5 \times 10^7,\ K_1 = 40,\ K_2 = 0$) on the critical time is significantly greater than the effect of the previous VE-F type, although the influence of the VE-F is quickly decreasing. In addition, it is found that the influence of the VE-F (for $K_0 = 4.5 \times 10^7$, $K_1 = 40$, $K_2 = 35$) on the critical time is smaller than the previous VE-F, and this effect also decreases with increasing a/h. Note that the effects of the FG profile on the critical time decrease for all soil types as a/h increases.

The distributions of critical times of FG-VE-Ps on VE-Fs versus a/b for FIC and SIC are plotted in Figure 7. The data required for the numerical analysis are: $a/h = 50$, $p^{VF} = 0.7$, $\gamma = 0.5$ and $K_0 = 2.5 \times 10^6$, $K_1 = 40$, $K_2 = 30$. The influence of VE-F (for $K_0 = 2.5 \times 10^6$, $K_1 = K_2 = 0$) on the critical time decreases with increasing a/b, whereas the influence of the VE-F (for $K_0 = 2.5 \times 10^6$, $K_1 = 40$, $K_2 = 0$) on the critical time is significantly greater than the influence of the previous VE-F type, and the influence of the VE-F increases as a/b increases. In addition, it is found that the influence of the VE-F (for $K_0 = 2.5 \times 10^6$, $K_1 = 40$, $K_2 = 30$) on the critical time is small compared to the previous VE-F, and this effect increases with increasing a/b. The influences of the FG profile on the critical time decrease for $K_0 = 2.5 \times 10^6$, $K_1 = K_2 = 0$, while they increase for $K_0 = 2.5 \times 10^6$, $K_1 = 40$, $K_2 = 0$ and $K_0 = 2.5 \times 10^6$, $K_1 = 40$, $K_2 = 30$ as a/b increases.

Table 1. Changes of critical times of FG-VE-Ps on VE-Fs depending on the viscoelastic parameter γ with FIC and SIC ($h/a = 0.02$, $b = 0.5a$, $p^{VF} = 0.7$).

		t_{11cr}^{VF}			t_{12cr}^{VF}	
	Ni	**FG-exp.**	**Si_3N_4**	**Ni**	**FG-exp.**	**Si_3N_4**
γ			$K_0 = K_1 = K_2 = 0$			
0.1	4.236	4.434	4.669	2.031	2.13	2.248
0.3	3.686	3.884	4.12	1.757	1.856	1.973
0.5	3.431	3.629	3.864	1.629	1.728	1.845
0.7	3.263	3.461	3.696	1.545	1.644	1.761
γ			$K_0 = 4.2 \times 10^7$, $K_1 = K_2 = 0$			
0.1	4.6	4.742	4.93	2.207	2.279	2.374
0.3	4.011	4.16	4.354	1.912	1.988	2.086
0.5	3.737	3.889	4.086	1.775	1.853	1.952
0.7	3.556	3.711	3.91	1.685	1.764	1.864
γ			$K_0 = 4.2 \times 10^7$, $K_1 = 10$, $K_2 = 0$			
0.1	3.971	3.705	3.136	1.918	1.797	1.529
0.3	3.807	3.8	3.648	1.821	1.825	1.762
0.5	3.62	3.679	3.659	1.724	1.759	1.758
0.7	3.476	3.565	3.607	1.65	1.699	1.728
γ			$K_0 = 4.2 \times 10^7$, $K_1 = 10$, $K_2 = 5$			
0.1	3.987	3.759	3.313	1.925	1.822	1.613
0.3	3.803	3.806	3.71	1.819	1.827	1.789
0.5	3.611	3.673	3.68	1.719	1.755	1.766
0.7	3.465	3.553	3.609	1.644	1.692	1.727

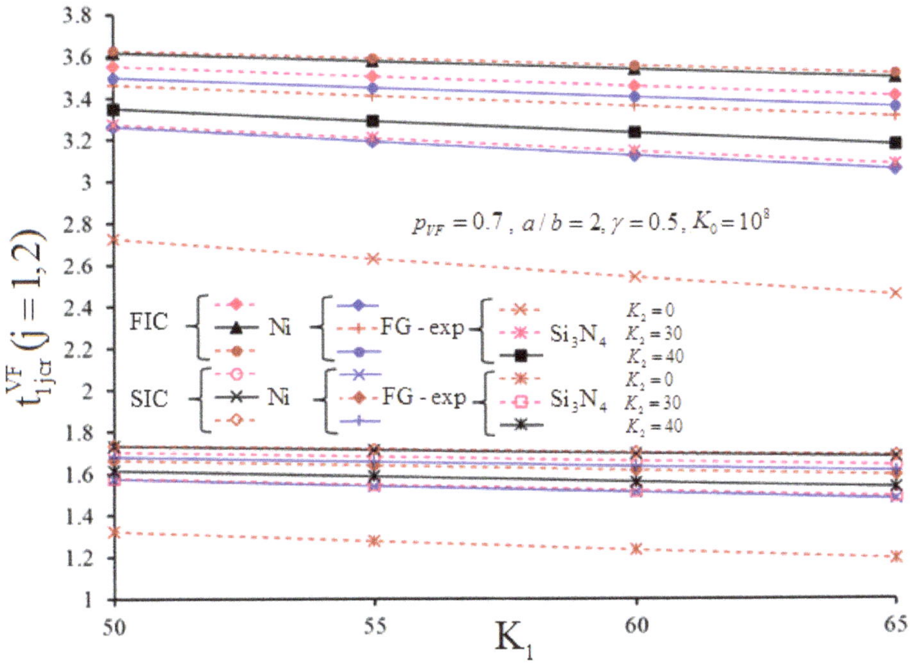

Figure 5. Changes of critical times of FG-VE-Ps on VE-Fs depending on K_1 with FIC and SIC for different K_2.

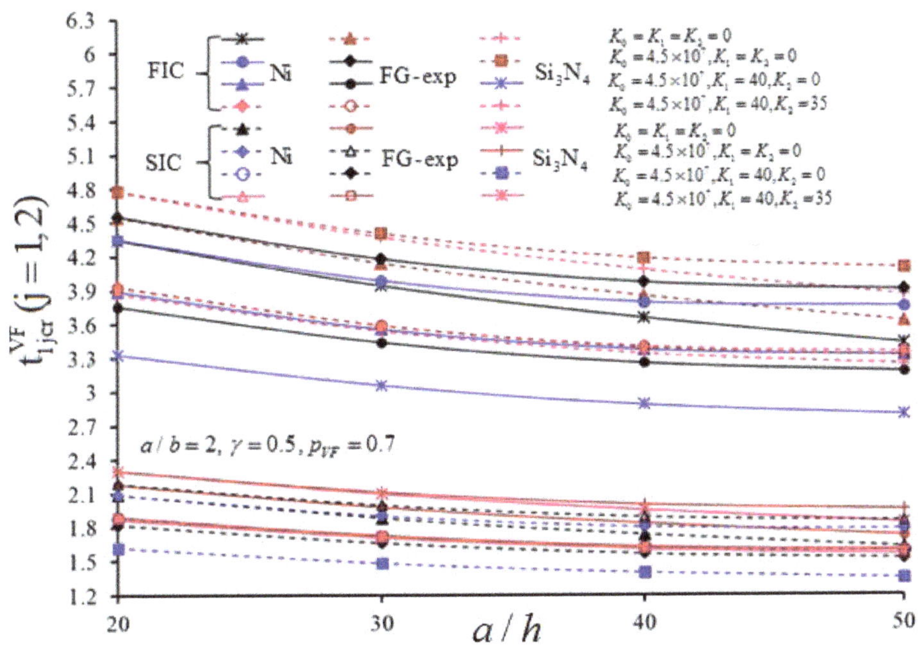

Figure 6. Changes of critical times of FG-VE-Ps on VE-Fs against a/h with FIC and SIC for various VE-Fs.

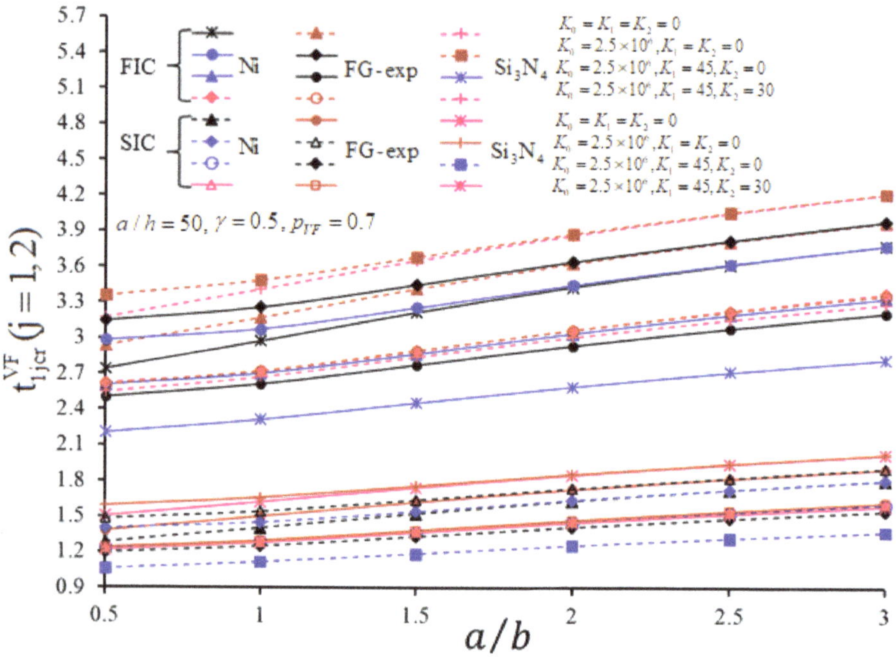

Figure 7. Distributions of critical times of FG-VE-Ps on VE-Fs versus a/b with FIC and SIC for various VE-Fs.

5. Conclusions

The dynamic stability of FG-VE-Ps with different initial conditions under compressive edge load resting on VE-Fs was solved. The basic equations for FG-VE-Ps on VE-Fs were derived using the concepts of Boltzmann and Volterra. The problem was reduced to the solution of an integro-differential equation system using the Galerkin method. By using Laplace transforms the new analytical expressions were obtained for deflection function and critical time with two initial conditions. The results were compared with the results obtained by various methods, and the accuracy of the results was confirmed. Finally, the effects of the VE-Fs, VE properties and the FG exponential profile on the dynamic characteristics of plates with various initial conditions were investigated numerically.

Funding: This research received no external funding.

Institutional Review Board Statement: Not related to our work.

Informed Consent Statement: Not applicable.

Data Availability Statement: This study does not report any data.

Conflicts of Interest: The author declares no conflict of interest.

References

1. Ogibalov, P.M.; Lomakin, V.A.; Kishkin, B.P. *Mechanics of Polymers*; Moscow State University: Moscow, Russia, 1975. (In Russian)
2. Christensen, R.M. *Theory of Viscoelasticity*; Dover: New York, NY, USA, 1982.
3. Drozdov, A.D.; Kolmanovskii, V.B. *Stability in Viscoelasticity*; Elsevier Science B.V.: Amsterdam, The Netherlands, 2013.
4. Matyash, V.I. Vibrations of isotropic viscoelastic shells. *Polym. Mech.* **1973**, *7*, 129–134. [CrossRef]
5. Ding, R.; Zhu, Z.; Cheng, C. Some dynamical properties of a viscoelastic cylindrical shell. *Appl. Math. Mech. Eng. Edit.* **1999**, *20*, 233–240.
6. Zenkour, A. Buckling of fiber-reinforced viscoelastic composite plates using various plate theories. *J. Eng. Math.* **2004**, *50*, 75–93. [CrossRef]

7. Ilyasov, M. Dynamic stability of viscoelastic plates. *Int. J. Eng. Sci.* **2007**, *45*, 111–122. [CrossRef]
8. Zhou, Y.F.; Wang, Z.M. Vibrations of axially moving viscoelastic plate with parabolically varying thickness. *J. Sound. Vib.* **2008**, *316*, 198–210.
9. Ferreira, A.; Araújo, A.; Neves, A.; Rodrigues, J.; Carrera, E.; Cinefra, M.; Soares, C.M.M. A finite element model using a unified formulation for the analysis of viscoelastic sandwich laminates. *Compos. Part B Eng.* **2012**, *45*, 1258–1264. [CrossRef]
10. Madeira, J.F.A.; Araujo, A.L.; Soares, C.M.M.; Soares, C.A.M.; Ferreira, A.J.M. Multi objective design of viscoelastic laminated composite sandwich panels. *Compos. Part B Eng.* **2015**, *77*, 391–401. [CrossRef]
11. Alibeigloo, A. Effect of viscoelastic interface on three-dimensional static and vibration behavior of laminated composite plate. *Compos. Part B Eng.* **2015**, *75*, 17–28. [CrossRef]
12. Zhou, X.; Yu, D.; Shao, X.; Zhang, S.; Wang, S. Research and applications of viscoelastic vibration damping materials: A review. *Compos. Struct.* **2016**, *136*, 460–480. [CrossRef]
13. Luis, N.F.; Madeira, J.F.A.; Araujo, A.L.; Ferreira, A.J.M. Active vibration attenuation in viscoelastic laminated composite panels using multi objective optimization. *Compos. Part B Eng.* **2017**, *28*, 53–66. [CrossRef]
14. Tekin, G.; Kadıoğlu, F. Viscoelastic behavior of shear-deformable plates. *Int. J. Appl. Mech.* **2017**, *09*, 1750085. [CrossRef]
15. Bacciocchi, M.; Tarantino, A.M. Time-dependent behavior of viscoelastic three-phase composite plates reinforced by Carbon nanotubes. *Compos. Struct.* **2019**, *216*, 20–31. [CrossRef]
16. Shen, H.S. *Functionally Graded Materials, Nonlinear Analysis of Plates and Shells*; CRC Press: Boca Raton, FL, USA, 2009.
17. Tornabene, F.; Fantuzzi, N.; Viola, E.; Batra, R.C. Stress and strain recovery for functionally graded free-form and doubly-curved sandwich shells using higher-order equivalent single layer theory. *Compos. Struct.* **2015**, *119*, 67–89. [CrossRef]
18. Mukherjee, S.; Paulino, G.H. The elastic-viscoelastic correspondence principle for functionally graded materials, revisited. *J. Appl. Mech.* **2003**, *70*, 359–363. [CrossRef]
19. Ashrafi, H.; Shariyat, M.; Khalili, S.M.R.; Asemi, K. A boundary element formulation for the heterogeneous functionally graded viscoelastic structures. *Appl. Math. Comput.* **2013**, *225*, 246–262. [CrossRef]
20. Zenkour, A.M.; Elsibai, K.A.; Mashat, D.S. Elastic and viscoelastic solutions to rotating functionally graded hollow and solid cylinders. *Appl. Math. Mech. Engl. Ed.* **2008**, *29*, 1601–1616. [CrossRef]
21. Shariyat, M.; Nasab, F.F. Low-velocity impact analysis of the hierarchical viscoelastic FGM plates, using an explicit shear-bending decomposition theory and the new DQ method. *Compos. Struct.* **2014**, *113*, 63–73. [CrossRef]
22. Barretta, R.; Feo, L.; Luciano, R. Torsion of functionally graded nonlocal viscoelastic circular nanobeams. *Compos. Part B Eng.* **2015**, *72*, 217–222. [CrossRef]
23. Deng, J.; Liu, Y.; Zhang, Z.; Liu, W. Stability analysis of multi-span viscoelastic functionally graded material pipes conveying fluid using a hybrid method. *Eur. J. Mech.-A/Solids* **2017**, *65*, 257–270. [CrossRef]
24. Sofiyev, A. On the solution of the dynamic stability of heterogeneous orthotropic viscoelastic cylindrical shells. *Compos. Struct.* **2018**, *206*, 124–130. [CrossRef]
25. Sofiyev, A. About an approach to the determination of the critical time of viscoelastic functionally graded cylindrical shells. *Compos. Part B Eng.* **2018**, *156*, 156–165. [CrossRef]
26. Kerr, A.D. Elastic and viscoelastic foundation models. *J. Appl. Mech.* **1964**, *31*, 491–498. [CrossRef]
27. Bajenov, V. *The Bending of the Cylindrical Shells in an Elastic Medium*; Visha Shkola: Kiev, Ukraine, 1975. (In Russian)
28. Pouresmaeeli, S.; Ghavanloo, E.; Fazelzadeh, S.A. Vibration analysis of viscoelastic orthotropic nanoplates resting on viscoelastic medium. *Compos. Struct.* **2013**, *96*, 405–410. [CrossRef]
29. Karličić, D.; Kozić, P.; Pavlović, R. Free transverse vibration of nonlocal viscoelastic orthotropic multi-nanoplate system (MNPS) embedded in a viscoelastic medium. *Compos. Struct.* **2014**, *115*, 89–99. [CrossRef]
30. Zhang, D.-P.; Lei, Y.-J.; Wang, C.; Shen, Z.-B. Vibration analysis of viscoelastic single-walled carbon nanotubes resting on a viscoelastic foundation. *J. Mech. Sci. Technol.* **2017**, *31*, 87–98. [CrossRef]
31. Zamani, H.A.; Aghdam, M.M.; Sadighi, M. Free vibration analysis of thick viscoelastic composite plates on vis-co-Pasternak foundation using higher-order theory. *Compos. Struct.* **2017**, *182*, 25–35. [CrossRef]
32. Zeighampour, H.; Beni, Y.T.; Dehkordi, M.B. Wave propagation in viscoelastic thin cylindrical nanoshell resting on a visco-Pasternak foundation based on nonlocal strain gradient theory. *Thin-Walled Struct.* **2018**, *122*, 378–386. [CrossRef]
33. Zenkour, A.M.; Sobhy, M. Nonlocal piezo-hygrothermal analysis for vibration characteristics of a piezoelectric Kelvin-Voigt viscoelastic nanoplate embedded in a viscoelastic medium. *Acta Mech.* **2018**, *229*, 3–19. [CrossRef]
34. Sophy, M.; Zenkour, A.M. The modified couple stress model for bending of normal deformable viscoelastic nanobeams resting on visco-Pasternak foundations. *Mech. Adv. Matr. Struct.* **2020**, *27*, 525–538.
35. Sobhy, M.; Radwan, A.F. Influence of a 2D magnetic field on hygrothermal bending of sandwich CNTs-reinforced microplates with viscoelastic core embedded in a viscoelastic medium. *Acta Mech.* **2020**, *231*, 71–99. [CrossRef]
36. Alazwari, M.A.; Zenkour, A.M.A. Quasi-3D refined theory for the vibration of functionally graded plates resting on vis-co-Winkler-Pasternak foundations. *Mathematics* **2022**, *10*, 716. [CrossRef]
37. Frahlia, H.; Bennai, R.; Nebab, M.; Atmane, H.A.; Tounsi, A. Assessing effects of parameters of viscoelastic foundation on the dynamic response of functionally graded plates using a novel HSDT theory. *Mech. Adv. Mater. Struct.* **2022**, *3*, 1–15. [CrossRef]
38. Zenkour, A.M.; Allam, M.N.M.; Sobhy, M. Bending analysis of FG viscoelastic sandwich beams with elastic cores resting on Pasternak's elastic foundations. *Acta Mech.* **2009**, *212*, 233–252. [CrossRef]

39. Shariyat, M.; Alipour, M.M. A power series solution for vibration and complex modal stress analyses of variable thickness viscoelastic two-directional FGM circular plates on elastic foundations. *Appl. Math. Model.* **2013**, *37*, 3063–3076. [CrossRef]
40. Liu, H.; Yang, J. Vibration of FG magneto-electro-viscoelastic porous nanobeams on visco-Pasternak foundation. *Compos. Part B Eng.* **2018**, *155*, 244–256. [CrossRef]
41. Sofiyev, A.H.; Zerin, Z.; Kuruoglu, N. Dynamic behavior of FGM viscoelastic plates resting on elastic foundations. *Acta Mech.* **2019**, *231*, 1–17. [CrossRef]
42. Zenkour, A.M.; El-Shahrany, H.D. Active control of a sandwich plate with reinforced magnetostrictive faces and viscoe-lastic core, resting on elastic foundation. *J. Intel. Mater. Sys. Struct.* **2021**, *33*, 1321–1337. [CrossRef]
43. Li, H.; Gao, Z.; Zhao, J.; Ma, H.; Han, Q.; Liu, J. Vibration suppression effect of porous graphene platelet coating on fiber reinforced polymer composite plate with viscoelastic damping boundary conditions resting on viscoelastic foundation. *Eng. Struct.* **2021**, *237*, 112167. [CrossRef]
44. Yuan, Y.; Niu, Z.; Smitt, J. Magneto-hygro-thermal vibration analysis of the viscoelastic nanobeams reinforcedwith carbon nanotubes resting on Kerr's elastic foundation based on NSGT. *Adv. Compos. Mater.* **2022**, 1–23. [CrossRef]

Disclaimer/Publisher's Note: The statements, opinions and data contained in all publications are solely those of the individual author(s) and contributor(s) and not of MDPI and/or the editor(s). MDPI and/or the editor(s) disclaim responsibility for any injury to people or property resulting from any ideas, methods, instructions or products referred to in the content.

mathematics MDPI

Article

Accurate Key Parameters Estimation of PEMFCs' Models Based on Dandelion Optimization Algorithm

Rabeh Abbassi [1,2,3,*], Salem Saidi [2,4], Abdelkader Abbassi [3,5], Houssem Jerbi [6], Mourad Kchaou [1] and Bilal Naji Alhasnawi [7]

1 Department of Electrical Engineering, College of Engineering, University of Ha'il, Ha'il City 81451, Saudi Arabia
2 LaTICE Laboratory, Higher National Engineering School of Tunis (ENSIT), University of Tunis, 5 Avenue Taha Hussein, P.O. Box 56, Tunis 1008, Tunisia
3 Institute of Applied Sciences and Technology of Kasserine (ISSATKas), University of Kairouan, P.O. Box 471, Kasserine 1200, Tunisia
4 National School of Advanced Sciences and Technologies of Borj Cédria (ENSTAB), University of Carthage, P.O. Box 122, Hammam-Chott 1164, Tunisia
5 Engineering Laboratory of Industrial Systems and Renewable Energies (LISIER), National Higher Engineering School of Tunis (ENSIT), University of Tunis, 5 Avenue Taha Hussein, P.O. Box 56, Tunis 1008, Tunisia
6 Department of Industrial Engineering, College of Engineering, University of Ha'il, Ha'il City 81451, Saudi Arabia
7 Department of Computer Technical Engineering, College of Information Technology, Imam Ja'afar Al-Sadiq University, Al-Muthanna 66002, Iraq
* Correspondence: r.abbassi@uoh.edu.sa

Abstract: With the increasing demand for electrical energy and the challenges related to its production, along with the need to be environmentally friendly to achieve sustainability for future generations, proton exchange membrane fuel cells (PEMFCs) are emerging as a clean energy source that can effectively replace conventional energy sources, in various fields of application and especially in the field of transportation exploiting electric vehicles (EVs). To improve the development and control of the PEMFCs, the precise determination of its mathematical model remains an essential task. Indeed, the accuracy of such a model depends on the ability to overcome the constraints associated with the nonlinearity and the numerous involved unknown parameters. The present paper proposes a new Dandelion Optimizer (DO) to accurately identify, for the first time, the parameters of the PEMFC model. The DO addresses the weaknesses of the majority of metaheuristic algorithms related to the self-adaptation of parameters, the stagnation of convergence to local minima, and the ability to refer to the whole population. The high ability of the proposed method is investigated using both steady-state and dynamic situations. The DO-based parameters estimation approach has been assessed through a specific comparative study with the most recently published techniques including GWO, GBO, HHO, IAEO, VSDE, and ABCDESC is performed using two typical PEMFC modules, namely 250 W PEMFC and NedStack PS6. The results obtained proved that the proposed approach obtained promising achievements and better performances comparatively with well-recognized and competitive methods.

Keywords: proton exchange membrane fuel cell; key parameters estimation; Hail region desert tourism; sum of square error; electric circuit model; dandelion optimization algorithm

MSC: 35Q93

1. Introduction

1.1. Motivation

Over the last three decades, global warming has become a major issue for humanity. Indeed, the main responsibility is committed by the resources of fossil origin which are currently ranked as the first sources of energy supply on a worldwide scale and which are becoming scarcer from one day to the next [1]. As such, developed and even developing countries are continuously adopting sustainable energy policies to achieve carbon dioxide (CO_2) emission reductions while ensuring a secure energy supply and a prosperous economy [2]. As a result, efforts have been intensified to promote the share of renewable energy to 30% by 2030. Recent studies have concluded that this target can even be exceeded towards achieving participation of RE in the global energy mix of about 36% if specific recommendations are properly addressed [3,4]. Among these recommendations, those related to the energy efficiency directive, improving access to energy, exploiting technological breakthroughs, consumer-driven societal developments, and the early retirement of conventional energy facilities, will effectively contribute to the achievement of such ecological and other goals [5].

Given the importance of the transport sector in the economic development of countries and its need for rapid economic expansion and urbanization as well as the necessity to improve people's livelihoods, the last few decades have been marked by a rapid increase in its energy consumption. This amounted to about 33% of the world's total, making it responsible for 37% of the total carbon dioxide emissions [6]. Faced with the serious environmental consequences of burning fossil fuels, the search for sustainable alternatives to provide energy in this sector becomes an urgent necessity. Therefore, one of the most relevant countermeasures is to shift the energy supply of the transport sector to renewable and clean energy sources, especially in oil-producing countries that depend mainly on it for consumption, such as the Kingdom of Saudi Arabia [7].

Within the framework of its Vision 2030 economic plan, the Saudi Commission for Tourism and National Heritage is working more and more to steadily increase the number of tourists visiting KSA. Therefore, the newest statistics of the World Tourism Organization (UNWTO) Tourism Barometer inform readers that KSA's tourism sector has risen rapidly to reach 121% compared to pre-COVID-19 pandemic international tourism.

In addition to religious tourism, desert tourism based primarily on electric vehicle (EV) transportation is a growing industry and a popular and sustainable option for exploring desert landscapes in the Hail region (HR) while reducing carbon emissions and noise pollution. Many tour agencies can offer electric vehicle tours, which makes the experience unique, enjoyable, and environmentally friendly since they can use zero-emission vehicles (ZEVs) including electric and hydrogen fuel cell vehicles [8].

Compared to combustion engines and electrochemical batteries, fuel cells are emerging as the most relevant choice in terms of environmental friendliness, durability, energy efficiency, autonomy and reliability [9–12]. In particular, proton exchange membrane fuel cells (PEMFCs) could be the leading candidate to power material handling applications and vehicles in the transportation sector [13].

1.2. Literature Review

Nowadays, PEMFCs are the best choice for future mobility and especially for hydrogen-powered vehicles. In order to master PEMFCs' operation and further push their development and efficiency, different modeling studies have been developed. A careful investigation allows for the classification of the analysis of PEMFCs in two main types of modeling, dynamic modeling, and steady-state modeling [14]. In this context, various published works have been focused on the PEMFCs modeling, control, and diagnosis to further advance their development and efficiency.

In [15], a real-time fault diagnostic/characterization of PEMFCs using a new concept combining a one-dimensional convolutional neural network and AC voltage response. For more complex applications, a diagnosis technique of faulty components of a 1 kW PEMFC-based system using energy analysis in [16]. In [17], a new robust estimator for the diagnosis and reconstruction of fault for a PEMFC air management system has been suggested under different conditions. The developed observer is able to accurately identify the state of the system even in case of any defects to achieve a tolerant control of the air supply. In [18], the feasibility of a reliable method for the detection of abnormal sensors during PEMFC operation has been investigated. After their identification, the sensors identified as faulty are no longer considered in the diagnosis to guarantee the reliability of the PEMFC state of health monitoring. Particular attention was devoted to humidity sensors that can generate misleading readings regarding flooding. In [13], Chen et al. focused on the performance assessment and the thermodynamics–economy–environment feasibility of a PEMFC-based vehicle under dynamic conditions. In [19], the main objective has been devoted to the laboratory investigation of the effect of dynamic load cycle and operational parameters on the PEMFCs lifetime.

In addition to the previously mentioned studies, the accurate extraction of PEMFCs parameters remains crucial for improving their performance and durability as a promising technology for clean and efficient energy production. Recently, metaheuristic optimizers have been considered among the most used methods for tackling global optimization problems [20–23]. In this context, various optimization approaches have been proposed to address the PEMFCs parameters estimation issue. In [24], 18 optimization algorithms have been applied to estimate the parameters of three following practical fuel cells: BCS 500-W PEM, 500 W SR-12PEM, and 250 W PEMFC, under various operating conditions. Mohamed et al. [25] proposed a modified gorilla troops optimizer (MGTO) to tackle the drawbacks of the GTO such as the low speed of the convergence to local optima. The proposed approach has been tested to estimate the parameters of three types of PEMFCs. Otherwise, a honey badger optimizer (HBO) is used to identify the parameters of three commercial PEMFC by the minimization of the SSEs. Various metrics such as Sobol sensitivity and statistical study and computational complexity have been conducted to confirm the HBO performance [26]. Another recent study [27] has proposed to identify the PEMFC parameters using the original Bonobo Optimization algorithm (BO) and its enhanced version named Quasi Oppositional BO (QOBO). Otherwise, Ibrahim et al. [28] suggested identifying the design parameters of PEMFCs through an optimization algorithm called Enhanced Bald Eagle Search (EBES), under different pressure and temperature conditions. In [29], PEMFC parameters estimation based on a hybrid artificial bee colony differential evolution (ABCDE) optimizer has been suggested. The algorithm was tested, and the results showed that it can effectively estimate the parameters with high accuracy. Otherwise, a significant improvement has been applied to the African vulture optimizer [30] to investigate the parameter value estimation and fitting for NedStackPS6, BCS 500 W, and SR-12 500 W.

In the literature, the behavior of dandelions has been exploited by researchers, like various other biological phenomena and behaviors, to propose new optimization algorithms inspired by nature. A highly developed research has unveiled the first approach inspired by the behavior of dandelion sowing. This approach is commonly known as the Dandelion Algorithm (DA) [31]. Within the DA, the evolutionary process involves classifying the dandelion population into excellent and poor seeds based on their fitness values. Then, it retains the excellent seeds and assesses them to participate in the evolutionary process and excludes the poor seeds without any evaluation. From its first proposal, the DA has been investigated in an application related to the classification of biomedical problems by optimizing the input weights and output offsets of the extreme learning machine. In the same study, the major concern was associated with premature convergence to local optima. To overcome this limitation, a modified version was proposed for mutation-based seeding [32]. Correspondingly, the generation of mutation seeding is ensured upon a probability model exploiting Levy mutations and Gaussian mutations. The most significant improvement is provided by the evaluation of excellent seeds using the number of evaluations recorded after classifying seeds, discarding the bad ones, and taking into account only the excellent ones, which thereby considerably decreases the consumption of evaluations.

Furthermore, the Extreme Learning Machine (ELM) is known as a neural network algorithm (NNA) that generates, during the training process, input weights and offsets randomly and without dynamic adjustments [33]. Indeed, with only one parameter to set (that materializes the hidden layer nodes), the ELM performs more efficiently and speedily than the traditional NNA. In order to benefit from its aforementioned strengths, ELM was proposed to take over the classification process and thus improve the dandelion DA algorithm (ELMDA) [34]. The fact that ELM's machine learning classifies dandelions into excellent and poor seeds according to their fitness and retains only the excellent ones motivates the evolution of the ELMDA algorithm.

Far from this theory and its applicability, a new concept inspired by the same natural phenomenon of a dandelion called Dandelion Optimizer (DO) has been investigated in the present work.

1.3. Contribution

The Dandelion Optimizer (DO) is a recent swarm intelligence bio-inspired optimizer developed by Zhao et al. [35]. It mimics the process of dandelion seeds' flight under the effect of the wind, to cross long distances. Such a process includes three main phases: ascent, descent, and landing. During the rising phase, the seeds drift along a localized community or spiral upwards under the effect of the whirlwinds deriving from the top to the ground. Then, according to the principles of Brownian motion and Levy's random walk, the seeds descend along a trajectory and land, respectively. Indeed, the flying seeds continue their descending by the adjustment of their trajectory in the global space and land at random to be able to grow again. The choice of the DO has been motivated by the fact that it has several strengths compared to other metaheuristic algorithms. These include:

- Low computational complexity: The evolution strategy used by the DO requires fewer computations than most other metaheuristic algorithms;
- Property of self-adaptation: The DO can self-adapt its parameters, allowing it to converge quickly and accurately to local minima and maximize the solution's performance;
- Minimization of stagnation of convergence: The DO utilizes a memory-based mechanism to identify stagnation of convergence and then takes steps to move away from a local minimum and towards a better solution;
- Ability to refer to an entire population: Unlike many other metaheuristic algorithms, the DO is able to refer to the entire population of solutions to best determine the optimal solution;
- Decentralized nature: The DO is a decentralized algorithm, meaning its components are distributed among multiple nodes or machines, making it less prone to failure than centralized algorithms.

The foremost contributions within the present work are:

- To adapt the DO algorithm, and benefit from its high exploitation and exploration abilities to address, for the first time, the issue of the PEMFC unidentified parameter estimation;
- Conducting a deep comparative study between DO and three recently published optimizers (Grey wolf optimizer (GWO), Gradient-based optimizer (GBO), and Harris hawks optimizer (HHO)) simulated under the same hypothesis;
- Comparing the DO performance with three competitive metaheuristic optimizers from the literature such as (Improved artificial ecosystem optimizer (IAEO), Vortex search-differential evolution (VSDE), and Artificial bee colony differential evolution shuffled complex (ABCDESC));
- The experimentation of two commercialized PEMFCs (EMFC 250 W, and NedStack PS6) has confirmed the superiority of the proposed DO in terms of stability, convergence speed, and absolute accuracy.

As shown in Figure 1, the proposed work design steps and flowchart are illustrated. Section 2 describes the mathematical modeling and the PEMFC; Section 3 formulates the investigated issue as an optimization problem; Section 4 discusses and analyses the main steps of the DO-based PEMFC parameter estimation; Section 5 is devoted to the validation of the DO, the discussions, and the comparative study with six well-known metaheuristic algorithms. Finally, the conclusions and future works are involved in Section 6.

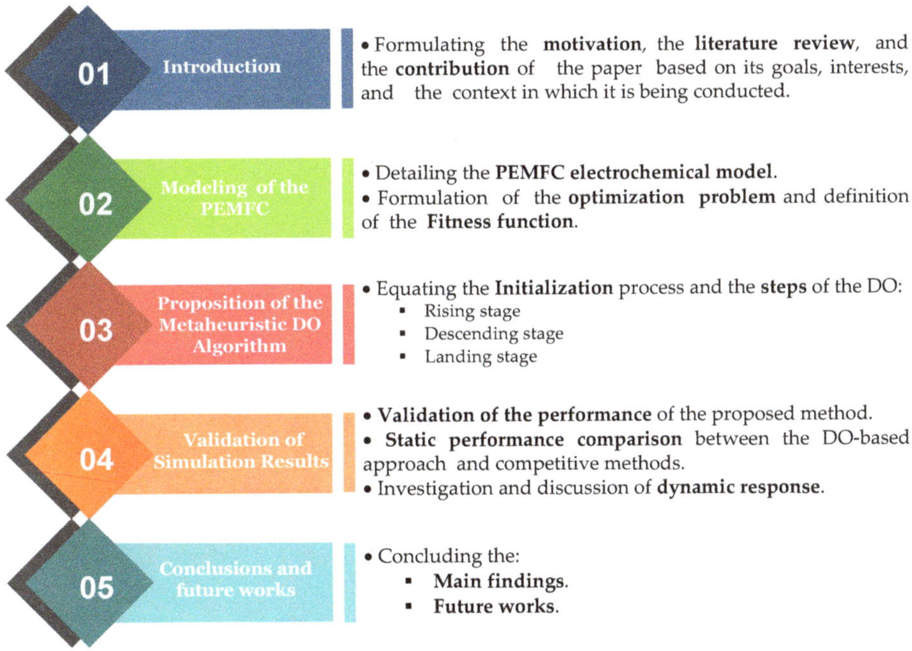

Figure 1. Flowchart illustrating the Research methodology .

2. General Model of PEM Fuel Cells

According to the literature, there are several types of models used to estimate the voltage–current relationship of the PEMFC. Amphlett's semi-empirical model is the most widely used thanks to its simplicity and efficiency [36,37]. In fact, this model presents the output voltage of a fuel cell as the sum of the thermodynamic Nernst voltage, the activation polarization, the concentration polarization, and the ohmic polarization (see Figure 2). Thus, the output voltage of the fuel cell can be written as Equation (1):

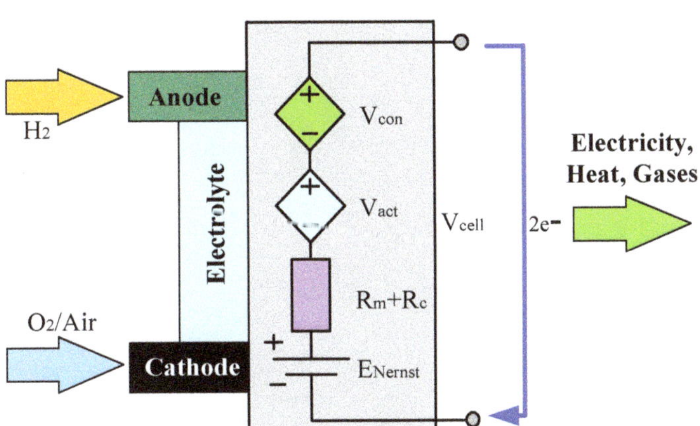

Figure 2. Electrical model of a PEM fuel cell.

$$V_{cell} = E_{Nernst} - V_{act} - V_{con} - V_{ohmic} \tag{1}$$

where V_{act} is the activation overpotential, V_{ohmic} is ohmic overpotential, V_{conc} denotes concentration loss, and E_{Nernst} is the theoretical voltage defined as follows [38–42]:

$$E_{Nernst} = 1.229 - 0.85 \times 10^{-3}(T - 298.15) + 4.308 \times 10^{-5} \times T \cdot \ln\left(P^*_{H2}\sqrt{P^*_{O_2}}\right) \quad (2)$$

where T corresponds to the cell temperature at Kelvin, $P^*_{H_2}$ and $P^*_{O_2}$ are the partial pressures of hydrogen and oxygen, which may be calculated according to (3):

$$P^*_{H_2} = 0.5RH_a \cdot P^{sat}_{H_2O}\left[\frac{1}{\left(\frac{RH_a \cdot P^{sat}_{H_2O}}{P_a}\exp\left(\frac{1.635(i/A)}{T^{1.334}}\right)\right)} - 1\right] \quad (3)$$

$$P^*_{O_2} = RH_c \cdot P^{sat}_{H_2O}\left[\frac{1}{\left(\frac{RH_c \cdot P^{sat}_{H_2O}}{P_c}\exp\left(\frac{4.192(i/A)}{T^{1.334}}\right)\right)} - 1\right] \quad (4)$$

where RH_c and RH_a are the relative humidity at anode and cathode, P_a and P_c are the anode and cathode inlet pressures in atm, and $P^{sat}_{H_2O}$ is the saturation pressure of water vapor, obtained, in atm units, by the following formula:

$$\begin{aligned}\log_{10}(p^{sat}_{H_2O}) = 2.95 \times 10^{-2}\ (T - 298.15) - 9.18 \times 10^{-5}(T - 298.15)^2 \\ +1.44 \times 10^{-5}(T - 298.15)^3 - 2.18\end{aligned} \quad (5)$$

The activation losses V_{act} can be determined as in (6):

$$V_{\text{act}} = -\left[\xi_1 + \xi_2 T + \xi_3 T \ln\left(C_{O_2}\right) + \xi_4 T \ln(i)\right] \quad (6)$$

where ξ_1, ξ_2, ξ_4 and ξ_4 represent semi-empirical factors of cell model and C_{O_2} is the oxygen concentration can be calculated by:

$$C_{O_2} = \frac{P^*_{O_2}}{5.08} \times 10^{-6}\exp\left(\frac{498}{T}\right) \quad (7)$$

Next, the formulation for the calculation of ohmic losses used in this model is presented below:

$$V_{ohmic} = i(R_m + R_c) \quad (8)$$

The contact resistance at the terminals of the bipolar plates is denoted by R_c, and R_m represents the equivalent resistance of the membrane as follows:

$$R_m = \frac{\rho_m}{A} l_m \quad (9)$$

where l_m is the membrane thickness in cm, and ρ_m is the resistivity of membrane in $\Omega.cm$, defined as:

$$\rho_m = \frac{181.6\left[1 + 0.03 \times \left(\frac{i}{A}\right) + 0.062 \times \left(\frac{T}{303}\right)^2\left(\frac{i}{A}\right)^{2.5}\right]}{[\lambda_m - 0.634 - 3] \times \left(\frac{i}{A}\right)\exp\left[\frac{4.18(T^4 - 303)}{T}\right]} \quad (10)$$

where λ_m is an adjustable parameter that specifies membrane content the water.

Finally, the concentration losses can be established mathematically as in (11).

$$V_{con} = -b \cdot \ln\left(\frac{J_{max} - J}{J_{max}}\right) \tag{11}$$

where J is the current density (A cm^{-2}), and J_{max} is the maximum current density generated by the PEM fuel cell (A cm^{-2}). In the mathematical model of the PEM fuel cell, b is presented as an unknown coefficient.

In practice, fuel cells are stacked together in series to obtain higher power output. Depending on the number of cells, the output voltage of the stack V_{stack} is given by the following equation:

$$V_{stack} = N_{cell} \cdot V_{cell} \tag{12}$$

where N_{cell} number of cells in the stack.

3. Problem Formulation

The mathematical model of Amphlett [36,37] presents the nonlinear characteristics of the PEMFC stack. Since the implementation of an accurate model is a challenging task, this model depends on seven key variables. These adjustable variables are those used in the optimization problem to find the best solution for the objective function. The objective function defined in this study is the sum of squared errors (SSE). These errors quantify the difference between the voltage values, which are calculated mathematically, and those obtained from the voltage data measured in the laboratory from a real PEMFC. The mathematical description of this objective function is as follows:

$$F_{obj}\left(\xi_{i(1:4)}, \lambda_m, R_c, b\right) = \min\left(\sum_{j=1}^{N} (\mathrm{V_{mes}}(j) - \mathrm{V_{est}}(j))^2\right) \tag{13}$$

Here, $\mathrm{V_{mes}}$ denotes the measured voltage of the PEMFC stack (V), $\mathrm{V_{est}}$ is the estimated voltage of the model (V), N is the number of measured data, and j is the counting factor. Depending on the type of the fuel cell and its operational state, b represents an empirical coefficient materializing the mass transport loss coefficient. The parameters of the PEMFC model are constrained by upper and lower boundaries that define the constraints of the problem in terms of inequality (14). The search ranges of ξ_i, λ_m, b and R_c are arranged in Table 1. These variables are those fitted by Dandelion Optimizer and some well-known algorithms.

$$\begin{array}{l} \xi_i^{\min} \leq \xi_i \leq \xi_i^{\max} \\ \lambda_m^{\min} \leq \lambda_m \leq \lambda_m^{\max} \\ b^{\min} \leq b \leq b^{\max} \\ R_c^{\min} \leq R_c \leq R_c^{\max} \end{array} \tag{14}$$

Table 1. Parameter range of the PEMFC.

Parameter	ξ_1	ξ_2	ξ_3	ξ_4	λ_m	R_c	b
Min	−1.19969	1×10^{-3}	3.6×10^{-5}	-2.6×10^{-4}	10	1×10^{-4}	0.0136
max	−0.8532	5×10^{-3}	9.8×10^{-5}	-9.54×10^{-4}	24	8×10^{-4}	0.5

4. Proposed DO-Based Approach

Having previously explained the general concept of the DO algorithm, the next section focuses on the mathematical formulation of the three steps crossed by the dandelion seeds during their lifetime journey, namely the rising, the descending, and the landing.

4.1. Initialization

Having the same principle as that of the metaheuristic algorithms inspired by nature, the proposed algorithm is based on the initialization of the population through its evolution and iterative optimization. Indeed, each seed of dandelion can be considered as a candidate solution. According to this, the population can be represented by the matrix representation (Equation (15)):

$$Pop = \begin{bmatrix} x_{1,1} & x_{1,2} & \cdots & x_{1,D} \\ x_{2,1} & x_{2,2} & \cdots & x_{2,D} \\ \vdots & \vdots & \ddots & \vdots \\ x_{NP,1} & x_{NP,2} & \cdots & x_{NP,D} \end{bmatrix} \quad (15)$$

Herein, D is the variable dimension. NP represents the size of the population.

By defining two boundary bands to the treated problem: an upper and a lower one, denoted Ub and Lb respectively, as shown in these equations:

$$\begin{cases} Ub_j = [ub_1, \cdots, ub_D] \\ Lb_j = [lb_1, \cdots, lb_D] \end{cases} \quad (16)$$

Here, j is an integer between 1 and NP. Any candidate solution is necessarily being generated at random between such boundaries so that each individual $X_{i,j}$ is expressed according to Equation (17):

$$x_{i,j} = Lb_j + rand \cdot (Ub_j - Lb_j) \quad (17)$$

$rand$ is a random number between 0 and 1.

During the initialization process, the algorithm starts by choosing the individual having the optimal fitness value. After locating it, it is regarded as the initial elite that approximates the best location for the flourishing of the seed of dandelion. If the minimum value is chosen, the initial elite x_{elite} can be expressed as:

$$\begin{cases} F_{best} = \min\left(F_{obj}(x_{i,j})\right) \\ x_{elite} = x\left(find\left(F_{best} == F_{obj}(x_{i,j})\right)\right) \end{cases} \quad (18)$$

with $find()$ being two equal indices.

4.2. Rising Stage

During the rising phase, the dandelion seed rises to a specific height and then moves away from its parent. Subsequently, depending on moisture factors and wind strength, the seeds mount to random heights according to two weather conditions.

- **Condition 1 :**
  On clear days without weather fluctuations, the wind speed is characterized by what can be modeled by a logarithmic distribution according to Equation (19):

  $$lnY = N(\mu, \sigma^2)) \quad (19)$$

  Under these conditions, the transmission by seeds is remote randomly because the distribution is mainly along the y-axis, which triggers the process of DO exploration. In the search area, the dispersion of dandelion seeds is closely matched to the wind speed, which influences their height and dispersion. Under this impact, the vortices above the seeds are continuously adjusted to force them to spiral upward, according to the following equation:

  $$X_{t+1} = X_t + \alpha \cdot v_x \cdot v_y \cdot \ln Y \cdot (X_s - X_t) \quad (20)$$

X_t and X_s denote the location of the dandelion seed and that of the search space for the iteration number t, respectively. As such, the location obtained by random is expressed by:

$$X_s = rand(1, \dim)(Ub - Lb) + Lb \tag{21}$$

It is important to mention that lnY is a lognormal distribution obeying the conditions $\sigma^2 = 1$ and $\mu = 0$, and so mathematically translated as:

$$\ln Y = \begin{cases} \frac{1}{y\sqrt{2\pi}} \exp\left[-\frac{1}{2\sigma^2}(\ln y)^2\right] & y \geq 0 \\ 0 & y \prec 0 \end{cases} \tag{22}$$

α is an adjustment parameter to adapt the search step length, and y is defined as the normal standard distribution $N(0,1)$. Accordingly, α is given by:

$$\alpha = rand() * \left(\frac{1}{T^2}t^2 - \frac{2}{T}t + 1\right) \tag{23}$$

It was shown in [35] that the parameter α behaves as a function of the number of iterations as a random fluctuation in the range [0, 1] that decreases nonlinearly toward 0. When defining v_x and v_y as the dandelion lift parameter coefficients under the effect of the whirlwind action, the force calculation on the variable dimension obeys:

$$\begin{cases} r = \frac{1}{e^\theta} \\ v_x = r * \cos\theta \\ u_y = r * \sin\theta \end{cases} \tag{24}$$

where θ denotes a random angle in the interval $[-\pi, \pi]$.

- **Condition 2**:
  During rainy days, the air resistance is increased due to the high humidity, and therefore the buoyancy of dandelion seeds and their height in space are restricted, which involves the need to process it in their local proximities, according to the following equation Equation (25):

$$X_{t+1} = X_t * k \tag{25}$$

where k defines the parameter responsible for setting the local search domain of a given dandelion and which is assessed by Equation (26):

$$\begin{cases} q = \left(\frac{1}{T^2-2T+1}t^2 - \frac{2}{T^2-2T+1}t + 1 + \frac{1}{T^2-2T+1}\right) \\ k = 1 - rand() * q \end{cases} \tag{26}$$

At this stage, the seeds that are undergoing the rising phase are approximated by Equation (27):

$$X_{t+1} = \begin{cases} X_t + \alpha * v_x * v_y * \ln Y * (X_s - X_t) & rand(n) \prec 1.5 \\ X_t * k & else \end{cases} \tag{27}$$

4.3. Descending Stage

With the careful attention that the DO pays to the process of exploration, the descending phase is governed in accordance with the following analysis reflected by Equation (28). The dandelion seeds, being at the end of their rising phase to a certain distance, start the phase of regular descent according to a moving trajectory approximated by Brown's motion. Such normally distributed motion with each change enables individuals to cross, through the process of iterative updating, growing search communities. In a further phase, the optimizer expands the whole population to promising communities considering the average location information after the ascension phase and all this for simulating the stability of the dandelion descending:

$$X_{t+1} = X_t - \alpha * \beta_t * (X_{mean\_t} - \alpha * \beta_t * X_t) \tag{28}$$

where β_t stands for a randomly generated number derived from the famous standard normal distribution and represents the Brownian movement. At the ith iteration, X_{mean_t} refers to the average population location according to Equation (29):

$$X_{mean\_t} = \frac{1}{pop} \sum_{i=1}^{pop} X_i \tag{29}$$

4.4. Landing Stage

The key to the successful implementation of metaheuristic algorithms is the balance between the two main search mechanisms, namely exploration and exploitation. In this context, the DO attempts, during the exploitation, to refine solutions already obtained during the exploration, to improve its fitness by searching the neighborhood of a promising region. The dandelion seeds land randomly in an unspecified location. However, as the iterations proceed, the algorithm converges to a globally optimal solution that pinpoints the approximate position that ensures the dandelion seeds germinate and continue their life cycle by borrowing the most relevant information from the actual elite by the search agents to exploit in their local neighborhoods. Assuming that, for the ith iteration, X_{elite} identifies the seed optimal position, the corresponding mathematical expression is as follows:

$$X_{t+1} = X_{elite} + levy(\lambda) * \alpha * (X_{elite} - \delta * X_t) \tag{30}$$

Herein, $levy(\lambda)$ denotes the Levy flight function given by:

$$levy(\lambda) = s \times \frac{w \times \sigma}{|t|^{\frac{1}{\beta}}} \tag{31}$$

The parameter β has been chosen randomly to equal 1.5, while s is fixed at 0.01 [35]. w and t are numbered in the interval [0, 1]. Accordingly, σ can be mathematically expressed by:

$$\sigma = \left(\frac{\Gamma(1+\beta) \times \sin\left(\frac{\pi\beta}{2}\right)}{\Gamma\left(\frac{1+\beta}{2}\right) \times \beta \times 2^{\left(\frac{\beta-1}{2}\right)}} \right) \tag{32}$$

Based on the previous value of β, σ increase linearly obeys Equation (33):

$$\delta = \frac{2t}{T} \tag{33}$$

4.5. Pseudo Code of the Proposed DO Algorithm

The Pseudo code of the proposed DO algorithm for PEMFC parameters estimation is summarized by Algorithm 1.

Algorithm 1 Pseudo-code of the proposed DO optimizer

Input: NP, T, D and measured V-I data
Output:$\boldsymbol{X}_{best}$ and $\boldsymbol{F}_{best}$
Initialize the initial dandelion seeds population in random way
Calculate the dandelion seeds fitness values f
Choose $\boldsymbol{X}_{elite}$ based on the fitness value f
while ($t < T$) **do**
  if $(rand() < 1.5)$ **then**
    Produce adaptive parameters using Equation (23)
    Update dandelion seeds by Equation (20)
    adaptive parameters using Equation (26)
    Update seeds by Equation (25)
  Update seeds by Equation (28)
  Update seeds by Equation (30)
  Arrange dandelion seeds based on fitness values
  Update $\boldsymbol{X}_{elite}$
  if $(f_{elite} = f(X_{best}))$ **then**
    $X_{Best} = X_{elite}$, $f_{Best} = f(X_{elite})$
Return $\boldsymbol{X}_{Best}$ and $\boldsymbol{F}_{best}$

5. Validation of Simulation Results

5.1. Identification of PEMFCs' Stack Parameters, Performance Measures and Comparisons

For a sufficiently rigorous validation, the proposed method is experimentally tested on two PEMFCs (PEMFC 250 W and NedStack PS6) whose electrical characteristics and operating conditions are shown in Table 2. The experimental data for the battery voltage versus the current are shown in [40] for different operating conditions. In addition, the DO Optimizer is compared with some well-functioning and competitive algorithms such as Harris Hawks Optimization (HHO), Grey Wolf Optimizer (GWO), and Gradient-based optimizer (GBO) through various statistical criteria such as accuracy, reliability, robustness, and stability. For a proper comparison, all of these algorithms were executed according to the same operating conditions, with the number of populations (N) fixed at 30 and the maximum number of iterations defined as 100. The best results of each algorithm are obtained after 30 executions. The simulations were performed using a Matlab 2019b environment on a laptop computer with an Intel Core i7-3630, 2.4 GHz processor, and 8 GB of RAM.

To further deepen the comparisons and prove the performance of the DO algorithm, its achieved results were also compared with those reached by three optimization methods well-cited in the literature such as improved artificial ecosystem optimizer (IAEO) [38], hybrid vortex search algorithm (VSDE) [39], and artificial bee colony differential evolution shuffled complex (ABCDESC) [40].

Table 2. The known parameters of PEMFCs.

Parameters	N_{cell}	A(cm^2)	l_m(μm)	J_{max}(A cm^2)	P_{H2}(bar)	P_{O2}(bar)	P_a(atm)	P_c(atm)	T(K)	P(kW)
250 W	24	27	127	0.86	3	5	-	-	353.15	0.25
NedSstack	65	240	178	1.2	-	-	1	1	343	6

The fitness function convergence curves of the different algorithms are shown for the two PEMFCs in Figure 3. In this figure, the convergence curve of the proposed DO algorithm reveals that it is much faster than the other three algorithms for the two investigated stacks. In both examples, the DO algorithm is computationally efficient, as it converges after a small number of iterations (27 iterations).

Tables 3 and 4 contain, respectively, the optimal parameters of the PEMFC 250 W and NedStack PS6 models estimated by the proposed DO and the other investigated algorithms.

To examine the superiority of the proposed DO, statistical measures, namely, best, worst, mean and standard deviation, are performed using the best fitness values obtained by each of the independent runs. Tables 3 and 4 summarize the values obtained for the two studied PEMFCs. It is worth highlighting that the proposed DO achieves the best value (0.158400329 PEMFC 250 W and 2.257565321 NedStack PS6) of the sum of square errors (SSE) as well as the lowest standard deviation (0.002660149 for PEMFC 250 W and 0.076297062 for NedStack PS6) compared to the other algorithms. The statistical results show that DO is consistent (in terms of robustness and efficiency) as the mean and standard deviation of SSE during 30 runs are lower than those obtained by the other algorithms for the two examined stacks.

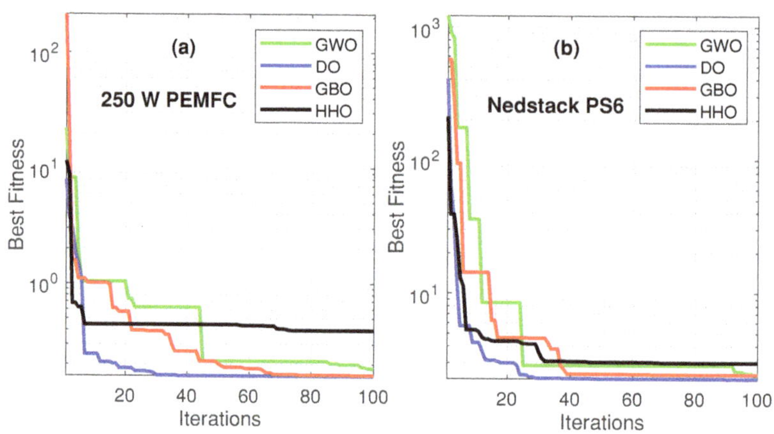

Figure 3. Convergence curve of fitness function: (**a**) 250 W fuel cell; (**b**) NedStack PS6 fuel cel.

Table 3. Optimal parameters of PEMFC 250 W.

Parameters	DO	GWO	GBO	HHO
ξ_1	−0.961592	−0.871596	−0.974457	−0.895253
ξ_2	0.00253443	0.00255737	0.00334035	0.00232372
ξ_3	3.6×10^{-5}	5.90919×10^{-5}	9.77117×10^{-5}	3.60984×10^{-5}
ξ_4	−0.000138245	−0.000141236	−0.000136735	−0.000100082
λ_m	13.3372	13.3735	13.9459	10.0273
R_c	0.000423201	0.000136504	0.0007994	0.000100273
b	0.0149649	0.0157339	0.0148931	0.0136372
Minimum SSE	0.158400329	0.160086164	0.158527784	0.276840933
Maximum SSE	0.166811864	0.353987785	0.272967021	2.136931329
Average SSE	0.160609673	0.194413051	0.18248663	0.983809404
Std SSE	0.002660149	0.046728642	0.033055337	0.488586136

Table 4. Optimal parameters of NedStack PS6.

Parameters	DO	GWO	GBO	HHO
ξ_1	−1.10823	−0.981556	−1.19841	−0.8532
ξ_2	0.00348488	0.0029638	0.00435526	0.00274411
ξ_3	5.23328×10^{-5}	4.10262×10^{-5}	9.40149×10^{-5}	5.17837×10^{-5}
ξ_4	-9.54×10^{-5}	-9.55047×10^{-5}	-9.54×10^{-5}	-9.54×10^{-5}
λ_m	23.0714	14.9218	23.95	14.3893
R_c	0.000127527	0.000198012	0.000327086	0.000186993
b	0.0835662	0.0236393	0.0539602	0.0195792

Table 4. *Cont.*

Parameters	DO	GWO	GBO	HHO
Minimum *SSE*	2.077565321	2.288386949	2.278642183	2.286126251
Maximum *SSE*	2.627548699	4.705647651	3.756412117	9.447348766
Average *SSE*	2.501037792	3.038447633	2.873919639	4.517318823
Std *SSE*	0.076297062	0.618991833	0.248397126	1.865763408

In order to evaluate the stability of the different algorithms, the boxplots, for the SSE after 30 repetitions of 100 iterations, are plotted in Figures 4 and 5. The interquartile ranges increase as one moves from the DO algorithm to the GBO algorithm and then GWO and HHO. The distribution of outcomes (SSE) built by the DO algorithm is around its median. Based on these comparisons, it can be concluded that the proposed DO algorithm achieves better performance in terms of accuracy and robustness compared to the other algorithms.

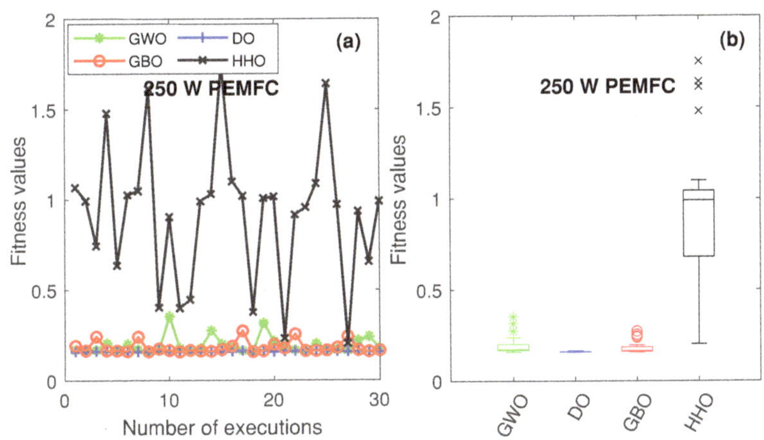

Figure 4. The statistical study of the 250 W after 30 repetitions: (**a**) best values of the objective function; (**b**) boxplot of SSE.

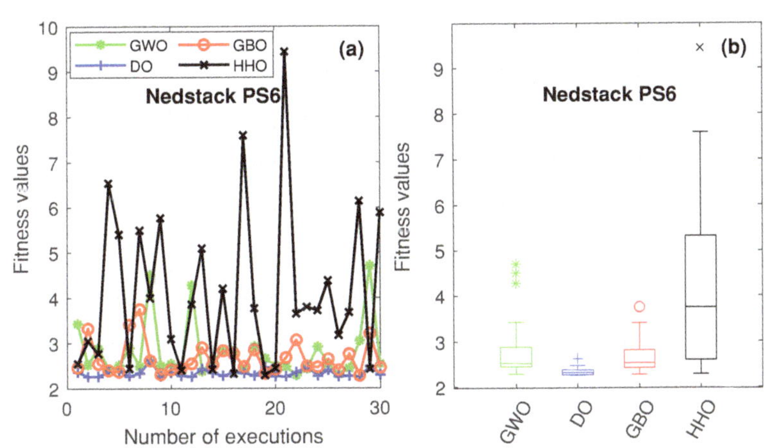

Figure 5. The statistical study of the NedStack PS6: (**a**) best values of the objective function; (**b**) boxplot of SSE.

Tables 5 and 6 summarize the results of the DO, IAEO, VSDE, and ABCDESC algorithms by illustrating the estimated parameters and SSE metric of the experimented PEMFC 250 W and NedStack PS6 fuel cells. In both case studies, the proposed DO algorithm reaches the best results with minimum SSE compared with other algorithms.

Table 5. Optimum values of unknown parameters and SSE of PEMFC 250 W.

Parameters	**DO**	**IAEO** [18]	**VSDE** [39]	**ABCDESC** [40]
ξ_1	−0.961592	−0.9991	−1.1921	−1.12806
ξ_2	0.00253443	0.002825	0.0031990	0.00394667
ξ_3	3.6×10^{-5}	4.47×10^{-5}	3.799×10^{-5}	9.777204×10^{-5}
ξ_4	−0.000138245	−0.00017	−0.000187	-0.000174889
λ_m	13.3372	19.99358	22.817	19.9358326
R_c	4.23201×10^{-4}	1.000×10^{-4}	1.202×10^{-4}	1×10^{-4}
b	0.0149649	0.0145	0.0290	0.014526
Minimum SSE	0.158400329	0.3360	1.0526	0.33597

Table 6. Optimum values of unknown parameters and SSE of NedStack PS6.

Parameters	**DO**	**IAEO** [18]	**VSDE** [39]	**ABCDESC** [40]
ξ_1	−1.10823	−0.9822	−1.1212	−0.9350526
ξ_2	0.00348488	0.0035957	0.00033487	0.0035035
ξ_3	5.23328×10^{-5}	9.48×10^{-5}	4.6787×10^{-5}	9.793216×10^{-5}
ξ_4	-9.54×10^{-5}	-9.54×10^{-5}	-9.5400×10^{-5}	-9.54×10^{-5}
λ_m	23.0714	13.4650	13.0000	13.094707
R_c	1.27527×10^{-4}	1.00×10^{-4}	1.00×10^{-4}	0.0001
b	0.0835662	0.0136	0.0494	0.0136
Minimum SSE	2.077565321	2.1459	2.088	2.079204604

Figures 6 and 7 show the experimental polarization curves and the best polarization curves obtained through the model of the I–V and I–P characteristics of the two studied PEMFCs. A closer examination of these graphs shows that the simulation results of the model with the parameters estimated using the proposed DO are very close to the experimental results. This further emphasizes the superiority of the DO to achieve a very accurate model.

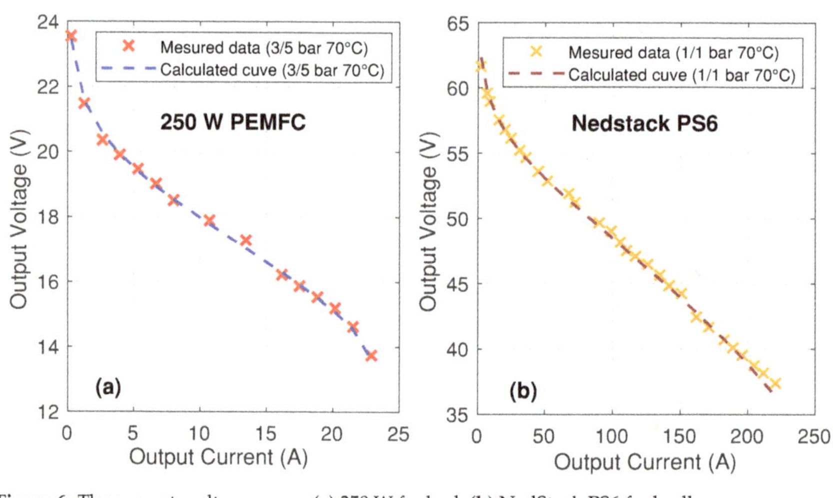

Figure 6. The current–voltage curve: (**a**) 250 W fuel cel; (**b**) NedStack PS6 fuel cell.

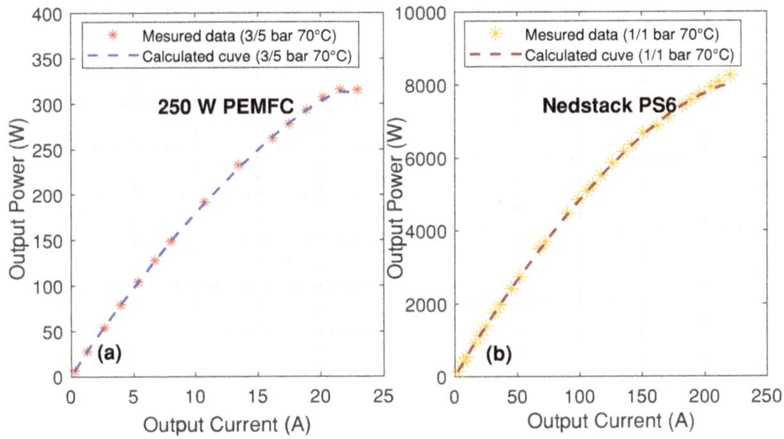

Figure 7. The current–power curve: (**a**) 250 W fuel cell; (**b**) NedStack PS6 fuel cell.

The absolute deviation of each voltage point between the real and estimated data $Div = V_{mes} - V_{est}$ of the two stacks (250 W PEMFC and NedStack PS6) for the best results of all 30 independent tests is displayed in Tables 7 and 8.

Table 7. Estimated voltage and absolute deviation of the 250 W PEMFC.

N	$i(A)$	$V_{mes}(V)$	$V_{est}(V)$	$Div(V)$	$(Div)^2(V)$
1	0.2729	23.5410	23.436884	0.1041	0.0108
2	1.2790	21.4756	21.552742	−0.0771	0.0060
3	2.6603	20.3484	20.542713	−0.1943	0.0378
4	3.9734	19.8969	19.913082	−0.0162	2.6186×10^{-4}
5	5.3547	19.4642	19.385395	0.0788	0.0062
6	6.7190	19.0127	18.934608	0.0781	0.0061
7	8.0321	18.5049	18.470406	0.0345	0.0012
8	10.7265	17.8835	17.792614	0.0909	0.0083
9	13.4720	17.2808	17.135401	0.1457	0.0449
10	16.1664	16.2089	15.996914	0.2120	0.0212
11	17.4966	15.8701	15.988641	−0.1185	0.0141
12	18.8608	15.5312	15.594024	−0.0628	0.0039
13	20.1910	15.1923	15.175456	0.01686	2.8372×10^{-4}
14	21.5553	14.6282	14.586637	0.0416	0.0017
15	22.9195	13.7450	13.693124	0.0519	0.0027
SSE	0.158400329				

Table 8. Estimated voltage and absolute deviation of the NedStack PS6.

N	$i(A)$	$V_{mes}(V)$	$V_{est}(V)$	$Div(V)$	$(Div)^2(V)$
1	2.25	61.64	62.452443	−0.8124	0.6600
2	6.75	59.57	59.873841	−0.3038	0.0923
3	9.00	58.94	59.140399	−0.2003	0.4877
4	15.75	57.54	57.582298	−0.04229	0.0017
5	20.25	56.80	56.799747	0.0002	6.36×10^{-8}
6	24.75	56.13	56.122583	0.0074	5.5×10^{-5}
7	31.50	55.23	55.729928	0.0003	1.37×10^{-7}
8	36.00	54.66	54,589203	0.0707	0.0050
9	45.00	53.61	53.604175	0.0058	3.39×10^{-5}
10	51.75	52.86	52,799762	0.0602	0.0036

Table 8. *Cont.*

N	$i(A)$	$V_{mes}(V)$	$V_{est}(V)$	$Div(V)$	$(Div)^2(V)$
11	67.50	51.91	51.48410	0.4258	0.1813
12	72.00	51.22	51.068878	0.1511	0.0228
13	90.00	49.66	49,452415	0.2075	0.04309
14	99.00	49.00	48.659847	0.3401	0.1157
15	105.80	48.15	48.064054	0.0859	0.0073
16	110.30	47.52	47.670360	−0.1503	0.0022
17	117.00	47.10	47.084098	0.0159	0.0002
18	126.00	46.48	46.294582	0.1854	0.0343
19	135.00	45.66	45.500518	0.1594	0.0254
20	141.80	44.85	44.799173	0.0508	0.0025
21	150.80	44.24	44,088817	0.1511	0.0228
22	162.00	42.45	43.069394	−0.6193	0.3836
23	171.00	41.66	42,235973	−0.5759	0.3317
24	182.30	40.68	40.708183	−0.0281	0.0007
25	189.00	40.09	40.102165	−0.0121	0.0001
26	195.80	39.51	39.455396	0.0546	0.0.0030
27	204.80	38.73	38.553613	0.1763	0.0311
28	211.50	38.15	38.696963	0.1837	0.0337
29	220.50	37.38	37.18800	0.1919	0.0368
SSE	2.257565321				

The previous results prove the excellent agreement between the measured voltage data of the two stacks (250 W PEMFC and NedStack PS6) and the model data found by the DO-based method. This is once again significant proof of the exactitude of the seven parameter values of the PEMFCs identified by DO.

5.2. Transient Response to Current Changes

The changing of the current level induces a variation of the cell voltage. Indeed, if the current varies, a time delay is required for the cell voltage to reach its steady-state value. This delay clearly affects the activation and concentration drops. However, the ohmic potential is not sensitive to this delay. To provide an approximate representation of this phenomenon, a first order transfer function cascaded with the activation and concentration potentials is adopted. In such a situation, Equations (6) and (11) are rewritten as indicated, respectively, in Equations (34) and (35):

$$V_{\text{act}} = -\left[\xi_1 + \xi_2 T + \xi_3 T \ln\left(C_{O_2}\right) + \xi_4 T \ln(i)\right] \cdot \frac{1}{1 + T_r \cdot s} \tag{34}$$

$$V_{con} = -b \cdot \ln\left(\frac{J_{max} - J}{J_{max}}\right) \cdot \frac{1}{1 + T_r \cdot s} \tag{35}$$

Herein, T_r represents the transfer function time constant.

The dynamic model is depicted in the diagram of Figure 8. It is worth mentioning that pressures, thermodynamics and valve handling are not considered in this simplified dynamic model. As illustrated in the figure, the irreversible voltage losses in the PEMFC are obtained via the "PEMFC voltage losses model" block, taking into consideration the response time of the stack. The open circuit voltage is represented by the "PEMFC Nernst output voltage model" block. It is important to remember that this voltage is determined by applying Equation (2).

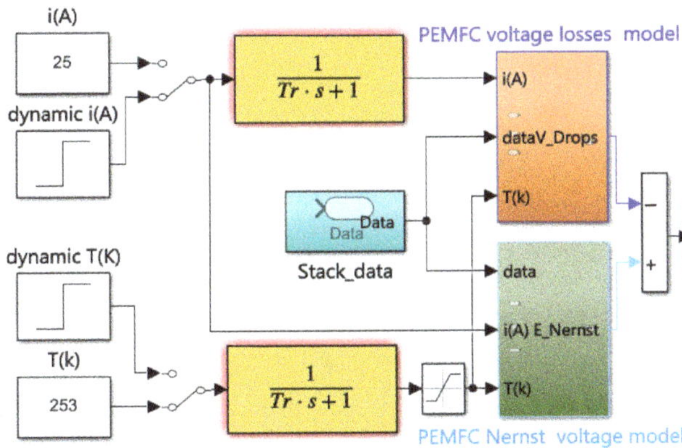

Figure 8. PEMFC simplified dynamic model.

In order to evaluate the degree of compatibility of the model based on the DO algorithm to the actual behavior of the stack, the NedStack PS6 stack is chosen to simulate the dynamic response due to changes in load current. Thus, the model based on the GBO algorithm, which has a better SSE compared to the other two methods (GWO and HHO), is simulated to perform such a comparison. Table 6 presents the best values of the unknown parameters obtained by the DO compared to those obtained by the GBO.

The experimental I–V characteristic as well as those obtained using the simulated BO-based model and the GBO-based model are depicted in Figure 9a. The results obtained are in full agreement with those shown previously; the plots show a good fit between the experimental I–V characteristics and those derived from the BO and GBO-based models. To investigate further, the unknown parameter values obtained are used in the dynamic model implemented in MATLAB/SIMULINK to examine the dynamic performance of the PS6 stack in the case where Tr equals 3 s.

To obtain an idea about the dynamic performance of the fuel cell, two load variation scenarios are applied to the generated model (increase and decrease) as shown in Figure 9b. The assumed increase and decrease time instants are 30 s and 60 s, respectively. Figure 9c shows the dynamic responses of the NedStack PS6 battery voltage as a function of load current variations. It is meaningfully clear that both models exhibit transient responses to these changes. As the load current increases, the stack voltage decreases until it reaches its steady-state value, as illustrated by the curves in Figure 9a,c.

On the other hand, when the current decreases, the stack reacts again to this change and, after a short time, the stack voltage rejoins the value of its steady-state voltage. In both cases, the performances shown are very satisfactory.

This is also confirmed by Figure 9d where the voltage errors between the real model and those generated from the BO and GBO-based models. It is shown in this figure that the voltage error generated by the developed DO model is lower.

In contrast to the optimization algorithms and the difficulties that can be encountered in their implementation for solving engineering problems, the implementation of the DO algorithm for extracting the unknown parameters of the PEMFC model allowed us to achieve the foregoing:

- Regarding the parameter settings, the population size, the mutation rate and the convergence criteria have been set appropriately for the present problem without any difficulties to be mentioned;
- For the implementation complexity, the complex operations involved in the whole process, i.e., the rising, descending, and landing stages, and the steps of generating the seeds and updating them, etc., the simplicity of the DO has allowed its implementation to be successful;

- Concerning memory usage, the dimensionality of the solved optimization problem did not cause any problems in this respect;
- The convergence speed of the DO has been satisfactory since it runs for a short period of time and achieves better results than the other tested algorithms.

Overall, with careful consideration and appropriate attention to the processes of the DO algorithm, its implementation to address the current research problem has achieved good results. Nevertheless, the concerns that may be raised will obviously be related to the cases of more complex and challenging problems with higher dimensionalities, requiring a larger amount of memory, and/or a longer execution period.

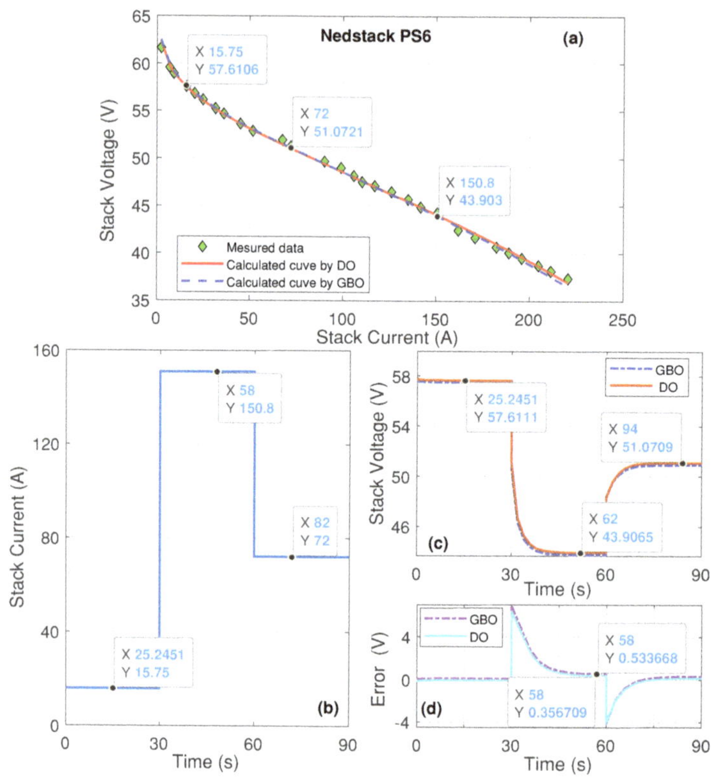

Figure 9. Characteristic and dynamic simulations of the PS6 stack: (**a**) I–V polarisation; (**b**) stack load current changes; (**c**) stack voltage responses; (**d**) voltage error.

6. Conclusions and Future Works

The research work presented in this paper deals with the development of a new optimization approach based on the DO algorithm to effectively address the (theoretical) problem of identifying the key parameters of the PEMFCs. The objective function presented aims to minimize the sum of squared deviations between the generated theoretical model and the experimental measurements of two PEM fuel cells, namely PEMFCs 250 W stack and NedStack PS6. The seven variables to be approximated are the following: ξ_1, ξ_2, ξ_3, ξ_4, λ_m, b and R_c. According to the proposed Do features, the results of its performance analysis are compared with several other programmed meta-heuristic approaches and others reported from the literature namely GWO, GBO, HHO, IAEO, VSDE, and ABCDESC under the conditions imposed by the constraints of the variables to be estimated.

The series of conducted tests and experiments showed that the proposed algorithm obtains better results, in comparison with those obtained by the competitive algorithms.

Indeed, the DO approach is faster than the other approaches in terms of generated outcomes for two tested stacks. Otherwise, it also obtained better solutions than the other methods, which shows the efficiency and robustness of the implemented approach. The superiority and efficiency of the DO are evident in terms of maximum, minimum, and median for the tested piles.

Although the performance of the proposed approach is significantly promising as a valuable tool, used for the first time, for solving the problem of nonlinear fuel cell model equations and estimating its unknown parameters, future recommendations are mainly targeted to its improvement and exploitation in this application and other fields related to renewable energy and power systems.

Author Contributions: All authors (R.A., S.S., A.A., H.J., M.K. and B.N.A.) contributed equally. All authors have read and agreed to the published version of the manuscript.

Funding: This research has been funded by Scientific Research Deanship at the University of Ha'il, Saudi Arabia through project number RD-21 083.

Data Availability Statement: Not applicable.

Conflicts of Interest: The authors declare no conflict of interest.

Abbreviations

The following abbreviations are used in this manuscript:

PEMFC	Proton exchange membrane fuel cell
DO	Dandelion optimizer
GWO	Grey wolf optimizer
GBO	Gradient-based optimizer
HHO	Harris Hawks optimizer
IAEO	Improved artificial ecosystem optimizer
VSDE	Vortex search-differential evolution
ABCDESC	Artificial bee colony differential evolution shuffled complex
HR	Hail region
CO_2	Carbon dioxide
CO	Carbon monoxide
H_2O	Water molecule
H_2	Hydrogen gas
O_2	Dioxygen gas
RE	Renewable energy
KSA	Kingdom of Saudi Arabia
UNWTO	World Tourism Organization
COVID-19	Coronavirus disease
EV	Electric vehicle
ZEVs	Zero-emission vehicles
AC	Alternative current
GTO	Gorilla troops optimizer
MGTO	Modified GTO
HBO	Honey badger optimizer
SSE	Sum of squared errors
BO	Bonobo optimizer
QOBO	Quasi oppositional bonobo optimizer
EBES	Enhanced bald eagle search
DA	Dandelion algorithm
ELM	Extreme learning machine
NNA	Neural network algorithm
ELMD	Dandelion algorithm with ELM

References

1. Zhao, L.; Jerbi, H.; Abbassi, R.; Liu, B.; Latifi, M.; Nakamura, H. Sizing renewable energy systems with energy storage systems based microgrids for cost minimization using hybrid shuffled frog-leaping and pattern search algorithm. *Sustain. Cities Soc.* **2021**, *73*, 103124. [CrossRef]
2. Li, N.; Su, Z.; Jerbi, H.; Abbassi, R.; Latifi, M.; Furukawa, N. Energy management and optimized operation of renewable sources and electric vehicles based on microgrid using hybrid gravitational search and pattern search algorithm. *Sustain. Cities Soc.* **2021**, *75*, 103279. [CrossRef]
3. Alturki, M.; Abbassi, R.; Albaker, A.; Jerbi, H. A New Hybrid Synchronization PLL Scheme for Interconnecting Renewable Energy Sources to an Abnormal Electric Grid. *Mathematics* **2022**, *10*, 1101. [CrossRef]
4. Abbassi, R.; Marrouchi, S.; Ben Hessine, M.; Chebbi, S.; Juini, H. Voltage Control Strategy of an Electrical Network by the Integration of the UPFC Compensator. *Int. Rev. Model. Simul.* **2012**, *5*, 380–384.
5. Abbassi, R.; Hammami, M.; Chebbi, S. Improvement of the integration of a grid-connected wind-photovoltaic hybrid system. In Proceedings of the International Conference on Electrical Engineering and Software Applications, Yasmine Hammamet, Tunisia, 17–19 March 2013.
6. Hong, M.D.; Yun, P.Z.; Jing, L.; Wei, T.G.; Chu, J.B. Research on energy saving potential and countermeasures in China's transport sector. *Energy Rep.* **2022**, *8*, 300–311.
7. Marko, M.; Maja, P.; Nikola, V.; Goran, K. Cross-sectoral integration for increased penetration of renewable energy sources in the energy system – Unlocking the flexibility potential of maritime transport electrification. *Smart Energy* **2022**, *8*, 100089.
8. Rasul, M.G.; Hazrat, M.A.; Sattar, M.A.; Jahirul, M.I.; Shearer, M.J. The future of hydrogen: Challenges on production, storage and applications. *Energy Convers. Manag.* **2022**, *272*, 116326. [CrossRef]
9. Hong, S.; Lee, J.; Cho, H.; Kim, M.; Moon, I.; Kim, J. Multi-objective optimization of CO_2 emission and thermal efficiency for on-site steam methane reforming hydrogen production process using machine learning. *J. Clean. Prod.* **2022**, *359*, 132133. [CrossRef]
10. Yan, X.; Li, Y.; Sun, C.; Zhang, C.; Yang, L.; Fan, X.; Chu, L. Enhanced H_2 production from steam gasification of biomass by red mud-doped Ca-Al-Ce bi-functional material. *Appl. Energy* **2022**, *312*, 118737. [CrossRef]
11. Zhang, X.Y.; Yu, W.L.; Zhao, J.; Dong, B.; Liu, C.G.; Chai, Y.M. Recent development on self-supported transition metal-based catalysts for water electrolysis at large current density. *Appl. Mater. Today* **2021**, *22*, 100913. [CrossRef]
12. Matoba, K.; Takahashi, M.; Matsuda, Y.; Higashimoto, S. Photoelectrochemical water splitting on the Pt-In2S3/CuInS2 photoelectrode under solar light irradiation: Effects of electrolytes on the solar energy to hydrogen conversion. *J. Electroanal. Chem.* **2021**, *895*, 115489. [CrossRef]
13. Chen, X.; Long, S.; He, L.; Wang, C.; Chai, F.; Kong, X.; Wan, Z.; Song, X.; Tu, Z. Performance evaluation on thermodynamics-economy-environment of PEMFC vehicle power system under dynamic condition. *Energy Convers. Manag.* **2022**, *269*, 116082. [CrossRef]
14. Ouaidat, G.; Cherouat, A.; Kouta, R.; Chamoret, D. Study of the effect of mechanical uncertainties parameters on performance of PEMFC by coupling a 3D numerical multiphysics model and design of experiment. *Int. J. Hydrogen Energy* **2022**, *47*, 23772–23786. [CrossRef]
15. Zhou, S.; Tranter, T.; Neville, T.P.; Shearing, P.R.; Brett, D.J.; Jervis, R. Fault diagnosis of PEMFC based on the AC voltage response and 1D convolutional neural network. *Cell Rep. Phys. Sci.* **2022**, *3*, 101052. [CrossRef]
16. Seo, S.H.; Oh, S.D.; Park, J.; Park, J.Y.; Lim, I.S.; Kim, M.S.; Kwak, H.Y. Diagnosis of a hydrogen-fueled 1-kW PEMFC system based on exergy analysis. *Int. J. Hydrogen Energy* **2020**, *45*, 17745–17758. [CrossRef]
17. Yang, D.; Wang, Y.; Chen, Z. Robust fault diagnosis and fault tolerant control for PEMFC system based on an augmented LPV observer. *Int. J. Hydrogen Energy* **2020**, *45*, 13508–13522. [CrossRef]
18. Mao, L.; Jackson, L.; Davies, B. Investigation of PEMFC fault diagnosis with consideration of sensor reliability. *Int. J. Hydrogen Energy* **2018**, *43*, 16941–16948. [CrossRef]
19. Chu, T.; Xie, M.; Yu, Y.; Wang, B.; Yang, D.; Li, B.; Ming, P.; Zhang, C. Experimental study of the influence of dynamic load cycle and operating parameters on the durability of PEMFC. *Energy* **2022**, *239*, 122356. [CrossRef]
20. Tang, S.; Jiang, M.; Abbassi, R.; Jerbi, H. A cost-oriented resource scheduling of a solar-powered microgrid by using the hybrid crow and pattern search algorithm. *J. Clean. Prod.* **2021**, *313*, 127853. [CrossRef]
21. Guo, S.; Abbassi, R.; Jerbi, H.; Rezvani, A.; Suzuki, K. Efficient maximum power point tracking for a photovoltaic using hybrid shuffled frog-leaping and pattern search algorithm under changing environmental conditions. *J. Clean. Prod.* **2021**, *297*, 126573. [CrossRef]
22. Abbassi, A.; Abbassi, R.; Heidari, A.A.; Oliva, D.; Chen, H.; Habib, A.; Jemli, M.; Wang, M. Parameters identification of photovoltaic cell models using enhanced exploratory salp chains-based approach. *Energy* **2020**, *198*, 117333. [CrossRef]
23. Abbassi, R.; Abbassi, A.; Heidari, A.A.; Mirjalili, S. An efficient salp swarm-inspired algorithm for parameters identification of photovoltaic cell models. *Energy Convers. Manag.* **2019**, *179*, 362–372. [CrossRef]
24. Diab, A.A.Z.; Ali, H.; Abdul-Ghaffar, H.I.; Abdelsalam, H.A.; Abd El Sattar, M. Accurate parameters extraction of PEMFC model based on metaheuristics algorithms. *Energy Rep.* **2021**, *7*, 6854–6867. [CrossRef]
25. Abdel-Basset, M.; Mohamed, R.; Chang, V. An Efficient Parameter Estimation Algorithm for Proton Exchange Membrane Fuel Cells. *Energies* **2021**, *14*, 7115. [CrossRef]

26. Ashraf, H.; Abdellatif, S.O.; Elkholy, M.M.; El-Fergany, A.A. Honey badger optimizer for extracting the ungiven parameters of PEMFC model: Steady-state assessment. *Energy Convers. Manag.* **2022**, *258*, 115521. [CrossRef]
27. Sultan, H.M.; Menesy, A.S.; Hassan, M.S.; Jurado, F.; Kamel, S. Standard and Quasi Oppositional bonobo optimizers for parameter extraction of PEM fuel cell stacks. *Fuel* **2023**, *340*, 127586. [CrossRef]
28. Alsaidan, I.; Shaheen, M.A.; Hasanien, H.M.; Alaraj, M.; Alnafisah, A.S. A PEMFC model optimization using the enhanced bald eagle algorithm. *Ain Shams Eng. J.* **2022**, *13*, 101749. [CrossRef]
29. Hachana, O.; El-Fergany, A.A. Efficient PEM fuel cells parameters identification using hybrid artificial bee colony differential evolution optimizer. *Energy* **2022**, *250*, 123830. [CrossRef]
30. Yongguang C.; Guanglei Z. New parameters identification of Proton exchange membrane fuel cell stacks based on an improved version of African vulture optimization algorithm. *Energy Rep.* **2022**, *8*, 3030–3040.
31. Li, X.; Han, S.; Zhao, L.; Gong, C.; Liu, X. New dandelion algorithm optimizes extreme learning machine for biomedical classification problems. *Comput. Intell. Neurosci.* **2017**, *2017*, 4523754. [CrossRef]
32. Zhu, H.; Liu, G.; Zhou, M.; Xie, Y.; Kang, Q. Dandelion Algorithm With Probability-Based Mutation. *IEEE Access* **2019**, *7*, 97974–97985. [CrossRef]
33. Wang, J.; Lu, S.; Wang, S.H.; Zhang, Y.D. A review on extreme learning machine. *Multimed. Tools Appl.* **2022**, *81*, 41611–41660. [CrossRef]
34. Han, S.; Zhu, K.; Wang, R. Improvement of evolution process of dandelion algorithm with extreme learning machine for global optimization problems. *Expert Syst. Appl.* **2021**, *163*, 113803. [CrossRef]
35. Zhao, S.; Zhang, T.; Ma, S.; Chen, M. Dandelion Optimizer: A nature-inspired metaheuristic algorithm for engineering applications. *Eng. Appl. Artif. Intell.* **2022**, *114*, 105075. [CrossRef]
36. Daeichian, A.; Ghaderi, R.; Kandidayeni, M.; Soleymani, M.; Trovão, J.P.; Boulon, L. Online characteristics estimation of a fuel cell stack through covariance intersection data fusion. *Appl. Energy* **2019**, *292*, 116907. [CrossRef]
37. Nóbrega, P.H.A. A review of physics-based low-temperature proton-exchange membrane fuel cell models for system-level water and thermal management studies. *J. Power Sources* **2019**, *558*, 232585. [CrossRef]
38. Rizk-Allah, R.M.; El-Fergany, A.A. Artificial ecosystem optimizer for parameters identification of proton exchange membrane fuel cells model. *Int. J. Hydrogen Energy* **2021**, *46*, 37612–37627. [CrossRef]
39. Fathy, A.; Abd Elaziz, M.; Alharbi, A.G. A novel approach based on hybrid vortex search algorithm and differential evolution for identifying the optimal parameters of PEM fuel cell. *Renew. Energy* **2020**, *146*, 1833–1845. [CrossRef]
40. Hachana, O. Accurate PEM fuel cells parameters estimation using hybrid artificial bee colony differential evolution shuffled complex optimizer. *Int. J. Energy Res.* **2022**, *46*, 6383–6405. [CrossRef]
41. Fathy, A.; Rezk, H. Multi-verse optimizer for identifying the optimal parameters of PEMFC model. *Energy* **2018**, *143*, 634–644. [CrossRef]
42. Rezaie, M.; karamnejadi azar, K.; Sani, A.K.; Akbari, E.; Ghadimi, N.; Razmjooy, N.; Ghadamyari, M. Model parameters estimation of the proton exchange membrane fuel cell by a Modified Golden Jackal Optimization. *Energy Technol. Assess.* **2022**, *53 Pt C*, 102657. [CrossRef]

Disclaimer/Publisher's Note: The statements, opinions and data contained in all publications are solely those of the individual author(s) and contributor(s) and not of MDPI and/or the editor(s). MDPI and/or the editor(s) disclaim responsibility for any injury to people or property resulting from any ideas, methods, instructions or products referred to in the content.

mathematics

MDPI

Article

Reinforcement-Learning-Based Level Controller for Separator Drum Unit in Refinery System

Anwer Abdulkareem Ali [1], Mofeed Turky Rashid [1,*], Bilal Naji Alhasnawi [2], Vladimír Bureš [3] and Peter Mikulecký [3,*]

[1] Electrical Engineering Department, University of Basrah, Basrah 61004, Iraq
[2] Department of Computer Technical Engineering, College of Information Technology, Imam Ja'afar Al-Sadiq University, Al-Muthanna 66002, Iraq
[3] Department of Information Technologies, Faculty of Informatics and Management, University of Hradec Králové, 500 03 Hradec Králové, Czech Republic
* Correspondence: mofeed.rashid@uobasrah.edu.iq (M.T.R.); peter.mikulecky@uhk.cz (P.M.)

Abstract: The Basrah Refinery, Iraq, similarly to other refineries, is subject to several industrial constraints. Therefore, the main challenge is to optimize the parameters of the level controller of the process unit tanks. In this paper, a PI controller is designed for these important processes in the Basrah Refinery, which is a separator drum (D5204). Furthermore, the improvement of the PI controller is achieved under several constraints, such as the inlet liquid flow rate to tank (m2) and valve opening in yi%, by using two different techniques: the first one is conducted using a closed-Loop PID auto-tuner that is based on a frequency system estimator, and the other one is via the reinforcement learning approach (RL). RL is employed through two approaches: the first is calculating the optimal PI parameters as an offline tuner, and the second is using RL as an online tuner to optimize the PI parameters. In this case, the RL system works as a PI-like controller of RD5204. The mathematical model of the RD5204 system is derived and simulated using MATLAB. Several experiments are designed to validate the proposed controller. Further, the performance of the proposed system is evaluated under several industrial constraints, such as disturbances and noise, in which the results indict that RL as a tuner for the parameters of the PI controller is superior to other methods. Furthermore, using RL as a PI-like controller increases the controller's robustness against uncertainty and perturbations.

Keywords: separator drum; level controller; process unit; refinery; PI controller; PID suto-tuner; reinforcement learning (RL)

MSC: 37N40; 93C80

1. Introduction

Working process units in an industrial treatment need vessels as essential components; these types of vessels may be categorized as tanks, reactors, drums, dryers, and cylinders. Of note, it is important to consider the pressure, temperature, and other variables related to the material state (liquid, gas, or solid) while designing a vessel [1]. Furthermore, in the processes of the control system, liquid level control is important because it can improve the quality of the products and make the operations safer for both workers and the equipment [2–5]. Recently in the industry, several methods and strategies for level control systems were developed, in which the performance of the level control system should meet the application requirements [6]. This manuscript represents a follow-up and extension of the study dealing with the design of PI controllers for tank level in the industrial process [7].

There are many types of industrial applications in which it is important to take into account non-linearity when looking at the stability margins or robustness requirements of a control system. In the refinery industry, tanks are used for separation purposes; they are referred to as "separator drums" or "flash drums". Separators are an essential component of the entire process of an oil refinery, in which an oil–gas separator is a pressurized vessel that is used to separate a liquid stream into its gas and liquid components; this type of separator is a two-phase separator [8,9]. It is noteworthy that physical changes in the fluid stream may lead to these types of separations, where there are no chemical interactions between the parts of these mixtures, and the boundaries of each phase are very clear. Moreover, the level, concentration, temperature, and mass flow in the feed stream all have a significant influence on the efficiency of the separator drums; therefore, a robust control system is needed to control the separation process [10]. To achieve this goal, the separation process should be modeled to design a high-performance controller for the separator drum [11].

Some of the major refineries in Iraq are the Southern Refineries, which are located in Basrah Province. These refineries include D5204, which is a recontacting drum, as a separator vessel used to improve the gasoline production unit. In this process unit, as long as the sensors and valves are working ideally, the controllers can keep the level, temperature, and pressure at or near their set points [12]. A combination of unpredictable circumstances might result in dangerously high drum pressure, such as faults in the valve of the top vapor effluent and the valve of the bottom liquid effluent, which leads to closing them [13]. These uncertain situations induce disturbances, which need a significant robust controller in order to be overcome.

In refinery stations, the Proportional-Integral-Derivative (PID) controller is mostly used, although more sophisticated control systems were developed in recent years [14]. To achieve a high-performance PID controller, three parameters of the PID controller must be carefully evaluated. These parameters are the proportional gain (KP), which influences the rising time but never eliminates steady-state inaccuracy; the integral gain (Ki), which eliminates the steady-state inaccuracy, albeit at the expense of the transient responsiveness; and the derivative gain (Kd), which can offer improved transient responsiveness, cut down on overshoot, and make the system more stable [15,16]. In noisy systems, due to the noise being amplified by the Kd parameter, the PI controller is used to handle variables of the industrial process, and the derivative portion of the controller is deactivated (level, velocity, pressure, location, temperature, etc.) [15]. Obtaining the optimal PID parameters to design a robust controller is the main challenge without significant knowledge of the plant. Over many years, several techniques were proposed to evaluate the optimum values of PID parameters [17,18]. There is a common aim in all tuning processes: reduce the overshoot, settle quicker, and achieve more robustness in the case of uncertainty. In general, most researchers focused on evaluating optimal performance have considered set-point tracking, disturbance rejection, and reducing noise effects.

Researchers have proposed many control strategies to regulate the liquid levels in drums; one of the main methods is a PID controller in which the research focuses on evaluating the optimum values of the PID parameters. These works are mentioned as follows.

Singh et al. proposed a new method to keep the levels in three tanks in a row under control. Approaches can be summed up by considering the three tanks as one large tank with one PI controller and two other PI controllers as support. This way, the three tanks appear almost as one. The main objective is to keep both the output flow rate and the level of the three tanks under control. The main advantages of this method are the simple structure of the PI controller and the ability to obtain specification requirements, but it has very high time consumption in tuning the PI controller, which uses the trial and error method [19]. In addition, Jáureguim et al. used PI/PID controllers to keep the level of a conical tank at the appropriate level. They used the PI/PID tuning method to examine how well the system worked in several cases. They used the first root locus for tuning, followed by the Ziegler and Nichols methods, and finally particle swarm optimization. They found that the last method was the best because it had the lowest integral absolute error (IAE) and also the least amount of energy used. This method does not give a clear picture of how well the whole system works because it only tests set-point tracking. In other words, it does not consider the disturbances during the validation of the system [20].

Simultaneously, in the process area, and particularly in the oil and gas fields, Christoph Josef Backi et al. developed a straightforward model based on a gravity separator for liquid and pressure management while improving the separation efficiency. The findings indicate that a considerably higher level of water is more advantageous for the separation process, although this is dependent on the level controller's accuracy. Because the restricted control range is irrelevant here, the control is useless for other forms of separation involving high pressure [21]. Edison R. Sásig et al. proposed a linear algebra-based technique for controlling quadruple tank systems. While this approach performed well in general, it had some limitations, including an inability to be used in industrial applications that need more precise control and precision. It may be useful for huge tanks (storage tanks) that require the controller to be turned on and off [22].

Reyes-La et al. suggested a straightforward approach that combines a PI controller for regular level management with additional PI controllers constraining the limit and surplus levels. The primary purpose of this technology is to minimize flow oscillations via liquid level control. This technique requires less modeling work and computing time, as well as extremely easy tuning procedures, but also provides less control over the efficiency level and is suitable for lower and higher bounds [23]. Again, in the separator industry, Sathasivam et al. employed particle swarm optimization (PSO) to tune the PI controller to enhance three-phase separator level control. The system responded with a smaller integral square error (ISE) and a shorter process settling time, but their work did not accurately assess the system in the presence of any disruption, such as instantly lowering the feed input or perturbing the output stream [24].

Additionally, Nath et al. used internal model control (IMC) to construct an auto-tuning level control loop with the goal of minimizing the discrepancy between the intended and measured levels, using twenty-five fuzzy rules for adaptive control. This approach is excellent for adjusting level control loops live, but it is computationally demanding and requires a large number of fuzzy rules, which is its primary drawback [25]. Shuyou Yu et al. proposed a feed-forward controller and a feedback controller for the control level for three tank systems. On the one hand, this method achieved high accuracy and matched the input constraints, but when measurement noises and mismatches were factored in, the model produced large errors [26]. Junjie et al. developed a technique for liquid level control in double capacity tanks based on a PID control theory algorithm. The form result indicates that the designed system is capable of maintaining the liquid level close to the desired level; however, the PID parameters were tuned using the trial and error method, which requires additional experimentation and time to obtain optimal values, and the system was not tested with external noise to determine its resistance [27].

Ujjwal Manikya Nath et al. designed a PID controller with a cascade lag filter. This design is applied to a very common integrator process system that is a level control loop. The method is based on the desired characteristics in a question. This question includes two parameters: the closed-loop time constant (k) and damping ratio (d). Values of (k) and (d) are obtained from perfect values of IAE. Robustness of the response is seen for upset samples; in addition, more stability can be provided [28]. Simultaneously, V.P. Singh et al. developed a PID controller-tuning algorithm for the hypothetical scenario of a control system consisting of three vertical tanks linked in series. Their concept was based on Box's evolutionary optimization and optimization based on teacher–learner relationships (BEO-TLBO). By reducing the unit step response's ISE, the TLBO algorithm and Box's evolutionary technique achieved the necessary specifications with high precision. The system's behavior is uncertain when used in conjunction with numerous hybrid algorithm applications [29].

Most industrial applications include integrator systems, such as process tanks, distillation columns, chemical reactors, and other oil industry applications, that cause many researchers to seek methods or algorithms to improve the control efficiency for integrator systems. Tomaž Kos et al. proposed an extension of the magnitude optimum multiple integrations (MOMI) tuning methods for integrator processes controlled by two degrees of freedom (2-DOF). When two processes are exactly equivalent, this extension can obtain controller parameters in two ways: the time domain and the process transfer function of a specified order with time delay. This method did not examine the system controller output's high-frequency disturbance or more diverse types of process noise [30]. A novel algorithm based on the machine learning technique, proposed by Ali Hussien Mary et al., includes an intelligent controller using adaptive neuro-fuzzy inference system-based reinforcement learning for the control of non-linear coupled tank systems. This work achieved good tracking and less settling time. On the other hand, this approach has many weaknesses, such as the method being applied to a very simple application and not being considered suitable for industrial application. The accuracy method is not useful with continuous control valves; therefore, it is only used with on/off valves and does not test the system with any type of industrial disturbance [31].

In this paper, the processing unit that is the improvement unit of gasoline production, located in the Basrah Refinery, Southern Iraq, was investigated to improve the performance of this system. In this operation process, a separator drum was employed to achieve the operation of improvement; therefore, the first step for this mission is deriving a mathematical model of the separator drum, after which the processing unit performance is evaluated. The PI control system was adopted to improve the overall system performance. To calculate the optimum values of the PI parameters, several approaches are utilized, which are the Ziegler and Nichols method [32] and the auto-tuning approach. Additionally, we describe the tuning and optimization of the parameters of a PI controller with the reinforcement learning technique. Further, the RL agent was used as a PI-like controller, in which the PI parameters were adapted during operation. According to the MATLAB simulations, the proposed system response has less overshoot, settles more quickly, and is more resilient to shocks. It is noteworthy that the system response in the case of evaluating the PI parameters by the RL approach is superior to the other methods under the effect of the disturbances. Further, using the RL system as a PI-like controller overcomes the noise effect. There are several contributions to this work, which can be summarized as follows:

1. To emulate the performance of the RD5204 system, it was mathematically modeled depending on the information of the existing system in the Basrah Refinery. Further, the system performance was evaluated in the case of using a conventional PI controller, and its parameters were evaluated by trial and error.
2. The auto-tuning method was used to evaluate the optimal PI parameters that achieve a performance improvement.
3. The reinforcement learning approach (as an offline tuner) was proposed to evaluate the optimal PI parameters that will increase the robustness of the system controller against perturbation.
4. Reinforcement learning (as an online tuner) was used as an adaptive PI-like controller; in this case, the system performance will be more robust against perturbation and noise.

This paper is organized as follows: Section 2 provides a brief background about the Basrah Refinery. Section 3 discusses the mathematical modeling for systems and controllers with various approaches; Section 4 contains all experiments and results that pertain to the different scenarios that are described later. Finally, Section 5 includes the conclusions and a discussion.

2. Background

In 1969, Southern Refineries Company was established with the building of the Basrah Refinery, which commenced operation in 1974 with the installation of Refining Unit No. 1, as seen in Figure 1. It is one of the country's largest manufacturing units, using cutting-edge scientific techniques and modern technology to produce oil derivatives that mimic its high-quality goods, including imported ones, and match customer criteria. They will continue to modernize and develop the business, broaden their product offerings, and enhance their quality. This was accomplished via the development of a refinery and a second unit dedicated to the improvement of gasoline and oil refineries, as well as the liquidator of Dhi Qar and Maysan, which is presently assisting the firm in obtaining a certificate of quality performance (ISO) [33].

Figure 1. UNIT 7501 in Basrah Refinery.

The naphtha HDS with a stabilization and splitting unit (U7501) was designed for preparing the feedstock of modern catalytic reforming and isomerization units within the Basrah Refinery. Naphtha receives input from U7501 and sends it to a catalytic reforming unit which comprises paraffin ranging from C6 to C11, naphthenes, and aromatics. The main objective of this reforming process can be summarized as generating high-octane aromatics to use as a blending component in gasoline of high octane. The hydrogen is created by the vapor phase of D5204. Hydrogen is used to generate an upstream to control the pressure of the valve that is used to power the naphtha hydrotreatment unit (Figure 2). RD-D5204 separated liquid is delivered to the stabilization section through the gas network that is rich in hydrogen at 24 bar g.

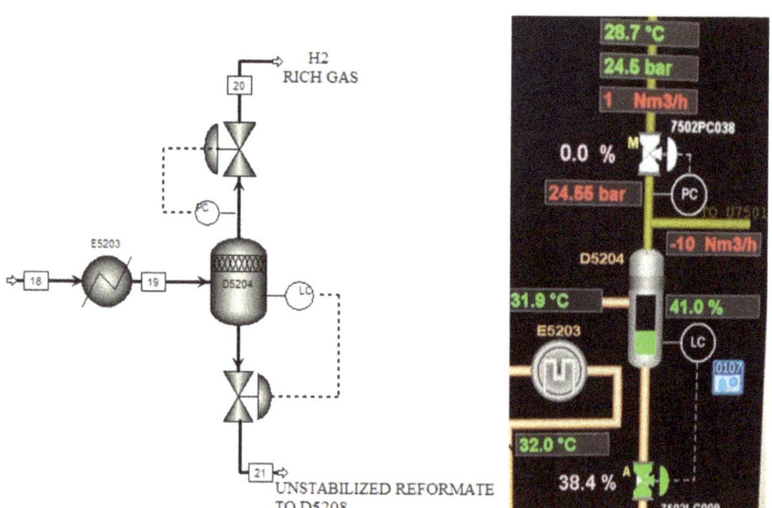

(a) (b)

Figure 2. DRUM D5204 schematic diagram: (**a**) schematic diagram; (**b**) graphical user interface (GUI).

3. Mathematical Model

3.1. RD 5204 Mathematical Model

Figure 3 shows the RD5204 (flash drum or separator) which has the following specifications [7]:

(a) (b)

Figure 3. D5204 in Basrah Refinery: (**a**) process tank; (**b**) electrival valve.

1. Item: 7502-D5204.
2. The mixture is readily accessible at (45) °C, (25) bar.
3. The gravity 759 kg/m^3 and molar inlet is 48,141 kg/h or (1159.01) kmole/h (constant pressure).
4. With pressure (25), this stream will be split into two phases, with 85% liquid and 15% vapor.
5. The physical separation is occurring in a flash drum with a height is 5.2 m and a diameter is 1.6 m.
6. In the flash drum, liquid–vapor equilibrium is achieved because the relative volatility of the liquids is sufficiently different.

To assist in the conservation of all processing systems (PS), each (PS) should have a unit comprehensive mass balance, one component of mass balance, and a comprehensive energy balance. Momentum balancing is used when there are large pressure or density differences. The dynamics balance equations (DBE) propose that each balance is initially dynamic. The static characteristic of a process may be transformed into a static equation. The flash process establishes the mass and energy balance [9].

- Balance over Total PS:
  - Total mass balance:

$$\frac{dM}{dt} = \dot{m}_{2V} + \dot{m}_{2L} - \dot{m}_3 - \dot{m}_4 \tag{1}$$

where M is the total mass, $\dot{m}_i$ is the current mass flow i, subscript V is the vapor, and L is the liquid in multiphase currents.

  - Energy balance:

$$\frac{dQ}{dt} - \frac{dW}{dt} + \dot{m}_{2L} * \widehat{H}_{2L} + \dot{m}_{2V} * \widehat{H}_{2V} - \dot{m}_3 * \widehat{H}_3 - \dot{m}_4 * \widehat{H}_4 = \frac{dE_T}{dt} \tag{2}$$

with $\frac{dQ}{dt}$ as the heat flow and $\frac{dW}{dt}$ as the work flow of the system, and $(\hat{H}_i)$ is the specific enthalpy of current E_T, the total energy of total PS.

- Balance over Liquid Process System (PS liquid):
  - Total mass balance:

$$\frac{dL_L}{dt} = \frac{1}{\rho L * \pi * r^2} * (\dot{m}_{2L} - \dot{m}_4) \tag{3}$$

with L_L as the liquid level in the tank, ρ_i as the phase density i (vapor or liquid), and r is the tank radius.

- Balance over Vapor Process System (PS vapor):
  - Total mass balance:

$$\frac{dP}{dt} = \frac{1}{V_V} * \left(\frac{R * T}{M_{mV}} * \dot{m}_{2V} - \frac{R * T}{M_{mV}} * \dot{m}_3 - P * \frac{dV_V}{dt} \right) \tag{4}$$

where P is the pressure of the vapor phase inside the tank, R is the universal gas constant and the operating temperature, M_{mV} is the molecular mass of vapor, and V_V is the volume of vapor phase inside the flash tank.
For liquid or vapor flow through the output flash tank valve, it is necessary to calculate $(\dot{m}_3)$ and $(\dot{m}_4)$, and the vapor and liquid flows exiting the flash tank are

$$\dot{m}_i = Cv_i * \frac{\gamma_i}{100} * \sqrt{\Delta P_i * \rho_i} \tag{5}$$

where Cv_i is the coefficient of the valve for phase i, γ_i is the valve opening percentage, and Δ_i is the pressure drop through the valve acting over phase i. In valve sizing, ρ_i is taken equal to 50% for a nominal or design flow.

3.2. Auto-Tuning PID Mathematical Model

In an ideal PID form, the output u(t) is the sum of the three proportional terms: (P) term, integral (I) term, and derivative (D) term [7].

$$u(t) = K_c e(t) + \frac{K_c}{\tau_1} \int_0^t e(\tau) d\tau + K_c \tau_D \frac{de(t)}{dt} \tag{6}$$

where $e(t) = r(t) - y(t)$ is the feedback error, and τ_D is the derivative control gain. The transfer function is

$$\frac{U(s)}{E(S)} = C(s) = K_c \left(1 + \frac{1}{\tau_1 s} + \tau_D S \right) \tag{7}$$

The controller's output is adjusted based on the amount of the mistake using the P action (mode). In certain cases, the steady-state offset can be eliminated with I action (mode), but the D action (mode) forecasts the future trend (mode). A wide range of process applications may benefit from these useful capabilities, and the features' openness ensures widespread user acceptability [34].

Two estimated frequency responses were evaluated from the relay testing data, which are the fundamental frequency $G_p(j\omega_1)$, $w_1 = \frac{2\pi}{N\Delta t}$ and $G_p(j\omega_2)$. In the case of the system having no disturbance, w_2 was selected as $3w_1$, otherwise, $2w_1$. The transfer function of the ideal PID will be as:

$$c(s) = \frac{c_2 s^2 + c_1 s + c_0}{s} \tag{8}$$

where $K_c = c_1$, $\tau_1 = c_1/c_0$, and $\tau_D = c_2/c_1$. To design a high-performance PID controller, the optimal parameters of c_2, c_1, and c_0 are evaluated based on the estimated frequency response.

We adjust the PID gains automatically in real time in response to the predicted plant frequency response in a closed-loop experiment. We utilize the frequency response estimator to obtain a real-time estimate of a physical plant's frequency response based on experiments.

- At the normal operating range, we inject sine wave test signals into the plant.
- We collect data on the reaction of the plant's performance.
- We estimate the frequency.

A recursive least squares (RLS) algorithm [35–38] is used to evaluate the predicted frequency response. The plant's frequency response $G(jw) = \gamma\angle j\theta$ was assumed; when the system is excited by a signal $u(t) = Asin(wt)$, the steady-state of system response is $y(t) = A\gamma\sin(jwt + \theta)$, as follows:

$$y(t) = (\gamma\cos\theta)A\sin(\omega t) + (\gamma\sin\theta)A\cos(\omega t) \tag{9}$$

For any time, $Asin(wt)$ and $Acos(wt)$ are known. So, they can be employed as regresses in an RLS algorithm to predict $\gamma cos(\theta)$ and $\gamma sin(\theta)$ based on system output $y(t)$ in real time.

In the case of the excitation signal containing an accumulation of multiple signals, then

$$u(t) = A_1\sin(\omega_1 t) + A_2\sin(\omega_2 t) + \cdots \tag{10}$$

The estimation algorithm uses $A_i sin(wt)$ and $A_i cos(wt)$ as regressors to estimate $\gamma_i cos(\gamma_i)$ and $\gamma_i sin(\gamma_i)$. For N frequencies, the algorithm uses 2N regresses. The calculation is performed on the assumption that a system with zero nominal input and output is feeding by perturbation signal u(t).

3.3. *The Twin-Delayed Deep Deterministic Policy Gradient (TD3) Algorithm*

The TD3 algorithm is a technique for off-policy reinforcement learning that is online and model-free. The TD3 agent is an RL agent that incorporates actor–critic skills and pursues the optimal policy that maximizes the expected cumulative long-term reward [39]. The TD3 algorithm is an elongation of the DDPG algorithm. DDPG agents can overvalue functions, which can produce suboptimal policies. To avoid overestimation of the value function, the TD3 method incorporates the following adjustments to the DDPG algorithm.

1. The TD3 agent learns two Q-value functions and changes policies based on the estimated minimum value function.
2. In contrast to Q functions, TD3 agents modify their policies and targets more slowly.
3. When the policy is updated, a TD3 agent introduces noise into the target action, making it less likely to exploit actions with high Q-value estimations.

TD3 agents use the following actor and critic representations.

Critic: One or more Q-value function critics Q (S, A).

Actor: Deterministic policy actor π (S).

The following training procedure is used by TD3 agents in which they update their actor and critic models at each time step.

- Initialize each critic Qk(S, A) with random parameter values ϕk, and initialize each target critic with the same random parameter values: $\phi tk = \phi k$.
- Initialize the actor $\pi(S)$ with random parameter values θ, and initialize the target actor with the same parameter values: $\theta t = \theta$.

For each time phase of training,

1. For the current monitoring S, select action $A = \pi(S) + N$, where N denotes stochastic noise as defined by the noise model.
2. Run action A. Observe the benefit R and next monitoring S′.
3. Store the knowledge (S, A, R, S') in the knowledge buffer.
4. Sample a random mini-batch of M knowledge (S_i, A_i, R_i, S'_i) from the knowledge buffer.
5. If S'_i is a terminal state, set the value function target y_i to R_i. Otherwise, set it to

$$y_i = R_i + \gamma * \min_k(Q_{tk}(S_i', \text{clip}(\pi_t(S_i' \mid \theta_t) + \varepsilon) \mid \varnothing_{tk})) \quad (11)$$

To compute the cumulative benefit, the agent first computes the next action by passing the next monitoring S_i' from the sampled knowledge to the target actor. The agent finds the cumulative rewards by passing the next action to the target critics.

1. Update the parameters of each critic at each time training step by minimizing the loss L_k over all sampled experiences.

$$L_K = \frac{1}{M}\sum_{i=1}^{M}(y_i - Q_k(S_i, A_i \mid \phi_k))^2 \quad (12)$$

2. At every D1 step, update the actor parameters using the following sampled policy gradient to maximize the expected discounted reward.

$$\nabla_\theta J \approx \frac{1}{M}\sum_{i=1}^{M} G_{ai}G_{\pi i} \quad (13)$$

$$G_{ai} = \nabla_A \min_K(Q_k(S_i, A \mid \varnothing))$$

where $A = \pi(S_i \mid \theta)$

$$G_{\pi i} = \nabla_\theta \pi(S_i \mid \theta)$$

where $G_a i$ is the gradient of the minimum critic output with respect to the action computed by the actor network, and $G_\pi i$ is the gradient of the actor output with respect to the actor parameters. Both gradients are evaluated for observation S_i.

3. At every D2 step, update the target actor and critics based on the technique used to update the target.

4. Experiments and Results

This section focuses on validating the D5204 system using MATLAB, as well as the simulation of the real industrial system by designing several experiments. Therefore, the first group of experiments evaluates the performance of the closed-loop system by using a PI controller, and then an auto-tuner is used to optimize the performance of the system; finally, we validate the use of RL to optimize the PI controller for the best performance. The second group of experiments uses the RL agent as an online tuner to optimize the PI parameters; in this case, the RL system works as an RL PI-like controller of RD5204. The D5204 system that is designed by Simulink is shown in Figure 4, and the real parameters of the D5204 system in the process unit of the Basrah Refinery are listed in Table 1 [7].

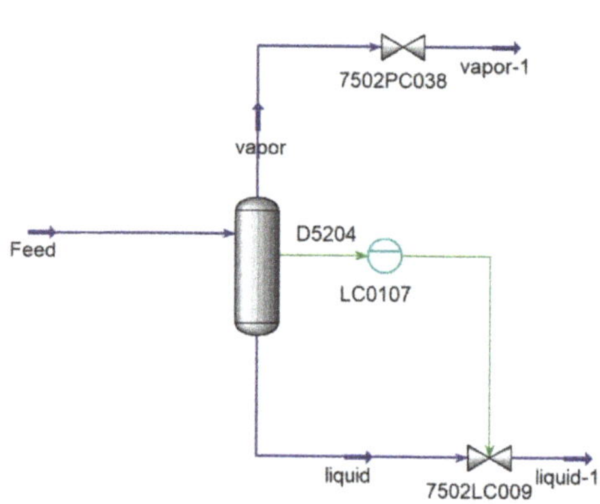

Figure 4. Graphical representation of model.

Table 1. Parameters of the D5204 system in process unit of Basrah Refinery.

Height:	5200 mm tang to tang
Diameter:	1600 mm
Total volume:	11.5 m^3
Operation pressure:	25 bar
Operation temperature:	45 °C
Liquid density at 45 °C:	759 kg/m^3
Liquid operation density for inlet stream:	650.52 kg/m^3
Liquid operation density for output stream:	722.8 kg/m^3
The level control valve coefficient:	cvi = 44.6
The pressure drop through the valve acting:	10 bar
Inlet liquid flow rate to tank m2:	600 Kmole/h
Valve opening in % yi:	50%
Desired level set point:	40%

Several scenarios were designed using Simulink in MATLAB to validate the proposed systems as follows:

1. Analyzing the performance of the D5204 system with a PI controller in which the PI parameters are manually tuned in the case of effect factors (inlet feed and opening valve);
2. Analyzing the performance of the D5204 system with a PI controller in which the PI parameters are optimized by an auto-tuner in the case of effect factors (inlet feed and opening valve);
3. Analyzing the performance of the D5204 system with a PI controller in which the PI parameters are optimized by the RL approach in the case of effect factors (inlet feed and opening valve);
4. Using an RL controller as a PI-like controller and analyzing the performance of the D5204 system in the case of effect factors (inlet feed and opening valve).

4.1. PI Controller (Evaluating PI Parameters by Manual Tuning) [7]

The system performance was enhanced by a PI controller, and it will be built in the manner seen in Figure 5. It is being developed at present to enhance the performance with this controller configuration. The settings for the PI will be determined by a trial and error method. This approach is widely used in practically every industrial application and has a high rate of success. There are many challenges, including having an expert and professional engineer available to observe the system's performance to tune the PI parameters by trial and error. Normally, this mission takes about 4 to 6 work hours to achieve an acceptable system response as that in Basrah Refinery which is shown in Figure 6.

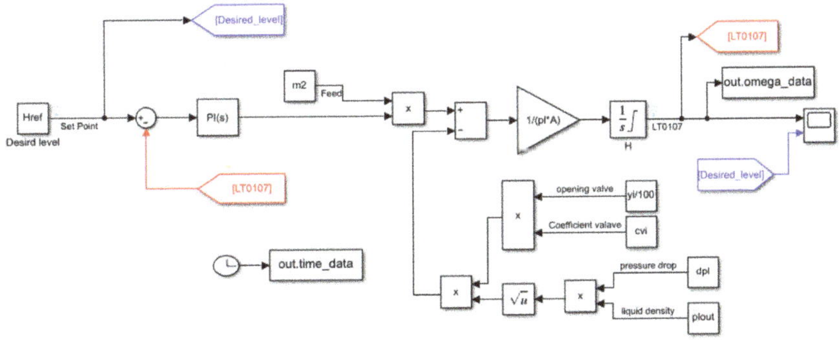

Figure 5. Overall system with PI control.

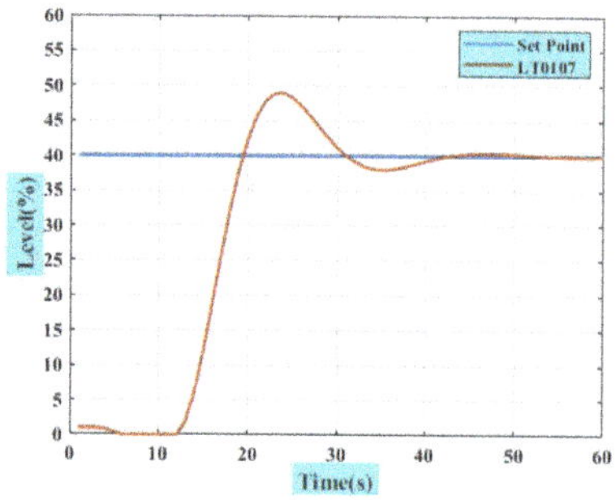

Figure 6. System response with manual tuning.

Rising-time and overshoot are the most critical components to examine when assessing the system's reaction and may be used to evaluate the system's overall performance, since the results indicate a high value for overshoot and other system characteristics. Certain issues arise often in refineries and other industries for a variety of reasons, including insufficient input supplies, valve failures, and so on. Due to this immediate failure happening while the system is running, the situational feed rate will decrease to 250 kg/h causing the level to deviate from the desired level, preventing the system from meeting the performance requirements for the desired process operation—as a result, affecting all product specifications. Another factor influencing system performance is the accuracy of the output control valve. Hence, any modification or failure in this component would decrease the system responsiveness. The result is shown in Figure 7 and Table 2, which show that the system responds to disturbances, such as changing the input feed m2 or opening the valve value and recording the system's response to these changes after modifying the PI controller.

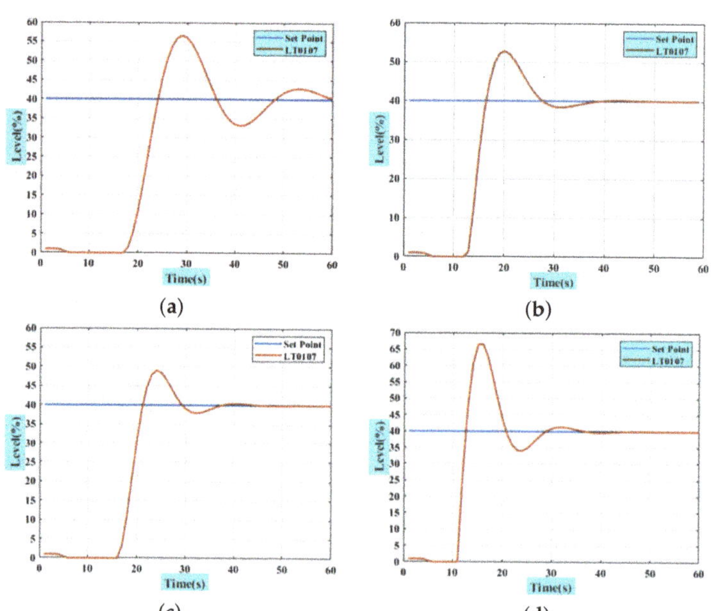

Figure 7. System response in case of several values of m2 and yi: (**a**) decrease m2 to 250 kmole/h; (**b**) increase m2 to 1000 kmole/h; (**c**) increase yi to 100%; (**d**) decrease yi to 0%.

Table 2. Step-response characteristics for system in Figure 7.

Parameters	m2 = 250 kmole/h	m2 = 1000 kmole/h	yi = 100%	yi = 0%
Rise Time	4.9	1.42	3.57	1.03
Transient Time	57.46	25.15	35.6	35.49
Settling Time	57.46	25.15	35.6	35.49
SettlingMin	33.10	38.28	37.97	34.23
SettlingMax	56.61	53.98	49.1	66.56
Overshoot	38.98%	34.96%	22.5%	86.46%
Undershoot	0	0	0	0
Peak	56.61	53.98	49.1	66.56
Peak Time	29	20	24	16

4.2. *PI Controller (Estimating PI Parameters by Auto-Tuning) [7]*

The system in Figure 5 was modified to include the closed-loop PID auto-tuner block, which is added between the PI controller and the plant to optimize the PI parameters, as illustrated in Figure 8. The closed-loop PID auto-tuner blocks functions are equivalent to a unity gain block, except that the u signal is wired directly to u + Δu. To configure the closed-loop PID auto-tuner block, the following settings should be implemented.

Target bandwidth: Determines the rate at which the controller should reply. The target bandwidth is roughly (2/desired rise time). For a 4 s rising time, set the target bandwidth = 0.5 rad/s.

Target phase margin: Determines the controller's robustness. Begin with the default setting of 75 degrees in this example.

Experiment sample time: Sample time for the experiment performed by the auto-tuner block. Use the recommended (0.02/bandwidth) for sample time = 0.04 s.

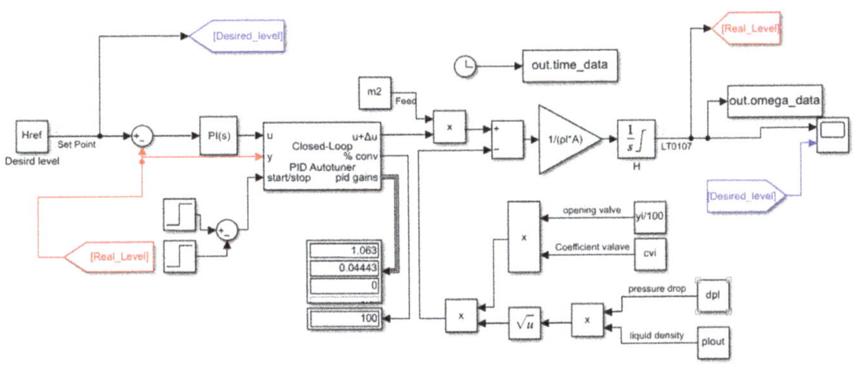

Figure 8. Overall system with closed-loop PID auto-tuning.

The experiment is started at 140 s to ensure that the material level has reached steady state H = 40. The recommended experiment duration is 200/bandwidth seconds = 200/0.4 = 500 s. With a start time of 140 s, the stop time is 640 s. The simulation stop time is further increased to capture the full experiment. For estimated PI gains, the PID auto-tuning block will employ several approaches, such as insinuating signals into the system to obtain a frequency response in real time. The overall system will be perturbed by a sinusoidal type of testing signal. After finishing the experiment, it is easy to obtain a PI parameter based on plant frequency estimation. The PI controller directly updates the values of the PI parameters. In order to obtain the best system response values, we must first compute the system response characteristic as below.

With a maximum of 60 s needed for system frequency estimation and PI gain values for optimum PI parameters, this tuning strategy has the significant advantage of taking less time to calculate the ideal PI parameters and improving other characteristics, such as the rising time and overshoot, which are shown in Figure 9. Validation of the control system with the same disturbance in the previous scenario was achieved, in which the behavior of the system is shown in Figure 10 and Table 3. From the results, it can be seen that the performance when using the auto-tuning method is superior to the manual tuning of the PI parameters.

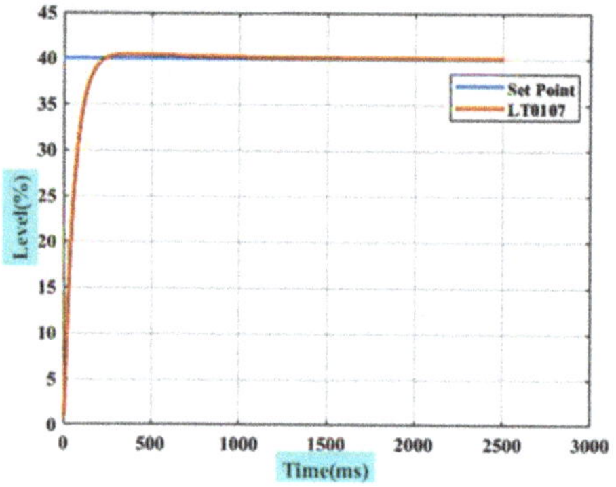

Figure 9. System response with closed-loop PID auto-tuning.

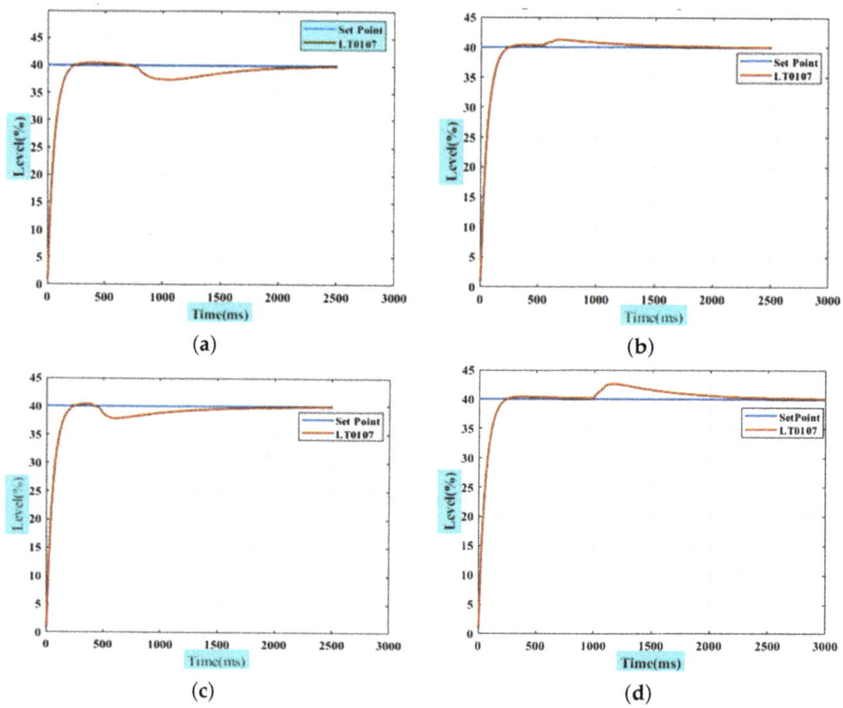

Figure 10. Response of system with closed-loop auto-tuning PID controller in the case of several values of m2 and yi; (**a**) decrease m2 to 250 kmole/h; (**b**) increase m2 to 1000 kmole/h; (**c**) increase yi to 100%; (**d**) decrease yi to 0%.

Table 3. Step-response characteristics for system in Figure 10.

Parameters	m2 = 250 kmole/h	m2 = 1000 kmole/h	yi = 100%	yi = 0%
Rise Time	116.54	116.54	116.54	116.54
Transient Time	2637.5	194.44	1642.7	5780
Settling Time	2626.3	193.60	1629	5766.1
SettlingMin	36.00	36.00	36.00	36.00
SettlingMax	41.04	40.72	40.39	42.39
Overshoot	0.98%	1.82%	0.98%	5.98%
Undershoot	0	0	0	0
Peak	40.39	40.72	40.39	42.39
Peak Time	388	6193	388	7633

4.3. *PI Controller (Estimating PI Parameters by RL Approach)*

In this section, the improvement of a PI controller using the RL approach (TD3) was considered. When comparing model-free RL with other techniques, model-based tuning strategies may provide acceptable results with a reduced tuning time for relatively simple control tasks involving only one or a few tunable parameters. RL techniques, on the other hand, may be more appropriate for highly non-linear systems or adaptive controller tuning. The system in Figure 5 was modified by using an RL block for the estimation of PI parameters via the following steps:

1. Delete the PI controller.
2. Insert an RL agent block.
3. Create the observation vector $[\int edte]^T$, where $e = r - h, h$ is the height of the tank, and r is the reference height. Connect the observation signal to the RL agent block.
4. Define the reward function for the RL agent as the negative, i.e.,

$$\text{Reward} = -\left((ref - h)^2(t) + 0.01u^2(t)\right) \tag{14}$$

The RL agent maximizes this reward, for which the resulting model is as shown in Figure 11.

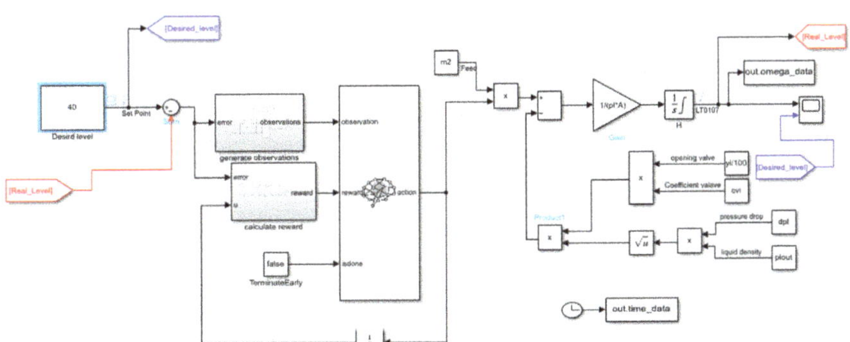

Figure 11. System with RL agent.

4.3.1. Create TD3 Agent

When we wish to create a TD3 agent that is given observations, a TD3 agent selects the action to perform using an actor. To build the actor, we first establish a deep neural network using the observation input and the action output. A PI controller can be modeled as a neural network (NN) with one fully connected layer with error and error integral observations: $u = [\int edte] * [K_i K_p]^T$. Here:

- U is the outlet of the actor NN.
- K_p and K_i are the absolute values of the neural network weights.
- $e = r - h, h$ is the height of the tank, and r is the reference height.

Using two critic value–function representations, a TD3 proxy approximates the long-term award associated with monitoring and actions. To begin, we construct a deep neural network with two inputs, observation and action, and a single output. We configure the agent using the following options:

- Set the agent to use the controller sample time Ts;
- Set the mini-batch size to 128 experience samples;
- Set the experience buffer length to 10^6;
- Set the exploration model and target policy smoothing model to use Gaussian noise with variance of 0.1.

4.3.2. Train Agent

To train the agent, first set the following:

- Run each training step for at most 1000 episodes, with every episode enduring at most 100 schedule steps.
- Show the training headway in the episode manager (set the plots option) and consult the command-line display.
- Stop training when the agent receives an average cumulative reward greater than −200 over 100 consecutive episodes.
- At this point, the agent can control the level in the tank.

Finally, the optimal PI parameters can be evaluated, which are $K_i = 0.3926$ and $K_p = 5.9828$. The parameters of the PI controller block shown in Figure 5 will be set by using the optimal parameters evaluated by RL. Therefore, the step response characteristics will be as shown in Figure 12.

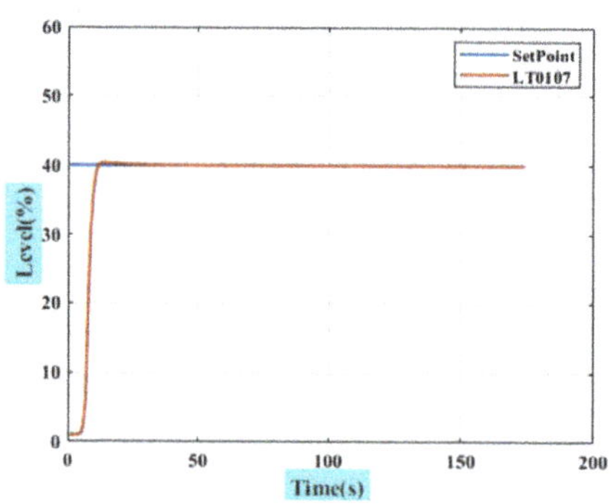

Figure 12. System response after tuning by RL.

Figure 13 and Table 4 show a system response in the case of disturbances. Different methods of disruption are included, such as increasing or decreasing the input feed (m2) and increasing or decreasing the opening valve (yi). After testing the system in the case of optimizing the PI parameters using the RL approach, the results reveal the good performance of the proposed system.

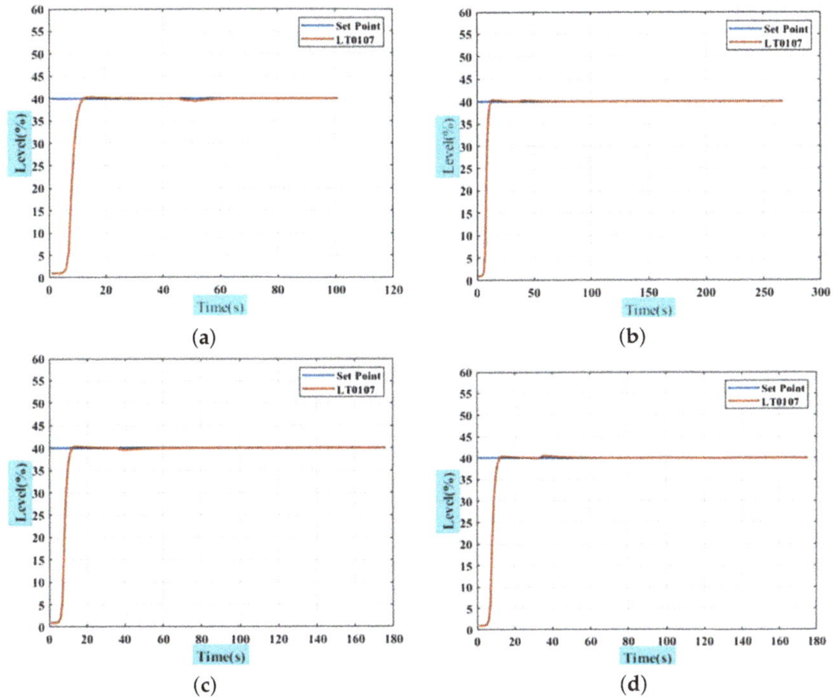

Figure 13. Response of system with reinforcement learning for optimization of PI in case of several values of m2 and yi: (a) decrease m2 to 250 kmole/h; (b) increase m2 to 1000 kmole/h; (c) decrease yi to 100%; (d) decrease yi to 0%.

Table 4. Step-response characteristics for system in Figure 13.

Parameters	m2 = 250 kmole/h	m2 = 1000 kmole/h	yi = 100%	yi = 0%
Rise Time	3.46	3.46	3.46	3.46
Transient Time	11.31	11.30	11.31	11.30
Settling Time	11.29	11.28	11.29	11.28
SettlingMin	36.27	36.27	36.27	36.27
SettlingMax	40.35	40.35	40.35	40.40
Overshoot	0.86%	0.88%	0.85%	0.93%
Undershoot	0	0	0	0
Peak	40.35	40.35	40.35	40.40
Peak Time	14	14	14	14

4.4. RL Agent as PI-like Controller

The objective of this part is to show how we can use RL as an online tuner to optimize the PI parameters; in this case, the RL system is working as an RL PI-like controller of RD5204, as shown in Figure 11, and we study the performance of the proposed system, which is shown in Figure 14. Further, the system was validated under the same condition as in previous scenarios; after applying disturbances, the response of the system is as shown in Figure 15 and Table 5. Although the system response seems similar to that in the previous setup (optimization of PI by using RL), there is an important difference. In scenario three, we obtain fixed parameters for the PI controller, but, in the case of using RL as a PI-Like controller, the agent will still learn online with a long period of system operation, which will offer the system more reliability and experience.

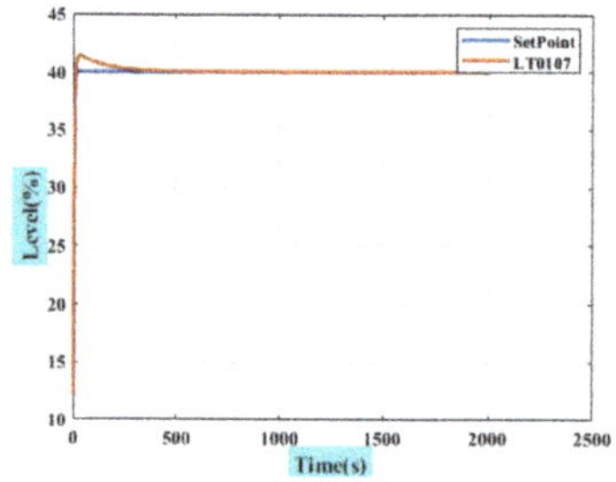

Figure 14. System response after being controlled by RL agent.

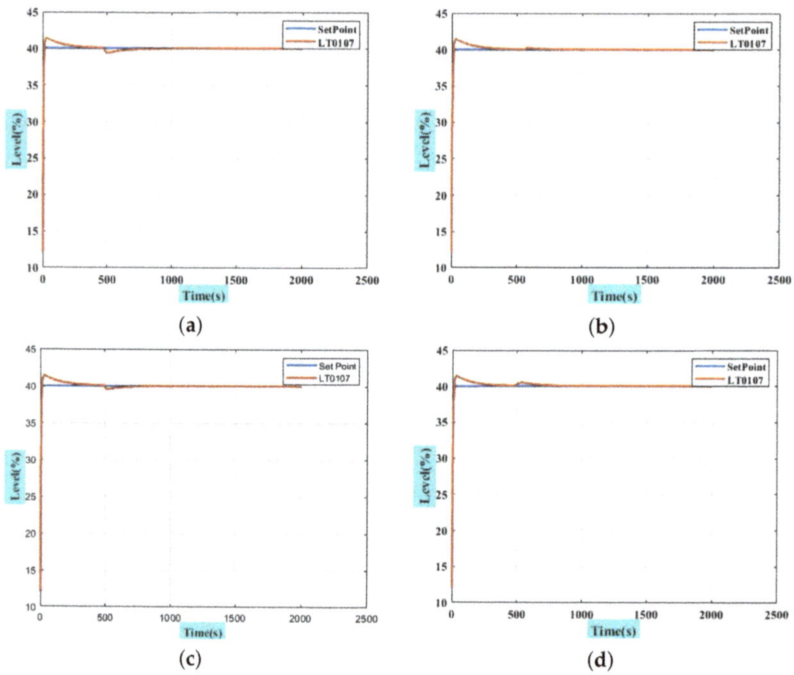

Figure 15. Response of system with reinforcement learning as controller in the case of several values of m2 and yi: (**a**) decrease m2 to 250 kmole/h; (**b**) increase m2 to 1000 kmole/h; (**c**) increase yi to 100%; (**d**) decrease yi to 0%.

Table 5. Step-response characteristics for system in Figure 15.

Parameters	m2 = 250 kmole/h	m2 = 1000 kmole/h	yi = 100%	yi = 0%
Rise Time	7.47	7.47	7.47	7.47
Transient Time	158.77	158.77	158.77	158.77
Settling Time	112.09	112.09	112.09	112.09
SettlingMin	36.57	36.57	36.57	36.57
SettlingMax	41.40	41.40	41.40	41.40
Overshoot	3.50%	3.50%	3.50%	3.50%
Undershoot	0	0	0	0
Peak	41.40	41.40	41.40	41.40
Peak Time	32	32	32	32

4.5. Comparison of Use of RL as an Offline Tuner and PI-like Controller

To compare the performance of RL as an online and offline tuner, RL is used as a particular optimization element for the PI controller and as a controller itself, which is known as the PI-like controller. To show that there is a large difference between these two methods, the system performance was tested in the case of using these controllers under the same conditions.

To achieve the mentioned comparison, the process noise was added to the system; this process noise was represented by the band-limited white noise block. Process noise exists in the real world and is manifested in various forms as a result of certain causes, such as physical aspects of electronic circuits, wires, or electrical and magnetic causes as a result of external influences on the signal, which in turn affects the overall operation of the system.

Figure 16 shows the performance of the PI controller in the case of using RL for offline parameter tuning and RL as a PI-like controller, in which the performance when using the RL as a PI-like controller is superior to the other method. In this figure, we show that the case of using RL as an offline tuner leads to the use of the conventional PI controller for process operation; therefore, there is no prediction for stochastic behavior, and the system will not overcome the external noise. Meanwhile, in the case of using RL as an online tuner, this leads to the use of RL as a PI-like controller during the operation of the process; therefore, the RL will optimize the PI parameters based on the prediction of the performance of the system in the future to improve the performance of the system. From this discussion, it can be concluded that the use of RL as a PI-like controller is more resistant to external noise.

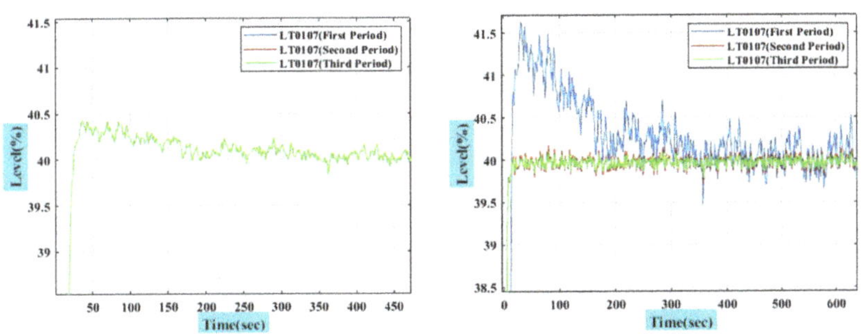

(a) (b)

Figure 16. System response under process noise for two approaches (online and offline tuning): (**a**) offline tuning with process noise; (**b**) online tuning with process noise.

Here, it is vital to identify the strengths and weaknesses of each method; therefore, each method may be introduced based on the controlled application requirement.

1. The values extracted from the offline tuner are fixed for a conventional PI controller during operation, but the values that are evaluated by the online tuner are changeable and improved during operation; therefore, it is more resistant to external noise due to continuous learning, improvement, exploration, and event anticipation.
2. Due to the additional complexity of the online tuner, the offline tuner has a faster reaction time than its online counterpart.
3. In the case of offline training, the duration of training is less than that of online training; thus, the best option is determined based on the requirements.
4. In certain industrial applications that require an auto-stop, the system's reaction speed is necessary; therefore, the online tuner is unsuitable in comparison to the offline case.
5. Economically, the offline tuner is more costly than the online tuner due to the increase in complexity and, thus, the need for more devices and capabilities, particularly in applications with a large number of control paths.

In addition, Table 6 illustrates the performance of the system with RL in the two methods, as a control and an optimization method. Some differences should be highlighted, such as the fact that the time of rising in the case of the online tuner is longer than in the case of the offline tuner, and this is therefore reflected in the stability of the system and its ability to reach a stable state, but this factor has no impact on the RD5204 application of the refinery. Further, the offline tuner is superior in terms of overshoot and settling values. These differences are considered acceptable due to the different nature of the internal formation of both the PI controller and the agent in RL, as the principal operation of RL is dependent on exploration and exploitation, which leads to approximation. However, the task of reinforcement learning as a controller remains the greatest in terms of the ability to modify the overall performance of the system throughout each operation.

Table 6. Step-response characteristics for systems in Figure 16.

Parameters	RL as Offline Tuner	RL as Online Tuner
Rise Time (s)	8.7	7.47
Transient Time (s)	20.08	158.77
Settling Time (s)	20	112.09
SettlingMin (%)	36.87	36.57
SettlingMax (%)	40.35	41.40
Overshoot (%)	0.88%	3.50%
Undershoot (%)	0	0
Peak (0–100)%	40.35	41.40

5. Conclusions

This paper focused on using the RL approach for the level control of the separator drum unit in a refinery system in which the mathematical model of Drum RD5204 is derived to study the response of the system. A PI controller is proposed to improve the system's response, in which the PI parameters are manually calculated. From the results, the system's response was superior to that of the conventional controller, but it did not achieve the required performance. In the case of using the auto-tuning method for PI parameter evaluation, the response is superior to the manual tuning method, where the system performance was significantly improved, and it is more reliable and robust against disturbances. The employment of reinforcement learning (RL) as an offline tuner leads to an enhancement in the system's performance and the system's ability to resist interruptions and unexpected changes, as well as return to a stable state. Utilizing the RL agent as an online tuner for the PI parameters, in which the online tuner values are adaptable during the operation, makes it more resistant to external noise as a result of continuous learning, exploration, and event anticipation. The validation of the system controller that uses online and offline reinforcement learning techniques for optimization against process noise showed that online tuning was able to attenuate the process noise and reduce it after certain operational periods, while its value was still constant in the case of using offline tuning; therefore, this is an advantage in favor of online tuners.

Author Contributions: Methodology, A.A.A. and M.T.R.; Validation, B.N.A.; Formal analysis, A.A.A. and M.T.R.; Investigation, A.A.A., M.T.R. and B.N.A.; Resources, V.B. and P.M.; Data curation, B.N.A.; Writing—original draft, A.A.A. and M.T.R.; Writing—review & editing, V.B. and P.M.; Project administration, V.B.; Funding acquisition, P.M. All authors have read and agreed to the published version of the manuscript.

Funding: This work has received no external funding.

Acknowledgments: The research was partially supported by the FIM UHK specific research project 2107 Integration of Departmental Research Activities and Students' Research Activities Support III. The authors also express their gratitude to Patrik Urbanik for his assistance and helpfulness.

Conflicts of Interest: The authors have no conflicts of interest relevant to this article.

References

1. Chirita, D.; Florescu, A.; Florea, B.C.; Ene, R.; Stoichescu, D.A. Liquid level control for industrial three tanks system based on sliding mode control. *Rev. Roum. Sci. Technol. Électrotechnol. Énerg.* **2015**, *60*, 437–446.
2. Dorf, R.C.; Bishop, R.H. *Modern Control Systems*; Prentice-Hall: Englewood Cliffs, NJ, USA, 2004.
3. Liptak, B.G. *Instrument Engineers, Volume Two: Process Control and Optimization*; CRC Press: Boca Raton, FL, USA, 2018.
4. Smith, R.S.; Doylel, J. The Two Tank Experiment: A Benchmark Control Problem. In Proceedings of the American Control Conference, Milwaukee, WI, USA, 27–29 June 2018.
5. Zhao, Z.; Zhang, X.; Li, Z. Tank-Level Control of Liquefied Natural Gas Carrier Based on Gaussian Function Nonlinear Decoration. *J. Mar. Sci. Eng.* **2020**, *8*, 695. [CrossRef]
6. Short, M.; Selvakumar, A.A. Non-Linear Tank Level Control for Industrial Applications. *Appl. Math.* **2020**, *11*, 876. [CrossRef]
7. Ali, A.A.; Rashid, M.T. Design PI Controller for Tank Level in Industrial Process. *Iraqi J. Electr. Electron. Eng.* **2022**, *18*, 82–92. [CrossRef]
8. Ademola, O.; Akpa, J.; Dagde, K. Modeling and Simulation of Two-Staged Separation Process for an Onshore Early Production Facility. *Adv. Chem. Eng. Sci.* **2019**, *9*, 127. [CrossRef]
9. Mokhatab, S.; Poe, W.A. *Handbook of Natural Gas Transmission and Processing*; Gulf Professional Publishing: Houston, TX, USA, 2012.
10. Keidy, R.; Morales, L.; Alvarez, H. Flash distillation modeling and a multiloop control proposal. In Proceedings of the IEEE 2nd Colombian Conference on Automatic Control (CCAC), Manizales, Colombia, 14–16 October 2015.
11. Seames, W. *Designing Controls for the Process Industries*; CRC Press: Boca Raton, FL, USA, 2017.
12. Marlin, T.E. *Process Control*; McGraw-Hill International Editions: New York, NY, USA, 2018.
13. Zhang, Z.; Wu, Z.; Dur, H.; Albalawi, F.; Christofides, P.D. On integration of feedback control and safety systems: Analyzing two chemical process applications. *Int. J. Control. Autom. Syst.* **2020**, *132*, 616–626. [CrossRef]
14. Xu, J.; Shao, H. A novel method of PID tuning for integrating processes. In Proceedings of the 42nd IEEE International Conference on Decision and Control, Maui, HI, USA, 9–12 December 2004.
15. Bucz, Š.; Kozáková, A. Advanced methods of PID controller tuning for specified performance. In *PID Control for Industrial Processes*; InTech Open: London, UK, 2018; pp. 73–119.
16. Chidambaram, M.; Saxena, N. *Relay Tuning of PID Controllers*; Springer: Tamil Nadu, India, 2018.
17. Pandey, S.K.; Veeranna, K.; Kumai, B.; Deshmukh, K.U. A Robust Auto-tuning Scheme for PID Controllers. In Proceedings of the 46th Annual Conference of the IEEE Industrial Electronics Society, Singapore, 18–21 October 2020.
18. Vilanova, R.; Arrieta, O.; Ponsa, P. Robust PI/PID controllers for load disturbance based on direct synthesis. *ISA Trans.* **2018**, *81*, 177–196. [CrossRef] [PubMed]
19. Singh, A.P.; Mukherjee, S.; Nikolaou, M. Debottlenecking level control for tanks in series. *J. Process. Control.* **2014**, *24*, 158–171. [CrossRef]
20. Jáuregui, C.; Duarte-Mermoud, M.A.; Oróstica, R.; Travieso-Torres, J.C.; Beytía, O. Conical tank level control using fractional order PID controllers: A simulated and experimental study. *Control. Theory Technol.* **2016**, *14*, 369–384. [CrossRef]
21. Backi, C.J.; Skogestad, S. A simple dynamic gravity separator model for separation efficiency evaluation incorporating level and pressure control. In Proceedings of the American Control Conference (ACC), Seattle, WA, USA, 24–26 May 2017.
22. Sásig, R.; Naranjo, C.; Pruna, E.; Chicaiza, W.D.; Chicaiza, F.A.; Carvajal, C.P.; Andaluz, V.H. An Implementation on Matlab Software for Non-linear Controller Design Based on Linear Algebra for Quadruple Tank Process. In Proceedings of the World Conference on Information Systems and Technologies, Naples, Italy, 27–29 March 2018.
23. Reyes-Lúa, A.; Backi, C.J.; Skogestad, S. Improved PI control for a surge tank satisfying level constraints. *IFAC-PapersOnLine* **2018**, *51*, 835–840. [CrossRef]
24. Sathasivam, L.; Elamvazuthi, I.; Ahamed Khan, M.K.A.; Parasuraman, S. Tuning a three-phase separator level controller via particle swarm optimizationalgorithm. In Proceedings of the International Conference on Recent Trends in Electrical, Control and Communication (RTECC), Malaysia, Malaysia, 20–22 March 2018.
25. Yu, S.; Lu, X., Zhou, Y.; Feng, Y.; Qu, T.; Chen, H. Liquid level tracking control of three-tank systems. *Int. J. Control. Autom. Syst.* **2020**, *18*, 2630–2640. [CrossRef]
26. Nath, U.M.; Dey, C.; Mudi, R.K. Fuzzy tuned model based control for level and temperature processes. *Microsyst. Technol.* **2019**, *25*, 819–827. [CrossRef]
27. Ye, J.; Zhang, X.; Lv, C.; Wang, P.; Lv, H. Design of liquid level control system for double tank. *IOP Conf. Ser. Mater. Sci. Eng.* **2020**, *740*, 012097. [CrossRef]
28. Nath, U.M.; Dey, C.; Mudi, R.K. Desired characteristic equation based PID controller tuning for lag-dominating processes with real-time realization on level control system. *IEEE Control. Syst. Lett.* **2020**, *5*, 1255–1260. [CrossRef]
29. Singh, V.P.; Patnana, N.; Singh, S. PID controller tuning using hybrid optimisation technique based on Box's evolutionary optimisation and teacher-learner-based-optimisation. *Int. J. Comput. Aided Eng. Technol.* **2020**, *13*, 258–270. [CrossRef]
30. Kos, T.; Huba, M.; Vrančić, D. Parametric and Nonparametric PID controller tuning method for integrating processes based on Magnitude Optimum. *Appl. Sci.* **2020**, *10*, 6012. [CrossRef]
31. Mary, A.H.; Miry, A.H.; Miry, M.H. ANFIS based reinforcement learning strategy for control a nonlinear coupled tanks system. *J. Electr. Eng. Technol.* **2022**, *17*, 1921–1929. [CrossRef]
32. Ziegler, J.G.; Nichols, N.B. Optimum settings for automatic controllers. *J. Dyn. Syst. Meas. Control.* **1993**, *115*, 759–765. [CrossRef]

33. Available online: http://www.src.gov.iq/en/about_us (accessed on 15 March 2023).
34. McDonald, K.A.; McAvoy, T.J. Decoupling Dual Composition Controllers 1. Steady State Results. In Proceedings of the American Control Conference, San Francisco, CA, USA, 22–24 June 1983.
35. Davis, M.; Vinter, R. Minimum-Variance and Self-Tuning Control. In *Stochastic Modelling and Control*; Springer: Berlin/Heidelberg, Germany, 1985.
36. Haykin, S. Recursive least squares adaptive filters. In *Adaptive Filter Theory*; Pearson Education India: Delhi, India , 2002; pp. 436–447.
37. Monson, H.H. *Recursive Least Squares. Statistical Digital Signal Processing and Modelling*; Wiley: Hoboken, NJ, USA, 1996.
38. Available online: https://en.wikipedia.org/w/index.php?title=Recursive_least_squares_filter&oldid=1059014247 (accessed on 20 February 2023).
39. Scott, F.; Hoof, H.; Meger, D. Addressing function approximation error in actor-critic methods. In Proceedings of the International Conference on Machine Learning, Stockholm, Sweden, 10–15 July 2018.

Disclaimer/Publisher's Note: The statements, opinions and data contained in all publications are solely those of the individual author(s) and contributor(s) and not of MDPI and/or the editor(s). MDPI and/or the editor(s) disclaim responsibility for any injury to people or property resulting from any ideas, methods, instructions or products referred to in the content.

mathematics

MDPI

Article

Fixed-Time Adaptive Chaotic Control for Permanent Magnet Synchronous Motor Subject to Unknown Parameters and Perturbations

Qijia Yao [1], Hadi Jahanshahi [2,*], Stelios Bekiros [3,4], Jinping Liu [5] and Abdullah A. Al-Barakati [6]

1 School of Automation and Electrical Engineering, University of Science and Technology Beijing, Beijing 100083, China; qijia_yao@ustb.edu.cn
2 Institute of Electrical and Electronics Engineers, Toronto, ON M5V 3T9, Canada
3 Faculty of Economics, Management & Accountancy (FEMA), University of Malta, MSD 2080 Msida, Malta; stelios.bekiros@um.edu.mt or s.bekiros@lse.ac.uk
4 LSE Health, Department of Health Policy, London School of Economics and Political Science, London WC2A 2AE, UK
5 College of Information Science and Engineering, Hunan Normal University, Changsha 410081, China; ljp@hunnu.edu.cn
6 Communication Systems and Networks Research Group, Department of Information Systems, Faculty of Computing and Information Technology, King Abdulaziz University, Jeddah 21589, Saudi Arabia; aaalbarakati@kau.edu.sa
* Correspondence: jahanshahi.hadi@ieee.org

Abstract: It is well known that the permanent magnet synchronous motor (PMSM) exhibits chaotic characteristics when its parameters fall within a certain range, which can lead to system instability. This article proposes an adaptive control strategy for achieving the fixed-time chaotic stabilization of PMSM, even in the presence of unknown parameters and perturbations. The developed controller is synthesized by combining a parametric adaptive mechanism with a fixed-time control technique. The stability analysis demonstrates that the system states under the developed controller can converge to small neighborhoods around the equilibrium point within a fixed time. Thanks to the adoption of the parametric adaptive mechanism, the developed controller is not only insensitive to unknown parameters but also robust against perturbations. Finally, simulated studies are conducted to verify and emphasize the effectiveness of the developed control strategy.

Keywords: permanent magnet synchronous motor; chaotic stabilization; fixed-time control; adaptive control

MSC: 34C28; 37D45; 93C40

1. Introduction

Permanent magnet synchronous motors (PMSMs) play a crucial role in various industrial applications. It is well-known that PMSMs can exhibit chaotic behavior when their parameters fall within a certain range, which may lead to system instability. Ensuring the safe operation of PMSMs requires the significant consideration of chaotic stabilization [1–3]. Chaotic systems exhibit irregular and unpredictable dynamic behavior, which is highly insensitive to initial conditions. To control or manipulate chaotic systems, two main approaches are commonly used. The first approach involves using feedback control techniques to regulate the system states from chaos to order. The second approach involves estimating the system states using filtering techniques and then utilizing these estimates for regulation. The chaotic stabilization of PMSMs falls under the first approach, where appropriate feedback control is added to achieve the desired behavior. Various methods have been extensively investigated for chaotic control, including adaptive control [4–6], backstepping control [7–14], sliding mode control [15–22], iterative learning control [23], and intelligent control [24–35].

Notably, most of the above controllers can only achieve asymptotic stabilization or, at best, exponential stabilization. In contrast, finite-time control can ensure that the system states stabilize to zero or small neighborhoods around zero within a bounded settling time. Finite-time control is mainly designed based on either the homogeneous system theory [36] or the finite-time Lyapunov stability theory [37]. Finite-time controllers have been utilized for the stabilization of chaotic systems in [38–46]. In [47], a finite-time adaptive control scheme was implemented for the chaotic stabilization of PMSM with uncertain parameters. Moreover, ref. [48] developed a terminal sliding mode controller for the finite-time synchronization of fractional-order PMSM.

However, finite-time control has the disadvantage of having the settling time heavily determined by the initial system states, which limits its practical application. Fortunately, fixed-time control can overcome this weakness, as its settling time is bounded and independent of the initial system states. Fixed-time control is primarily designed based on the bilimit homogeneous system theory [49] or the fixed-time Lyapunov stability theory [50,51]. Fixed-time controllers have been developed for the stabilization of chaotic systems in [52–57]. For instance, ref. [58] proposed a fixed-time adaptive control approach for the stabilization of the Lorenz system, while a similar controller was applied to the stabilization and synchronization of hyperchaotic Lü systems in [59]. However, these studies [58,59] did not consider perturbations, and the performance of the controllers in the presence of perturbations cannot be guaranteed.

Inspired by the aforementioned content, in this article, we propose an adaptive control strategy for achieving the fixed-time chaotic stabilization of PMSM in the presence of unknown parameters and perturbations. The developed controller is a combination of the parametric adaptive mechanism and fixed-time control technique. The major contributions of this work are two-fold.

- The developed controller is designed within the fixed-time control framework. Stability analysis demonstrates that the developed controller can ensure the system states stabilize within a fixed time to small neighborhoods around the equilibrium point.
- The parametric adaptive mechanism is incorporated into the developed controller to estimate the unknown parameters and perturbations, respectively. Unlike the controllers in [58,59], this design ensures that the developed controller is not only insensitive to unknown parameters but also robust against perturbations.

The remainder of this paper is organized as follows: Section 2 describes the problem and presents some preliminaries. Section 3 presents the main results. Section 4 conducts the simulated studies. Finally, Section 5 summarizes the main conclusions.

2. Preliminaries and Problem Description

2.1. Preliminaries

The following lemmas can support to obtain the main results.

Lemma 1 (Ref. [51]). *Consider the nonlinear system:*

$$\dot{x} = f(x), \;\; x(0) = 0, \;\; x \in \mathbb{R}^n, \tag{1}$$

where $f(\cdot)$ is a continuous function vector and $\mathbb{R}$ stands for the set of real numbers. If there is a positive definite function $V(x)$, such that $\dot{V}(x) \leq -\rho_1 V^p(x) - \rho_2 V^q(x) + \Delta$, where $\rho_1 > 0$, $\rho_2 > 0$, $0 < p < 1$, $q > 1$, and $\Delta > 0$, then system (1) is practically fixed-time stable and $V(x)$ can stabilize to the following small neighborhood about zero:

$$V(x) \leq \min\left\{ \left(\frac{\Delta}{\rho_1(1-\varepsilon)} \right)^{\frac{1}{p}}, \left(\frac{\Delta}{\rho_2(1-\varepsilon)} \right)^{\frac{1}{q}} \right\}, \tag{2}$$

where $0 < \varepsilon < 1$, *in fixed time* $T_c \leq \frac{1}{\rho_1 \varepsilon (1-p)} + \frac{1}{\rho_2 \varepsilon (q-1)}$.

Lemma 2 (Ref. [60]). *For* $x_1 \in \mathbb{R}, x_2 \in \mathbb{R}, p > 0, q > 0, \xi > 0$, *the following inequality is true:*

$$|x_1|^p |x_2|^q \leq \frac{p}{p+q} \xi |x_1|^{p+q} + \frac{q}{p+q} \xi^{-\frac{p}{q}} |x_2|^{p+q}. \tag{3}$$

Lemma 3 (Ref. [60]). *For* $x_i \in \mathbb{R}, i = 1, 2, \ldots, n, 0 < p \leq 1$, *and* $q > 1$, *the following inequalities are true:*

$$\left(\sum_{i=1}^{n} |x_i| \right)^p \leq \sum_{i=1}^{n} |x_i|^p, \quad n^{1-q} \left(\sum_{i=1}^{n} |x_i| \right)^q \leq \sum_{i=1}^{n} |x_i|^q. \tag{4}$$

2.2. Problem Description

Referring to [1,2], the PMSM system can be expressed as

$$\begin{cases} \dot{i}_d = -i_d + i_q w, \\ \dot{i}_q = -i_q - i_d w + \gamma w, \\ \dot{w} = \sigma (i_q - w), \end{cases} \tag{5}$$

where i_d is the quadrature-axis current, i_q is the direct-axis current, w is the motor angular frequency, and γ and σ are the system parameters. When $\gamma = 20$ and $\sigma = 5.46$, the PMSM system has the chaotic characteristics. The chaotic phenomena are illustrated in Figure 1 with the initial states set as $i_d(0) = 5$, $i_q(0) = 1$, and $w(0) = -1$. Let $\dot{i}_d = \dot{i}_q = \dot{w} = 0$. It is easy to find that the PMSM system has three equilibrium points $O(0,0,0)$, $E^+\left(19, \sqrt{19}, \sqrt{19}\right)$, and $E^-\left(19, -\sqrt{19}, -\sqrt{19}\right)$.

The PMSM system in the presence of controls and perturbations can be described as

$$\begin{cases} \dot{i}_d = -i_d + i_q w + u_1 + d_1, \\ \dot{i}_q = -i_q - i_d w + \gamma w + u_2 + d_2, \\ \dot{w} = \sigma (i_q - w) + u_3 + d_3, \end{cases} \tag{6}$$

where u_1, u_2, and u_3 are the control inputs and d_1, d_2, and d_3 are the perturbations. The parameters γ and σ and the perturbations d_1, d_2, and d_3 are supposed to be unknown in the control design.

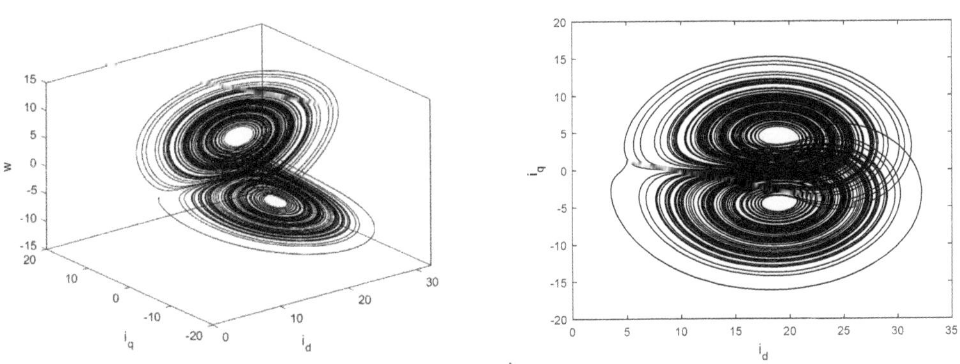

(a) (b)

Figure 1. *Cont.*

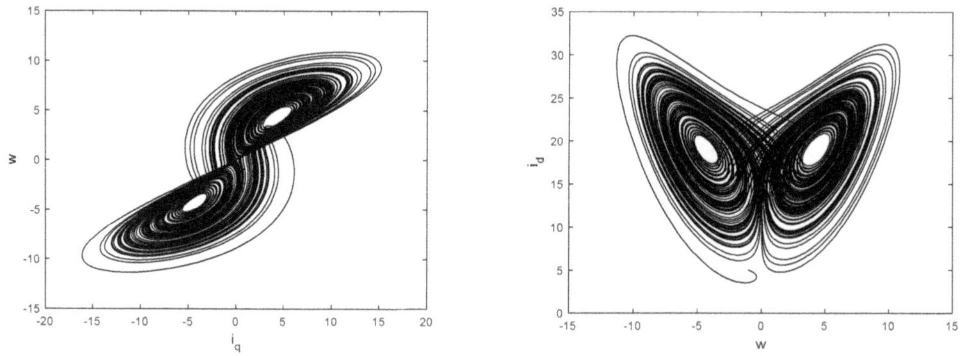

(c) **(d)**

Figure 1. Chaos of the PMSM system: (**a**) projection on the XYZ space; (**b**) projection on the XY plane; (**c**) projection on the YZ plane; (**d**) projection on the ZX plane.

The objective is to develop an appropriate controller such that the system states can stabilize to the small neighborhoods about the specific equilibrium point in fixed time.

3. Main Results

The main results are provided in this section. First, the controller is developed for the chaotic stabilization about the equilibrium point $O(0,0,0)$. Then, the controllers for the chaotic stabilization about the equilibrium points $E^{+}\left(19,\sqrt{19},\sqrt{19}\right)$ and $E^{-}\left(19,-\sqrt{19},-\sqrt{19}\right)$ are designed in a similar way.

3.1. Chaotic Control about $O(0,0,0)$

Theorem 1. *For PMSM system (6), if the fixed-time adaptive controller is developed as*

$$\begin{cases} u_1 = -k_{11}\mathrm{sig}^p(i_d) - k_{12}\mathrm{sig}^q(i_d) + i_d - i_q w - \hat{d}_1, \\ u_2 = -k_{21}\mathrm{sig}^p(i_q) - k_{22}\mathrm{sig}^q(i_q) + i_q + i_d w - \hat{\gamma} w - \hat{d}_2, \\ u_3 = -k_{31}\mathrm{sig}^p(w) - k_{32}\mathrm{sig}^q(w) - \hat{\sigma}(i_q - w) - \hat{d}_3, \end{cases} \tag{7}$$

where $k_{11}>0$, $k_{12}>0$, $k_{21}>0$, $k_{22}>0$, $k_{31}>0$, $k_{32}>0$, $0<p<1$, $q>1$, $\hat{\gamma}$, $\hat{\sigma}$, $\hat{d}_1$, $\hat{d}_2$, *and* $\hat{d}_3$ *are the estimations of* γ, σ, d_1, d_2, *and* d_3, $\mathrm{sig}^p(\cdot)$ *is defined as* $\mathrm{sig}^p(x) = |x|^p \mathrm{sgn}(x)$, *and the parametric adaptive mechanism is provided as*

$$\begin{cases} \dot{\hat{\gamma}} = -\eta_{11}\hat{\gamma} + \eta_{12} w i_q, \\ \dot{\hat{\sigma}} = -\eta_{21}\hat{\sigma} + \eta_{22}(i_q - w)w, \\ \dot{\hat{d}}_1 = -\eta_{31}\hat{d}_1 + \eta_{32} i_d, \\ \dot{\hat{d}}_2 = -\eta_{41}\hat{d}_2 + \eta_{42} i_q, \\ \dot{\hat{d}}_3 = -\eta_{51}\hat{d}_3 + \eta_{52} w, \end{cases} \tag{8}$$

where $\eta_{11}>0$, $\eta_{12}>0$, $\eta_{21}>0$, $\eta_{22}>0$, $\eta_{31}>0$, $\eta_{32}>0$, $\eta_{41}>0$, $\eta_{42}>0$, $\eta_{51}>0$, *and* $\eta_{52}>0$, *then the system states can stabilize to the small neighborhoods about the equilibrium point* $O(0,0,0)$ *in fixed time.*

Proof. The Lyapunov function is involved as

$$V = \frac{1}{2}i_d^2 + \frac{1}{2}i_q^2 + \frac{1}{2}w^2 + \frac{1}{2\eta_{12}}\tilde{\gamma}^2 + \frac{1}{2\eta_{22}}\tilde{\sigma}^2 + \frac{1}{2\eta_{32}}\tilde{d}_1^2 + \frac{1}{2\eta_{42}}\tilde{d}_2^2 + \frac{1}{2\eta_{52}}\tilde{d}_3^2, \tag{9}$$

where $\widetilde{\gamma}, \widetilde{\sigma}, \widetilde{d}_1, \widetilde{d}_2$, and $\widetilde{d}_3$ are the estimation errors of $\widetilde{\gamma} = \gamma - \hat{\gamma}, \widetilde{\sigma} = \sigma - \hat{\sigma}, \widetilde{d}_1 = d_1 - \hat{d}_1$, $\widetilde{d}_2 = d_2 - \hat{d}_2$, and $\widetilde{d}_3 = d_3 - \hat{d}_3$. Evaluating the time differentiation of V yields

$$\begin{aligned}\dot{V} = \; & i_d(-i_d + i_q w + u_1 + d_1) + i_q(-i_q - i_d w + \gamma w + u_2 + d_2) + w(\sigma(i_q - w) + u_3 + d_3) \\ & -\tfrac{1}{\eta_{12}}\widetilde{\gamma}\dot{\hat{\gamma}} - \tfrac{1}{\eta_{22}}\widetilde{\sigma}\dot{\hat{\sigma}} - \tfrac{1}{\eta_{32}}\widetilde{d}_1\dot{\hat{d}}_1 - \tfrac{1}{\eta_{42}}\widetilde{d}_2\dot{\hat{d}}_2 - \tfrac{1}{\eta_{52}}\widetilde{d}_3\dot{\hat{d}}_3.\end{aligned} \tag{10}$$

Substituting the fixed-time adaptive controller (7) and the parametric adaptive mechanism (8) into (10), we have

$$\begin{aligned}\dot{V} = \; & i_d\Big(-k_{11}\mathrm{sig}^p(i_d) - k_{12}\mathrm{sig}^q(i_d) + \widetilde{d}_1\Big) + i_q\Big(-k_{21}\mathrm{sig}^p(i_q) - k_{22}\mathrm{sig}^q(i_q) + \widetilde{\gamma}w + \widetilde{d}_2\Big) \\ & + w\Big(-k_{31}\mathrm{sig}^p(w) - k_{32}\mathrm{sig}^q(w) + \widetilde{\sigma}(i_q - w) + \widetilde{d}_3\Big) - \tfrac{1}{\eta_{12}}\widetilde{\gamma}(-\eta_{11}\hat{\gamma} + \eta_{12} i_q w) \\ & -\tfrac{1}{\eta_{22}}\widetilde{\sigma}(-\eta_{21}\hat{\sigma} + \eta_{22} w(i_q - w)) - \tfrac{1}{\eta_{32}}\widetilde{d}_1\Big(-\eta_{31}\hat{d}_1 + \eta_{32} i_d\Big) \\ & -\tfrac{1}{\eta_{42}}\widetilde{d}_2\Big(-\eta_{41}\hat{d}_2 + \eta_{42} i_q\Big) - \tfrac{1}{\eta_{52}}\widetilde{d}_3\Big(-\eta_{51}\hat{d}_3 + \eta_{52} w\Big) \\ = \; & -k_{11}|i_d|^{p+1} - k_{12}|i_d|^{q+1} - k_{21}|i_q|^{p+1} - k_{22}|i_q|^{q+1} - k_{31}|w|^{p+1} - k_{32}|w|^{q+1} \\ & + \tfrac{\eta_{11}}{\eta_{12}}\widetilde{\gamma}\hat{\gamma} + \tfrac{\eta_{21}}{\eta_{22}}\widetilde{\sigma}\hat{\sigma} + \tfrac{\eta_{31}}{\eta_{32}}\widetilde{d}_1\hat{d}_1 + \tfrac{\eta_{41}}{\eta_{42}}\widetilde{d}_2\hat{d}_2 + \tfrac{\eta_{51}}{\eta_{52}}\widetilde{d}_3\hat{d}_3.\end{aligned} \tag{11}$$

It is not difficult to derive the following inequalities:

$$\frac{\eta_{11}}{\eta_{12}}\widetilde{\gamma}\hat{\gamma} \le -\frac{\eta_{11}}{2\eta_{12}}\widetilde{\gamma}^2 + \frac{\eta_{11}}{2\eta_{12}}\gamma^2, \tag{12}$$

$$\frac{\eta_{21}}{\eta_{22}}\widetilde{\sigma}\hat{\sigma} \le -\frac{\eta_{21}}{2\eta_{22}}\widetilde{\sigma}^2 + \frac{\eta_{21}}{2\eta_{22}}\sigma^2, \tag{13}$$

$$\frac{\eta_{31}}{\eta_{32}}\widetilde{d}_1\hat{d}_1 \le -\frac{\eta_{31}}{2\eta_{32}}\widetilde{d}_1^2 + \frac{\eta_{31}}{2\eta_{32}}d_1^2, \tag{14}$$

$$\frac{\eta_{41}}{\eta_{42}}\widetilde{d}_2\hat{d}_2 \le -\frac{\eta_{41}}{2\eta_{42}}\widetilde{d}_2^2 + \frac{\eta_{41}}{2\eta_{42}}\widetilde{d}_2^2, \tag{15}$$

$$\frac{\eta_{51}}{\eta_{52}}\widetilde{d}_3\hat{d}_3 \le -\frac{\eta_{51}}{2\eta_{52}}\widetilde{d}_3^2 + \frac{\eta_{51}}{2\eta_{52}}d_3^2, \tag{16}$$

Substituting the above inequalities into (11), we have

$$\begin{aligned}\dot{V} = \; & -k_{11}|i_d|^{p+1} - k_{12}|i_d|^{q+1} - k_{21}|i_q|^{p+1} - k_{22}|i_q|^{q+1} - k_{31}|w|^{p+1} - k_{32}|w|^{q+1} \\ & -\Big(\tfrac{\eta_{11}}{4\eta_{12}}\widetilde{\gamma}^2\Big)^{\frac{p+1}{2}} - \Big(\tfrac{\eta_{11}}{4\eta_{12}}\widetilde{\gamma}^2\Big)^{\frac{q+1}{2}} - \Big(\tfrac{\eta_{21}}{4\eta_{22}}\widetilde{\sigma}^2\Big)^{\frac{p+1}{2}} - \Big(\tfrac{\eta_{21}}{4\eta_{22}}\widetilde{\sigma}^2\Big)^{\frac{q+1}{2}} \\ & -\Big(\tfrac{\eta_{31}}{4\eta_{32}}\widetilde{d}_1^2\Big)^{\frac{p+1}{2}} - \Big(\tfrac{\eta_{31}}{4\eta_{32}}\widetilde{d}_1^2\Big)^{\frac{q+1}{2}} - \Big(\tfrac{\eta_{41}}{4\eta_{42}}\widetilde{d}_2^2\Big)^{\frac{p+1}{2}} - \Big(\tfrac{\eta_{41}}{4\eta_{42}}\widetilde{d}_2^2\Big)^{\frac{q+1}{2}} \\ & -\Big(\tfrac{\eta_{51}}{4\eta_{52}}\widetilde{d}_3^2\Big)^{\frac{p+1}{2}} - \Big(\tfrac{\eta_{51}}{4\eta_{52}}\widetilde{d}_3^2\Big)^{\frac{q+1}{2}} + \Delta,\end{aligned} \tag{17}$$

where Δ is defined as

$$\begin{aligned}\Delta = \; & \Big(\tfrac{\eta_{11}}{4\eta_{12}}\widetilde{\gamma}^2\Big)^{\frac{p+1}{2}} + \Big(\tfrac{\eta_{11}}{4\eta_{12}}\widetilde{\gamma}^2\Big)^{\frac{q+1}{2}} - \tfrac{\eta_{11}}{2\eta_{12}}\widetilde{\gamma}^2 + \Big(\tfrac{\eta_{21}}{4\eta_{22}}\widetilde{\sigma}^2\Big)^{\frac{p+1}{2}} + \Big(\tfrac{\eta_{21}}{4\eta_{22}}\widetilde{\sigma}^2\Big)^{\frac{q+1}{2}} \\ & -\tfrac{\eta_{21}}{2\eta_{22}}\widetilde{\sigma}^2 + \Big(\tfrac{\eta_{31}}{4\eta_{32}}\widetilde{d}_1^2\Big)^{\frac{p+1}{2}} + \Big(\tfrac{\eta_{31}}{4\eta_{32}}\widetilde{d}_1^2\Big)^{\frac{q+1}{2}} - \tfrac{\eta_{31}}{2\eta_{32}}\widetilde{d}_1^2 + \Big(\tfrac{\eta_{41}}{4\eta_{42}}\widetilde{d}_2^2\Big)^{\frac{p+1}{2}} \\ & + \Big(\tfrac{\eta_{41}}{4\eta_{42}}\widetilde{d}_2^2\Big)^{\frac{q+1}{2}} - \tfrac{\eta_{41}}{2\eta_{42}}\widetilde{d}_2^2 + \Big(\tfrac{\eta_{51}}{4\eta_{52}}\widetilde{d}_3^2\Big)^{\frac{p+1}{2}} + \Big(\tfrac{\eta_{51}}{4\eta_{52}}\widetilde{d}_3^2\Big)^{\frac{q+1}{2}} - \tfrac{\eta_{51}}{2\eta_{52}}\widetilde{d}_3^2.\end{aligned} \tag{18}$$

Consider the item $\Big(\frac{\eta_{11}}{4\eta_{12}}\widetilde{\gamma}^2\Big)^{\frac{p+1}{2}} + \Big(\frac{\eta_{11}}{4\eta_{12}}\widetilde{\gamma}^2\Big)^{\frac{q+1}{2}} - \frac{\eta_{11}}{2\eta_{12}}\widetilde{\gamma}^2$ in the above inequality. Two cases are discussed in the sequel. For the case that $\frac{\eta_{11}}{4\eta_{12}}\widetilde{\gamma}^2 \ge 1$, we have

$$\Big(\frac{\eta_{11}}{4\eta_{12}}\widetilde{\gamma}^2\Big)^{\frac{p+1}{2}} + \Big(\frac{\eta_{11}}{4\eta_{12}}\widetilde{\gamma}^2\Big)^{\frac{q+1}{2}} - \frac{\eta_{11}}{2\eta_{12}}\widetilde{\gamma}^2 \le \Big(\frac{\eta_{11}}{4\eta_{12}}\widetilde{\gamma}^2\Big)^{\frac{q+1}{2}} - \frac{\eta_{11}}{4\eta_{12}}\widetilde{\gamma}^2. \tag{19}$$

For the case that $\frac{\eta_{11}}{4\eta_{12}}\tilde{\gamma}^2 < 1$, recalling Lemma 2, we have

$$\left(\frac{\eta_{11}}{4\eta_{12}}\tilde{\gamma}^2\right)^{\frac{p+1}{2}} + \left(\frac{\eta_{11}}{4\eta_{12}}\tilde{\gamma}^2\right)^{\frac{q+1}{2}} - \frac{\eta_{11}}{2\eta_{12}}\tilde{\gamma}^2 \leq \left(\frac{\eta_{11}}{4\eta_{12}}\tilde{\gamma}^2\right)^{\frac{p+1}{2}} - \frac{\eta_{11}}{4\eta_{12}}\tilde{\gamma}^2 \leq (1-\overline{p})\overline{p}^{\frac{\overline{p}}{1-\overline{p}}}, \quad (20)$$

where $\overline{p} = \frac{p+1}{2}$. Construct a compact set Θ_1 satisfying $\Theta_1 = \{\tilde{\gamma} \in \mathbb{R} | |\tilde{\gamma}| \leq \theta_1\}$, where $\theta_1 > 0$. Combining (19) and (20), we have the following inequality:

$$\left(\frac{\eta_{11}}{4\eta_{12}}\tilde{\gamma}^2\right)^{\frac{p+1}{2}} + \left(\frac{\eta_{11}}{4\eta_{12}}\tilde{\gamma}^2\right)^{\frac{q+1}{2}} - \frac{\eta_{11}}{2\eta_{12}}\tilde{\gamma}^2 \leq \mu_1, \quad (21)$$

where μ_1 is defined as

$$\mu_1 = \begin{cases} (1-\overline{p})\overline{p}^{\frac{\overline{p}}{1-\overline{p}}}, & \theta_1 < 2\sqrt{\frac{\eta_{12}}{\eta_{11}}}, \\ \left(\frac{\eta_{11}}{4\eta_{12}}\theta_1^2\right)^{\frac{q+1}{2}} - \frac{\eta_{11}}{4\eta_{12}}\theta_1^2, & \theta_1 \geq 2\sqrt{\frac{\eta_{12}}{\eta_{11}}}. \end{cases} \quad (22)$$

Likewise, the following inequalities can be easily derived:

$$\left(\frac{\eta_{21}}{4\eta_{22}}\tilde{\sigma}^2\right)^{\frac{p+1}{2}} + \left(\frac{\eta_{21}}{4\eta_{22}}\tilde{\sigma}^2\right)^{\frac{q+1}{2}} - \frac{\eta_{21}}{2\eta_{22}}\tilde{\sigma}^2 \leq \mu_2, \quad (23)$$

$$\left(\frac{\eta_{31}}{4\eta_{32}}\tilde{d}_1^2\right)^{\frac{p+1}{2}} + \left(\frac{\eta_{31}}{4\eta_{32}}\tilde{d}_1^2\right)^{\frac{q+1}{2}} - \frac{\eta_{31}}{2\eta_{32}}\tilde{d}_1^2 \leq \mu_3, \quad (24)$$

$$\left(\frac{\eta_{41}}{4\eta_{42}}\tilde{d}_2^2\right)^{\frac{p+1}{2}} + \left(\frac{\eta_{41}}{4\eta_{42}}\tilde{d}_2^2\right)^{\frac{q+1}{2}} - \frac{\eta_{41}}{2\eta_{42}}\tilde{d}_2^2 \leq \mu_4, \quad (25)$$

$$\left(\frac{\eta_{51}}{4\eta_{52}}\tilde{d}_3^2\right)^{\frac{p+1}{2}} + \left(\frac{\eta_{51}}{4\eta_{52}}\tilde{d}_3^2\right)^{\frac{q+1}{2}} - \frac{\eta_{51}}{2\eta_{52}}\tilde{d}_3^2 \leq \mu_5. \quad (26)$$

Substituting the above inequalities into (17) and recalling Lemma 3, we have

$$\dot{V} \leq -\rho_1 V^{\frac{p+1}{2}} - \rho_2 V^{\frac{q+1}{2}} + \overline{\Delta}, \quad (27)$$

where ρ_1, ρ_2, and $\overline{\Delta}$ are defined as

$$\rho_1 = \min\left\{2^{\frac{p+1}{2}}k_{11}, 2^{\frac{p+1}{2}}k_{21}, 2^{\frac{p+1}{2}}k_{31}, \left(\frac{\eta_{11}}{2}\right)^{\frac{p+1}{2}}, \left(\frac{\eta_{21}}{2}\right)^{\frac{p+1}{2}}, \left(\frac{\eta_{31}}{2}\right)^{\frac{p+1}{2}}, \left(\frac{\eta_{41}}{2}\right)^{\frac{p+1}{2}}, \left(\frac{\eta_{51}}{2}\right)^{\frac{p+1}{2}}\right\}, \quad (28)$$

$$\rho_2 = 8^{\frac{1-q}{2}}\min\left\{2^{\frac{q+1}{2}}k_{12}, 2^{\frac{q+1}{2}}k_{22}, 2^{\frac{q+1}{2}}k_{32}, \left(\frac{\eta_{12}}{2}\right)^{\frac{q+1}{2}}, \left(\frac{\eta_{22}}{2}\right)^{\frac{q+1}{2}}, \left(\frac{\eta_{32}}{2}\right)^{\frac{q+1}{2}}, \left(\frac{\eta_{42}}{2}\right)^{\frac{q+1}{2}}, \left(\frac{\eta_{52}}{2}\right)^{\frac{q+1}{2}}\right\}, \quad (29)$$

$$\overline{\Delta} = \mu_1 + \mu_2 + \mu_3 + \mu_4 + \mu_5 + \frac{\eta_{11}}{2\eta_{12}}\gamma^2 + \frac{\eta_{21}}{2\eta_{22}}\sigma^2 + \frac{\eta_{31}}{2\eta_{32}}d_1^2 + \frac{\eta_{41}}{2\eta_{42}}d_2^2 + \frac{\eta_{51}}{2\eta_{52}}d_3^2. \quad (30)$$

By Lemma 1, the closed-loop system is practically fixed-time stable and V can stabilize to the following small neighborhood about zero:

$$V \leq \min\left\{\left(\frac{\overline{\Delta}}{\rho_1(1-\varepsilon)}\right)^{\frac{p+1}{2}}, \left(\frac{\overline{\Delta}}{\rho_2(1-\varepsilon)}\right)^{\frac{q+1}{2}}\right\}, \quad (31)$$

where $0 < \varepsilon < 1$, in fixed time, $T_c \leq \frac{2}{\rho_1\varepsilon(1-p)} + \frac{2}{\rho_2\varepsilon(q-1)}$. Recalling the definition of V, it follows that all error variables i_d, i_q, w, $\widetilde{\gamma}$, $\widetilde{\sigma}$, $\widetilde{d}_1$, $\widetilde{d}_2$, and $\widetilde{d}_3$ can stabilize to the small neighborhoods about zero in fixed time. This completes the proof. □

3.2. Chaotic Control about $E^+\left(19, \sqrt{19}, \sqrt{19}\right)$ and $E^-\left(19, -\sqrt{19}, -\sqrt{19}\right)$

Similarly, the controllers for the chaotic stabilization about the equilibrium points $E^+\left(19, \sqrt{19}, \sqrt{19}\right)$ and $E^-\left(19, -\sqrt{19}, -\sqrt{19}\right)$ are provided in Theorems 2 and 3, respectively.

Theorem 2. *For PMSM system (6), if the fixed-time adaptive controller is developed as*

$$\begin{cases} u_1 = -k_{11}\mathrm{sig}^p(i_d - 19) - k_{12}\mathrm{sig}^q(i_d - 19) + i_d - i_q w - \hat{d}_1, \\ u_2 = -k_{21}\mathrm{sig}^p\left(i_q - \sqrt{19}\right) - k_{22}\mathrm{sig}^q\left(i_q - \sqrt{19}\right) + i_q + i_d w - \hat{\gamma} w - \hat{d}_2, \\ u_3 = -k_{31}\mathrm{sig}^p\left(w - \sqrt{19}\right) - k_{32}\mathrm{sig}^q\left(w - \sqrt{19}\right) - \hat{\sigma}(i_q - w) - \hat{d}_3, \end{cases} \tag{32}$$

and the parametric adaptive mechanism is provided as

$$\begin{cases} \dot{\hat{\gamma}} = -\eta_{11}\hat{\gamma} + \eta_{12} w\left(i_q - \sqrt{19}\right), \\ \dot{\hat{\sigma}} = -\eta_{21}\hat{\sigma} + \eta_{22}(i_q - w)\left(w - \sqrt{19}\right), \\ \dot{\hat{d}}_1 = -\eta_{31}\hat{d}_1 + \eta_{32}(i_d - 19), \\ \dot{\hat{d}}_2 = -\eta_{41}\hat{d}_2 + \eta_{42}\left(i_q - \sqrt{19}\right), \\ \dot{\hat{d}}_3 = -\eta_{51}\hat{d}_3 + \eta_{52}\left(w - \sqrt{19}\right), \end{cases} \tag{33}$$

then the system states can stabilize to the small neighborhoods about the equilibrium point $E^+\left(19, \sqrt{19}, \sqrt{19}\right)$ in fixed time.

Theorem 3. *For PMSM system (6), if the fixed-time adaptive controller is developed as*

$$\begin{cases} u_1 = -k_{11}\mathrm{sig}^p(i_d - 19) - k_{12}\mathrm{sig}^q(i_d - 19) + i_d - i_q w - \hat{d}_1, \\ u_2 = -k_{21}\mathrm{sig}^p\left(i_q + \sqrt{19}\right) - k_{22}\mathrm{sig}^q\left(i_q + \sqrt{19}\right) + i_q + i_d w - \hat{\gamma} w - \hat{d}_2, \\ u_3 = -k_{31}\mathrm{sig}^p\left(w + \sqrt{19}\right) - k_{32}\mathrm{sig}^q\left(w + \sqrt{19}\right) - \hat{\sigma}(i_q - w) - \hat{d}_3, \end{cases} \tag{34}$$

and the parametric adaptive mechanism is provided as

$$\begin{cases} \dot{\hat{\gamma}} = -\eta_{11}\hat{\gamma} + \eta_{12} w\left(i_q + \sqrt{19}\right), \\ \dot{\hat{\sigma}} = -\eta_{21}\hat{\sigma} + \eta_{22}(i_q - w)\left(w + \sqrt{19}\right), \\ \dot{\hat{d}}_1 = -\eta_{31}\hat{d}_1 + \eta_{32}(i_d - 19), \\ \dot{\hat{d}}_2 = -\eta_{41}\hat{d}_2 + \eta_{42}\left(i_q + \sqrt{19}\right), \\ \dot{\hat{d}}_3 = -\eta_{51}\hat{d}_3 + \eta_{52}\left(w + \sqrt{19}\right), \end{cases} \tag{35}$$

then the system states can stabilize to the small neighborhoods about the equilibrium point $E^-\left(19, -\sqrt{19}, -\sqrt{19}\right)$ in fixed time.

Remark 1. *It is worth noting that perturbations were not considered in [58,59], and as a result, the performance of the controllers in those studies in the presence of perturbations cannot be guaranteed. In contrast, in this article, we have embedded the parametric adaptive mechanism (Equation (8))* *to estimate the unknown parameters and perturbations. This design ensures that the developed controller is not only insensitive to unknown parameters, but also robust against perturbations.*

Remark 2. *The dynamic behavior of chaotic systems, such as the PMSM system, is irregular, unpredictable, and highly insensitive to initial conditions. Due to this inherent nature, achieving complete stabilization of chaotic systems is impossible. In fact, the developed controller cannot stabilize the attractor itself but can only guide the system states to achieve the desired behavior.*

4. Simulated Studies

Simulated studies are carried out to demonstrate the developed control strategy in this section. Without loss of generality, we take account of the chaotic stabilization about the equilibrium point $O(0,0,0)$. The following simulations are deployed though two scenarios. Scenario 1 is the performance comparisons and Scenario 2 is the fixed-time stability tests.

4.1. Performance Comparisons

In Scenario 1, the performance comparisons are made to show the advantages of the developed controller. In the simulations, the parameters are set as $\gamma = 20$ and $\sigma = 5.46$, and the perturbations are given as $d_1 = 0.2\sin(0.8t)$, $d_2 = 0.3\cos(0.9t)$, and $d_3 = 0.2\sin(0.9t)$. The parameters and perturbations are supposed to be unknown in the control design. The initial system states are chosen as $i_d(0) = 1$, $i_q(0) = 3$, and $w(0) = -2$.

Besides the developed controller (7), the existing linear feedback controller is also utilized for comparisons, which is presented as

$$\begin{cases} u_1 = -k_1 i_d, \\ u_2 = -k_2 i_q, \\ u_3 = -k_3 w, \end{cases} \tag{36}$$

where $k_1 > 0$, $k_2 > 0$, and $k_3 > 0$.

In the simulations, the parameters of the developed controller (7) are made as $k_{11} = 10$, $k_{12} = 10$, $k_{21} = 10$, $k_{22} = 10$, $k_{31} = 10$, $k_{32} = 10$, $p = 9/11$, $q = 13/11$, $\eta_{11} = 0.01$, $\eta_{12} = 1$, $\eta_{21} = 0.01$, $\eta_{22} = 1$, $\eta_{31} = 0.01$, $\eta_{32} = 1$, $\eta_{41} = 0.01$, $\eta_{42} = 1$, $\eta_{51} = 0.01$, and $\eta_{52} = 1$. The initial values of the adaptive parameters are set as $\hat{\gamma}(0) = 18$, $\hat{\sigma}(0) = 5$, $\hat{d}_1(0) = 0$, $\hat{d}_2(0) = 0$, and $\hat{d}_3(0) = 0$. The parameters of the existing controller (36) are made as $k_1 = 12$, $k_2 = 12$, and $k_3 = 12$.

The simulation results of Scenario 1 are given in Figures 2–4. Specifically, Figure 2 shows the time history of the system states. It is desirable that both the developed and existing controllers can fulfill the chaotic stabilization successfully. Quantitatively, the steady-state state errors i_d, i_q, and w under the developed controller are within the ranges of ± 0.008, ± 0.016, and ± 0.01, and under the existing controller are within the ranges of ± 0.02, ± 0.06, and ± 0.04. The existing controller can attain the much larger steady-state state errors than the developed controller. This implies that the stabilization performance of the developed controller is better than that of the existing controller in terms of higher control accuracy. The time history of the control inputs is presented in Figure 3. The control inputs under the existing controller even have a larger magnitude than those under the developed controller. This means that comparisons are quite fair or at least not partial to the developed controller. Figure 4 gives the time history of the adaptive parameters. These adaptive parameters are changing smoothly with time. Owing to the utilization of the parametric adaptive mechanism, the developed controller is not only insensitive to unknown parameters but also robust against perturbations. By contrast, the disturbance rejection property of the existing linear feedback controller is really poor.

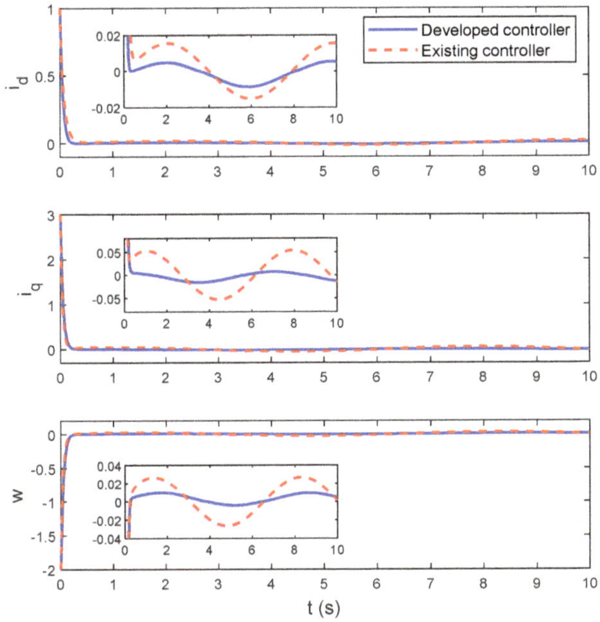

Figure 2. System states (Scenario 1).

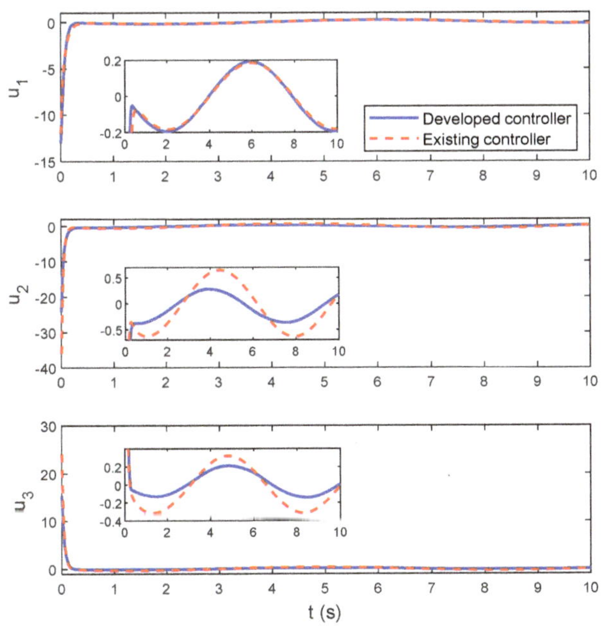

Figure 3. Control inputs (Scenario 1).

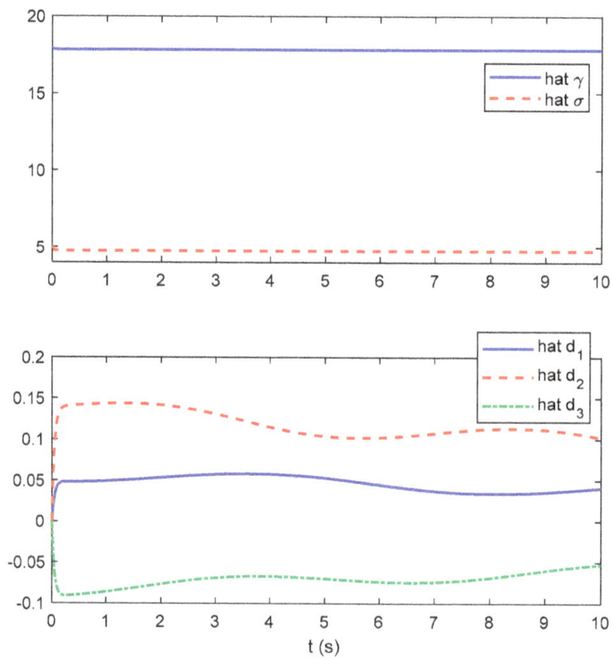

Figure 4. Adaptive parameters (Scenario 1).

4.2. Fixed-Time Stability Tests

In Scenario 2, the tests with different initial system states are provided to examine the fixed-time stability capability of the developed controller. Three groups of initial system states are considered. In Group 1, the initial system states are chosen as $i_d(0) = 1$, $i_q(0) = 3$, and $w(0) = -2$. In Group 2, the initial system states are chosen as $i_d(0) = -1.5$, $i_q(0) = -0.5$, and $w(0) = 1$. In Group 3, the initial system states are chosen as $i_d(0) = 3$, $i_q(0) = -2.5$, and $w(0) = 2.5$. In Group 4, the initial system states are chosen as $i_d(0) = -2.5$, $i_q(0) = 2$, and $w(0) = 0.5$. The perturbations and parameters of the developed controller (7) are chosen in the same way as those in Scenario 1.

The simulation results of Scenario 2 are provided in Figures 5 and 6. It is clearly seen that the developed controller can realize the chaotic stabilization within the similar settling time $T_c = 0.25$ s in the presence of different initial system states. This means that the settling time is bounded and particularly the upper bound is irrelevant to the initial system states. Therefore, it can be derived that the developed controller has the fixed-time stability capability.

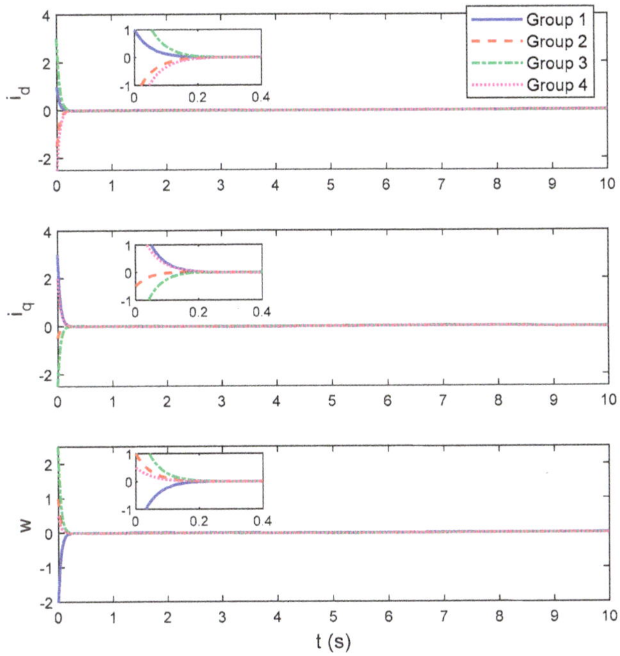

Figure 5. System states (Scenario 2).

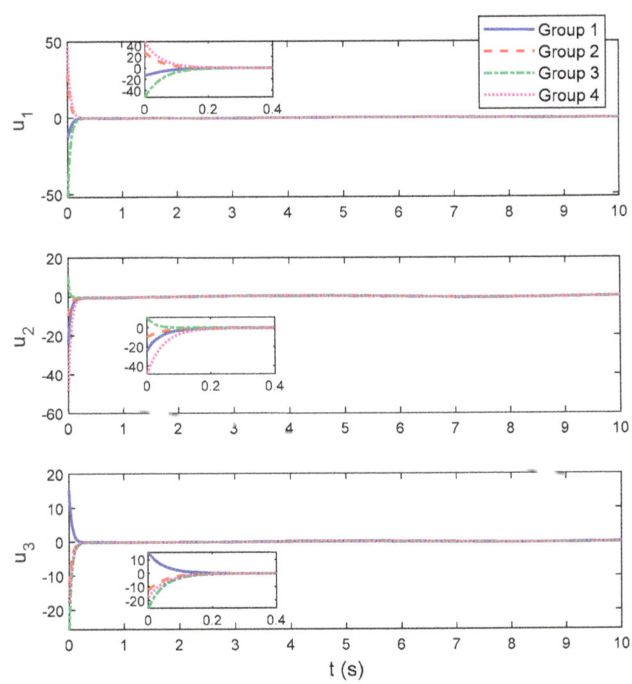

Figure 6. Control inputs (Scenario 2).

5. Conclusions

This article addresses the fixed-time chaotic stabilization of PMSM subject to unknown parameters and perturbations by developing an adaptive control strategy. The developed controller is synthesized by combining it with the parametric adaptive mechanism under the fixed-time control framework. Stability analysis demonstrates that the system states under the developed controller can stabilize within fixed time to small neighborhoods around the equilibrium point. A distinctive advantage of the developed controller is its insensitivity to unknown parameters and robustness against perturbations. Finally, the developed control strategy is verified and highlighted through simulated studies.

Author Contributions: Conceptualization, Q.Y., H.J., S.B., J.L. and A.A.A.-B.; methodology, Q.Y., H.J., S.B., J.L. and A.A.A.-B.; software, Q.Y., H.J., S.B., J.L. and A.A.A.-B.; validation, Q.Y., H.J., S.B., J.L. and A.A.A.-B.; formal analysis, Q.Y., H.J., S.B., J.L. and A.A.A.-B.; writing—original draft, Q.Y., H.J., S.B., J.L. and A.A.A.-B.; writing—review & editing, Q.Y., H.J., S.B., J.L. and A.A.A.-B.; supervision, Q.Y. and H.J. All authors have read and agreed to the published version of the manuscript.

Funding: This research work was funded by Institutional Fund Projects under grant no. (IFPIP: 600-611-1443). The authors gratefully acknowledge technical and financial support provided by the Ministry of Education and King Abdulaziz University, DSR, Jeddah, Saudi Arabia.

Data Availability Statement: Not applicable.

Conflicts of Interest: The authors declare no conflict of interest.

References

1. Jing, Z.; Park, J.B.; Joo, Y.H.; Zhang, B.; Chen, G. Bifurcations and chaos in a permanent-magnet synchronous motor. *IEEE Trans. Circuits Syst. I Fundam. Theory Appl.* **2002**, *49*, 383–387.
2. Jing, Z.; Yu, C.; Chen, G. Complex dynamics in a permanent-magnet synchronous motor model. *Chaos Solitons Fractals* **2004**, *22*, 831–848. [CrossRef]
3. Zribi, M.; Oteafy, A.; Smaoui, N. Controlling chaos in the permanent magnet synchronous motor. *Chaos Solitons Fractals* **2009**, *41*, 1266–1276. [CrossRef]
4. Chen, S.; Lü, J. Synchronization of an uncertain unified chaotic system via adaptive control. *Chaos Solitons Fractals* **2002**, *14*, 643–647. [CrossRef]
5. Chen, S.; Lü, J. Parameters identification and synchronization of chaotic systems based upon adaptive control. *Phys. Lett. A* **2002**, *299*, 353–358. [CrossRef]
6. Yau, H.-T.; Chen, C.-L. Chaos control of Lorenz systems using adaptive controller with input saturation. *Chaos Solitons Fractals* **2007**, *34*, 1567–1574. [CrossRef]
7. Wang, C.; Ge, S.S. Adaptive synchronization of uncertain chaotic systems via backstepping design. *Chaos Solitons Fractals* **2001**, *12*, 1199–1206. [CrossRef]
8. Yu, Y.; Zhang, S. Adaptive backstepping synchronization of uncertain chaotic system. *Chaos Solitons Fractals* **2004**, *21*, 643–649. [CrossRef]
9. Bowong, S.; Kakmeni, F.M.M. Synchronization of uncertain chaotic systems via backstepping approach. *Chaos Solitons Fractals* **2004**, *21*, 999–1011. [CrossRef]
10. Bowong, S. Adaptive synchronization of chaotic systems with unknown bounded uncertainties via backstepping approach. *Nonlinear Dyn.* **2007**, *49*, 59–70. [CrossRef]
11. Peng, C.-C.; Chen, C.-L. Robust chaotic control of Lorenz system by backstepping design. *Chaos Solitons Fractals* **2008**, *37*, 598–608. [CrossRef]
12. Yu, S.-H.; Hyun, C.-H.; Park, M. Control and synchronization of new hyperchaotic system using active backstepping design. *Int. J. Fuzzy Log. Intell. Syst.* **2011**, *11*, 77–83. [CrossRef]
13. Yu, S.-H.; Hyun, C.-H.; Park, M. Backstepping control and synchronization for 4-D Lorenz-Stenflo chaotic system with single input. *Int. J. Fuzzy Log. Intell. Syst.* **2011**, *11*, 143–148. [CrossRef]
14. Tu, J.; He, H.; Xiong, P. Adaptive backstepping synchronization between chaotic systems with unknown Lipschitz constant. *Appl. Math. Comput.* **2014**, *236*, 10–18. [CrossRef]
15. Yau, H.-T. Design of adaptive sliding mode controller for chaos synchronization with uncertainties. *Chaos Solitons Fractals* **2004**, *22*, 341–347. [CrossRef]
16. Yan, J.-J.; Yang, Y.-S.; Chiang, T.-Y.; Chen, C.-Y. Robust synchronization of unified chaotic systems via sliding mode control. *Chaos Solitons Fractals* **2007**, *34*, 947–954. [CrossRef]
17. Li, W.-L.; Chang, K.-M. Robust synchronization of drive-response chaotic systems via adaptive sliding mode control. *Chaos Solitons Fractals* **2009**, *39*, 2086–2092. [CrossRef]

18. Wang, B.; Wen, G. On the synchronization of uncertain master-slave chaotic systems with disturbance. *Chaos Solitons Fractals* **2009**, *41*, 145–151. [CrossRef]
19. Feki, M. Sliding mode control and synchronization of chaotic systems with parametric uncertainties. *Chaos Solitons Fractals* **2009**, *41*, 1390–1400. [CrossRef]
20. Zribi, M.; Smaoui, N.; Salim, H. Synchronization of the unified chaotic systems using a sliding mode controller. *Chaos Solitons Fractals* **2009**, *42*, 3197–3209. [CrossRef]
21. Pourmahmood, M.; Khanmohammadi, S.; Alizadeh, G. Synchronization of two different uncertain chaotic systems with unknown parameters using a robust adaptive sliding mode controller. *Commun. Nonlinear Sci. Numer. Simul.* **2011**, *16*, 2853–2868. [CrossRef]
22. Liu, H.; Yang, J. Sliding-mode synchronization control for uncertain fractional-order chaotic systems with time delay. *Entropy* **2015**, *17*, 4202–4214. [CrossRef]
23. Cheng, C.-K.; Chao, P.C.-P. Trajectory tracking between Josephson junction and classical chaotic system via iterative learning control. *Appl. Sci.* **2018**, *8*, 1285. [CrossRef]
24. Kim, J.-H.; Park, C.-W.; Kim, E.; Park, M. Fuzzy adaptive synchronization of uncertain chaotic systems. *Phys. Lett. A* **2005**, *334*, 295–305. [CrossRef]
25. Liu, Y.-J.; Zheng, Y.-Q. Adaptive robust fuzzy control for a class of uncertain chaotic systems. *Nonlinear Dyn.* **2009**, *57*, 431–439. [CrossRef]
26. Lin, D.; Wang, X. Self-organizing adaptive fuzzy neural control for the synchronization of uncertain chaotic systems with random-varying parameters. *Neurocomputing* **2011**, *74*, 2241–2249. [CrossRef]
27. Lin, D.; Wang, X.; Yao, Y. Fuzzy neural adaptive tracking control of unknown chaotic systems with input saturation. *Nonlinear Dyn.* **2012**, *67*, 2889–2897. [CrossRef]
28. Jahanshahi, H.; Shahriari-Kahkeshi, M.; Alcaraz, R.; Wang, X.; Singh, V.P.; Pham, V.-T. Entropy analysis and neural network-based adaptive control of a non-equilibrium four-dimensional chaotic system with hidden attractors. *Entropy* **2019**, *21*, 156. [CrossRef]
29. Le, T.-L.; Huynh, T.-T.; Nguyen, V.-Q.; Lin, C.-M.; Hong, S.-K. Chaotic synchronization using a self-evolving recurrent interval type-2 Petri cerebellar model articulation controller. *Mathematics* **2020**, *8*, 219. [CrossRef]
30. Zhu, Z.-Y.; Zhao, Z.-S.; Zhang, J.; Wang, R.-K.; Li, Z. Adaptive fuzzy control design for synchronization of chaotic time-delay system. *Inf. Sci.* **2020**, *535*, 225–241. [CrossRef]
31. Jahanshahi, H.; Yousefpour, A.; Munoz-Pacheco, J.M.; Moroz, I.; Wei, Z.; Castillo, O. A new multi-stable fractional-order four-dimensional system with self-excited and hidden chaotic attractors: Dynamic analysis and adaptive synchronization using a novel fuzzy adaptive sliding mode control method. *Appl. Soft Comput.* **2020**, *87*, 105943. [CrossRef]
32. Wang, S.-Y.; Lin, C.-M.; Li, C.-H. Design of adaptive TSK fuzzy self-organizing recurrent cerebellar model articulation controller for chaotic systems control. *Mathematics* **2021**, *11*, 1567. [CrossRef]
33. Xiong, P.-Y.; Jahanshahi, H.; Alcaraz, R.; Chu, Y.-M.; Gómez-Aguilar, J.F.; Alsaadi, F.E. Spectral entropy analysis and synchronization of a multi-stable fractional-order chaotic system using a novel neural network-based chattering-free sliding mode technique. *Chaos Solitons Fractals* **2021**, *144*, 110576. [CrossRef]
34. Yao, Q. Neural adaptive learning synchronization of second-order uncertain chaotic systems with prescribed performance guarantees. *Chaos Solitons Fractals* **2021**, *152*, 111434. [CrossRef]
35. Zaqueros-Martinez, J.; Rodriguez-Gomez, G.; Tlelo-Cuautle, E.; Orihuela-Espina, F. Fuzzy synchronization of chaotic systems with hidden attractors. *Entropy* **2023**, *25*, 495. [CrossRef] [PubMed]
36. Bhat, S.P.; Bernstein, D.S. Geometric homogeneity with applications to finite-time stability. *Math. Control Signals Syst.* **2005**, *17*, 101–127. [CrossRef]
37. Bhat, S.P.; Bernstein, D.S. Finite-time stability of continuous autonomous systems. *SIAM J. Control Optim.* **2000**, *38*, 751–766. [CrossRef]
38. Li, S.; Tian, Y.-P. Finite time synchronization of chaotic systems. *Chaos Solitons Fractals* **2003**, *15*, 303–310. [CrossRef]
39. Aghababa, M.P.; Khanmohammadi, S.; Alizadeh, G. Finite-time synchronization of two different chaotic with unknown parameters via sliding mode technique. *Appl. Math. Model.* **2011**, *35*, 3080–3091. [CrossRef]
40. Aghababa, M.P.; Aghababa, H.P. Chaos suppression of rotational machine systems via finite-time control method. *Nonlinear Dyn.* **2012**, *69*, 1881–1888. [CrossRef]
41. Aghababa, M.P.; Aghababa, H.P. A general nonlinear adaptive control scheme for finite-time synchronization of chaotic systems with uncertain parameters and nonlinear inputs. *Nonlinear Dyn.* **2012**, *69*, 1903–1914. [CrossRef]
42. Wang, S.; Yousefpour, A.; Yusuf, A.; Jahanshahi, H.; Alcaraz, R.; He, S.; Munoz-Pacheco, J.M. Synchronization of a non-equilibrium four-dimensional chaotic system using a disturbance-observer-based adaptive terminal sliding mode control method. *Entropy* **2020**, *22*, 271. [CrossRef] [PubMed]
43. Wei, Z.; Yousefpour, A.; Jahanshahi, H.; Kocamaz, U.E.; Moroz, I. Hopf bifurcation and synchronization of a five-dimensional self-exciting homopolar disc dynamo using a new fuzzy disturbance-observer-based terminal sliding mode control. *J. Frankl. Inst.* **2021**, *358*, 814–833. [CrossRef]
44. Narayanan, G.; Ali, M.S.; Alam, M.I.; Rajchakit, G.; Boonsatit, N.; Kumar, P.; Hammachukiattikul, P. Adaptive fuzzy feedback controller design for finite-time Mittag-Leffler synchronization of fractional-order quaternion-valued reaction-diffusion fuzzy molecular modeling of delayed neural networks. *IEEE Access* **2021**, *9*, 130862–130883. [CrossRef]

45. Wang, Y.-L.; Jahanshahi, H.; Bekiros, S.; Bezzina, F.; Chu, Y.-M.; Aly, A.A. Deep recurrent neural networks with finite-time terminal sliding mode control for a chaotic fractional-order financial system with market confidence. *Chaos Solitons Fractals* **2021**, *146*, 110881. [CrossRef]
46. Alsaadi, F.E.; Jahanshahi, H.; Yao, Q.; Mou, J. Recurrent neural networkbased technique for synchronization of fractional-order systems subject to control input limitations and faults. *Chaos Solitons Fractals* **2023**, *173*, 113717. [CrossRef]
47. Wang, J.; Chen, X.; Fu, J. Adaptive finite-time control of chaos in permanent magnet synchronous motor with uncertain parameters. *Nonlinear Dyn.* **2014**, *78*, 1321–1328. [CrossRef]
48. Narayanan, G.; Ali, M.S.; Iqbal, M.M.; Kumar, P. Synchronization of fractional-order permanent magnet synchronous generator model based on terminal sliding mode control with switching surface. *Math. Eng. Sci. Aerosp.* **2021**, *12*, 655–667.
49. Andrieu, V.; Praly, L.; Astolfi, A. Homogeneous approximation, recursive observer design, and output feedback. *SIAM J. Control Optim.* **2008**, *47*, 1814–1850. [CrossRef]
50. Polyakov, A. Nonlinear feedback design for fixed-time stabilization of linear control systems. *IEEE Trans. Autom. Control.* **2012**, *57*, 2106–2110. [CrossRef]
51. Jiang, B.; Hu, Q.; Friswell, M.I. Fixed-time attitude control for rigid spacecraft with actuator saturation and faults. *IEEE Trans. Control Syst. Technol.* **2016**, *51*, 332–340. [CrossRef]
52. Ni, J.; Liu, L.; Liu, C.; Hu, X.; Li, S. Fast fixed-time nonsingular terminal sliding mode control and its application to chaos suppression in power system. *IEEE Trans. Circuits Syst. II Exp. Briefs* **2017**, *64*, 151–155. [CrossRef]
53. Yao, Q. Synchronization of second-order chaotic systems with uncertainties and disturbances using fixed-time adaptive sliding mode control. *Chaos Solitons Fractals* **2021**, *142*, 110372. [CrossRef]
54. Yao, Q.; Jahanshahi, H.; Batrancea, L.M.; Alotaibi, N.D.; Rus, M.-I. Fixed-time output-constrained synchronization of unknown chaotic financial systems using neural learning. *Mathematics* **2022**, *10*, 3682. [CrossRef]
55. Alsaade, F.W.; Yao, Q.; Bekiros, S.; Al-zahrani, M.S.; Alzahrani, A.S.; Jahanshahi, H. Chaotic attitude synchronization and anti-synchronization of master-slave satellites using a robust fixed-time adaptive controller. *Chaos Solitons Fractals* **2022**, *165*, 112883. [CrossRef]
56. Yao, Q.; Alsaade, F.W.; Al-zahrani, M.S.; Jahanshahi, H. Fixed-time neural control for output-constrained synchronization of second-order chaotic systems. *Chaos Solitons Fractals* **2023**, *169*, 113284. [CrossRef]
57. Bekiros, S.; Yao, Q.; Mou, J.; Alkhateeb, A.F.; Jahanshahi, H. Adaptive fixed-time robust control for function projective synchronization of hyperchaotic economic systems with external perturbations. *Chaos Solitons Fractals* **2023**, *172*, 113609. [CrossRef]
58. Wang, H.; Yue, H.; Liu, S.; Li, T. Adaptive fixed-time control for Lorenz systems. *Nonlinear Dyn.* **2020**, *102*, 2617–2625. [CrossRef]
59. Wang, H.; Ai, Y. Adaptive fixed-time control and synchronization for hyperchaotic Lü systems. *Appl. Math. Comput.* **2022**, *433*, 127388. [CrossRef]
60. Hardy, G.H.; Littlewood, J.E.; Pólya, G. *Inequalities*; Cambridge University Press: Cambridge, UK, 1952.

Disclaimer/Publisher's Note: The statements, opinions and data contained in all publications are solely those of the individual author(s) and contributor(s) and not of MDPI and/or the editor(s). MDPI and/or the editor(s) disclaim responsibility for any injury to people or property resulting from any ideas, methods, instructions or products referred to in the content.

mathematics

MDPI

Article

An Improved Mathematical Theory for Designing Membrane Deflection-Based Rain Gauges

Jun-Yi Sun [1,2,*], Ning Li [1] and Xiao-Ting He [1,2]

1 School of Civil Engineering, Chongqing University, Chongqing 400045, China; 202116131316@cqu.edu.cn (N.L.); hexiaoting@cqu.edu.cn (X.-T.H.)
2 Key Laboratory of New Technology for Construction of Cities in Mountain Area (Chongqing University), Ministry of Education, Chongqing 400045, China
* Correspondence: sunjunyi@cqu.edu.cn; Tel.: +86-023-65120720

Abstract: This paper is devoted to developing a more refined mathematical theory for designing the previously proposed membrane deflection-based rain gauges. The differential-integral equations governing the large deflection behavior of the membrane are improved by modifying the geometric equations, and more accurate power-series solutions of the large deflection problem are provided, resulting in a new and more refined mathematical theory for designing such rain gauges. Examples are presented to illustrate how to analyze the convergence of the power-series solutions and how to numerically calibrate membrane deflection-based linear rain gauges. In addition, some important issues are demonstrated, analyzed, and discussed, such as the superiority of the new mathematical theory over the old one, the reason why the classical geometric equations cause errors, and the influence of changing design parameters on the input–output relationships of rain gauges.

Keywords: conductive membrane; transversely loading; axisymmetric deformation; large deflection; power-series solution

MSC: 74G10; 74K15

1. Introduction

Many thin films are able to exhibit large elastic deflections when subjected to external loads [1–6], which makes it possible to develop devices or instruments based on film deflection [7–12]. In our previous study [13], to overcome the shortcomings of the existing rain gauges, a new type of membrane deflection-based rain gauge was proposed, which involves a liquid–structure interaction of a peripherally fixed circular membrane under liquid weight loading. Such a fluid–solid coupling problem presents serious analytical difficulties, which involves the analytical solution to differential-integral governing equations. The mathematical theory for designing such rain gauges, which is presented in our previous study [13], is observed to be inaccurate. It is suitable only for the design of nonlinear (rather than linear) rain gauges, because the ranges of the nearly-linear (seemingly following a linear-dependent relationship) segments in the nonlinear input–output relationships of the rain gauges, which it can provide, are too small or too narrow. The main purpose of this study is to present a new and more accurate mathematical theory suitable for the design of both nonlinear and linear rain gauges.

The precipitation sensors are generally divided into three major standard categories: manual rain gauges, tipping-bucket rain gauges [14–18], and weighing rain gauges [19,20], in addition to novel optical infrared sensors [21–23]. Among them, the most popular are the tipping-bucket rain gauges, as they are simple, robust, suitable for different data loggers, and provide an available point measurement, especially suitable for installation in remote areas. Applications of tipping-bucket gauges (also including weighing rain gauges) usually presuppose the static or dynamic calibrations in the laboratory and in the field [24–27], and although very troublesome, they are necessary to do, otherwise, the measurements of precipitation will be accompanied by errors [28–31]. In general, due to various factors, such as calibration errors, the measurements of precipitation may be underestimated by 5% to 40% [32]. In our previous study [13], we proposed developing a new type of rain gauge using the elastic deflection of conductive membranes, namely the membrane elastic deflection-based rain gauge. As opposed to tipping-bucket or weighing rain gauges, this new type of rain gauge does not require performing the calibration for volumetric metering of rainwater, thus avoiding the measurement errors of precipitation caused by this.

The basic configuration and working principle of a membrane deflection-based rain gauge are shown in Figure 1. The rainwater is collected by the rainwater collector funnel that is placed outside. The area of the upward opening of the rainwater collector funnel will be used to determine the amount of rainfall per unit area. The conductive circular membrane is used as the upper electrode plate of capacitors and is fixed to the wall of the circular tank when it is initially flat, resulting in the circular rainwater-collecting tank. The collected rainwater flows into the circular rainwater-collecting tank from the rainwater collector funnel, resulting in the deflection of the conductive circular membrane. Therefore, the upper electrode plate is called a movable electrode plate due to the membrane deflection, while the lower electrode plate, thickly coated with the insulator layer, which is made of a conductive circular thin plate, is an unmovable electrode plate because it is fixed on the substrate. The non-parallel plate variable capacitor between the upper and lower electrode plates is made of two capacitors in series: one is the non-parallel plate variable capacitor between the movable upper electrode plate and the insulator layer, and the other is the parallel plate fixed capacitor between the insulator layer and the unmovable lower electrode plate. The dielectric material between the upper electrode plate and the insulator layer is air, and a small hole is opened in the wall of the circular tank to allow air to pass through, which is located between the upper electrode plate and the insulator layer (see Figure 1).

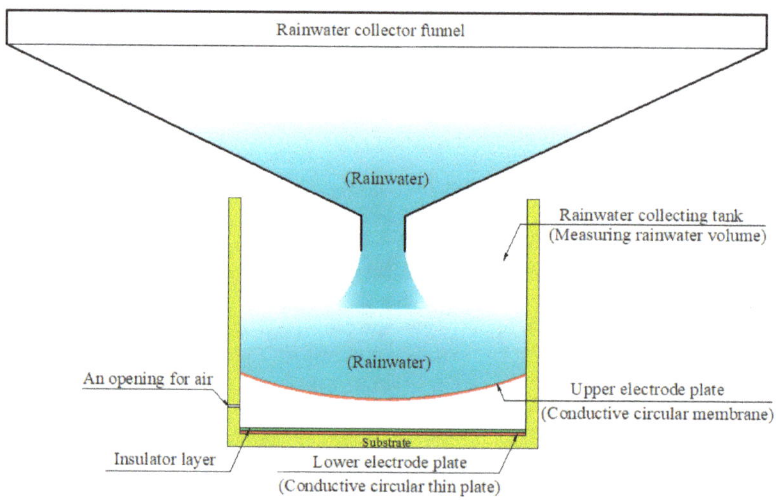

Figure 1. The configuration and working principle of a membrane deflection-based rain gauge.

Obviously, the collected rainwater in the circular rainwater-collecting tank, as an external load acting on the conductive circular membrane, causes the elastic deflection of the conductive circular membrane, determines the spatial geometry of the movable upper electrode plate (i.e., the deflected conductive circular membrane), and thus, determines the capacitance of the non-parallel plate variable capacitor between the movable upper electrode plate and the insulator layer. Therefore, if the magnitude of the external loads acting on the conductive circular membrane is defined by the volume of the collected rainwater in the circular rainwater-collecting tank, then, once the elastic behavior of the conductive circular membrane under the external loads is analytically solved, the volume of the collected rainwater in the circular rainwater-collecting tank can be determined by using the deflection analytical solution. At the same time, the spatial geometry of the deflected conductive circular membrane (i.e., the movable upper electrode plate) can also be determined by using the deflection analytical solution; that is, the capacitance of the non-parallel plate variable capacitor between the movable upper electrode plate and the insulator layer can be determined by using the deflection analytical solution. On the other hand, the capacitance of the parallel plate fixed capacitor between the insulator layer and the unmovable lower electrode plate is constant and, for given design parameters, can be determined by calculation. Therefore, the total capacitance of the non-parallel plate variable capacitor between the upper and lower electrode plates, which can be determined by measurements, is in one-to-one correspondence with the volume of the collected rainwater in the circular rainwater-collecting tank. In other words, the volume of the collected rainwater in the circular rainwater-collecting tank can be determined by measuring the total capacitance of the non-parallel plate variable capacitor between the upper and lower electrode plates. Usually, it is customary to express the rainfall in terms of the height of rainfall per unit area per unit time. Therefore, since any two capacitance measurements will result in two values of volume of the collected rainwater in the circular rainwater-collecting tank, the height of rainfall per unit area per unit time can finally be determined by the volume difference between the two measurements divided by the upward opening area of the rainwater collector funnel, and by the time difference between the two measurements.

However, it can be seen from Figure 1 that there is an interaction between the applied rainwater loads and the deflected conductive circular membrane. The rainwater applied to the conductive circular membrane, as an external load acting on the membrane, gives rise to the deflection of the membrane. In turn, the deflection change gives rise to the distribution change of the rainwater on the conductive circular membrane, i.e., the change in the external loads acting on the membrane. In other words, the liquid action causes the solid response, and in turn, the solid response changes the liquid action, which is commonly referred to as the fluid–solid coupling or interaction problem. Previous studies have shown that the elastic behavior of the conductive circular membrane can be described or governed by a set of differential-integral equations, and the size of membrane deflections has a great influence on the accuracy of the established governing equations [33–35]. In general, it is sufficient to formulate governing equations with lower precision for small deflection problems, because high-precision governing equations will bring difficulties to the subsequent analytical solution. However, if the governing equations with low precision are used for large deflection problems, errors are inevitable. The governing equations used in [13] are the governing equations with low precision, and therefore, only apply to small deflection problems, not to large deflection problems. However, the elastic deflection exhibited by the conductive circular membrane in Figure 1 may reach half of the radius of the circular membrane; therefore, the governing equations used in [13] are practically inapplicable in this case. Therefore, it is recommended that the mathematical theory for designing membrane deflection-based rain gauges, presented in [13], should not be used to avoid causing errors.

In this paper, the differential-integral equations governing the large deflection behavior of the conductive circular membrane are improved by modifying the geometric equations, and more accurate power-series solutions of the large deflection problem are presented, resulting in a new and more refined mathematical theory for designing membrane deflection-based rain gauges. The remainder of this paper is organized as follows. In the following section, the liquid–structure coupling problem in Figure 1: the large deflection problem of the peripherally fixed conductive circular membrane under liquid weight loading, is reformulated, the power-series method for differential equations is used to analytically solve the resulting differential-integral governing equations, and examples are presented to illustrate how to numerically analyze the convergence of the resulting power-series solutions. In Section 3, the analytical relationships between the input capacitance and the output rainwater volume are derived. Examples are provided to illustrate how to numerically calculate the nonlinear input–output relationships of the membrane deflection-based linear rain gauges, and the clear differences between the numerical results calculated by using the new and old mathematical theories are graphically shown. Then, an example is presented to illustrate how to numerically calibrate a membrane deflection-based linear rain gauge. In Section 4, some important issues are analyzed and discussed, such as the reason why the classical geometric equations cause errors, and the influence of changing design parameters on the input–output relationships of membrane deflection-based rain gauges. The concluding remarks are presented in Section 5.

2. Governing Equations and Power-Series Solutions

2.1. Governing Equations

Suppose that an initially flat, conductive, circular membrane with radius a, thickness h, Poisson's ratio v, and Young's modulus of elasticity E is fixed peripherally at the inner wall of the rainwater-collecting tank, as shown in Figure 1, and then it is deflected toward the insulator layer due to the action of the collected rainwater in the rainwater-collecting tank; that is, the action of the so-called liquid weight loading, denoted by $q(r)$, where the height of the rainwater above the plane in which the initially flat, peripherally fixed, conductive, circular membrane is located is denoted by H. A free body is taken from the central portion of the deflected circular membrane in Figure 1, whose radius is $0 \leq r \leq a$, to study its static problem of equilibrium, as shown in Figure 2, where the origin, o, of the introduced cylindrical coordinate system (r, φ, w) is placed in the centroid of the initially flat circular membrane. The dash-dotted line represents the geometric middle plane of the initially flat circular membrane in which the polar coordinate plane (r, φ) is located, r, φ, and w are the radial, circumferential, and transverse coordinates, respectively, w also denotes the transverse displacement of the deflected circular membrane under the action of the loads, $q(r)$, σ_r denotes the radial stress, and θ denotes the slope angle at a point on the geometric middle plane of the deflected circular membrane.

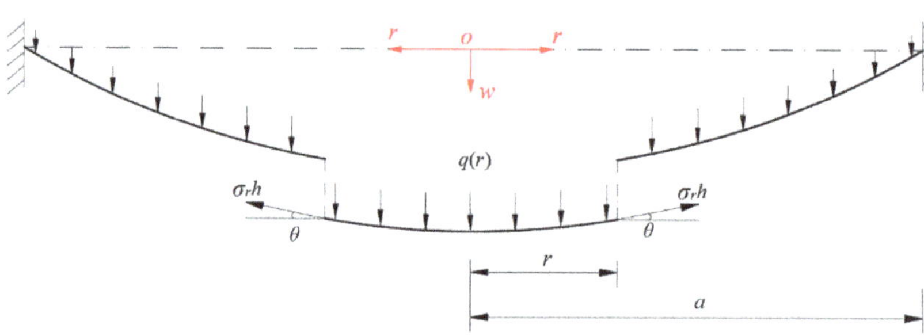

Figure 2. Sketch of a free body with radius $0 \leq r \leq a$.

In particular, it is noted that the external loads, $q(r)$, acting on the conductive circular membrane should include the actions of two parts of rainwater: one is the rainwater with the height H above the polar plane (r, φ), and the other is the rainwater with the height $w(r)$ below the polar plane (r, φ). At point r, the total height of the collected rainwater is equal to H plus $w(r)$.

The out-of-plane equilibrium equation can be derived as follows. The external force $F(r)$ acting on the free body, no matter how the circular membrane is deflected, is always downward, and is given by

$$F(r) = \int_0^r q(r)\mathrm{d}r = \rho\,\mathrm{g}\int_0^r [H + w(r)]\cdot 2\pi r\mathrm{d}r = \rho\,\mathrm{g}\pi r^2 H + 2\pi\rho\,\mathrm{g}\int_0^r w(r)r\mathrm{d}r. \quad (1)$$

The upward force is only the component of the membrane force $\sigma_r h$ acting on the boundary r. Therefore, the out-of-plane equilibrium condition, when the resultant force in the vertical direction is equal to zero, yields

$$2\pi r\sigma_r h\sin\theta = F(r) = \rho\, g\pi r^2 H + 2\pi\rho\, g\int_0^r w(r)r\mathrm{d}r, \tag{2}$$

where

$$\sin\theta = 1/\sqrt{1+1/\tan^2\theta} = 1/\sqrt{1+1/(-\mathrm{d}w/\mathrm{d}r)^2}. \tag{3}$$

After substituting Equation (3) into Equation (2), the out-of-plane equilibrium equation may finally be written as

$$\frac{2r\sigma_r h}{\sqrt{1+1/(-\mathrm{d}w/\mathrm{d}r)^2}} = \rho g r^2 H + 2\rho g\int_0^r w(r)r\mathrm{d}r. \tag{4}$$

The in-plane equilibrium equation is [13]

$$\frac{\mathrm{d}}{\mathrm{d}r}(r\sigma_r) - \sigma_t = 0, \tag{5}$$

where σ_t denotes the circumferential stress.

The classic geometric equations used in [13] do not fully consider the contribution of deflection to the geometric relationship between radial strain and radial displacement. The classical geometric equations have been improved in [34]. If the radial and circumferential strains are denoted by e_r and e_t, and the radial displacement is denoted by u, then the improved geometric equations may be written as

$$e_r = [(1+\frac{\mathrm{d}u}{\mathrm{d}r})^2 + (\frac{\mathrm{d}w}{\mathrm{d}r})^2]^{1/2} - 1 \tag{6}$$

and

$$e_t = \frac{u}{r}. \tag{7}$$

By comparing Equation (6) here with Equation (6) presented in [13], it can be seen that the radial geometric equation here more fully considers the contribution of deflection to the geometric relationship between radial strain and radial displacement.

In addition, the physical equations, i.e., the relations of stress and strain, are still assumed to follow the generalized Hooke's law,

$$\sigma_r = \frac{E}{1-\nu^2}(e_r + \nu e_t) \tag{8}$$

and

$$\sigma_t = \frac{E}{1-\nu^2}(e_t + \nu e_r). \tag{9}$$

2.2. Boundary Conditions

Equations (4)–(9) are six governing equations for solving stresses σ_r and σ_t, strains e_r and e_t, and displacements u and w. Equations (4)–(19) can be solved by using the following boundary conditions

$$\frac{\mathrm{d}w}{\mathrm{d}r} = 0 \text{ at } r = 0, \tag{10}$$

$$e_t = 0 \text{ at } r = a \tag{11}$$

and

$$w = 0 \text{ at } r = a. \tag{12}$$

2.3. Power-Series Solutions

Substituting Equations (6) and (7) into Equations (8) and (9) to eliminate e_r and e_t in Equations (8) and (9) yields

$$\sigma_r = \frac{E}{1-\nu^2}\left\{[(1+\frac{du}{dr})^2 + (\frac{dw}{dr})^2]^{1/2} - 1 + \nu\frac{u}{r}\right\} \tag{13}$$

and

$$\sigma_t = \frac{E}{1-\nu^2}\left\{\frac{u}{r} + \nu[(1+\frac{du}{dr})^2 + (\frac{dw}{dr})^2]^{1/2} - \nu\right\}. \tag{14}$$

Eliminating " $\left[\left(1+\frac{du}{dr}\right)^2 + \left(\frac{dw}{dr}\right)^2\right]^{1/2}$ " from Equations (13) and (14) and then further eliminating σ_t by Equation (5) yields

$$\frac{u}{r} = \frac{1}{E}(\sigma_t - \nu\sigma_r) = \frac{1}{E}[\frac{d}{dr}(r\sigma_r) - \nu\sigma_r]. \tag{15}$$

After substituting the u in Equation (15) into Equation (14), the usually so-called consistency equation can be written as

$$\begin{gathered}\left\{\tfrac{d}{dr}[r\tfrac{d}{dr}(r\sigma_r h)]\right\}^2 + 2Eh\tfrac{d}{dr}[r\tfrac{d}{dr}(r\sigma_r h)] - 2v\tfrac{d}{dr}(r\sigma_r h) \times \tfrac{d}{dr}[r\tfrac{d}{dr}(r\sigma_r h)] \\ +2v\sigma_r h\tfrac{d}{dr}(r\sigma_r h) - 2Eh(\sigma_r h) - (\sigma_r h)^2 + E^2h^2(\tfrac{dw}{dr})^2 = 0\end{gathered}. \tag{16}$$

Let us proceed to the following nondimensionalization

$$W = \frac{w}{a}, S_r = \frac{\sigma_r}{E}, S_t = \frac{\sigma_t}{E}, x = \frac{r}{a}, H_0 = \frac{H}{a}, G = \frac{\rho g a^2}{Eh}, \tag{17}$$

and transform Equations (4), (5), and (16) into

$$4x^2S_r^2(-\frac{dW}{dx})^2 - G^2[(-\frac{dW}{dx})^2 + 1][\int_0^x 2xW(x)dx + x^2H_0]^2 = 0, \tag{18}$$

$$S_t = S_r + x\frac{dS_r}{dx} \tag{19}$$

and

$$\begin{gathered}\left\{\tfrac{d}{dx}[x\tfrac{d}{dx}(xS_r)]\right\}^2 + 2\tfrac{d}{dx}[x\tfrac{d}{dx}(xS_r)] - 2v\tfrac{d}{dx}(xS_r) \times \tfrac{d}{dx}[x\tfrac{d}{dx}(xS_r)] \\ +2vS_r\tfrac{d}{dx}(xS_r) - 2S_r - S_r^2 + (\tfrac{dW}{dx})^2 = 0\end{gathered}. \tag{20}$$

After considering Equations (7) and (15), the boundary conditions, Equations (10)–(12) can be further transformed into

$$\frac{dW}{dx} = 0 \text{ at } x = 0, \tag{21}$$

$$(1-\nu)S_r + x\frac{dS_r}{dx} = 0 \text{ at } x = 1 \tag{22}$$

and

$$W = 0 \text{ at } x = 1. \tag{23}$$

S_r and W can be solved from Equations (18) and (20). To this end, let us expand S_r and W into the power series in powers of the x, i.e., let

$$S_r = \sum_{i=0}^{\infty} c_i x^i \tag{24}$$

and

$$W = \sum_{i=0}^{\infty} d_i x^i. \tag{25}$$

The recursion formulas for the coefficients c_i and d_i in Equations (24) and (25) can be determined as follows. After substituting Equations (24) and (25) into Equations (18) and (20), the similar terms are combined to obtain the sums of coefficients of the x with the same powers. To ensure that Equations (18) and (20), after being substituted into Equations (24) and (25), still hold regardless of the value taken by the x in the interval [0, 1], all the sums of coefficients of the x with the same powers have to simultaneously be equal to zero. This gives rise to a system containing infinitely more equations with respect to the power-series coefficients c_i and d_i. The recursion formulas for the coefficients c_i and d_i can be determined by successively solving this infinite system of equations, as shown in Appendix A, where the coefficients c_i and d_i are always equal to zero when i is odd, or are expressed as the polynomials of c_0 and d_0 when i is even.

The remaining two coefficients, c_0 and d_0, are usually known as the undetermined constants, and they can be determined by using the boundary conditions at $x = 1$ as follows. From Equation (24), the boundary condition Equation (22) gives

$$(1-\nu)\sum_{i=0}^{\infty} c_i + \sum_{i=1}^{\infty} i c_i = 0, \tag{26}$$

and from Equation (25), the boundary condition Equation (23) gives

$$\sum_{i=0}^{\infty} d_i = 0. \tag{27}$$

Since all the coefficients c_i and d_i can be expressed as the polynomials of c_0 and d_0 (see the recursion formulas in Appendix A), Equations (26) and (27) contain only the undetermined constants c_0 and d_0. As a result, the undetermined constants c_0 and d_0 can be determined by simultaneously solving Equations (26) and (27), and with the known c_0 and d_0, the expressions of S_r and W can finally be determined. The problem under consideration is thus solved analytically, where the external loads $q(r)$ applied to the circular membrane are defined by the parameter H, i.e., the height of the collected rainwater above the polar plane (r, φ).

2.4. *Convergence Analysis of Power-Series Solutions*

As can be seen from the Appendix A, the recursion formulas for the coefficients c_i and d_i are so complicated that the convergences of the power-series solutions S_r and W have to be numerically analyzed. To this end, a conductive circular membrane with radius $a = 70$ mm, thickness $h = 0.3$ mm, Young's modulus of elasticity $E = 3.05$ MPa, and Poisson's ratio $\nu = 0.45$, which is subjected to the actions of the collected rainwater with the height $H = 300$ mm and $H = 1000$ mm, respectively, is used as an example to illustrate how to conduct a convergence analysis of the power-series solutions S_r and W.

For the convenience of practical calculation operation, all the infinite power series in Equations (26) and (27) have to be truncated and replaced with their nth partial sums, i.e.,

$$(1-\nu)\sum_{i=0}^{n} c_i + \sum_{i=1}^{n} i c_i = 0 \tag{28}$$

and

$$\sum_{i=0}^{n} d_i = 0. \tag{29}$$

The undetermined constants c_0 and d_0 are calculated by using Equations (28) and (29), where the value of the parameter n begins first with 2, then $n = 4$, $n = 6$, …, and does not stop until the calculated numerical values of c_0 and d_0 are sufficiently saturated, as shown in Table 1, where $H = 300$ mm. The variations of c_0 and d_0 with n are shown in Figures 3 and 4. It can be seen from Figures 3 and 4 that c_0 and d_0 converge very well as the parameter n progressively increases. Therefore, the coefficients c_i and d_i can be calculated using $c_0 = 0.19801$ and $d_0 = 0.38702301$, i.e., the saturated values of b_0 and d_0 when $n = 34$ in Table 1, and the calculated results of c_i and d_i are listed in Table 2. The variations of c_i and d_i with i are shown in Figures 5 and 6. It can be seen from Figures 5 and 6 that c_i and d_i converge very quickly as i progressively increases. This means that the power-series solutions of stress and deflection converge very well at the right end of the interval $x \in [0, 1]$, i.e., at $x = 1$. On the other hand, the power-series solutions of stress and deflection converge to c_0 and d_0 at the left end of the interval $x \in [0, 1]$ (i.e., at $x = 0$, see Equations (24) and (25)); therefore, they converge in the whole interval $x \in [0, 1]$.

Table 1. The numerical values of c_0 and d_0 calculated using different n when $a = 70$ mm, $h = 0.3$ mm, $E = 3.05$ MPa, $\nu = 0.45$, and $H = 300$ mm.

n	c_0	d_0
2	1.6096321×10^{-1}	3.8879863×10^{-1}
4	1.8256583×10^{-1}	4.0353242×10^{-1}
6	1.8997545×10^{-1}	4.0096550×10^{-1}
8	1.9331984×10^{-1}	3.9755283×10^{-1}
10	1.9507474×10^{-1}	3.9487555×10^{-1}
12	1.9608889×10^{-1}	3.9291886×10^{-1}
14	1.9671601×10^{-1}	3.9135900×10^{-1}
16	1.9712404×10^{-1}	3.9006109×10^{-1}
18	1.9739921×10^{-1}	3.8969211×10^{-1}
20	1.9759256×10^{-1}	3.8911582×10^{-1}
22	1.9773075×10^{-1}	3.8857772×10^{-1}
24	1.9783209×10^{-1}	3.8804093×10^{-1}
26	1.9790780×10^{-1}	3.8747951×10^{-1}
28	1.9796534×10^{-1}	3.8727428×10^{-1}
30	1.9799512×10^{-1}	3.8715202×10^{-1}
32	1.9800913×10^{-1}	3.8703145×10^{-1}
34	1.9801000×10^{-1}	3.8702301×10^{-1}

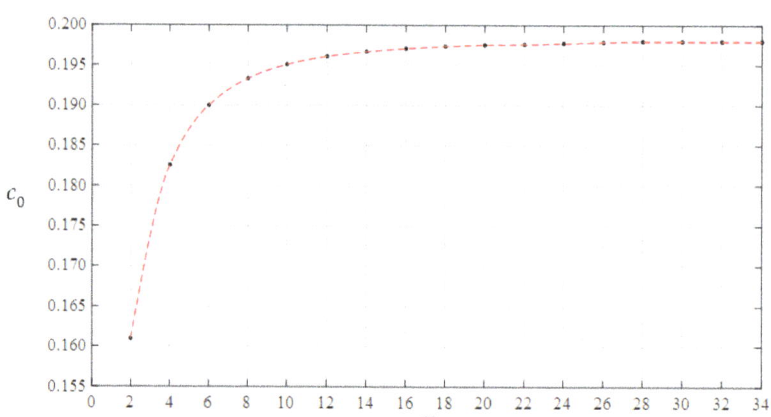

Figure 3. Variation of c_0 with n when $a = 70$ mm, $h = 0.3$ mm, $E = 3.05$ MPa, $\nu = 0.45$, and $H = 300$ mm.

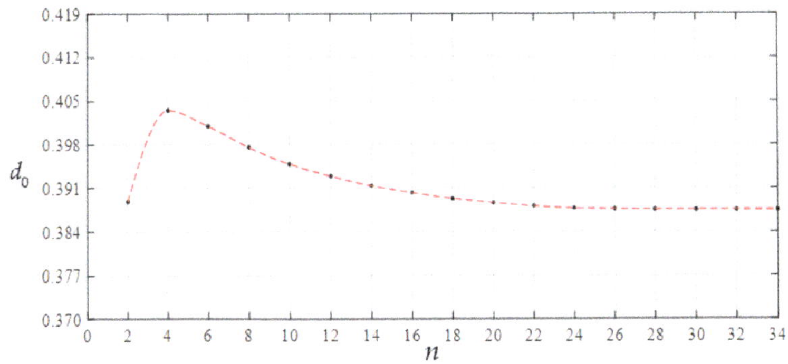

Figure 4. Variation of d_0 with n when a = 70 mm, h = 0.3 mm, E = 3.05 MPa, ν = 0.45, and H = 300 mm.

Table 2. The numerical values of c_i and d_i calculated using c_0 = 0.19801 and d_0 = 0.38702301 when a = 70 mm, h = 0.3 mm, E = 3.05 MPa, ν = 0.45, and H = 300 mm.

i	c_i	d_i
0	1.9801000×10^{-1}	3.8702301×10^{-1}
2	$-2.2503182 \times 10^{-2}$	$-3.1593609 \times 10^{-1}$
4	$-4.7482704 \times 10^{-3}$	$-4.4147582 \times 10^{-2}$
6	$-1.6728142 \times 10^{-3}$	$-1.4480307 \times 10^{-2}$
8	$-7.4018474 \times 10^{-4}$	$-6.0976418 \times 10^{-3}$
10	$-3.7351168 \times 10^{-4}$	$-3.0261953 \times 10^{-3}$
12	$-2.0567441 \times 10^{-4}$	$-1.4010811 \times 10^{-3}$
14	$-1.2065107 \times 10^{-4}$	$-7.9474886 \times 10^{-4}$
16	$-7.4301711 \times 10^{-5}$	$-4.2051265 \times 10^{-4}$
18	$-4.7576760 \times 10^{-5}$	$-2.1235107 \times 10^{-4}$
20	$-3.5862468 \times 10^{-5}$	$-1.9217554 \times 10^{-4}$
22	$-2.1382054 \times 10^{-5}$	$-1.1071414 \times 10^{-4}$
24	$-1.4877621 \times 10^{-5}$	$-7.7178828 \times 10^{-5}$
26	$-1.0567262 \times 10^{-5}$	$-5.0111706 \times 10^{-5}$
28	$-7.6436405 \times 10^{-6}$	$-3.2987094 \times 10^{-5}$
30	$-5.6194073 \times 10^{-6}$	$-2.1986210 \times 10^{-5}$
32	$-4.1919107 \times 10^{-6}$	$-1.4822624 \times 10^{-5}$
34	$-3.1684580 \times 10^{-6}$	$-1.0100267 \times 10^{-5}$

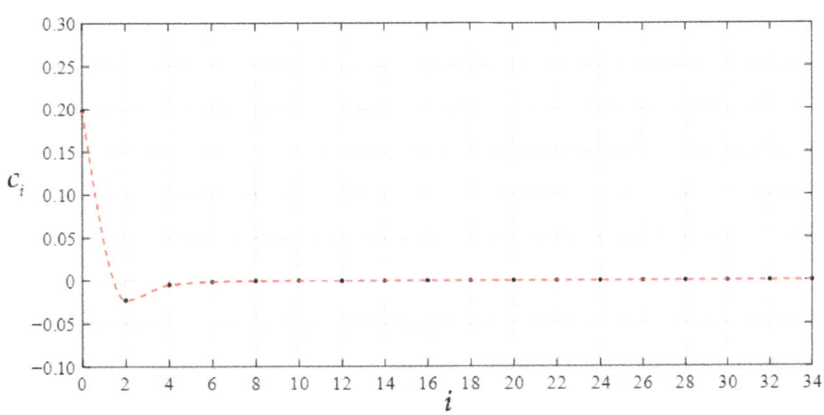

Figure 5. Variation of c_i with i when a = 70 mm, h = 0.3 mm, E = 3.05 MPa, ν = 0.45, and H = 300 mm.

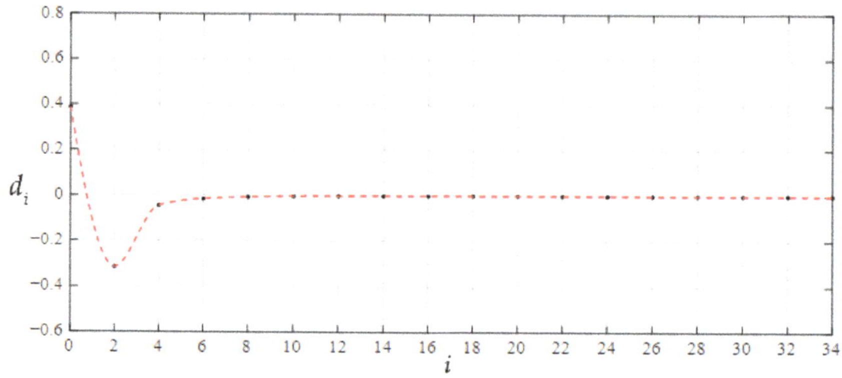

Figure 6. Variation of d_i with i when a = 70 mm, h = 0.3 mm, E = 3.05 MPa, v = 0.45, and H = 300 mm.

Moreover, the calculated numerical values of c_0 and d_0 for H = 1000 mm are listed in Table 3. The variations of c_0 and d_0 with n are shown in Figures 7 and 8. It can be seen from Figures 7 and 8 that c_0 and d_0 also converge very well for H = 1000 mm. The coefficients c_i and d_i are calculated using c_0 = 0.49259866 and d_0 = 0.55707220, i.e., the saturated values of b_0 and d_0 when n = 40 in Table 3, and the calculated results of c_i and d_i are listed in Table 4. The variations of c_i and d_i with i are shown in Figures 9 and 10. It can be seen from Figures 9 and 10 that c_i and d_i also converge very quickly. Therefore, when H = 1000 mm, the power-series solutions of stress and deflection also converge in the whole interval $x \in [0, 1]$.

Table 3. The numerical values of c_0 and d_0 calculated using different n when a = 70 mm, h = 0.3 mm, E = 3.05 MPa, v = 0.45, and H = 1000 mm.

n	c_0	d_0
2	3.3839845×10^{-1}	5.8846359×10^{-1}
4	4.0702919×10^{-1}	6.3457560×10^{-1}
6	4.3696963×10^{-1}	6.3275950×10^{-1}
8	4.5326724×10^{-1}	6.2343005×10^{-1}
10	4.6334148×10^{-1}	6.1364387×10^{-1}
12	4.7011936×10^{-1}	6.0483459×10^{-1}
14	4.7496794×10^{-1}	5.9718707×10^{-1}
16	4.7860304×10^{-1}	5.9059016×10^{-1}
18	4.8143206×10^{-1}	5.8407944×10^{-1}
20	4.8380208×10^{-1}	5.7830109×10^{-1}
22	4.8587068×10^{-1}	5.7262599×10^{-1}
24	4.8774255×10^{-1}	5.6754944×10^{-1}
26	4.8932959×10^{-1}	5.6428763×10^{-1}
28	4.9000625×10^{-1}	5.6247383×10^{-1}
30	4.9075866×10^{-1}	5.6025188×10^{-1}
32	4.9149346×10^{-1}	5.5858188×10^{-1}
34	4.9227867×10^{-1}	5.5723711×10^{-1}
36	4.9240450×10^{-1}	5.5719711×10^{-1}
38	4.9253201×10^{-1}	5.5713711×10^{-1}
40	4.9259866×10^{-1}	5.5707220×10^{-1}

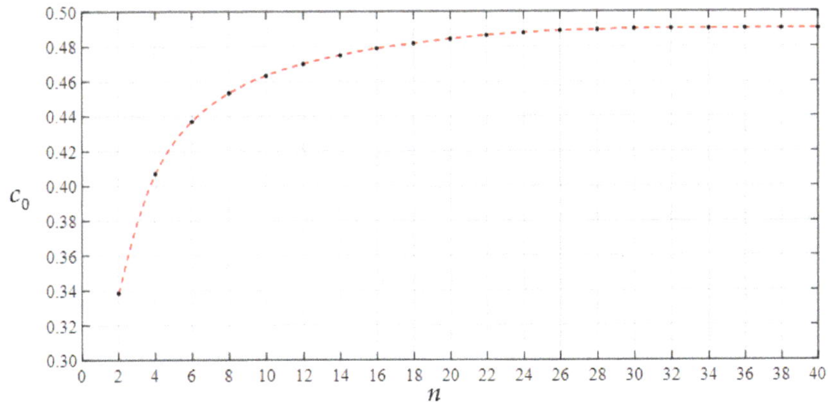

Figure 7. Variation of c_0 with n when a = 70 mm, h = 0.3 mm, E = 3.05 MPa, ν = 0.45, and H = 1000 mm.

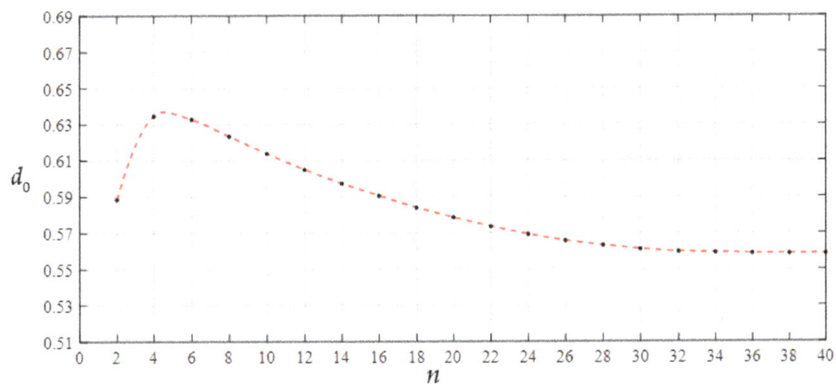

Figure 8. Variation of d_0 with n when a = 70 mm, h = 0.3 mm, E = 3.05 MPa, ν = 0.45, and H = 1000 mm.

Table 4. The numerical values of c_i and d_i calculated using c_0 = 0.49259866 and d_0 = 0.5570722 when a = 70 mm, h = 0.3 mm, E = 3.05 MPa, ν = 0.45, and H = 1000 mm.

i	c_i	d_i
0	4.9259866×10^{-1}	5.5707220×10^{-1}
2	$-3.2010543 \times 10^{-2}$	$-4.0340122 \times 10^{-1}$
4	$-9.0232331 \times 10^{-3}$	$-7.6012684 \times 10^{-2}$
6	$-4.0233576 \times 10^{-3}$	$-3.0795960 \times 10^{-2}$
8	$-2.2202114 \times 10^{-3}$	$-1.6031626 \times 10^{-2}$
10	$-1.3908635 \times 10^{-3}$	$-9.4849784 \times 10^{-3}$
12	$-9.4956383 \times 10^{-4}$	$-6.0706292 \times 10^{-3}$
14	$-6.9066665 \times 10^{-4}$	$-4.0999474 \times 10^{-3}$
16	$-5.2777370 \times 10^{-4}$	$-2.8805707 \times 10^{-3}$
18	$-4.1977975 \times 10^{-4}$	$-2.0867243 \times 10^{-3}$
20	$-3.0524980 \times 10^{-4}$	$-1.3494309 \times 10^{-3}$
22	$-2.5218835 \times 10^{-4}$	$-1.1744272 \times 10^{-3}$
24	$-2.3349516 \times 10^{-4}$	$-8.0307410 \times 10^{-4}$
26	$-2.2477177 \times 10^{-4}$	$-6.1001658 \times 10^{-4}$
28	$-2.0318916 \times 10^{-4}$	$-5.5124579 \times 10^{-4}$

Table 4. *Cont.*

i	c_i	d_i
30	$-1.7687008 \times 10^{-4}$	$-4.4422360 \times 10^{-4}$
32	$-1.3653613 \times 10^{-4}$	$-3.5009484 \times 10^{-4}$
34	$-1.0429799 \times 10^{-4}$	$-3.0502913 \times 10^{-4}$
36	$-6.5852655 \times 10^{-5}$	$-2.3420090 \times 10^{-4}$
38	$-4.3771181 \times 10^{-5}$	$-2.0414329 \times 10^{-4}$
40	$-3.0706861 \times 10^{-5}$	$-1.8232860 \times 10^{-4}$

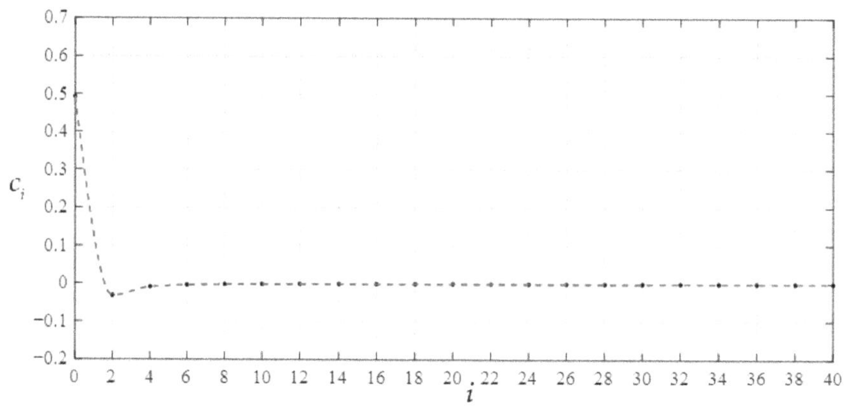

Figure 9. Variation of c_i with i when a = 70 mm, h = 0.3 mm, E = 3.05 MPa, ν = 0.45, and H = 1000 mm.

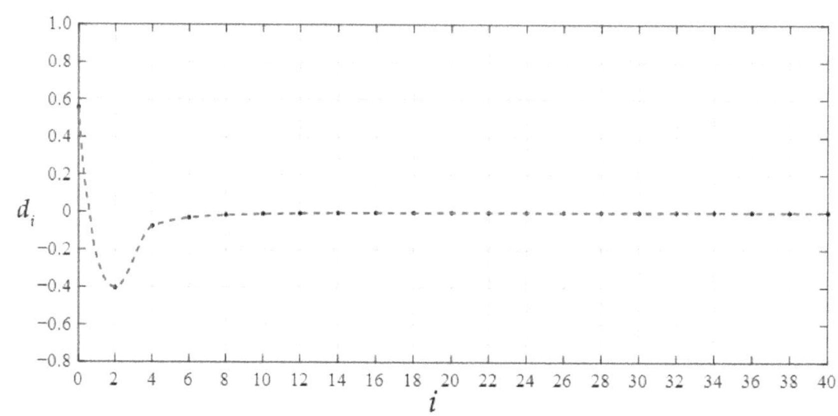

Figure 10. Variation of d_i with i when a = 70 mm, h = 0.3 mm, E = 3.05 MPa, ν = 0.45, and H = 1000 mm.

3. Numerical Calibration of Membrane Deflection-Based Linear Rain Gauges

3.1. Input–Output Analytical Relationships of Membrane Deflection-Based Rain Gauges

Figure 11 shows the states of a membrane deflection-based rain gauge, where the initial state refers to the case without the rainwater, and the operating state refers to the case of the conductive circular membrane (the upper electrode plate) under the rainwater.

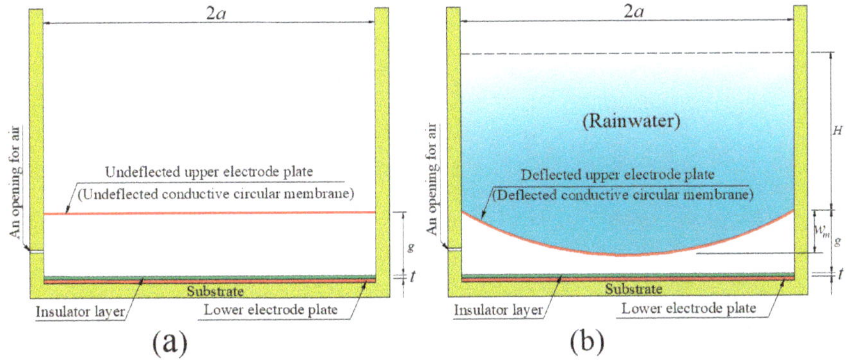

Figure 11. Sketch of a rain gauge: (**a**) initial state and (**b**) operating state.

As shown in Figure 11a, before application of the collected rainwater, the conductive circular membrane (the upper electrode plate) is in its initially flat, undeflected state, maintains an initial parallel gap g with the insulator layer with thickness t, and forms a parallel plate capacitor with the insulator layer. Obviously, the total parallel plate capacitor between the upper and lower electrode plates, whose capacitance is assumed to be denoted as C_0, is comprised of two parallel plate capacitors in series: one is the parallel plate capacitor between the initially undeflected upper electrode plate and the insulator layer, whose capacitance is denoted by C_1, and the other is the one between the insulator layer and the lower electrode plate fixed to the substrate, whose capacitance is denoted by C_2. If the vacuum permittivity is denoted by ε_0, the relative permittivity of air is ε_{r1}, and the relative permittivity of the insulator layer with thickness t is ε_{r2}, then, the capacitance of the parallel plate capacitor between the initially undeflected upper electrode plate and the insulator layer may be written as:

$$C_1 = \frac{\varepsilon_0 \varepsilon_{r1} \pi a^2}{g}, \tag{30}$$

and the capacitance of the parallel plate capacitor between the insulator layer and the lower electrode plate may be written as:

$$C_2 = \frac{\varepsilon_0 \varepsilon_{r2} \pi a^2}{t}. \tag{31}$$

Since the reciprocal of the equivalent capacitance of a series capacitor is equal to the sum of the reciprocal of each series capacitor, the total capacitance of the parallel plate capacitor between the initially undeflected upper electrode plate and the lower electrode plates may be written as:

$$C_0 = \frac{C_1 C_2}{C_1 + C_2} = \frac{\frac{\varepsilon_0 \varepsilon_{r1} \pi a^2}{g} \frac{\varepsilon_0 \varepsilon_{r2} \pi a^2}{t}}{\frac{\varepsilon_0 \varepsilon_{r1} \pi a^2}{g} + \frac{\varepsilon_0 \varepsilon_{r2} \pi a^2}{t}} = \frac{\pi a^2 \varepsilon_0 \varepsilon_{r1} \varepsilon_{r2}}{\varepsilon_{r1} t + \varepsilon_{r2} g}. \tag{32}$$

On the other hand, after application of the collected rainwater, as shown in Figure 11b, the conductive circular membrane (the upper electrode plate) is in a deflected state, whose spatial geometry is governed by the deflection solution: $w(r) = a\sum_{i=0}^{\infty} d_i (\frac{r}{a})^i$, see Equations (17) and (25). Therefore, at this time, the capacitor between the upper electrode plate and the insulator layer is changed from the original parallel plate capacitor with the capacitance C_1 to the current, non-parallel plate capacitor with the capacitance C_1'. The expression of capacitance C_1' can be derived as follows. A micro-area element, which is formed by the increments of radial coordinate Δr and circumferential coordinate $\Delta\varphi$, is taken, whose area ΔS may be written as:

$$\Delta S = \frac{(r+\Delta r)^2\Delta\varphi}{2} - \frac{r^2\Delta\varphi}{2} = r\Delta r\Delta\varphi + \frac{1}{2}(\Delta r)^2\Delta\varphi. \quad (33)$$

Therefore, ΔS can be reduced to $r\Delta r\Delta\varphi$ after ignoring the higher-order terms in Equation (33). Obviously, this micro-area element still corresponds to a non-parallel plate capacitor. However, since it can be made very small, this non-parallel plate capacitor can be approximately regarded as a parallel plate capacitor with a parallel gap g-$w(r)$, whose capacitance $\Delta C_1'$ may be approximated as:

$$\Delta C_1' = \varepsilon_0\varepsilon_{r1}\frac{r\Delta r\Delta\varphi}{g-w(r)}. \quad (34)$$

By integrating both sides of Equation (34), the capacitance C_1' of the non-parallel plate capacitor between the deflected upper electrode plate and the insulator layer may finally be written as:

$$C_1' = \int_0^a\int_0^{2\pi}\varepsilon_0\varepsilon_{r1}\frac{r}{g-w(r)}\mathrm{d}\varphi\mathrm{d}r = 2\pi\varepsilon_0\varepsilon_{r1}\int_0^a\frac{r}{g-w(r)}\mathrm{d}r. \quad (35)$$

Therefore, the total capacitance C of the non-parallel plate capacitor between the deflected upper electrode plate and the lower electrode plate may finally be written as:

$$C = \frac{C_1'C_2}{C_1'+C_2} = \frac{2\pi a^2\varepsilon_0\varepsilon_{r1}\varepsilon_{r2}\int_0^a\frac{r}{g-w(r)}\mathrm{d}r}{2\varepsilon_{r1}t\int_0^a\frac{r}{g-w(r)}\mathrm{d}r+\varepsilon_{r2}a^2}. \quad (36)$$

Obviously, before application of the collected rainwater, the upper electrode plate (the conductive circular membrane) is in its initially flat, undeflected state, that is, $w(r) \equiv 0$. Therefore, it can be seen by comparing Equation (36) with Equation (32), such that Equation (36) is able to regress to Equation (32) if $w(r)$ in Equation (36) is set equal to 0. This implies that the derivation of Equation (36) is correct.

However, as seen in Section 2, the closed-form solutions of the conductive circular membrane under the action of the liquid loads $q(r)$ are presented in power-series form, the external loads $q(r)$ applied to the conductive circular membrane are defined by the parameter H (the height of the collected rainwater above the polar plane (r, φ)), and all the power-series coefficients of the stress and deflection solutions are dependent on the parameter H (see Appendix A). This means that Equation (36) yields the analytical relationship between the total capacitance C and the rainwater height H, rather than the desired analytical relationship between the total capacitance C and the rainwater volume V, which is essential to the numerical calibration of the rain gauge to be designed. Therefore, the volume V of the rainwater collected in the rainwater-collecting tank can only be determined after the deflection solution $w(r)$ is determined with the parameter H. To this end, a micro-volume element, which is formed by the approximate height, $H + w(r)$, and the increments of the radial coordinate Δr and circumferential coordinate $\Delta\varphi$, is taken, whose volume ΔV may be approximated as:

$$\Delta V = [H+w(r)][\frac{(r+\Delta r)^2\Delta\varphi}{2} - \frac{r^2\Delta\varphi}{2}] = [H+w(r)][r\Delta\varphi\Delta r + \frac{1}{2}\Delta\varphi(\Delta r)^2]. \quad (37)$$

Therefore, ΔV can be reduced to $[H + w(r)]r\Delta r\Delta\varphi$ after ignoring the higher-order terms in Equation (37). By integrating both sides of Equation (37), the volume V of the rainwater collected in the rainwater-collecting tank may finally be written as:

$$V = \int_0^a\int_0^{2\pi}[H+w(r)]r\mathrm{d}\varphi\mathrm{d}r = \pi r^2 H + 2\pi\int_0^a w(r)r\mathrm{d}r. \quad (38)$$

As stated in the Introduction Section, the basic principle of this rain gauge is to determine the rainwater volume V by measuring the total capacitance C, which implies that the measured capacitance C is used as input and the volume V to be determined is used as output. This can be achieved by substituting the $w(r)$ in Equations (36)–(38). Obviously, however, doing so works only in theory, not in practice, due to the strong nonlinearity therein; that is, the relationship between the input capacitance C and output volume V has strong nonlinearity.

3.2. Numerical Calculation of Nonlinear Input–Output Relationships

The proposed membrane deflection-based rain gauges generally need to first be numerically calibrated before the experimental calibration. In other words, in order to reduce unnecessary economic losses, material purchase, fabrication, and experimental calibration can only be considered on the basis of sufficient numerical design and calibration. During the design stage of a membrane deflection-based rain gauge, the stress solution provided in Section 2 is used to calculate the maximum stress, σ_m, of the conductive circular membrane under the action of the collected rainwater, to ensure that the membrane will not yield during normal operation. The relationship between input capacitance C and output volume V has to be graphically presented based on numerical calculations, due to its strong nonlinearity (see Equations (36) and (38)). In the following, an example is provided to illustrate how to carry out the numerical calculation and calibration of the relationship between input capacitance C and output volume V.

The total capacitance C of the non-parallel plate capacitor between the deflected upper electrode plate and the lower electrode plate (see Figure 11) can be calculated by Equation (36), while the volume V of the rainwater collected in the rainwater-collecting tank can be calculated by Equation (38). For comparison under the same conditions, the $w(r)$ in Equations (36) and (38) is determined by using the deflection solutions provided in this paper and in [13], respectively. Finally, using the calculated results of input capacitance C and output volume V, the relationships between the input capacitance C and output volume V can be graphically presented. Suppose that in Figure 11, the conductive circular membrane with radius a = 70 mm, thickness h = 0.3 mm, and Poisson's ratio ν = 0.45 is subjected to the action of the collected rainwater with the height H that progressively increases from 0 mm to 1160 mm, and its Young's modulus of elasticity, E, is 7.84 MPa, 3.05 MPa, and 1.55 MPa, respectively. The initial parallel gap between the initially undeflected upper electrode plate (the undeflected conductive circular membrane) and the insulator layer, g, is 45 mm, the thickness of the insulator layer, t, is 0.1 mm, the vacuum permittivity, ε_0, is $8.854187817 \times 10^{-12}$ F/m, the relative permittivity of air, ε_{r1}, is 1.000585, and the relative permittivity of the insulator layer (polystyrene), ε_{r2}, is 2.5.

The numerical results calculated by using the deflection solutions presented in Section 2, including the volume V and height H of the applied rainwater, the undetermined constants c_0 and d_0, the maximum stress σ_m and maximum deflection w_m of the conductive circular membrane, and the total capacitance C, are listed in Table 5 for E = 7.84 MPa, in Table 6 for E = 3.05 MPa, and in Table 7 for E = 1.55 MPa, respectively. The numerical results calculated by using the deflection solutions presented in [13] are listed in Table 8 for E = 7.84 MPa, in Table 9 for E = 3.05 MPa, and in Table 10 for E = 1.55 MPa, respectively. The graphical relationships between the input capacitance C and output volume V are shown in Figure 12 for E = 7.84 MPa, in Figure 13 for E = 3.05 MPa, and in Figure 14 for E = 1.55 MPa, respectively, where "Solution 1" refers to the results calculated by using the deflection solution provided in Section 2, and "Solution 2" refers to the results calculated by using the deflection solution presented in [13].

Table 5. The calculation results obtained by using the deflection solution presented in Section 2, when a = 70 mm, h = 0.3 mm, E = 7.84 MPa, ν = 0.45, t = 0.1 mm, and g = 45 mm.

V/mm^3	H/mm	c_0	d_0	σ_m/MPa	w_m/mm	C/pF
0	0	0	0	0	0	3.031
124,575	5	0.00912651	0.08928599	0.072	6.250	3.260
375,589	20	0.01804884	0.12363215	0.142	8.654	3.372
858,653	50	0.03086522	0.16028735	0.242	11.220	3.501
1,334,678	80	0.04136554	0.18472239	0.324	12.931	3.595
1,650,327	100	0.04768439	0.19800761	0.374	13.861	3.649
2,435,732	150	0.06208688	0.22478540	0.487	15.735	3.766
3,218,327	200	0.07514752	0.24648209	0.589	17.254	3.869
4,778,253	300	0.09889744	0.28076362	0.775	19.653	4.049
6,333,912	400	0.12044591	0.30814841	0.944	21.570	4.210
7,888,224	500	0.14112447	0.33158565	1.106	23.211	4.369
9,439,805	600	0.16035428	0.35188757	1.257	24.632	4.515
10,991,294	700	0.17927879	0.37051281	1.406	25.936	4.668
12,542,859	800	0.19780640	0.38824460	1.551	27.177	4.833
14,090,957	900	0.21564079	0.40241204	1.691	28.169	4.967
15,639,301	1000	0.23265806	0.41685058	1.824	29.180	5.117
17,184,907	1100	0.25131599	0.42593509	1.970	29.815	5.221
18,736,165	1200	0.26785971	0.44219936	2.100	30.954	5.462
20,281,633	1300	0.28472526	0.45204828	2.232	31.644	5.670
21,832,194	1400	0.30154191	0.46626571	2.364	32.638	5.848
23,377,102	1500	0.31713399	0.47601986	2.486	33.321	5.058
24,920,726	1600	0.33252186	0.48436690	2.607	33.906	6.251
26,267,341	1700	0.34772280	0.49535388	2.726	34.675	6.451
27,516,958	1800	0.36575166	0.50602041	2.867	35.421	6.637
28,760,027	1900	0.38062130	0.51340029	2.984	35.938	6.860
30,006,149	2000	0.39534296	0.52352253	3.099	36.647	7.082
31,248,954	2100	0.40992652	0.53041230	3.213	37.129	7.347
32,197,815	2200	0.42738078	0.54009150	3.351	37.806	7.582
33,140,390	2300	0.44171346	0.54657935	3.463	38.261	7.840
34,450,957	2400	0.45593168	0.55589281	3.575	38.912	8.214
35,634,503	2500	0.47304169	0.56504691	3.709	39.553	8.586
36,780,016	2600	0.48704925	0.57405502	3.818	40.184	9.068
37,723,326	2700	0.50095953	0.58092913	3.928	40.665	9.546
38,467,637	2800	0.51477727	0.58867998	4.036	41.208	10.288
39,207,668	2900	0.53050684	0.60001726	4.159	42.001	11.555

Table 6. The calculation results obtained by using the deflection solution presented in Section 2, when a = 70 mm, h = 0.3 mm, E = 3.05 MPa, ν = 0.45, t = 0.1 mm, and g = 45 mm.

V/mm^3	H/mm	c_0	d_0	σ_m/MPa	w_m/mm	C/pF
0	0	0	0	0	0	3.031
146,691	5	0.01970885	0.13184277	0.060	9.229	3.385
404,127	20	0.03649575	0.17618466	0.111	12.333	3.549
895,034	50	0.06113101	0.22518344	0.186	15.763	3.758
1,376,699	80	0.08160197	0.25830933	0.249	18.082	3.918
1,695,396	100	0.09405417	0.27623054	0.287	19.336	4.014
2,487,441	150	0.12268822	0.31281998	0.374	21.897	4.232
3,275,452	200	0.14901856	0.34230622	0.455	23.961	4.435
4,842,819	300	0.19812768	0.38702300	0.604	27.091	4.802
6,409,229	400	0.24266300	0.42806925	0.740	29.965	5.232
7,969,683	500	0.28553745	0.46027746	0.871	32.219	5.653
9,527,928	600	0.32846954	0.48689881	1.002	34.083	6.094
11,080,313	700	0.36913154	0.50797866	1.126	35.556	6.496

Table 6. *Cont.*

V/mm^3	H/mm	c_0	d_0	σ_m/MPa	w_m/mm	C/pF
12,632,618	800	0.40776782	0.52917831	1.244	37.042	6.989
14,184,999	900	0.45054965	0.54504372	1.374	38.153	7.479
15,733,468	1000	0.49259866	0.55707220	1.502	38.995	8.067
17,293,779	1100	0.52902425	0.58434882	1.614	40.904	9.136
18,219,213	1159	0.55081967	0.59296547	1.680	41.508	9.784

Table 7. The calculation results obtained by using the deflection solution presented in Section 2, when a = 70 mm, h = 0.3 mm, E = 1.55 MPa, ν = 0.45, t = 0.1 mm, and g = 45 mm.

V/mm^3	H/mm	c_0	d_0	σ_m/MPa	w_m/mm	C/pF
0	0	0	0	0	0	3.031
169,813	5	0.03504216	0.17636915	0.054	12.346	3.530
433,003	20	0.06160905	0.22908031	0.095	16.036	3.758
931,308	50	0.10161546	0.28875958	0.157	20.213	4.069
1,418,300	80	0.13536348	0.32949594	0.209	23.065	4.327
1,740,528	100	0.15660160	0.35132099	0.243	24.592	4.491
2,539,208	150	0.20501025	0.39658974	0.318	27.761	4.882
3,332,226	200	0.24990568	0.43276906	0.387	30.294	5.272
4,911,306	300	0.33517697	0.49068028	0.519	34.348	6.145
6,485,216	400	0.41408249	0.54065885	0.642	37.846	7.336
8,057,472	500	0.49541046	0.58106523	0.768	40.674	9.070
8,843,439	550	0.53204470	0.60338329	0.824	42.237	10.704
9,623,917	600	0.56810397	0.62001403	0.880	43.401	12.794

Table 8. The calculation results obtained by using the deflection solution presented in [13], when a = 70 mm, h = 0.3 mm, E = 7.84 MPa, ν = 0.45, t = 0.1 mm, and g = 45 mm.

V/mm^3	H/mm	c_0	d_0	σ_m/MPa	w_m/mm	C/pF
0	0	0	0	0	0	3.031
124,588	5	0.00913051	0.08929323	0.072	6.251	3.261
375,633	20	0.01806282	0.12365775	0.142	8.656	3.375
858,691	50	0.03089858	0.16029982	0.242	11.221	3.504
1,334,723	80	0.04141489	0.18475348	0.325	12.933	3.599
1,650,384	100	0.04775642	0.19802746	0.374	13.862	3.657
2,435,884	150	0.06217947	0.22494449	0.487	15.741	3.777
3,218,461	200	0.07526571	0.24665732	0.590	17.260	3.881
4,778,663	300	0.09906146	0.28128970	0.777	19.690	4.073
6,335,174	400	0.12084574	0.30925282	0.944	21.648	4.245
7,889,134	500	0.14131148	0.33286392	1.108	23.300	4.409
9,441,679	600	0.16090029	0.35370677	1.261	24.759	4.575
10,992,711	700	0.17955734	0.37244376	1.408	26.071	4.732
12,543,452	800	0.19807130	0.38955350	1.553	27.269	4.905
14,092,787	900	0.21580643	0.40516165	1.692	28.361	5.091
15,641,994	1000	0.23326902	0.42000069	1.829	29.400	5.349
17,191,522	1100	0.25243719	0.43374474	1.971	30.362	5.649
18,739,873	1200	0.27177709	0.44517926	2.131	31.162	5.958
20,290,603	1300	0.29002133	0.47212330	2.274	33.049	6.315
21,850,279	1400	0.30683175	0.49023351	2.406	34.316	6.770
23,810,192	1500	0.31957734	0.51393343	2.505	35.975	7.440
24,921,876	1600	0.33516431	0.53469018	2.628	37.428	8.040
26,273,301	1700	0.35079983	0.55535388	2.750	38.875	8.850
27,526,771	1800	0.36873324	0.58255698	2.891	40.779	9.950
28,771,321	1900	0.38242337	0.60046679	2.998	42.033	11.221
30,029,618	2000	0.39749640	0.62254338	3.116	43.578	12.750

Table 9. The calculation results obtained by using the deflection solution presented in [13], when a = 70 mm, h = 0.3 mm, E = 3.05 MPa, ν = 0.45, t = 0.1 mm, and g = 45 mm.

V/mm^3	H/mm	c_0	d_0	σ_m/MPa	w_m/mm	C/pF
0	0	0	0	0	0	3.031
146,724	5	0.06016640	0.13186295	0.060	9.230	3.386
404,212	20	0.03655238	0.17621740	0.111	12.335	3.551
895,253	50	0.06128064	0.22528736	0.187	15.770	3.759
1,376,928	80	0.08183265	0.25841407	0.250	18.092	3.920
1,695,731	100	0.09432359	0.27647647	0.288	19.353	4.017
2,488,099	150	0.12303213	0.31351195	0.375	21.946	4.238
3,276,555	200	0.14965178	0.34321310	0.456	24.025	4.446
4,846,461	300	0.19821688	0.39148280	0.605	27.404	4.850
6,411,526	400	0.24471626	0.42924903	0.746	30.047	5.261
7,978,001	500	0.29208802	0.46270729	0.891	32.389	5.755
9,540,106	600	0.33782439	0.49102081	1.030	34.371	6.272
11,101,273	700	0.38000127	0.51981346	1.159	36.387	6.926
12,661,746	800	0.42426305	0.54443643	1.294	38.111	7.690
14,221,573	900	0.46737880	0.56833220	1.426	39.783	8.692
15,776,926	1000	0.50487106	0.59139964	1.540	41.398	10.034
17,328,075	1100	0.54153188	0.61012303	1.652	42.709	11.750
18,253,522	1159	0.56126944	0.62057931	1.712	43.441	13.246

Table 10. The calculation results obtained by using the deflection solution presented in [13], when a = 70 mm, h = 0.3 mm, E = 1.55 MPa, ν = 0.45, t = 0.1 mm, and g = 45 mm.

V/mm^3	H/mm	c_0	d_0	σ_m/MPa	w_m/mm	C/pF
0	0	0	0	0	0	3.031
169,902	5	0.03509797	0.17643908	0.054	12.351	3.530
433,137	20	0.06176587	0.22910474	0.096	16.037	3.759
931,759	50	0.10190303	0.28922995	0.158	20.246	4.074
1,419,348	80	0.13587112	0.33052673	0.211	23.137	4.338
1,741,524	100	0.15675307	0.35309502	0.243	24.717	4.504
2,541,171	150	0.20535898	0.39945876	0.318	27.962	4.953
3,335,829	200	0.25076296	0.43702251	0.389	30.592	5.503
4,917,064	300	0.33611589	0.49773713	0.521	34.846	6.827
6,491,273	400	0.41649287	0.54717865	0.646	38.303	8.776
8,061,359	500	0.49382544	0.58981307	0.765	41.287	11.898
8,845,243	550	0.53214314	0.60880232	0.825	42.616	14.857
9,629,215	600	0.56999709	0.62751931	0.883	43.926	18.896

It can be seen from Figures 12–14 that the C-V relationships are indeed nonlinear, and that the difference between the C-V relationship calculated by using the deflection solution provided in this paper and that calculated by using the deflection solution in [13], i.e., the difference between "Solution 1" and "Solution 2" in Figures 12–14, is very clear, and it increases with the increase of the Young's modulus of elasticity E. This difference is caused by the use of the improved differential-integral governing equations (see Section 2). In addition, from Figures 12–14, it can be observed that the ranges of the nearly-linear segments (which seem to follow a linear variation trend) in the nonlinear C-V relationships calculated by using the deflection solution in this paper are wider than the ranges of the nearly-linear segments (which seem to follow a linear variation trend) in the nonlinear C-V relationships calculated by using the deflection solution presented in [13] (see "Solution 1" and "Solution 2" in Figures 12–14). For instance, the ranges of the nearly-linear segments of E = 3.05 MPa are about C = 3.5 pF–8 pF and V = 15,733,468 mm^3 in "Solution 1", and C = 3.5 pF–6 pF and V = 9,540,106 mm^3 in "Solution 2", respectively (see Figure 13). The differences of 2 pF and 6,193,362 mm^3 are very valuable for designing linear rain gauges, especially the 2 pF input capacitance, C. This is caused by the use of the improved differential-integral governing equations in Section 2.

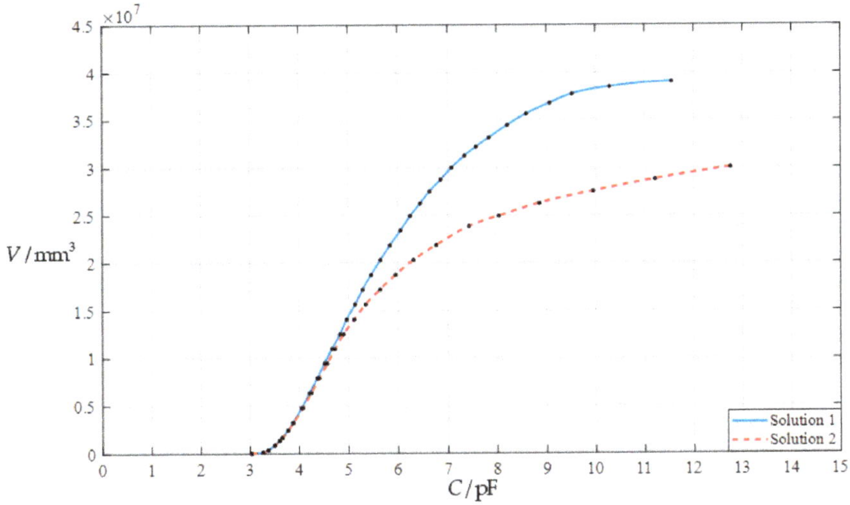

Figure 12. The relationships between the input capacitance C and output volume V when $a = 70$ mm, $h = 0.3$ mm, $E = 7.84$ MPa, $\nu = 0.45$, $t = 0.1$ mm, and $g = 45$ mm, where "Solution 1" refers to the results calculated by using the deflection solution presented in Section 2, and "Solution 2" refers to the results calculated by using the deflection solution provided in [13].

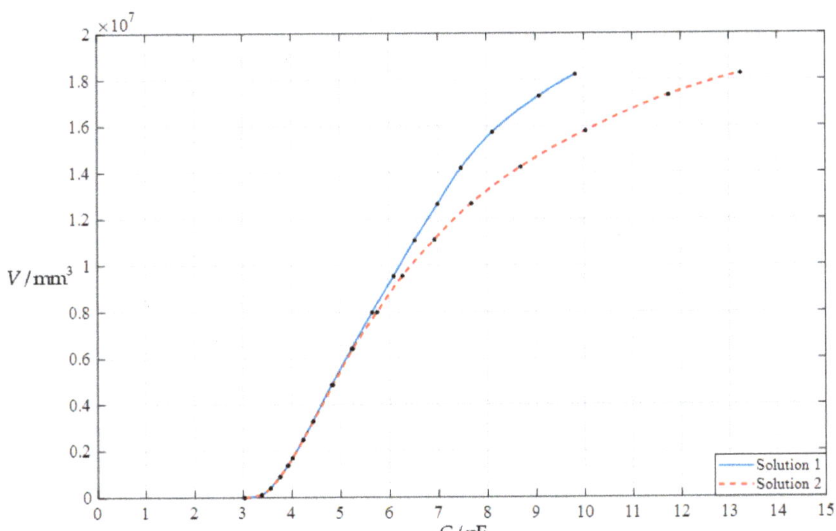

Figure 13. The relationships between the input capacitance C and output volume V when $a = 70$ mm, $h = 0.3$ mm, $E = 3.05$ MPa, $\nu = 0.45$, $t = 0.1$ mm, and $g = 45$ mm, where "Solution 1" refers to the results calculated by using the deflection solution presented in Section 2, and "Solution 2" refers to the results calculated by using the deflection solution provided in [13].

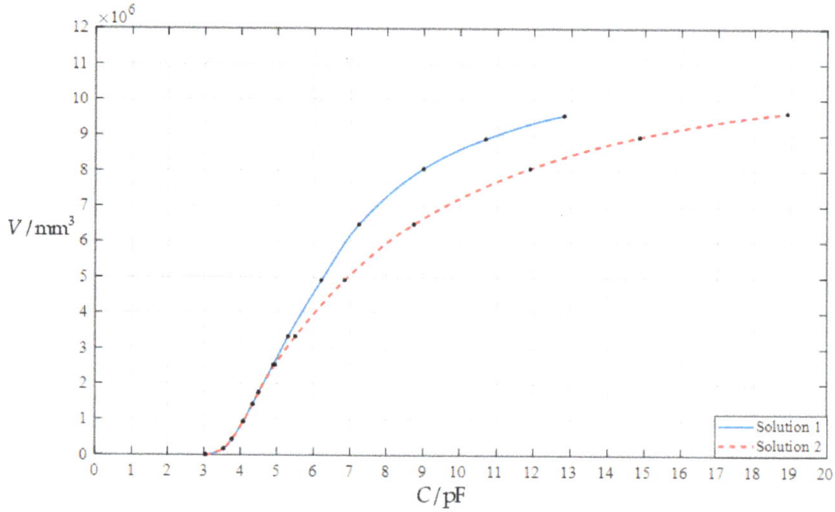

Figure 14. The relationships between the input capacitance C and output volume V when $a = 70$ mm, $h = 0.3$ mm, $E = 1.55$ MPa, $\nu = 0.45$, $t = 0.1$ mm, and $g = 45$ mm, where "Solution 1" refers to the results calculated by using the deflection solution presented in Section 2, and "Solution 2" refers to the results calculated by using the deflection solution provided in [13].

3.3. An Example of Numerical Calibration for Linear Rain Gauges

The reason why in [13], only nonlinear rain gauges are discussed, and linear rain gauges are not considered, is that the range of the nearly-linear segment obtained is too narrow for linear fitting. We will not discuss nonlinear fitting here, but only provide an example to illustrate how to conduct the linear fitting for numerically calibrating a linear rain gauge. The data for the output volume V and input capacitance C in Table 6, i.e., 146,691 mm^3–15,733,468 mm^3 for the output volume V and 3.385 pF–8.067 pF for the input capacitance C, are used to numerically calibrate a linear rain gauge, and the obtained linear relationship between the output volume V and input capacitance C is, via least-squares straight-line-fitting,

$$V = 3524947C - 12176469. \tag{39}$$

The fitting effect is shown in Figure 15. Therefore, such a linear rain gauge should be calibrated to about 3525 mm^3 per 1 pF input capacitance C, when designing its analog circuit. Obviously, for any two capacitance measurements, the difference in measured capacitances, ΔC, corresponds to the difference in the rainwater volumes to be measured, ΔV, while the volume difference, ΔV, divided by the time difference between the two capacitance measurements, Δt, is the rainfall volume per unit time. However, it is usually customary to express rainfall by the height of the rainfall per unit area per unit time. For example, if the upward opening area A of the rainwater collector funnel (see Figure 1) is equal to one square meter, and if the height of rainfall is expressed in centimeters, then the rainfall R_f, measured by this linear rain gauge, can be simply calibrated as:

$$R_f = (0.352\Delta C - 1.218) / \Delta t, \tag{40}$$

where R_f is measured in units per centimeter per square meter per unit time, and Δt can be measured in units per second, per minute, per hour, per day, per month, or even per year.

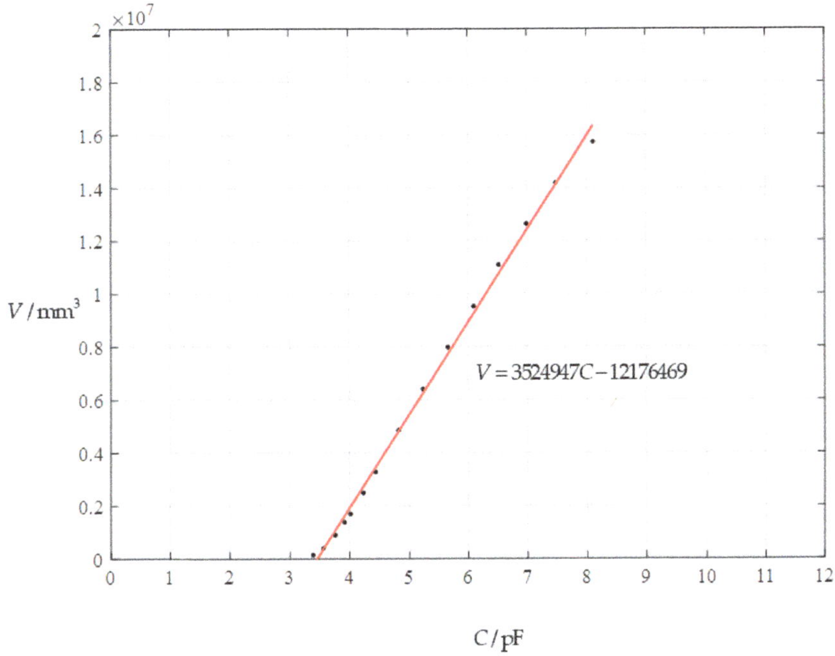

Figure 15. The least-squares straight-line-fitting for the nearly-linear segment of "Solution 1" in Figure 13.

4. Results and Discussion

The membrane elastic deflection-based rain gauges proposed here have the following advantages, in comparison to the traditional tipping-bucket rain gauges (TBRGs) [14–18]. First, unlike tipping-bucket rain gauges, these new types of rain gauges do not need to conduct the calibration for volumetric metering of rainwater, thus avoiding the measurement errors of precipitation caused by this. Second, these new types of rain gauges can achieve continuous rainfall measurements, because the magnitude of the time interval Δt between two measurements of the input capacitance C can be arbitrary, while the time taken to fill a TBRG bucket with rainwater under a given rainfall intensity is basically constant (i.e., the time between two rainfall measurements is basically constant for TBRGs, so the continuous rainfall measurements cannot be achieved.) Therefore, these new types of rain gauges can be used in cases where continuous rainfall measurements are required but cannot be satisfied by TBRGs.

It can be seen from Section 3.2 that the closed-form solution presented in Section 2 is more suitable for designing linear rain gauges, in comparison to the closed-form solution in [13]. It can be seen by comparing Section 2 in this paper with Section 2 in [13] that the out-of-plane and in-plane equilibrium equations, physical equations, and circumferential geometric equation used in this paper are the same as those used in [13], and only the radial geometric equation used in this paper is different from that used in [13]. Therefore, the difference between the power-series solutions presented in this paper and those in [13] is entirely caused by the different radial geometric equations used. The difference between the radial geometric equation used in this paper and that used in [13] can be seen in Section 4.1 below.

The reason for the emphasis on linear rain gauges is that the circuit design of linear sensors is much easier than that of nonlinear sensors. Linear sensors can use analog circuit technology, while nonlinear sensors often can only use digital circuits. Therefore, under the same conditions, the use of a linear sensor has more advantages than the use of a nonlinear sensor, such as simple, easy to implement, low cost, good stability, and strong adaptability to the use environment. However, if a linear rain gauge is to be designed and calibrated, then the ranges of the input capacitance C as well as the output volume V are usually difficult to fully meet the actual use requirements. At this time, it is often necessary to consider making some compromises, otherwise, the rain gauge design cannot proceed, as is often the case with the solutions of many engineering problems [35–40]. Therefore, in this sense, linear rain gauge designs are usually much more difficult, in comparison to nonlinear rain gauge designs.

In addition, it is obvious that the power-series solutions must be shown to converge before they can be used in practical computational applications. In other words, a particular solution in the form of a power series must be analyzed for convergence before it can be used, otherwise it cannot be used. However, the problem dealt with here, the liquid–structure interaction of the circular membrane under liquid weight loading (see Figure 1 and Equation (1)), presents a strong nonlinearity. This leads to the phenomenon that the characteristic parameters of the problem, the undetermined constants c_0 and d_0, strictly depend on the external action $q(r)$ applied to the circular membrane, which is defined by the height H of the collected rainwater above the polar plane (r, φ) (see Figure 11). Therefore, every value of H corresponds to a statics problem, a pair of saturated values of c_0 and d_0, which are calculated by progressively increasing the parameter n, and a pair of particular solutions of stress and deflection, which need to be shown to converge, as detailed in Section 2.4. As a result, a lot of numerical calculations and convergence analyses are needed to obtain a usable pair of particular solutions of stress and deflection. Therefore, from this point of view, it is very important to carry out research on various computational approaches [41,42].

As can be seen in Section 3.2, the closed-form solution presented in this paper has a positive effect on changing the range of the nearly-linear segment. In addition, changing some design parameters, such as Young's modulus of elasticity E and Poisson's ratio ν, can also influence the range of the nearly-linear segment in the nonlinear relationships between the input capacitance C and the output volume V, as can be seen in Sections 4.2 and 4.3 below.

4.1. Difference between Geometric Equations Used Here and Those Used in [13]

The geometric equations, i.e., the analytical relationships between displacements and strains, are derived by taking radial and circumferential micro-line elements on the circular membrane before and after deformation. Imagine that the conductive circular membrane undergoes an axisymmetric deformation with large deflection under the collected rainwater (see Figure 11); therefore, a radial micro-straight-line element $\overline{A'B'}$ on the initially flat circular membrane before deformation becomes a radial micro-curve element $\overset{\frown}{AB}$ on the circular membrane after deformation, as shown in Figure 16a, while a circumferential micro-curve element $\overset{\frown}{A'D'}$ on the initially flat circular membrane before deformation becomes a circumferential micro-curve element $\overset{\frown}{AD}$ on the circular membrane after deformation, as shown in Figure 16b. The initial length of $\overline{A'B'}$ is Δr, see Figure 16a, and the increment of the polar angle coordinate φ is $\Delta\varphi$; that is, the angle of counterclockwise rotation from the point A' to the point D', see Figure 16b. The coordinate of the point A' is $(r, \varphi, 0)$, and its radial and transverse displacements are denoted by u and w, respectively; that is, the coordinate of the point A is $(r + u, \varphi, w)$. The coordinate of the point B' is $(r + \Delta r, \varphi, 0)$, and its radial and transverse displacements may be expressed as $u(r + \Delta r)$ and $w(r + \Delta r)$, respectively. Therefore, after expanding $u(r + \Delta r)$ and $w(r + \Delta r)$ into the Taylor series and ignoring the higher-order terms therein, that is, letting

$$u(r+\Delta r) = u(r) + \frac{\mathrm{d}u(r)}{\mathrm{d}r}\Delta r + \frac{1}{2!}\frac{\mathrm{d}^2u(r)}{\mathrm{d}r^2}(\Delta r)^2 + \ldots \cong u(r) + \frac{\mathrm{d}u(r)}{\mathrm{d}r}\Delta r \tag{41}$$

and

$$w(r+\Delta r) = w(r) + \frac{\mathrm{d}w(r)}{\mathrm{d}r}\Delta r + \frac{1}{2!}\frac{\mathrm{d}^2 w(r)}{\mathrm{d}r^2}(\Delta r)^2 + \ldots \cong w(r) + \frac{\mathrm{d}w(r)}{\mathrm{d}r}\Delta r, \tag{42}$$

the geometric dimensions marked on Figure 16a can be obtained.

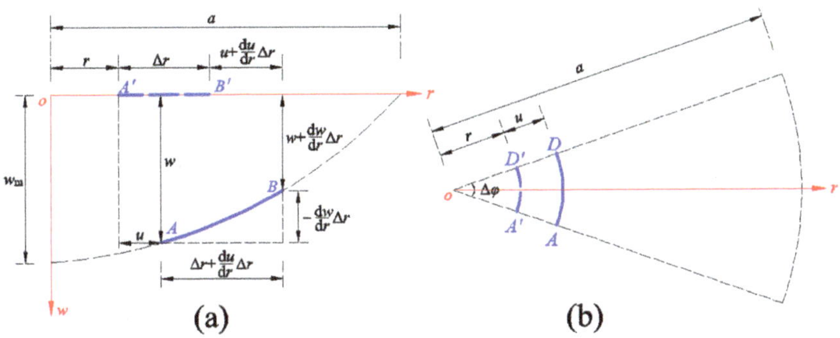

Figure 16. Geometrical relationships of micro-line elements before and after deformation: (**a**) The geometrical relationship between a radial micro-straight-line element $\overline{A'B'}$ before deformation and a radial micro-curve element $\overset{\frown}{AB}$ after deformation. (**b**) The geometrical relationship between a circumferential micro-curve element $\overset{\frown}{A'D'}$ before deformation and a circumferential micro-curve element $\overset{\frown}{AD}$ after deformation.

According to the definition of line strain, the radial line strain when the radial micro-straight-line element $\overline{A'B'}$ becomes the radial micro-curve element $\overset{\frown}{AB}$ may be written as (see Figure 16a)

$$e_r = \frac{L_{\overset{\frown}{AB}} - L_{\overline{A'B'}}}{L_{\overline{A'B'}}}, \tag{43}$$

while the circumferential line strain when the circumferential micro-curve element $\overset{\frown}{A'D'}$ becomes the circumferential micro-curve element $\overset{\frown}{AD}$ may be written as (see Figure 16b)

$$e_t = \frac{L_{\overset{\frown}{AD}} - L_{\overset{\frown}{A'D'}}}{L_{\overset{\frown}{A'D'}}}. \tag{44}$$

Obviously, the length of the curve $\overset{\frown}{AB}$ may be approximated by that of the straight line $\overline{AB}$ (see Figure 16a), that is,

$$L_{\overset{\frown}{AB}} \cong L_{\overline{AB}} = \sqrt{\left(\Delta r + \frac{\mathrm{d}u}{\mathrm{d}r}\Delta r\right)^2 + \left(-\frac{\mathrm{d}w}{\mathrm{d}r}\Delta r\right)^2}. \tag{45}$$

Therefore, the radial line strain e_r may finally be written as

$$e_r = \frac{L_{\overset{\frown}{AB}} - L_{\overline{A'B'}}}{L_{\overline{A'B'}}} = \frac{\sqrt{\left(\Delta r + \frac{\mathrm{d}u}{\mathrm{d}r}\Delta r\right)^2 + \left(-\frac{\mathrm{d}w}{\mathrm{d}r}\Delta r\right)^2} - \Delta r}{\Delta r} = \sqrt{\left(1 + \frac{\mathrm{d}u}{\mathrm{d}r}\right)^2 + \left(-\frac{\mathrm{d}w}{\mathrm{d}r}\right)^2} - 1. \tag{46}$$

On the other hand, due to $L_{\overset{\frown}{AD}} = (r+u)\cdot\Delta\varphi$ and $L_{\overset{\frown}{A'D'}} = r\cdot\Delta\varphi$ (see Figure 16b), the circumferential line strain e_t may finally be written as

$$e_t = \frac{L_{\overset{\frown}{AD}} - L_{\overset{\frown}{A'D'}}}{L_{\overset{\frown}{A'D'}}} = \frac{(r+u)\cdot\Delta\varphi - r\cdot\Delta\varphi}{r\cdot\Delta\varphi} = \frac{u}{r}. \tag{47}$$

Equations (46) and (47) are the radial and circumferential geometric equations used in this paper, see Equations (6) and (7) in Section 2.1. However, in the derivation of the classical radial geometric equation, a very inappropriate "assumption", instead of the "approximation" in Equation (45), is used. The classical radial geometric equation is derived as follows. With the assumption of $L_{\overset{\frown}{AB}} = L_{\overline{A'B'}}$, it is found that, from Equation (43)

$$e_r = \frac{L_{\overset{\frown}{AB}} - L_{\overline{A'B'}}}{L_{\overline{A'B'}}} = \frac{(L_{\overset{\frown}{AB}} + L_{\overline{A'B'}})\bullet(L_{\overset{\frown}{AB}} - L_{\overline{A'B'}})}{(L_{\overset{\frown}{AB}} + L_{\overline{A'B'}})\bullet L_{\overline{A'B'}}} = \frac{L^2_{\overset{\frown}{AB}} - L^2_{\overline{A'B'}}}{(L_{\overset{\frown}{AB}} + L_{\overline{A'B'}})\bullet L_{\overline{A'B'}}} \approx \frac{L^2_{\overset{\frown}{AB}} - L^2_{\overline{A'B'}}}{(2L_{\overline{A'B'}})\bullet L_{\overline{A'B'}}} = \frac{L^2_{\overset{\frown}{AB}} - L^2_{\overline{A'B'}}}{2L^2_{\overline{A'B'}}}. \tag{48}$$

After considering Equation (45) and $L_{\overline{A'B'}} = \Delta r$ (see Figure 16a), the classical radial geometric equation is finally written as

$$e_r = \frac{L_{\overset{\frown}{AB}} - L_{\overline{A'B'}}}{L_{\overline{A'B'}}} \approx \frac{L^2_{\overset{\frown}{AB}} - L^2_{\overline{A'B'}}}{2L^2_{\overline{A'B'}}} = \frac{(\Delta r + \frac{du}{dr}\Delta r)^2 + (-\frac{dw}{dr}\Delta r)^2 - (\Delta r)^2}{2(\Delta r)^2} = \frac{du}{dr} + \frac{1}{2}(\frac{du}{dr})^2 + \frac{1}{2}(-\frac{dw}{dr})^2 \cong \frac{du}{dr} + \frac{1}{2}(-\frac{dw}{dr})^2. \tag{49}$$

From the above derivation, it can be concluded that the classical radial geometric equation used in [13], i.e., Equation (6) in [13], or Equation (49) in this paper, only applies to small deflection membranes, and that, no matter how small the deflections, it is essentially invalid, because the adopted assumption of $L_{\overset{\frown}{AB}} = L_{\overline{A'B'}}$ does not hold, even for very small deflections. On the other hand, however, the radial geometric equation used in this paper, i.e., Equation (6) or (46), is not affected by the size of the deflections, because it uses only the "approximation" in Equation (45). It is worth noting that the smaller Δr is, the more accurate Equation (45) is, and the length of the taken radial micro-straight-line element $\overline{A'B'}$, Δr, itself is a quantity that can be as small as expected, because the "micro" here means $\Delta r \to 0$. Therefore, in this sense, the radial geometric equation used in this paper, i.e., Equation (6) or (46), is, in fact, an exact geometric equation for the large deflection problems of thin plates or membranes, while the classical one, i.e., Equation (6) in [13] or Equation (49) in this paper, should be abandoned.

By comparing the governing equations used in Section 2.1 in this paper with those used in Section 2 in [13], it can be seen that only the radial geometric equation is different, while other governing equations, such as the circumferential geometry equation, out-of-plane and in-plane equilibrium equations, and radial and circumferential physical equations, are completely the same. Therefore, the radial geometric equation used in this paper, i.e., Equation (6) or (46), plays a crucial role in improving the performance of the obtained closed-form solutions, in comparison to the classical radial geometric equation used in [13], i.e., Equation (6) in [13], or Equation (49) in this paper. Such an improvement results in a wider range of the nearly-linear segment in the nonlinear *C-V* relationship calculated by using the deflection solution obtained in this paper, in comparison with the range calculated by using the deflection solution obtained in [13] (see Figures 12–14). Such a wider range of the nearly-linear segment can be used to develop linear rain gauges; therefore, the closed-form solutions obtained in Section 2 in this paper open up a larger research and development space for linear rain gauges, while the closed-form solutions in [13] should be abandoned.

4.2. Effect of Changes in Elasticity Modulus on Input–Output Relationships

The results of the numerical calculation, which are listed in Table 5 for E = 7.84 MPa, in Table 6 for E = 3.05 MPa, and in Table 7 for E = 1.55 MPa, are used here. The influence of changing Young's modulus of elasticity E on the relationships of the input capacitance C and output volume V is shown in Figure 17, showing that the degree of linearization of the C-V relationships can be improved by increasing the value of the Young's modulus of elasticity E; in other words, the nonlinearity of the C-V relationships becomes stronger with the decrease of Young's modulus of elasticity E. From Figure 17, it can be observed that the nearly-linear segments in the C-V relationships are about 3–5.6 pF and 18,126,666 mm^3 for E = 7.84 MPa, 3–8 pF and 15,733,468 mm^3 for E = 3.05 MPa, and 3–5.6 pF and 4,911,306 mm^3 for E = 1.55 MPa.

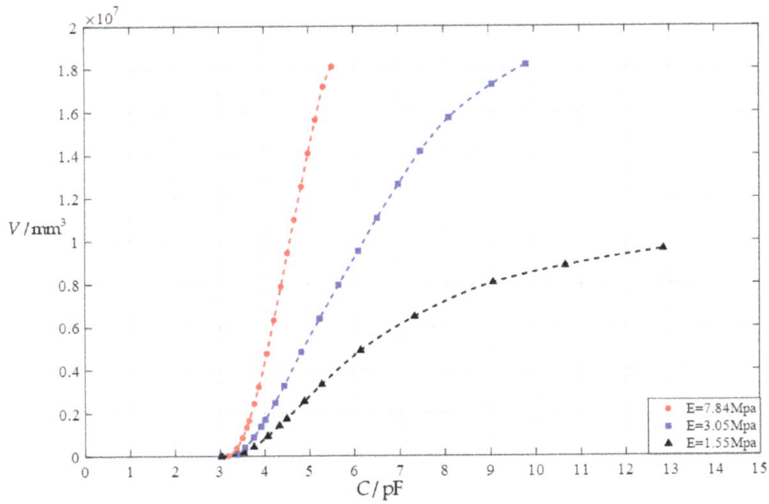

Figure 17. The relationships between the input capacitance C and output volume V, when a = 70 mm, h = 0.3 mm, ν = 0.45, t = 0.1 mm, g = 45 mm, and E = 1.55 MPa, 3.05 MPa, and 7.84 MPa, respectively.

4.3. Effect of Changes in Poisson's Ratio on Input–Output Relationships

In this section, the parameters used in Section 3.2 are still used, except for the Poisson's ratio ν; that is, a = 70 mm, thickness h = 0.3 mm, E = 3.05 MPa, t = 0.1 mm, g = 45 mm, $\varepsilon_0 = 8.854187817 \times 10^{-12}$ F/m, ε_{r1} = 1.0000585, and ε_{r2} = 2.5. Poisson's ratio ν here is 0.35 and 0.25, respectively, in order to compare with the case of using v = 0.45 in Section 3.2. The numerical results calculated by using the deflection solution in Section 2 are listed in Table 11 for v = 0.35, and in Table 12 for v = 0.25, in addition to the results of numerical calculation for v = 0.45, which are listed in Table 6. The influence of changing Poisson's ratio ν on the relationships of the input capacitance C and output volume V is shown in Figure 18, showing that the degree of linearization of the C-V relationships can be improved by increasing the value of Poisson's ratio ν. In other words, the nonlinearity of the C-V relationships becomes stronger with the decrease of Poisson's ratio ν. From Figure 18, it can be observed that the nearly-linear segments of the C-V relationships are about 3–8 pF and 15,733,468 mm^3 for v = 0.45, 3–6.7 pF and 9,547,325 mm^3 for v = 0.35, and 3–6.3 pF and 6,436,267 mm^3 for v = 0.25.

Table 11. The calculation results obtained by using the deflection solution presented in Section 2, when a = 70 mm, h = 0.3 mm, E = 3.05 MPa, ν = 0.35, t = 0.1 mm, and g = 45 mm.

V/mm^3	H/mm	c_0	d_0	σ_m/MPa	w_m/mm	C/pF
0	0	0	0	0	0	3.031
151,249	5	0.01960065	0.13970727	0.060	9.779	3.412
409,891	20	0.03584467	0.18571549	0.109	13.001	3.616
902,358	50	0.05981112	0.23675734	0.182	16.573	3.831

Table 11. *Cont.*

V/mm^3	H/mm	c_0	d_0	σ_m/MPa	w_m/mm	C/pF
1,385,079	80	0.07975804	0.27130274	0.243	18.991	4.045
1,704,436	100	0.09193828	0.29000494	0.280	20.301	4.145
2,498,392	150	0.11995604	0.32807286	0.366	22.965	4.422
3,287,069	200	0.14605552	0.35864799	0.445	25.105	4.650
4,862,035	300	0.19400944	0.40680981	0.592	28.477	5.121
6,428,063	400	0.23822218	0.44559751	0.726	31.192	5.610
7,973,715	500	0.28096429	0.47906534	0.857	33.534	6.106
9,547,325	600	0.32334823	0.50876616	0.982	35.614	6.658
11,103,956	700	0.36364397	0.53606178	1.109	37.524	7.361
12,660,576	800	0.40189638	0.56152032	1.226	39.306	8.287
14,215,831	900	0.44027831	0.58559057	1.343	40.991	9.758
15,652,977	1000	0.47591760	0.61058872	1.4515	42.741	11.896

Table 12. The calculation results obtained by using the deflection solution presented in Section 2, when a = 70 mm, h = 0.3 mm, E = 3.05 MPa, ν = 0.25, t = 0.1 mm, and g = 45 mm.

V/mm^3	H/mm	c_0	d_0	σ_m/MPa	w_m/mm	C/pF
0	0	0	0	0	0	3.031
155,370	5	0.01955022	0.14669016	0.059	10.268	3.436
415,069	20	0.03537019	0.19413305	0.107	13.589	3.694
908,752	50	0.05875659	0.24695086	0.179	17.286	3.966
1,392,544	80	0.07835133	0.28269779	0.239	19.789	4.190
1,712,554	100	0.09031799	0.30215501	0.275	21.151	4.326
2,507,038	150	0.11785215	0.34171298	0.359	23.920	4.651
3,296,568	200	0.14306985	0.37344014	0.436	26.141	4.953
4,869,168	300	0.19031987	0.42400135	0.580	29.680	5.545
6,436,267	400	0.23500158	0.46421485	0.717	32.495	6.251
8,002,575	500	0.27645352	0.50295479	0.843	35.207	7.114
9,560,993	600	0.31807374	0.53012719	0.970	37.109	8.122
11,129,019	700	0.34882488	0.57852073	1.064	40.496	9.503
12,031,455	750	0.37620298	0.58646151	1.147	41.052	10.904
12,702,326	800	0.39534789	0.60851844	1.206	42.596	13.009

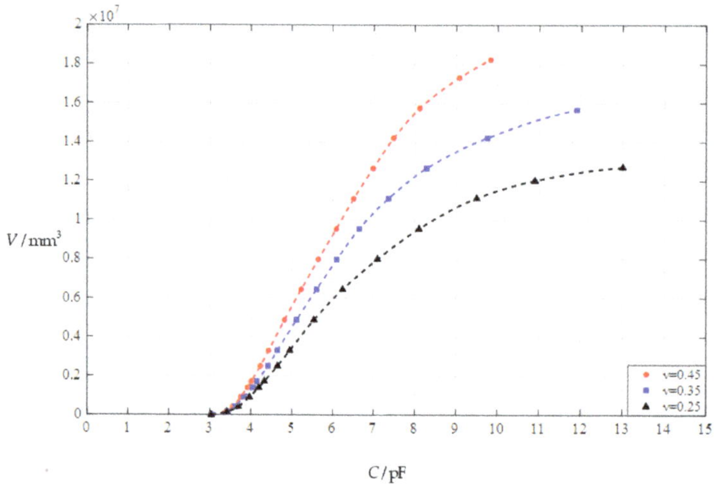

Figure 18. The relationships between the input capacitance C and output volume V, when a = 70 mm, h = 0.3 mm, E = 3.05 MPa, t = 0.1 mm, g = 45 mm, and ν = 0.45, 0.35, and 0.25, respectively.

5. Concluding Remarks

The main contribution of this paper is that by modifying the geometric equations, the differential-integral equations governing the elastic behavior of the deflected membrane were improved, new and more accurate closed-form solutions were presented, and a new and more accurate mathematical theory for designing membrane deflection-based rain gauges was provided. The newly provided mathematical theory can be used to design and numerically calibrate both nonlinear and linear membrane deflection-based rain gauges. From this study, the following conclusions were drawn.

The classical geometric equations are only applicable to small deflection problems due to the use of an inappropriate assumption, while the geometric equations used here abandoned this inappropriate assumption and fully considered the influence of deflection on geometric relationships, and thus apply to the case of arbitrary deflections.

The ranges of the nearly-linear segments in the nonlinear input–output relationships of membrane deflection-based rain gauges, obtained by using the newly presented mathematical theory, were indeed larger or wider than those obtained by using the previously presented mathematical theory. This leads to greater possibilities for developing membrane deflection-based linear rain gauges.

The nonlinear input–output relationships of membrane deflection-based rain gauges can be adjusted by changing some important design parameters, such as Young's modulus of elasticity E and Poisson's ratio v, which provides a direction for selecting an appropriate conductive circular membrane to meet the range requirements of the input capacitance C and output volume V, when designing linear or nonlinear rain gauges.

The work presented here is still in the stage of theoretical design, and the future works will focus on the dynamic problems that may arise when the conductive circular membrane is loaded by the collected rainwater, as well as the fabrication and experimental calibration of the rain gauges. In short, there may be some potential limitations or challenges that need to be addressed.

Author Contributions: Conceptualization, J.-Y.S.; methodology, N.L. and J.-Y.S.; validation, X.-T.H.; writing—original draft preparation, N.L.; writing—review and editing, N.L. and X.-T.H.; visualization, N.L.; funding acquisition, J.-Y.S. All authors have read and agreed to the published version of the manuscript.

Funding: This research was funded by the National Natural Science Foundation of China (Grant No. 11772072).

Data Availability Statement: Not applicable.

Conflicts of Interest: The authors declare no conflict of interest.

Appendix A

$$d_2 = -\frac{G(d_0+H_0)}{4c_0}$$
$$d_4 = \frac{G^2d_0-32c_0c_2d_2+4G^2d_0^2d_2+G^2H_0+8G^2d_0d_2H_0+4G^2d_2H_0^2}{64c_0^2}$$
$$d_6 = \frac{1}{1152c_0^2d_2}(3G^2d_2^2-192c_2^2d_2^2-384c_0c_4d_2^2+48G^2d_0d_2^3+8G^2d_0d_4-1536c_0c_2d_2d_4$$
$$+192G^2d_0^2d_2d_4-768c_0^2d_4^2+48G^2d_2^3H_0+8G^2d_4H_0+384G^2d_0d_2d_4H_0+192G^2d_2d_4H_0^2)$$
$$d_8 = \frac{1}{768c_0^3d_2}(-192c_2c_4d_2^2-192c_0c_6d_2^2+6G^2d_2^4+2G^2d_2d_4-384c_2^2d_2d_4-768c_0c_4d_2d_4$$
$$+112G^2d_0d_2^2d_4-768c_0c_2d_4^2+96G^2d_0^2d_4^2+3G^2d_0d_6-1152c_0c_2d_2d_6+144G^2d_0^2d_2d_6$$
$$-1152c_0^2d_4d_6+112G^2d_2^2d_4H_0+192G^2d_0d_4^2H_0+3G^2d_6H_0+288G^2d_0d_2d_6H_0+96G^2d_4^2H_0^2$$
$$+144G^2d_2d_6H_0^2)$$
$$d_{10} = \frac{1}{28800c_0^2d_2}(-2880c_4^2d_2^2-5760c_2c_6d_2^2-5760c_0c_8d_2^2-23040c_2c_4d_2d_4-23040c_0c_6d_2d_4$$
$$+960G^2d_2^3d_4+20G^2d_4^2-11520c_2^2d_4^2-23040c_0c_4d_4^2+4800G^2d_0d_2d_4^2+45G^2d_2d_6-17280c_2^2d_2d_6$$
$$-34560c_0c_4d_2d_6+4680G^2d_0d_2^2d_6-69120c_0c_2d_4d_6+8640G^2d_0^2d_4d_6-25920c_0^2d_6^2+72G^2d_0d_8$$
$$-46080c_0c_2d_2d_8+5760G^2d_0^2d_2d_8-46080c_0^2d_4d_8+4800G^2d_2d_4^2H_0+4680G^2d_2^2d_6H_0$$
$$+17280G^2d_0d_4d_6H_0+72G^2d_8H_0+11520G^2d_0d_2d_8H_0+8640G^2d_4d_6H_0^2+5760G^2d_2d_8H_0^2)$$

$$
\begin{aligned}
&d_{12} = \tfrac{1}{17280c_0^2d_2}(-2880c_4c_6d_2^2 - 2880c_2c_8d_2^2 - 2880c_0c_{10}d_2^2 - 5760c_4^2d_2d_4 - 11520c_2c_6d_2d_4 \\
&-11520c_0c_8d_2d_4 - 11520c_2c_4d_4^2 - 11520c_0c_6d_4^2 + 880G^2d_2^2d_4^2 + 960G^2d_0d_4^3 - 17280c_2c_4d_2d_6 \\
&-17280c_0c_6d_2d_6 + 630G^2d_2^3d_6 + 15G^2d_4d_6 - 17280c_2^2d_4d_6 - 34560c_0c_4d_4d_6 + 6480G^2d_0d_2d_4d_6 \\
&-25920c_0c_2d_6^2 + 3240G^2d_0^2d_6^2 + 18G^2d_2d_8 - 11520c_2^2d_2d_8 - 23040c_0c_4d_2d_8 + 3024G^2d_0d_2^2d_8 \\
&-46080c_0c_2d_4d_8 + 5760G^2d_0^2d_4d_8 - 34560c_0^2d_6d_8 + 30G^2d_0d_{10} - 28800c_0c_2d_2d_{10} \\
&+3600G^2d_0^2d_2d_{10} - 28800c_0^2d_4d_{10} + 960G^2d_4^3H_0 + 6480G^2d_2d_4d_6H_0 + 6480G^2d_0d_6^2H_0 \\
&+3024G^2d_2^2d_8H_0 + 11520G^2d_0d_4d_8H_0 + 30G^2d_{10}H_0 + 7200G^2d_0d_2d_{10}H_0 + 3240G^2d_6^2H_0^2 \\
&+5760G^2d_4d_8H_0^2 + 3600G^2d_2d_{10}H_0^2)
\end{aligned}
$$

$$
\begin{aligned}
&d_{14} = \tfrac{1}{1128960c_0^2d_2}(-80640c_6^2d_2^2 - 161280c_4c_8d_2^2 - 161280c_2c_{10}d_2^2 - 161280c_0c_{12}d_2^2 \\
&-645120c_4c_6d_2d_4 - 645120c_2c_8d_2d_4 - 645120c_0c_{10}d_2d_4 - 322560c_4^2d_4^2 - 645120c_2c_6d_4^2 \\
&-645120c_0c_8d_4^2 + 35840G^2d_2d_4^3 - 483840c_4^2d_2d_6 - 967680c_2c_6d_2d_6 - 967680c_0c_8d_2d_6 \\
&-1935360c_2c_4d_4d_6 - 1935360c_0c_6d_4d_6 + 124320G^2d_2^2d_4d_6 + 201600G^2d_0d_4^2d_6 + 315G^2d_6^2 \\
&-725760c_2^2d_6^2 - 1451520c_0c_4d_6^2 + 241920G^2d_0d_2d_6^2 - 1290240c_2c_4d_2d_8 - 1290240c_0c_6d_2d_8 \\
&+44352G^2d_2^3d_8 + 672G^2d_4d_8 - 1290240c_2^2d_4d_8 - 2580480c_0c_4d_4d_8 + 462336G^2d_0d_2d_4d_8 \\
&-3870720c_0c_2d_6d_8 + 483840G^2d_0^2d_6d_8 - 1290240c_0^2d_8^2 + 840G^2d_2d_{10} - 806400c_2^2d_2d_{10} \\
&-1612800c_0c_4d_2d_{10} + 208320G^2d_0d_2^2d_{10} - 3225600c_0c_2d_4d_{10} + 403200G^2d_0^2d_4d_{10} \\
&-2419200c_0^2d_6d_{10} + 1440G^2d_0d_{12} - 1935360c_0c_2d_2d_{12} + 241920G^2d_0^2d_2d_{12} - 1935360c_0^2d_4d_{12} \\
&+201600G^2d_4^2d_6H_0 + 241920G^2d_2d_6^2H_0 + 462336G^2d_2d_4d_8H_0 + 967680G^2d_0d_6d_8H_0 \\
&+208320G^2d_2^2d_{10}H_0 + 806400G^2d_0d_4d_{10}H_0 + 1440G^2d_{12}H_0 + 483840G^2d_0d_2d_{12}H_0 \\
&+483840G^2d_6d_8H_0^2 + 403200G^2d_4d_{10}H_0^2 + 241920G^2d_2d_{12}H_0^2)
\end{aligned}
$$

$$
\begin{aligned}
&d_{16} = \tfrac{1}{322560c_0^2d_2}(-40320c_6c_8d_2^2 - 40320c_4c_{10}d_2^2 - 40320c_2c_{12}d_2^2 - 40320c_0c_{14}d_2^2 \\
&-80640c_6^2d_2d_4 - 161280c_4c_8d_2d_4 - 161280c_2c_{10}d_2d_4 - 161280c_0c_{12}d_2d_4 - 161280c_4c_6d_4^2 \\
&-161280c_2c_8d_4^2 - 161280c_0c_{10}d_4^2 + 2240G^2d_4^4 - 241920c_4c_6d_2d_6 - 241920c_2c_8d_2d_6 \\
&-241920c_0c_{10}d_2d_6 - 241920c_4^2d_4d_6 - 483840c_2c_6d_4d_6 - 483840c_0c_8d_4d_6 + 31920G^2d_2d_4^2d_6 \\
&-362880c_2c_4d_6^2 - 362880c_0c_6d_6^2 + 19215G^2d_2^2d_6^2 + 60480G^2d_0d_4d_6^2 - 161280c_4^2d_2d_8 \\
&-322560c_2c_6d_2d_8 - 322560c_0c_8d_2d_8 - 645120c_2c_4d_4d_8 - 645120c_0c_6d_4d_8 + 38304G^2d_2^2d_4d_8 \\
&+61824G^2d_0d_4^2d_8 + 126G^2d_6d_8 - 483840c_2^2d_6d_8 - 967680c_0c_4d_6d_8 + 153216G^2d_0d_2d_6d_8 \\
&-645120c_0c_2d_8^2 + 80640G^2d_0^2d_8^2 - 403200c_2c_4d_2d_{10} - 403200c_0c_6d_2d_{10} + 13440G^2d_2^3d_{10} \\
&+140G^2d_4d_{10} - 403200c_2^2d_4d_{10} - 806400c_0c_4d_4d_{10} + 141120G^2d_0d_2d_4d_{10} - 1209600c_0c_2d_6d_{10} \\
&+151200G^2d_0^2d_6d_{10} - 806400c_0^2d_8d_{10} + 180G^2d_2d_{12} - 241920c_2^2d_2d_{12} - 483840c_0c_4d_2d_{12} \\
&+61920G^2d_0d_2^2d_{12} - 967680c_0c_2d_4d_{12} + 120960G^2d_0^2d_4d_{12} - 725760c_0^2d_6d_{12} + 315G^2d_0d_{14} \\
&-564480c_0c_2d_2d_{14} + 70560G^2d_0^2d_2d_{14} - 564480c_0^2d_4d_{14} + 60480G^2d_4d_6^2H_0 + 61824G^2d_4^2d_8H_0 \\
&+153216G^2d_2d_6d_8H_0 + 161280G^2d_0d_8^2H_0 + 141120G^2d_2d_4d_{10}H_0 + 302400G^2d_0d_6d_{10}H_0 \\
&+61920G^2d_2^2d_{12}H_0 + 241920G^2d_0d_4d_{12}H_0 + 315G^2d_{14}H_0 + 141120G^2d_0d_2d_{14}H_0 + 80640G^2d_8^2H_0^2 \\
&+151200G^2d_6d_{10}H_0^2 + 120960G^2d_4d_{12}H_0^2 + 70560G^2d_2d_{14}H_0^2)
\end{aligned}
$$

$$
\begin{aligned}
&d_{18} = \tfrac{1}{3628800c_0^2d_2}(-201600c_8^2d_2^2 - 403200c_6c_{10}d_2^2 - 403200c_4c_{12}d_2^2 - 403200c_2c_{14}d_2^2 \\
&-403200c_0c_{16}d_2^2 - 1612800c_6c_8d_2d_4 - 1612800c_4c_{10}d_2d_4 - 1612800c_2c_{12}d_2d_4 \\
&-806400c_6^2d_4^2 - 1612800c_4c_8d_4^2 - 1612800c_2c_{10}d_4^2 - 1612800c_0c_{12}d_4^2 - 1209600c_6^2d_2d_6 \\
&-2419200c_4c_8d_2d_6 - 2419200c_2c_{10}d_2d_6 - 2419200c_0c_{12}d_2d_6 - 4838400c_4c_6d_4d_6 \\
&-4838400c_0c_{10}d_4d_6 + 100800G^2d_4^3d_6 - 1814400c_4^2d_6^2 - 3628800c_2c_6d_6^2 - 3628800c_0c_8d_6^2 \\
&+365400G^2d_2d_4d_6^2 + 226800G^2d_0d_6^3 - 3225600c_4c_6d_2d_8 - 3225600c_2c_8d_2d_8 \\
&-3225600c_4^2d_4d_8 - 6451200c_2c_6d_4d_8 - 6451200c_0c_8d_4d_8 + 380800G^2d_2d_4^2d_8 \\
&-9676800c_0c_6d_6d_8 + 468720G^2d_2^2d_6d_8 + 1451520G^2d_0d_4d_6d_8 + 504G^2d_8^2 - 3225600c_2^2d_8^2 \\
&-6451200c_0c_4d_8^2 + 967680G^2d_0d_2d_8^2 - 2016000c_4^2d_2d_{10} - 4032000c_2c_6d_2d_{10} \\
&-8064000c_2c_4d_4d_{10} - 8064000c_0c_6d_4d_{10} + 459200G^2d_2^2d_4d_{10} + 739200G^2d_0d_4^2d_{10} \\
&-6048000c_2^2d_6d_{10} - 12096000c_0c_4d_6d_{10} + 1864800G^2d_0d_2d_6d_{10} - 16128000c_0c_2d_8d_{10} \\
&+2016000G^2d_0^2d_8d_{10} - 5040000c_0^2d_{10}^2 - 4838400c_2c_4d_2d_{12} - 4838400c_0c_6d_2d_{12} \\
&+158400G^2d_2^3d_{12} + 1200G^2d_4d_{12} - 4838400c_2^2d_4d_{12} - 9676800c_0c_4d_4d_{12} \\
&-14515200c_0c_2d_6d_{12} + 1814400G^2d_0^2d_6d_{12} - 9676800c_0^2d_8d_{12} + 1575G^2d_2d_{14} \\
&-5644800c_0c_4d_2d_{14} + 718200G^2d_0d_2^2d_{14} - 11289600c_0c_2d_4d_{14} + 1411200G^2d_0^2d_4d_{14} \\
&+2800G^2d_0d_{16} - 6451200c_0c_2d_2d_{16} + 806400G^2d_0^2d_2d_{16} - 6451200c_0^2d_4d_{16} \\
&+1451520G^2d_4d_6d_8H_0 + 967680G^2d_2d_8^2H_0 + 739200G^2d_4^2d_{10}H_0 + 1864800G^2d_2d_6d_{10}H_0 \\
&+4032000G^2d_0d_8d_{10}H_0 + 1670400G^2d_2d_4d_{12}H_0 + 3628800G^2d_0d_6d_{12}H_0+ \\
&718200G^2d_2^2d_{14}H_0 + 2822400G^2d_0d_4d_{14}H_0 + 2800G^2d_{16}H_0 + 1612800G^2d_0d_2d_{16}H_0 \\
&-1612800c_0c_{14}d_2d_4 - 4838400c_2c_8d_4d_6 - 3225600c_0c_{10}d_2d_8 - 9676800c_2c_4d_6d_8
\end{aligned}
$$

$$-4032000c_0c_8d_2d_{10}+1050G^2d_6d_{10}+1670400G^2d_0d_2d_4d_{12}-2822400c_2^2d_2d_{14}$$
$$-8467200c_0^2d_6d_{14}+2016000G^2d_8d_{10}H_0^2+1814400G^2d_6d_{12}H_0^2+1411200G^2d_4d_{14}H_0^2$$
$$+226800G^2d_6^3H_0+806400G^2d_2d_{16}H_0^2)$$
$$d_{20}=\frac{1}{2016000c_0^2d_2}(-201600c_8c_{10}d_2^2-201600c_6c_{12}d_2^2-201600c_4c_{14}d_2^2-201600c_2c_{16}d_2^2$$
$$-201600c_0c_{18}d_2^2-403200c_8^2d_2d_4-806400c_6c_{10}d_2d_4-806400c_4c_{12}d_2d_4-806400c_2c_{14}d_2d_4$$
$$-806400c_0c_{16}d_2d_4-806400c_6c_8d_4^2-806400c_4c_{10}d_4^2-806400c_2c_{12}d_4^2-806400c_0c_{14}d_4^2$$
$$-1209600c_6c_8d_2d_6-1209600c_4c_{10}d_2d_6-1209600c_2c_{12}d_2d_6-1209600c_0c_{14}d_2d_6$$
$$-2419200c_4c_8d_4d_6-2419200c_2c_{10}d_4d_6-2419200c_0c_{12}d_4d_6-1814400c_4c_6d_6^2$$
$$-1814400c_0c_{10}d_6^2+81900G^2d_4^2d_6^2+66150G^2d_2d_6^3-806400c_6^2d_2d_8-1612800c_4c_8d_2d_8$$
$$-1612800c_2c_{10}d_2d_8-1612800c_0c_{12}d_2d_8-3225600c_4c_6d_4d_8-3225600c_2c_8d_4d_8$$
$$+58240G^2d_4^3d_8-2419200c_4^2d_6d_8-4838400c_2c_6d_6d_8-4838400c_0c_8d_6d_8$$
$$+393120G^2d_0d_6^2d_8-3225600c_2c_4d_8^2-3225600c_0c_6d_8^2+142128G^2d_2^2d_8^2$$
$$-2016000c_4c_6d_2d_{10}-2016000c_2c_8d_2d_{10}-2016000c_0c_{10}d_2d_{10}-2016000c_4^2d_4d_{10}$$
$$-4032000c_2c_6d_4d_{10}-4032000c_0c_8d_4d_{10}+224000G^2d_2d_4^2d_{10}-6048000c_2c_4d_6d_{10}$$
$$-6048000c_0c_6d_6d_{10}+279300G^2d_2^2d_6d_{10}+856800G^2d_0d_4d_6d_{10}+420G^2d_8d_{10}$$
$$-4032000c_2^2d_8d_{10}-8064000c_0c_4d_8d_{10}+1176000G^2d_0d_2d_8d_{10}-5040000c_0c_2d_{10}^2$$
$$+630000G^2d_0^2d_{10}^2-1209600c_4^2d_2d_{12}-2419200c_2c_6d_2d_{12}-2419200c_0c_8d_2d_{12}$$
$$-4838400c_2c_4d_4d_{12}-4838400c_0c_6d_4d_{12}+268800G^2d_2^2d_4d_{12}+432000G^2d_0d_4^2d_{12}$$
$$+450G^2d_6d_{12}-3628800c_2^2d_6d_{12}-7257600c_0c_4d_6d_{12}+1101600G^2d_0d_2d_6d_{12}$$
$$+1209600G^2d_0^2d_8d_{12}-6048000c_0^2d_{10}d_{12}-2822400c_2c_4d_2d_{14}-2822400c_0c_6d_2d_{14}$$
$$+91350G^2d_2^3d_{14}+525G^2d_4d_{14}-2822400c_2^2d_4d_{14}-5644800c_0c_4d_4d_{14}+966000G^2d_0d_2d_4d_{14}$$
$$-8467200c_0c_2d_6d_{14}+1058400G^2d_0^2d_6d_{14}-5644800c_0^2d_8d_{14}+700G^2d_2d_{16}-1612800c_2^2d_2d_{16}$$
$$-3225600c_0c_4d_2d_{16}+408800G^2d_0d_2^2d_{16}-6451200c_0c_2d_4d_{16}+806400G^2d_0^2d_4d_{16}$$
$$-4838400c_0^2d_6d_{16}+1260G^2d_0d_{18}-3628800c_0c_2d_2d_{18}+453600G^2d_0^2d_2d_{18}-3628800c_0^2d_4d_{18}$$
$$+393120G^2d_6^2d_8H_0+430080G^2d_4d_8^2H_0+856800G^2d_4d_6d_{10}H_0+1176000G^2d_2d_8d_{10}H_0$$
$$+1260000G^2d_0d_{10}^2H_0+432000G^2d_4^2d_{12}H_0+1101600G^2d_2d_6d_{12}H_0+2419200G^2d_0d_8d_{12}H_0$$
$$+966000G^2d_2d_4d_{14}H_0+2116800G^2d_0d_6d_{14}H_0+408800G^2d_2^2d_{16}H_0+1612800G^2d_0d_4d_{16}H_0$$
$$+1260G^2d_{18}H_0+907200G^2d_0d_2d_{18}H_0+630000G^2d_{10}^2H_0^2+1209600G^2d_8d_{12}H_0^2$$
$$-1209600c_6^2d_4d_6-1814400c_2c_8d_6^2-3225600c_0c_{10}d_4d_8+426720G^2d_2d_4d_6d_8$$
$$+430080G^2d_0d_4d_8^2-9676800c_0c_2d_8d_{12}+1058400G^2d_6d_{14}H_0^2+806400G^2d_4d_{16}H_0^2$$
$$+453600G^2d_2d_{18}H_0^2)$$

Appendix B

$$c_2=\frac{G^2(H_0+d_0)^2}{64{c_0}^2(vc_0-c_0-1)}$$
$$c_4=\frac{4G^2{H_0}^2{d_2}^2+8G^2H_0d_0{d_2}^2+4G^2{d_0}^2{d_2}^2-192v{c_0}^2{c_2}^2+G^2H_0d_2+G^2d_0d_2+320{c_0}^2{c_2}^2-32c_0c_2{d_2}^2}{192{c_0}^2(vc_0-c_0-1)}$$
$$c_6=\frac{1}{4608{c_0}^2(vc_0-c_0-1)}(192G^2{H_0}^2d_2d_4+384G^2H_0d_0d_2d_4+48G^2H_0{d_2}^3+192G^2{d_0}^2d_2d_4$$
$$+48G^2d_0{d_2}^3-10752v{c_0}^2c_2c_4+8G^2H_0d_4+8G^2d_0d_4+3G^2{d_2}^2+21504{c_0}^2c_2c_4-1536c_0c_2d_2d_4$$
$$-384c_0c_4{d_2}^2-192{c_2}^2{d_2}^2)$$
$$c_8=\frac{1}{3840{c_0}^2(vc_0-c_0-1)}(144G^2{H_0}^2d_2d_6+96G^2{H_0}^2{d_4}^2+288G^2H_0d_0d_2d_6+192G^2H_0d_0{d_4}^2$$
$$+112G^2H_0{d_2}^2d_4+144G^2{d_0}^2d_2d_6+96G^2{d_0}^2{d_4}^2+112G^2d_0{d_2}^2d_4+6G^2{d_2}^4-9600v{c_0}^2c_2c_6$$
$$-5760v{c_0}^2{c_4}^2+3G^2H_0d_6+3G^2d_0d_6+2G^2d_2d_4+21120{c_0}^2c_2c_6+14976{c_0}^2{c_4}^2-1152c_0c_2d_2d_6$$
$$-768c_0c_2{d_4}^2-768c_0c_4d_2d_4-192c_0c_6{d_2}^2-384{c_2}^2d_2d_4-192c_2c_4{d_2}^2)$$
$$c_{10}=\frac{1}{172800{c_0}^2(vc_0-c_0-1)}(5760G^2{H_0}^2d_2d_8+8640G^2{H_0}^2d_4d_6+11520G^2H_0d_0d_2d_8$$
$$+17280G^2H_0d_0d_4d_6+4680G^2H_0{d_2}^2d_6+4800G^2H_0d_2{d_4}^2+5760G^2{d_0}^2d_2d_8+8640G^2{d_0}^2d_4d_6$$
$$+4680G^2d_0{d_2}^2d_6+4800G^2d_0d_2{d_4}^2+960G^2{d_2}^3d_4-449280v{c_0}^2c_2c_8-587520v{c_0}^2c_4c_6$$
$$+72G^2H_0d_8+72G^2d_0d_8+45G^2d_2d_6+20G^2{d_4}^2+1048320{c_0}^2c_2c_8+1762560{c_0}^2c_4c_6$$
$$-46080c_0c_2d_2d_8-69120c_0c_2d_4d_6-34560c_0c_4d_2d_6-23040c_0c_4{d_4}^2-23040c_0c_6d_2d_4$$
$$-5760c_0c_8{d_2}^2-17280{c_2}^2d_2d_6-11520{c_2}^2{d_4}^2-23040c_2c_4d_2d_4-5760c_2c_6{d_2}^2-2880{c_4}^2{d_2}^2)$$
$$c_{12}=\frac{1}{120960{c_0}^2(vc_0-c_0-1)}(3600G^2{H_0}^2d_2d_{10}+5760G^2{H_0}^2d_4d_8+3240G^2{H_0}^2{d_6}^2+7200G^2H_0d_0d_2d_{10}$$
$$+11520G^2H_0d_0d_4d_8+6480G^2H_0d_0{d_6}^2+3024G^2H_0{d_2}^2d_8+6480G^2H_0d_2d_4d_6+960G^2H_0{d_4}^3$$
$$+3600G^2{d_0}^2d_2d_{10}+5760G^2{d_0}^2d_4d_8+3240G^2{d_0}^2{d_6}^2+3024G^2d_0{d_2}^2d_8+6480G^2d_0d_2d_4d_6+960G^2d_0{d_4}^3$$
$$+630G^2{d_2}^3d_6+880G^2{d_2}^2{d_4}^2-322560v{c_0}^2c_2c_{10}-443520v{c_0}^2c_4c_8-241920v{c_0}^2{c_6}^2+30G^2H_0d_{10}$$
$$+30G^2d_0d_{10}+18G^2d_2d_8+15G^2d_4d_6+783360{c_0}^2c_2c_{10}+1457280{c_0}^2c_4c_8+864000{c_0}^2{c_6}^2$$
$$-28800c_0c_2d_2d_{10}-46080c_0c_2d_4d_8-25920c_0c_2{d_6}^2-23040c_0c_4d_2d_8-34560c_0c_4d_4d_6-17280c_0c_6d_2d_6$$
$$-11520c_0c_6{d_4}^2-11520c_0c_8d_2d_4-2880c_0c_{10}{d_2}^2-11520{c_2}^2d_2d_8-17280{c_2}^2d_4d_6-17280c_2c_4d_2d_6$$
$$-11520c_2c_4{d_4}^2-11520c_2c_6d_2d_4-2880c_2c_8{d_2}^2-5760{c_4}^2d_2d_4-2880c_4c_6{d_2}^2)$$

$$c_{14} = \frac{1}{9031680c_0{}^2(vc_0-c_0-1)}(241920G^2H_0{}^2d_2d_{12} + 403200G^2H_0{}^2d_4d_{10} + 483840G^2H_0{}^2d_6d_8$$
$$+483840G^2H_0d_0d_2d_{12} + 806400G^2H_0d_0d_4d_{10} + 967680G^2H_0d_0d_6d_8 + 208320G^2H_0d_2{}^2d_{10}$$
$$+462336G^2H_0d_2d_4d_8 + 241920G^2H_0d_2d_6{}^2 + 201600G^2H_0d_4{}^2d_6 + 241920G^2d_0{}^2d_2d_{12}$$
$$+403200G^2d_0{}^2d_4d_{10} + 483840G^2d_0{}^2d_6d_8 + 208320G^2d_0d_2{}^2d_{10} + 462336G^2d_0d_2d_4d_8$$
$$+241920G^2d_0d_2d_6{}^2 + 201600G^2d_0d_4{}^2d_6 + 44352G^2d_2{}^3d_8 + 124320G^2d_2{}^2d_4d_6$$
$$+35840G^2d_2d_4{}^3 - 24514560vc_0{}^2c_2c_{12} - 34836480vc_0{}^2c_4c_{10} - 39997440vc_0{}^2c_6c_8 + 1440G^2H_0d_{12}$$
$$+1440G^2d_0d_{12} + 840G^2d_2d_{10} + 672G^2d_4d_8 + 315G^2d_6{}^2 + 61286400c_0{}^2c_2c_{12} + 121927680c_0{}^2c_4c_{10}$$
$$+159989760c_0{}^2c_6c_8 - 1935360c_0c_2d_2d_{12} - 3225600c_0c_2d_4d_{10} - 3870720c_0c_2d_6d_8$$
$$-1612800c_0c_4d_2d_{10} - 2580480c_0c_4d_4d_8 - 1451520c_0c_4d_6{}^2 - 1290240c_0c_6d_2d_8 - 1935360c_0c_6d_4d_6$$
$$-967680c_0c_8d_2d_6 - 645120c_0c_8d_4{}^2 - 645120c_0c_{10}d_2d_4 - 161280c_0c_{12}d_2{}^2 - 806400c_2{}^2d_2d_{10}$$
$$-1290240c_2{}^2d_4d_8 - 725760c_2{}^2d_6{}^2 - 1290240c_2c_4d_2d_8 - 1935360c_2c_4d_4d_6 - 967680c_2c_6d_2d_6$$
$$-645120c_2c_6d_4{}^2 - 645120c_2c_8d_2d_4 - 161280c_2c_{10}d_2{}^2 - 483840c_4{}^2d_2d_6 - 322560c_4{}^2d_4{}^2$$
$$-645120c_4c_6d_2d_4 - 161280c_4c_8d_2{}^2 - 80640c_6{}^2d_2{}^2)$$

$$c_{16} = \frac{1}{2903040c_0{}^2(vc_0-c_0-1)}(70560G^2H_0{}^2d_2d_{14} + 120960G^2H_0{}^2d_4d_{12} + 151200G^2H_0{}^2d_6d_{10}$$
$$+80640G^2H_0{}^2d_8{}^2 + 141120G^2H_0d_0d_2d_{14} + 241920G^2H_0d_0d_4d_{12} + 302400G^2H_0d_0d_6d_{10}$$
$$+161280G^2H_0d_0d_8{}^2 + 61920G^2H_0d_2{}^2d_{12} + 141120G^2H_0d_2d_4d_{10} + 153216G^2H_0d_2d_6d_8$$
$$+61824G^2H_0d_4{}^2d_8 + 60480G^2H_0d_4d_6{}^2 + 70560G^2d_0{}^2d_2d_{14} + 120960G^2d_0{}^2d_4d_{12} + 151200G^2d_0{}^2d_6d_{10}$$
$$+80640G^2d_0{}^2d_8{}^2 + 61920G^2d_0d_2{}^2d_{12} + 141120G^2d_0d_2d_4d_{10} + 153216G^2d_0d_2d_6d_8 + 61824G^2d_0d_4{}^2d_8$$
$$+60480G^2d_0d_4d_6{}^2 + 13440G^2d_2{}^3d_{10} + 38304G^2d_2{}^2d_4d_8 + 19215G^2d_2{}^2d_6{}^2 + 31920G^2d_2d_4{}^2d_6$$
$$+2240G^2d_4{}^4 - 7983360vc_0{}^2c_2c_{14} - 11612160vc_0{}^2c_4c_{12} - 13789440vc_0{}^2c_6c_{10} - 7257600vc_0{}^2c_8{}^2$$
$$+315G^2H_0d_{14} + 315G^2d_0d_{14} + 180G^2d_2d_{12} + 140G^2d_4d_{10} + 126G^2d_6d_8 + 20401920c_0{}^2c_2c_{14}$$
$$+42577920c_0{}^2c_4c_{12} + 59754240c_0{}^2c_6c_{10} + 33062400c_0{}^2c_8{}^2 - 564480c_0c_2d_2d_{14} - 967680c_0c_2d_4d_{12}$$
$$-1209600c_0c_2d_6d_{10} - 645120c_0c_2d_8{}^2 - 483840c_0c_4d_2d_{12} - 806400c_0c_4d_4d_{10} - 967680c_0c_4d_6d_8$$
$$-403200c_0c_6d_2d_{10} - 645120c_0c_6d_4d_8 - 362880c_0c_6d_6{}^2 - 322560c_0c_8d_2d_8 - 483840c_0c_8d_4d_6$$
$$-241920c_0c_{10}d_2d_6 - 161280c_0c_{10}d_4{}^2 - 161280c_0c_{12}d_2d_4 - 40320c_0c_{14}d_2{}^2 - 241920c_2{}^2d_2d_{12}$$
$$-403200c_2{}^2d_4d_{10} - 483840c_2{}^2d_6d_8 - 403200c_2c_4d_2d_{10} - 645120c_2c_4d_4d_8 - 362880c_2c_4d_6{}^2$$
$$-322560c_2c_6d_2d_8 - 483840c_2c_6d_4d_6 - 241920c_2c_8d_2d_6 - 161280c_2c_8d_4{}^2 - 161280c_2c_{10}d_2d_4$$
$$-40320c_2c_{12}d_2{}^2 - 161280c_4{}^2d_2d_8 - 241920c_4{}^2d_4d_6 - 241920c_4c_6d_2d_6 - 161280c_4c_6d_4{}^2 - 161280c_4c_8d_2d_4$$
$$-40320c_4c_{10}d_2{}^2 - 80640c_6{}^2d_2d_4 - 40320c_6c_8d_2{}^2)$$

$$c_{18} = \frac{1}{36288000c_0{}^2(vc_0-c_0-1)}(806400G^2H_0{}^2d_2d_{16} + 1411200G^2H_0{}^2d_4d_{14} + 1814400G^2H_0{}^2d_6d_{12}$$
$$+2016000G^2H_0{}^2d_8d_{10} + 1612800G^2H_0d_0d_2d_{16} + 2822400G^2H_0d_0d_4d_{14} + 3628800G^2H_0d_0d_6d_{12}$$
$$+4032000G^2H_0d_0d_8d_{10} + 718200G^2H_0d_2{}^2d_{14} + 1670400G^2H_0d_2d_4d_{12} + 1864800G^2H_0d_2d_6d_{10}$$
$$+967680G^2H_0d_2d_8{}^2 + 739200G^2H_0d_4{}^2d_{10} + 1451520G^2H_0d_4d_6d_8 + 226800G^2H_0d_6{}^3$$
$$+806400G^2d_0{}^2d_2d_{16} + 1411200G^2d_0{}^2d_4d_{14} + 1814400G^2d_0{}^2d_6d_{12} + 2016000G^2d_0{}^2d_8d_{10}$$
$$+718200G^2d_0d_2{}^2d_{14} + 1670400G^2d_0d_2d_4d_{12} + 1864800G^2d_0d_2d_6d_{10} + 967680G^2d_0d_2d_8{}^2$$
$$+739200G^2d_0d_4{}^2d_{10} + 1451520G^2d_0d_4d_6d_8 + 226800G^2d_0d_6{}^3 + 158400G^2d_2{}^3d_{12} + 459200G^2d_2{}^2d_4d_{10}$$
$$+468720G^2d_2{}^2d_6d_8 + 380800G^2d_2d_4{}^2d_8 + 365400G^2d_2d_4d_6{}^2 + 100800G^2d_4{}^3d_6 - 100800000vc_0{}^2c_2c_{16}$$
$$-149184000vc_0{}^2c_4c_{14} - 181440000vc_0{}^2c_6c_{12} - 197568000vc_0{}^2c_8c_{10} + 2800G^2H_0d_{16} + 2800G^2d_0d_{16}$$
$$+1575G^2d_2d_{14} + 1200G^2d_4d_{12} + 1050G^2d_6d_{10} + 504G^2d_8{}^2 + 262080000c_0{}^2c_2c_{16} + 566899200c_0{}^2c_4c_{14}$$
$$+834624000c_0{}^2c_6c_{12} + 987840000c_0{}^2c_8c_{10} - 6451200c_0c_2d_2d_{16} - 11289600c_0c_2d_4d_{14}$$
$$-14515200c_0c_2d_6d_{12} - 16128000c_0c_2d_8d_{10} - 5644800c_0c_4d_2d_{14} - 9676800c_0c_4d_4d_{12}$$
$$-12096000c_0c_4d_6d_{10} - 6451200c_0c_4d_8{}^2 - 4838400c_0c_6d_2d_{12} - 8064000c_0c_6d_4d_{10} - 9676800c_0c_6d_6d_8$$
$$-4032000c_0c_8d_2d_{10} - 6451200c_0c_8d_4d_8 - 3628800c_0c_8d_6{}^2 - 3225600c_0c_{10}d_2d_8 - 4838400c_0c_{10}d_4d_6$$
$$-2419200c_0c_{12}d_2d_6 - 1612800c_0c_{12}d_4{}^2 - 1612800c_0c_{14}d_2d_4 - 403200c_0c_{16}d_2{}^2 - 2822400c_2{}^2d_2d_{14}$$
$$-4838400c_2{}^2d_4d_{12} - 6048000c_2{}^2d_6d_{10} - 3225600c_2{}^2d_8{}^2 - 4838400c_2c_4d_2d_{12} - 8064000c_2c_4d_4d_{10}$$
$$-9676800c_2c_4d_6d_8 - 4032000c_2c_6d_2d_{10} - 6451200c_2c_6d_4d_8 - 3628800c_2c_6d_6{}^2 - 3225600c_2c_8d_2d_8$$
$$-4838400c_2c_8d_4d_6 - 2419200c_2c_{10}d_2d_6 - 1612800c_2c_{10}d_4{}^2 - 1612800c_2c_{12}d_2d_4 - 403200c_2c_{14}d_2{}^2$$
$$-2016000c_4{}^2d_2d_{10} - 3225600c_4{}^2d_4d_8 - 1814400c_4{}^2d_6{}^2 - 3225600c_4c_6d_2d_8 - 4838400c_4c_6d_4d_6$$
$$-2419200c_4c_8d_2d_6 - 1612800c_4c_8d_4{}^2 - 1612800c_4c_{10}d_2d_4 - 403200c_4c_{12}d_2{}^2 - 1209600c_6{}^2d_2d_6$$
$$-806400c_6{}^2d_4{}^2 - 1612800c_6c_8d_2d_4 - 403200c_6c_{10}d_2{}^2 - 201600c_8{}^2d_2{}^2)$$

$$c_{20} = \frac{1}{22176000c_0{}^2(vc_0-c_0-1)}(453600G^2H_0{}^2d_2d_{18} + 806400G^2H_0{}^2d_4d_{16} + 1058400G^2H_0{}^2d_6d_{14}$$
$$+1209600G^2H_0{}^2d_8d_{12} + 630000G^2H_0{}^2d_{10}{}^2 + 907200G^2H_0d_0d_2d_{18} + 1612800G^2H_0d_0d_4d_{16}$$
$$+2116800G^2H_0d_0d_6d_{14} + 2419200G^2H_0d_0d_8d_{12} + 1260000G^2H_0d_0d_{10}{}^2 + 408800G^2H_0d_2{}^2d_{16}$$
$$+966000G^2H_0d_2d_4d_{14} + 1101600G^2H_0d_2d_6d_{12} + 1176000G^2H_0d_2d_8d_{10} + 432000G^2H_0d_4{}^2d_{12}$$
$$+856800G^2H_0d_4d_6d_{10} + 430080G^2H_0d_4d_8{}^2 + 393120G^2H_0d_6{}^2d_8 + 453600G^2d_0{}^2d_2d_{18}$$
$$+806400G^2d_0{}^2d_4d_{16} + 1058400G^2d_0{}^2d_6d_{14} + 1209600G^2d_0{}^2d_8d_{12} + 630000G^2d_0{}^2d_{10}{}^2$$
$$+408800G^2d_0d_2{}^2d_{16} + 966000G^2d_0d_2d_4d_{14} + 1101600G^2d_0d_2d_6d_{12} + 1176000G^2d_0d_2d_8d_{10}$$
$$+432000G^2d_0d_4{}^2d_{12} + 856800G^2d_0d_4d_6d_{10} + 430080G^2d_0d_4d_8{}^2 + 393120G^2d_0d_6{}^2d_8 + 91350G^2d_2{}^3d_{14}$$
$$+268800G^2d_2{}^2d_4d_{12} + 279300G^2d_2{}^2d_6d_{10} + 142128G^2d_2{}^2d_8{}^2 + 224000G^2d_2d_4{}^2d_{10} + 426720G^2d_2d_4d_6d_8$$
$$+66150G^2d_2d_6{}^3 + 58240G^2d_4{}^3d_8 + 81900G^2d_4{}^2d_6{}^2 - 62092800vc_0{}^2c_2c_{18} - 93139200vc_0{}^2c_4c_{16}$$
$$-115315200vc_0{}^2c_6c_{14} - 128620800vc_0{}^2c_8c_{12} - 66528000vc_0{}^2c_{10}{}^2 + 1260G^2H_0d_{18} + 1260G^2d_0d_{18}$$
$$+700G^2d_2d_{16} + 525G^2d_4d_{14} + 450G^2d_6d_{12} + 420G^2d_8d_{10} + 163699200c_0{}^2c_2c_{18} + 364089600c_0{}^2c_4c_{16}$$
$$+555609600c_0{}^2c_6c_{14} + 689875200c_0{}^2c_8c_{12} + 368928000c_0{}^2c_{10}{}^2 - 3628800c_0c_2d_2d_{18} - 6451200c_0c_2d_4d_{16}$$
$$-8467200c_0c_2d_6d_{14} - 9676800c_0c_2d_8d_{12} - 5040000c_0c_2d_{10}{}^2 - 3225600c_0c_4d_2d_{16} - 5644800c_0c_4d_4d_{14}$$
$$-7257600c_0c_4d_6d_{12} - 8064000c_0c_4d_8d_{10} - 2822400c_0c_6d_2d_{14} - 4838400c_0c_6d_4d_{12} - 6048000c_0c_6d_6d_{10}$$
$$-3225600c_0c_6d_8{}^2 - 2419200c_0c_8d_2d_{12} - 4032000c_0c_8d_4d_{10} - 4838400c_0c_8d_6d_8 - 2016000c_0c_{10}d_2d_{10}$$

$$
\begin{aligned}
&-3225600c_0c_{10}d_4d_8 - 1814400c_0c_{10}{d_6}^2 - 1612800c_0c_{12}d_2d_8 - 2419200c_0c_{12}d_4d_6 - 1209600c_0c_{14}d_2d_6 \\
&-806400c_0c_{14}{d_4}^2 - 806400c_0c_{16}d_2d_4 - 201600c_0c_{18}{d_2}^2 - 1612800{c_2}^2d_2d_{16} - 2822400{c_2}^2d_4d_{14} \\
&-3628800{c_2}^2d_6d_{12} - 4032000{c_2}^2d_8d_{10} - 2822400c_2c_4d_2d_{14} - 4838400c_2c_4d_4d_{12} - 6048000c_2c_4d_6d_{10} \\
&-3225600c_2c_4{d_8}^2 - 2419200c_2c_6d_2d_{12} - 4032000c_2c_6d_4d_{10} - 4838400c_2c_6d_6d_8 - 2016000c_2c_8d_2d_{10} \\
&-3225600c_2c_8d_4d_8 - 1814400c_2c_8{d_6}^2 - 1612800c_2c_{10}d_2d_8 - 2419200c_2c_{10}d_4d_6 - 1209600c_2c_{12}d_2d_6 \\
&-806400c_2c_{12}{d_4}^2 - 806400c_2c_{14}d_2d_4 - 201600c_2c_{16}{d_2}^2 - 1209600{c_4}^2d_2d_{12} - 2016000{c_4}^2d_4d_{10} \\
&-2419200{c_4}^2d_6d_8 - 2016000c_4c_6d_2d_{10} - 3225600c_4c_6d_4d_8 - 1814400c_4c_6{d_6}^2 - 1612800c_4c_8d_2d_8 \\
&-2419200c_4c_8d_4d_6 - 1209600c_4c_{10}d_2d_6 - 806400c_4c_{10}{d_4}^2 - 806400c_4c_{12}d_2d_4 - 201600c_4c_{14}{d_2}^2 \\
&-806400{c_6}^2d_2d_8 - 1209600{c_6}^2d_4d_6 - 1209600c_6c_8d_2d_6 - 806400c_6c_8{d_4}^2 - 806400c_6c_{10}d_2d_4 \\
&-201600c_6c_{12}{d_2}^2 - 403200{c_8}^2d_2d_4 - 201600c_8c_{10}{d_2}^2)
\end{aligned}
$$

References

1. Zhang, C.H.; Fan, L.J.; Tan, Y.F. Sequential limit analysis for clamped circular membranes involving large deformation subjected to pressure load. *Int. J. Mech. Sci.* **2019**, *155*, 440–449. [CrossRef]
2. Li, X.; Sun, J.-Y.; Lu, X.-C.; Yang, Z.-X.; He, X.-T. Steady fluid–structure coupling interface of circular membrane under liquid weight loading: Closed-form solution for differential-integral equations. *Mathematics* **2021**, *9*, 1105. [CrossRef]
3. Bernardo, P.; Iulianelli, A.; Macedonio, F.; Drioli, E. Membrane technologies for space engineering. *J. Membr. Sci.* **2021**, *626*, 119177. [CrossRef]
4. Ma, Y.; Wang, G.R.; Chen, Y.L.; Long, D.; Guan, Y.C.; Liu, L.Q.; Zhang, Z. Extended Hencky solution for the blister test of nanomembrane. *Extrem. Mech. Lett.* **2018**, *22*, 69–78. [CrossRef]
5. Dai, Z.; Lu, N. Poking and bulging of suspended thin sheets: Slippage, instabilities, and metrology. *J. Mech. Phys. Solids* **2021**, *149*, 104320. [CrossRef]
6. Tai, Y.; Zhou, K.; Chen, N. Dynamic Properties of Microresonators with the Bionic Structure of Tympanic Membrane. *Sensors* **2020**, *20*, 6958. [CrossRef]
7. Lian, Y.-S.; Sun, J.-Y.; Zhao, Z.-H.; Li, S.-Z.; Zheng, Z.-L. A refined theory for characterizing adhesion of elastic coatings on rigid substrates based on pressurized blister test methods: Closed-form solution and energy release rate. *Polymers* **2020**, *12*, 1788. [CrossRef]
8. Li, X.; Sun, J.-Y.; Shi, B.-B.; Zhao, Z.-H.; He, X.-T. A theoretical study on an elastic polymer thin film-based capacitive wind-pressure sensor. *Polymers* **2020**, *12*, 2133. [CrossRef] [PubMed]
9. Jindal, S.K.; Varma, M.A.; Thukral, D. Comprehensive assessment of MEMS double touch mode capacitive pressure sensor on utilization of SiC film as primary sensing element: Mathematical modelling and numerical simulation. *Microelectron. J.* **2018**, *73*, 30–36. [CrossRef]
10. Lee, H.Y.; Choi, B. Theoretical and experimental investigation of the trapped air effect on air-sealed capacitive pressure sensor. *Sens. Actuat. A-Phys.* **2015**, *221*, 104–114. [CrossRef]
11. Jindal, S.K.; Mahajan, A.; Raghuwanshi, S.K. A complete analytical model for clamped edge circular diaphragm non-touch and touch mode capacitive pressure sensor. *Microsyst. Technol.* **2016**, *22*, 1143–1150. [CrossRef]
12. Li, F.-Y.; Zhang, Q.; Li, X.; He, X.-T.; Sun, J.-Y. Polymer conductive membrane-based non-touch mode circular capacitive pressure sensors: An analytical solution-based method for design and numerical calibration. *Polymers* **2022**, *14*, 3087. [CrossRef]
13. Sun, J.-Y.; Zhang, Q.; Wu, J.; Li, X.; He, X.-T. Large Deflection Analysis of Peripherally Fixed Circular Membranes Subjected to Liquid Weight Loading: A Refined Design Theory of Membrane Deflection-Based Rain Gauges. *Materials* **2021**, *14*, 1023. [CrossRef]
14. Humphrey, M.D.; Istok, J.D.; Lee, J.Y.; Hevesi, J.A.; Flint, A.L. A new method for automated dynamic calibration of tipping-bucket rain gauges. *J. Atmos. Ocean. Technol.* **1997**, *14*, 1513–1519. [CrossRef]
15. Habib, E.; Krajewski, W.F.; Kruger, A. Sampling errors of tipping-bucket rain gauge measurements. *J. Hydrol. Eng.* **2001**, *6*, 159–166. [CrossRef]
16. Molini, A.; Lanza, L.G.; La Barbera, P. Improving the accuracy of tipping-bucket rain records using disaggregation techniques. *Atmos. Res.* **2005**, *77*, 203–217. [CrossRef]
17. Vasvári, V. Calibration of tipping bucket rain gauges in the Graz urban research area. *Atmos. Res.* **2005**, *77*, 18–28. [CrossRef]
18. Habib, E.; Meselhe, E.A.; Aduvala, A.V. Effect of local errors of tipping-bucket rain gauges on rainfall-runoff simulations. *J. Hydrol. Eng.* **2008**, *13*, 488–496. [CrossRef]
19. Colli, M.; Lanza, L.G.; La Barbera, P. Performance of a weighing rain gauge under laboratory simulated time-varying reference rainfall rates. *Atmos. Res.* **2013**, *131*, 3–12. [CrossRef]
20. Colli, M.; Lanza, L.G.; La Barbera, P.; Chan, P.W. Measurement accuracy of weighing and tipping-bucket rainfall intensity gauges under dynamic laboratory testing. *Atmos. Res.* **2014**, *144*, 186–194. [CrossRef]
21. Colli, M.; Lanza, L.G.; Chan, P.W. Co-located tipping-bucket and optical drop counter RI measurements and a simulated correction algorithm. *Atmos. Res.* **2013**, *119*, 3–12. [CrossRef]
22. Bin Afzal, M.H. Effective application of optical sensing technology for sustainable liquid level sensing and rainfall measurement. In *Optical Sensors*; SPIE: Bellingham, DC, USA, 2015; p. 9506.
23. Borup, M.; Grum, M.; Linde, J.J.; Mikkelsen, P.S. Dynamic gauge adjustment of high-resolution X-band radar data for convective rain storms: Model-based evaluation against measured combined sewer overflow. *J. Hydrol.* **2016**, *539*, 687–699. [CrossRef]

24. Bergmann, H.; Breinhllter, H.; Hahle, O.; Krainer, R. Calibration of tipping bucket hyetographs. *Phys. Chem. Earth (C)* **2001**, *26*, 731–736. [CrossRef]
25. Segovia-Cardozo, D.A.; Rodriguez-Sinobas, L.; Diez-Herrero, A.; Zubelzu, S.; Canales-Ide, F. Understanding the Mechanical Biases of Tipping-Bucket Rain Gauges: A Semi-Analytical Calibration Approach. *Water* **2021**, *13*, 2285. [CrossRef]
26. Liao, M.; Liao, A.; Liu, J.; Cai, Z.; Liu, H.; Ma, T. A novel method and system for the fast calibration of tipping bucket rain gauges. *J. Hydrol.* **2021**, *597*, 125782. [CrossRef]
27. Schwamback, D.; Anache, J.A.A.; Wendland, E.C. Calibration and error investigation of large tipping bucket flow meters. *Catena* **2022**, *209*, 105834. [CrossRef]
28. Sevruk, B. Adjustment of tipping-bucket precipitation gauge measurements. *Atmos. Res.* **1996**, *42*, 237–246. [CrossRef]
29. Fankhauser, R. Influence of systematic errors from tipping bucket rain gauges on recorded rainfall data. *Water Sci. Technol.* **1998**, *37*, 121–129. [CrossRef]
30. Shedekar, V.S.; King, K.W.; Fausey, N.R.; Soboyejo, A.B.O.; Harmel, R.D.; Brown, L.C. Assessment of measurement errors and dynamic calibration methods for three different tipping bucket rain gauges. *Atmos. Res.* **2016**, *178*, 445–458. [CrossRef]
31. Sypka, P. Dynamic real-time volumetric correction for tipping-bucket rain gauges. *Agric. For. Meteorol.* **2019**, *271*, 158–167. [CrossRef]
32. Hoffmann, M.; Schwartengräber, R.; Wessolek, G.; Peters, A. Comparison of simple rain gauge measurements with precision lysimeter data. *Atmos. Res.* **2016**, *174*, 120–123. [CrossRef]
33. Lian, Y.-S.; Sun, J.-Y.; Yang, Z.-X.; He, X.-T.; Zheng, Z.-L. Closed-form solution of well-known Hencky problem without small-rotation-angle assumption. *Z. Angew. Math. Mech.* **2016**, *96*, 1434–1441. [CrossRef]
34. Lian, Y.-S.; Sun, J.-Y.; Zhao, Z.-H.; He, X.-T.; Zheng, Z.-L. A revisit of the boundary value problem for Föppl–Hencky membranes: Improvement of geometric equations. *Mathematics* **2020**, *8*, 631. [CrossRef]
35. Moghadam, R.A.; Ebrahimi, S. Design and Analysis of a Torsional Mode MEMS Disk Resonator for RF Applications. *J. Multidiscip. Eng. Sci. Technol.* **2021**, *8*, 14300–14303.
36. Mojtahedi, A.; Hokmabady, H.; Kouhi, M.; Mohammadyzadeh, S. A novel ANN-RDT approach for damage detection of a composite panel employing contact and non-contact measuring data. *Compos. Struct.* **2022**, *279*, 114794. [CrossRef]
37. Ghasemvand, M.; Behjat, B.; Ebrahimi, S. Experimental investigation of the effects of adhesive defects on the strength and creep behavior of single-lap adhesive joints at various temperatures. *J. Adhes.* **2023**, *99*, 1227–1243. [CrossRef]
38. Ahmadi, Z.; Haghighi, M.; Validi, Z. A Novel Approach for Energy Optimization in Distributed Databases in Wireless Network Applications. *J. Manag. Account. Stud.* **2020**, *8*, 50–55. [CrossRef]
39. Velidi, G. Pressure and Velocity Variation in Remote-Controlled Plane Using CFD Analysis. *J. Airl. Oper. Aviat. Manag.* **2022**, *1*, 9–18. [CrossRef]
40. Bhosale, A.; Patil, S.; Dhepe, V.; Banosde, K.; Kakde, R.; Teltumade, R.; Lengare, D. 3-D Numerical Study of Effect of Urea Injector Location and Intake Cone Geometry on SCR Performance. *Int. J. Innov. Res. Sci. Stud.* **2022**, *5*, 47–58. [CrossRef]
41. Moghaddam, B.P.; Tenreiro Machado, J.A. A computational approach for the solution of a class of variable-order fractional integro-differential equations with weakly singular kernels. *Fract. Calc. Appl. Anal.* **2017**, *20*, 1023–1042. [CrossRef]
42. Mokhtary, P.; Moghaddam, B.P.; Lopes, A.M.; Tenreiro Machado, J.A. A computational approach for the non-smooth solution of non-linear weakly singular Volterra integral equation with proportional delay. *Numer. Algorithms* **2020**, *83*, 987–1006. [CrossRef]

Disclaimer/Publisher's Note: The statements, opinions and data contained in all publications are solely those of the individual author(s) and contributor(s) and not of MDPI and/or the editor(s). MDPI and/or the editor(s) disclaim responsibility for any injury to people or property resulting from any ideas, methods, instructions or products referred to in the content.

mathematics

MDPI

Article

Global Asymptotic Stability and Synchronization of Fractional-Order Reaction–Diffusion Fuzzy BAM Neural Networks with Distributed Delays via Hybrid Feedback Controllers

M. Syed Ali [1], Gani Stamov [2,*], Ivanka Stamova [2], Tarek F. Ibrahim [3], Arafa A. Dawood [4] and Fathea M. Osman Birkea [5]

1 Department of Mathematics, Thiruvalluvar University, Vellore 632115, Tamil Nadu, India; syed@tvu.edu.in
2 Department of Mathematics, University of Texas at San Antonio, San Antonio, TX 78249, USA; ivanka.stamova@utsa.edu
3 Department of Mathematics, Faculty of Sciences and Arts (Mahayel), King Khalid University, Abha 62529, Saudi Arabia; tfoze@kku.edu.sa
4 Department of Mathematics, Faculty of Sciences and Arts in Sarat Abeda, King Khalid University, Abha 62529, Saudi Arabia; adawood@kku.edu.sa
5 Department of Mathematics, Faculty of Science, Northern Border University, Arar 1321, Saudi Arabia; fathia.birkia@nbu.edu.sa
* Correspondence: gani.stamov@utsa.edu

Abstract: In this paper, the global asymptotic stability and global Mittag–Leffler stability of a class of fractional-order fuzzy bidirectional associative memory (BAM) neural networks with distributed delays is investigated. Necessary conditions are obtained by means of the Lyapunov functional method and inequality techniques. The hybrid feedback controllers are then developed to ensure the global asymptotic synchronization of these neural networks, resulting in two additional synchronization criteria. The derived conditions are applied to check the fractional-order fuzzy BAM neural network's Mittag–Leffler stability and synchronization. Three examples are given to demonstrate the effectiveness of the achieved results.

Keywords: fractional-order system; bidirectional associative memory neural networks; distributed delays; global asymptotic stability; global Mittag–Leffler stability; reaction–diffusion terms

MSC: 26A33; 34K36; 34K37; 34K20; 93D20

1. Introduction

On the parallel perspective, neural networks having fractional-order derivatives generally possess boundless memory, which finds an advantage in comparison with common integer-order neural networks. In fact, the memory and heredity properties of certain materials and processes are known to be better represented by fractional-order derivatives [1,2]. Because of its wide range of applications in areas such as neural networks, quantum physics, optical systems, and optical image processing, fractional-order systems have been extensively investigated during the last several decades as a technique for precisely describing real systems [3–11].

In addition, there is a class of fuzzy cellular neural networks with delays that has been studied by numerous researchers using a variety of analytical and numerical methodologies. In comparison to normal cellular neural networks, a fuzzy cellular neural network uses fuzzy logic between its template input and/or output in addition to the sum of product operations. Hence, there has been a lot of research activity in the area of delayed fuzzy cellular neural networks [12–14], including recently studied fractional-order cases [15,16].

Bidirectional associative memory (BAM) neural networks with two layers of neuronal cells were first introduced by Kosko [17]. The neurons in the first layer are fully interconnected with the neurons in the second layer, but there is no interconnect between neurons in the same layer. Due to their application in numerous disciplines such as image and signal processing, pattern recognition, optimization, and autonomous control, BAM neural networks have received a lot of attention in the last decade [18,19]. As a result, the stability of BAM neural networks has been extensively studied, and many stability requirements for BAM neural networks have been published [20–22].

Global asymptotic stability is one of the most investigated stability behavior of real-world neural systems and artificial neural network systems. This is due to the fact that a globally asymptotically stable neural network system is promising for a fast convergence rate to a state of interest. The global asymptotic stability of an error neural network is closely related to the global asymptotic synchronization of the master and response systems. That is why global asymptotic stability and global asymptotic synchronization have received much attention among researchers [1,13,20,22]. Both notions are studied for integer-order as well as for fractional-order problems.

Podlubny and his coauthors proposed in [23] the Mittag–Leffler stability notion and the fractional Lyapunov direct approach to extend the use of fractional calculus in nonlinear systems, with the goal of improving both system theory and fractional calculus knowledge. Since then, the stability of Mittag–Leffler, generalized Mittag–Leffler stability, and synchronization have been examined for different classes of fractional-order neural networks [24–27], including BAM neural network models [28,29].

It is evident from the literature that most research work on delayed neural networks are devoted to simple cases of discrete delays. However, due to the presence of numerous parallel ways, neural networks usually exhibit a unique nature, resulting in a distribution of conduction velocities and propagation delays along these pathways. Due to the presence of a large number of parallel routes with different axon diameters and lengths, neural networks usually have a spatial extent. As a result, there will be a distribution of conduction velocities and propagation delays along these pathways. In these cases, signal transmission is not instantaneous and cannot be described using discrete delays; instead, continuously distributed and infinite delays are more appropriate [1,16,22,30–33].

When electrons move in asymmetric electromagnetic fields, diffusion effects cannot be avoided in the complex network models strictly speaking [2,12,34–39]. In signal transmission, the signal becomes weak due to diffusion, so it is very important to consider that the activation varies in space as well as in time, and the reaction–diffusion effects cannot be neglected in both biological and man-made networks [40]. The models covering time delay and reaction–diffusion are good mimicry for real neural networks in terms of application, but the existence of time delays and reaction–diffusion could bring about some undesirable behavior.

Motivated by the above considerations, we have studied the global asymptotic stability of fractional-order fuzzy BAM reaction–diffusion neural networks with discrete and distributed delays via hybrid feedback controllers. The main contributions of this research are:

1. The global asymptotic stability and synchronization of fractional-order fuzzy BAM neural networks with reaction–diffusion terms and mixed delays, including distributed ones, are investigated via hybrid feedback controllers.

2. By applying of stability theory for fractional models together with some inequality strategies, efficient criteria are obtained to guarantee the global Mittag–Leffler stability and synchronization.

3. We establish a uniform approach to dealing with discrete and distributed time delays under more general activation function assumptions.

4. The established conditions include the positive influence of reaction–diffusion terms on the stability and synchronization behavior and reduce the conservatism of the existing ones.

5. Finally, numerical examples are provided to demonstrate the correctness of the proposed results.

The rest of the paper is organized as follows. Some preliminary definitions and results related to fractional calculus are given in Section 2. The fractional-order fuzzy BAM neural network model, together with the controlled one are also introduced. Section 3 is devoted to our global asymptotic stability results. Global Mittag–Leffler synchronization criteria are established in Section 4. In Section 5, we elaborate some examples to demonstrate the validity and feasibility of the established results. Some conclusion notes and future directions of our research are discussed in Section 6.

2. Preliminaries and Problem Definition

In the present section, we first introduce some basic definitions and the corresponding results that are used later. Then, the fractional-order fuzzy BAM neural network model is formulated.

Definition 1 ([41]). *The Caputo fractional derivative of order β for a function $f(t)$ is defined by*

$$D^{\beta}f(t)=\frac{1}{\Gamma(n-\beta)}\int_{b}^{t}(t-\tau)^{n-\beta-1}f^{(n)}(\tau)d\tau,$$

in which $t \geq b, t \in \mathbb{R}, n-1<\beta<n \in \mathbb{N}$, and Γ is the standard Gamma function.

In this paper, we consider the following fractional-order reaction–diffusion fuzzy BAM neural network with mixed delays

$$\begin{aligned}
\frac{\partial^{\lambda}\zeta_{\varphi}(t,\wp)}{\partial t^{\lambda}} &= \sum_{k=1}^{q}\frac{\partial}{\partial\zeta_k}(m_{\varphi k}\frac{\partial\zeta_{\varphi}(t,\wp)}{\partial\wp_k})-d_{\varphi}\zeta_{\varphi}(t,\wp)+\sum_{\varpi=1}^{n}c_{\varphi\varpi}f_{\varpi}(\Im_{\varpi}(t,\wp))\\
&+\sum_{\varpi=1}^{n}a_{\varphi\varpi}f_{\varpi}(\Im_{\varpi}(t-\tau,\wp))\\
&+\bigwedge_{\varpi=1}^{n}u_{\varphi\varpi}\int_0^{\infty}k_{\varphi\varpi}(s)f_{\varpi}(\Im_{\varpi}(s-\tau,\wp))ds+\bigwedge_{\varpi=1}^{n}P_{\varphi\varpi}\Im_{\varpi}(t,\wp)\\
&+\bigvee_{\varpi=1}^{n}v_{\varphi\varpi}\int_0^{\infty}k_{\varphi\varpi}(s)f_{\varpi}(\Im_{\varpi}(s-\tau,\wp))ds+\bigvee_{\varpi=1}^{n}Q_{\varphi\varpi}\Im_{\varpi}(t,\wp)+I_{\varphi},\ \varphi=1,2,\ldots,o,\\
\frac{\partial^{\lambda}\Im_{\varpi}(t,\wp)}{\partial t^{\lambda}} &= \sum_{k=1}^{q}\frac{\partial}{\partial\Im_k}(\tilde{m}_{\varpi k}\frac{\partial\Im_{\varpi}(t,\wp)}{\partial\wp_k})-\tilde{d}_{\varpi}\Im_{\varpi}(t,\wp)+\sum_{\varphi=1}^{o}\tilde{c}_{\varpi\varphi}g_{\varphi}(\zeta_{\varphi}(t,\wp))\\
&+\sum_{\varphi=1}^{o}\tilde{a}_{\varpi\varphi}g_{\varphi}(\zeta_{\varphi}(t-\tau,\wp))\\
&+\bigwedge_{\varphi=1}^{o}\tilde{u}_{\varpi\varphi}\int_0^{\infty}k_{\varpi\varphi}(s)g_{\varphi}(\zeta_{\varpi}(s-\tau,\wp))ds+\bigwedge_{\varphi=1}^{o}\tilde{P}_{\varpi\varphi}\zeta_{\varphi}(t,\wp)\\
&+\bigvee_{\varphi=1}^{o}\tilde{v}_{\varpi\varphi}\int_0^{\infty}k_{\varpi\varphi}(s)g_{\varphi}(\zeta_{\varphi}(s-\tau,\wp))ds+\bigvee_{\varphi=1}^{o}\tilde{Q}_{\varpi\varphi}\zeta_{\varphi}(t,\wp)+I_{\varpi},\ \varpi=1,2,\ldots,n,
\end{aligned}\qquad(1)$$

where n and o denote the number of neurons in the $\Im$-layer and ζ-layer, respectively. For $\varphi=1,2,\ldots,o$, $\varpi=1,2,\ldots,n$, and $\wp=(\wp_1,\wp_2,\ldots,\wp_q)^T\in\Omega\subset R^q$, Ω is a bounded compact set with a smooth boundary $\partial\Omega$, and mess$(\Omega)>0$ in the space R^q; $\zeta_{\varphi}(t,\wp)$ and $\Im_{\varpi}(t,\wp)$ are the states of the φth neuron and the ϖth neurons at time t and space $\wp$, respectively; d_{φ} and $\tilde{d}_{\varpi}$ indicate the rates with which the φth neuron and ϖth neuron will reset their potentials to the resting states in isolation when disconnecting the network and external inputs; $c_{\varphi\varpi}$, $a_{\varphi\varpi}$, $\tilde{c}_{\varpi\varphi}$, and $\tilde{a}_{\varpi\varphi}$ are elements of the fuzzy feedback MIN template and fuzzy feedback MAX template, fuzzy feed-forward MIN template and fuzzy feed-forward MAX template, respectively; τ is the discrete transmission delay; $\bigwedge$ and $\bigvee$ denote the fuzzy AND and fuzzy OR operations, respectively; I_φ and J_ϖ denote the external inputs on the φth neurons in the $\Im$-layer and the ϖth neurons in the ζ-layer, respectively. The smooth functions $m_{\varphi k} \geq 0$ and $\tilde{m}_{\varpi k} \geq 0$ correspond to the transmission diffusion operators along the φth neurons and the ϖth neurons, respectively, $u_{\varphi\varpi}$, $v_{\varpi\varphi}$, $P_{\varpi\varphi}$, and $Q_{\varpi\varphi}$ are elements of the fuzzy feedback MIN template and fuzzy feedback MAX template in the $\Im$-layer, respectively. $\tilde{u}_{\varphi\varpi}$, $\tilde{v}_{\varpi\varphi}$, $\tilde{P}_{\varphi\varpi}$, and $\tilde{Q}_{\varphi\varpi}$ are elements of the fuzzy feedback MIN template and fuzzy feedback MAX template in the ζ-layer. $k_{\varphi\varpi}(\cdot)$ and $k_{\varpi\varphi}(\cdot)$ are delay kernels functions. $f_\varpi(\cdot)$ and $g_\varphi(\cdot)$ are signal transmission functions of ϖth neurons and φth neurons, respectively, and

$$\frac{\partial^\lambda p(t,\wp)}{\partial t^\lambda} = \frac{1}{\Gamma(1-\lambda)} \int_0^t \frac{\partial p(s,\wp)}{\partial s} \frac{ds}{(t-s)^\lambda},\ t > 0,\ 0 < \lambda < 1$$

for a function $p \in C^1[[0,b] \times \Omega, \mathbb{R}]$, $b > 0$ [7].

The corresponding response system with feedback controllers $\mathcal{U}_\varphi(t,\wp)$ and $\mathcal{U}_\varpi(t,\wp)$ is described by

$$\begin{aligned}
\frac{\partial^\lambda \bar{\zeta}_\varphi(t,\wp)}{\partial t^\lambda} &= \sum_{k=1}^{q} \frac{\partial}{\partial \wp_k}\Big(m_{\varphi k}\frac{\partial \bar{\zeta}_\varphi(t,\wp)}{\partial \wp_k}\Big) - d_\varphi \bar{\zeta}_\varphi(t,\wp) + \sum_{\varpi=1}^{n} c_{\varphi\varpi} f_\varpi(\bar{\Im}_\varpi(t,\wp)) \\
&+ \sum_{\varpi=1}^{n} a_{\varphi\varpi} f_\varpi(\bar{\Im}_\varpi(t-\tau,\wp)) + \bigwedge_{\varpi=1}^{n} u_{\varphi\varpi} \int_0^\infty k_{\varphi\varpi}(s) f_\varpi(\bar{\Im}_\varpi(s-\tau,\wp))ds \\
&+ \bigwedge_{\varpi=1}^{n} P_{\varphi\varpi} \bar{\Im}_\varpi(t,\wp) + \bigvee_{\varpi=1}^{n} v_{\varphi\varpi} \int_0^\infty k_{\varphi\varpi}(s) f_\varpi(\bar{\Im}_\varpi(s-\tau,\wp))ds \\
&+ \bigvee_{\varpi=1}^{n} Q_{\varphi\varpi} \bar{\Im}_\varpi(t,\wp) + I_\varphi + \mathcal{U}_\varphi(t,\wp),\ \varphi = 1,2,\ldots,o, \\
\frac{\partial^\lambda \bar{\Im}_\varpi(t,\wp)}{\partial t^\lambda} &= \sum_{k=1}^{q} \frac{\partial}{\partial \wp_k}\Big(\tilde{m}_{\varpi k}\frac{\partial \bar{\Im}_\varpi(t,\wp)}{\partial \wp_k}\Big) - \tilde{d}_\varpi \bar{\Im}_\varpi(t,\wp) + \sum_{\varphi=1}^{o} \tilde{c}_{\varpi\varphi} g_\varphi(\bar{\zeta}_\varphi(t,\wp)) \\
&+ \sum_{\varphi=1}^{o} \tilde{a}_{\varpi\varphi} g_\varphi(\bar{\zeta}_\varphi(t-\tau,\wp)) + \bigwedge_{\varphi=1}^{o} \tilde{u}_{\varpi\varphi} \int_0^\infty k_{\varpi\varphi}(s) g_\varphi(\bar{\zeta}_\varphi(s-\tau,\wp))ds \\
&+ \bigwedge_{\varphi=1}^{o} \tilde{P}_{\varpi\varphi} \bar{\zeta}_\varphi(t,\wp) + \bigvee_{\varphi=1}^{o} \tilde{v}_{\varpi\varphi} \int_0^\infty k_{\varpi\varphi}(s) g_\varphi(\bar{\zeta}_\varphi(s-\tau,\wp))ds \\
&+ \bigvee_{\varphi=1}^{o} \tilde{Q}_{\varpi\varphi} \bar{\zeta}_\varphi(t,\wp) + J_\varpi + \mathcal{U}_\varpi(t,\wp),\ \varpi = 1,2,\ldots,n.
\end{aligned} \tag{2}$$

For $\xi_\varphi(t,\wp) = \bar{\zeta}_\varphi(t,\wp) - \zeta_\varphi(t,\wp)$ and $\bar{\xi}_\varpi(t,\wp) = \bar{\Im}_\varpi(t,\wp) - \Im_\varpi(t,\wp)$, the error system is defined by

$$\begin{aligned}
\frac{\partial^\lambda \xi_\varphi(t,\wp)}{\partial t^\lambda} &= \sum_{k=1}^{q} \frac{\partial}{\partial \wp_k}\Big(m_{\varphi k}\frac{\partial \xi_\varphi(t,\wp)}{\partial \wp_k}\Big) - d_\varphi \xi_\varphi(t,\wp) \\
&+ \Big[\sum_{\varpi=1}^{n} c_{\varphi\varpi} f_\varpi(\bar{\Im}_\varpi(t,\wp)) - \sum_{\varpi=1}^{n} c_{\varphi\varpi} f_\varpi(\Im_\varpi(t,\wp))\Big] \\
&+ \Big[\sum_{\varpi=1}^{n} a_{\varphi\varpi} f_\varpi(\bar{\Im}_\varpi(t-\tau,\wp)) - \sum_{\varpi=1}^{n} a_{\varphi\varpi} f_\varpi(\Im_\varpi(t-\tau,\wp))\Big] \\
&+ \Big[\bigwedge_{\varpi=1}^{n} u_{\varphi\varpi} \int_0^\infty k_{\varphi\varpi}(s) f_\varpi(\bar{\Im}_\varpi(s-\tau,\wp))ds - \bigwedge_{\varpi=1}^{n} u_{\varphi\varpi} \int_0^\infty k_{\varphi\varpi}(s) f_\varpi(\Im_\varpi(s-\tau,\wp))ds\Big] \\
&+ \Big[\bigvee_{\varpi=1}^{n} v_{\varphi\varpi} \int_0^\infty k_{\varphi\varpi}(s) f_\varpi(\bar{\Im}_\varpi(s-\tau,\wp))ds - \bigvee_{\varpi=1}^{n} v_{\varphi\varpi} \int_0^\infty k_{\varphi\varpi}(s) f_\varpi(\Im_\varpi(s-\tau,\wp))ds\Big] \\
&+ \mathcal{U}_\varphi(t,\wp),\ \varphi = 1,2,\ldots,o,
\end{aligned}$$

$$\begin{aligned}\frac{\partial^{\lambda}\bar{\xi}_{\varpi}(\mathrm{t},\wp)}{\partial \mathrm{t}^{\lambda}} &= \sum_{k=1}^{q}\frac{\partial}{\partial \wp_k}(\tilde{m}_{\varpi k}\frac{\partial \bar{\xi}_{\varpi}(t,\wp)}{\partial \wp_k}) - \tilde{d}_{\varpi}\bar{\xi}_{\varpi}(t,\wp) \\ &+ [\sum_{\varphi=1}^{o}\tilde{c}_{\varpi\varphi}g_{\varphi}(\bar{\zeta}_{\varphi}(t,\wp)) - \sum_{\varphi=1}^{o}\tilde{c}_{\varpi\varphi}g_{\varphi}(\zeta_{\varphi}(\mathrm{t},\wp))] \\ &+ [\sum_{\varphi=1}^{o}\tilde{a}_{\varpi\varphi}g_{\varphi}(\bar{\zeta}_{\varphi}(\mathrm{t}-\tau,\wp)) - \sum_{\varphi=1}^{o}\tilde{a}_{\varpi\varphi}g_{\varphi}(\zeta_{\varphi}(t-\tau,\wp))] \\ &+ [\bigwedge_{\varphi=1}^{o}\tilde{u}_{\varpi\varphi}\int_0^{\infty}k_{\varpi\varphi}(s)g_{\varphi}(\bar{\zeta}_{\varphi}(s-\tau,\wp))ds - \bigwedge_{\varphi=1}^{o}\tilde{u}_{\varpi\varphi}\int_0^{\infty}k_{\varpi\varphi}(s)g_{\varphi}(\zeta_{\varphi}(s-\tau,\wp))ds] \\ &+ [\bigvee_{\varphi=1}^{o}\tilde{v}_{\varpi\varphi}\int_0^{\infty}k_{\varpi\varphi}(s)g_{\varphi}(\bar{\zeta}_{\varphi}(s-\tau,\wp))ds - \bigvee_{\varphi=1}^{o}\tilde{v}_{\varpi\varphi}\int_0^{\infty}k_{\varpi\varphi}(s)g_{\varphi}(\zeta_{\varphi}(s-\tau,\wp))ds] \\ &+ \mathcal{U}_{\varpi}(\mathrm{t},\wp),\ \varpi = 1,2,\ldots,n. \end{aligned} \tag{3}$$

We design a suitable controller for the error system (3). Let $\mathcal{U}_{\varphi}(\mathrm{t},\wp) = \mathcal{U}_{1\varphi}(\mathrm{t},\wp) + \mathcal{U}_{2\varphi}(\mathrm{t},\wp)$, where $\mathcal{U}_{1\varphi}(\mathrm{t},\wp) = -\mathrm{t}_{\varphi}\xi_{\varphi}(\mathrm{t},\wp)$ and $\mathcal{U}_{2\varphi}(\mathrm{t},\wp) = -\Psi_{\varphi}\xi_{\varphi}(\mathrm{t},\wp)$ and $\mathcal{U}_{\varpi}(\mathrm{t},\wp) = \mathcal{U}_{1\varpi}(\mathrm{t},\wp) + \mathcal{U}_{2\varpi}(\mathrm{t},\wp)$, where $\mathcal{U}_{1\varpi}(\mathrm{t},\wp) = -\varpi_{\varpi}\bar{\xi}_{\varpi}(\mathrm{t},\wp)$ and $\mathcal{U}_{2\varpi}(\mathrm{t},\wp) = -\varrho_{\varpi}\bar{\xi}_{\varpi}(\mathrm{t},\wp)$, where $\mathrm{t}_{\varphi},\Psi_{\varphi},\varpi_{\varpi}$, and ϱ_{ϖ} are positive constants. Then, system (3) has the form

$$\begin{aligned}\frac{\partial^{\lambda}\xi_{\varphi}(\mathrm{t},\wp)}{\partial \mathrm{t}^{\lambda}} &= \sum_{k=1}^{q}\frac{\partial}{\partial \wp_k}(m_{\varphi k}\frac{\partial \xi_{\varphi}(\mathrm{t},\wp)}{\partial \wp_k}) - d_{\varphi}\xi_{\varphi}(\mathrm{t},\wp) \\ &+ [\sum_{\varpi=1}^{n}c_{\varphi\varpi}f_{\varpi}(\bar{\Im}_{\varpi}(\mathrm{t},\wp)) - \sum_{\varpi=1}^{n}c_{\varphi\varpi}f_{\varpi}(\Im_{\varpi}(\mathrm{t},\wp))] \\ &+ [\sum_{\varpi=1}^{n}a_{\varphi\varpi}f_{\varpi}(\bar{\Im}_{\varpi}(\mathrm{t}-\tau,\wp)) - \sum_{\varpi=1}^{n}a_{\varphi\varpi}f_{\varpi}(\Im_{\varpi}(t-\tau,\wp))] \\ &+ [\bigwedge_{\varpi=1}^{n}u_{\varphi\varpi}\int_0^{\infty}k_{\varphi\varpi}(s)f_{\varpi}(\bar{\Im}_{\varpi}(s-\tau,\wp))ds - \bigwedge_{\varpi=1}^{n}u_{\varphi\varpi}\int_0^{\infty}k_{\varphi\varpi}(s)f_{\varpi}(\Im_{\varpi}(s-\tau,\wp))ds] \\ &+ [\bigvee_{\varpi=1}^{n}v_{\varphi\varpi}\int_0^{\infty}k_{\varphi\varpi}(s)f_{\varpi}(\bar{\Im}_{\varpi}(s-\tau,\wp))ds - \bigvee_{\varpi=1}^{n}v_{\varphi\varpi}\int_0^{\infty}k_{\varphi\varpi}(s)f_{\varpi}(\Im_{\varpi}(s-\tau,\wp))ds] \\ &- \mathrm{t}_{\varphi}\xi_{\varphi}(t,\wp) - \Psi_{\varphi}\xi_{\varphi}(t,\wp),\ \varphi = 1,2,\ldots,o, \end{aligned}$$

$$\begin{aligned}\frac{\partial^{\lambda}\bar{\xi}_{\varpi}(\mathrm{t},\wp)}{\partial \mathrm{t}^{\lambda}} &= \sum_{k=1}^{q}\frac{\partial}{\partial \wp_k}(\tilde{m}_{\varpi k}\frac{\partial \bar{\xi}_{\varpi}(\mathrm{t},\wp)}{\partial \wp_k}) - \tilde{d}_{\varpi}\bar{\xi}_{\varpi}(\mathrm{t},\wp) \\ &+ [\sum_{\varphi=1}^{o}\tilde{c}_{\varpi\varphi}g_{\varphi}(\bar{\zeta}_{\varphi}(t,\wp)) - \sum_{\varphi=1}^{o}\tilde{c}_{\varpi\varphi}g_{\varphi}(\zeta_{\varphi}(t,\wp))] \\ &+ [\sum_{\varphi=1}^{o}\tilde{a}_{\varpi\varphi}g_{\varphi}(\bar{\zeta}_{\varphi}(\mathrm{t}-\tau,\wp)) - \sum_{\varphi=1}^{o}\tilde{a}_{\varpi\varphi}g_{\varphi}(\zeta_{\varphi}(\mathrm{t}-\tau,\wp))] \\ &+ [\bigwedge_{\varphi=1}^{o}\tilde{u}_{\varpi\varphi}\int_0^{\infty}k_{\varpi\varphi}(s)g_{\varphi}(\bar{\zeta}_{\varphi}(s-\tau,\wp))ds - \bigwedge_{\varphi=1}^{o}\tilde{u}_{\varpi\varphi}\int_0^{\infty}k_{\varpi\varphi}(s)g_{\varphi}(\zeta_{\varphi}(s-\tau,\wp))ds] \\ &+ [\bigvee_{\varphi=1}^{o}\tilde{v}_{\varpi\varphi}\int_0^{\infty}k_{\varpi\varphi}(s)g_{\varphi}(\bar{\zeta}_{\varphi}(s-\tau,\wp))ds - \bigvee_{\varphi=1}^{o}\tilde{v}_{\varpi\varphi}\int_0^{\infty}k_{\varpi\varphi}(s)g_{\varphi}(\zeta_{\varphi}(s-\tau,\wp))ds] \\ &- \varpi_{\varpi}\bar{\xi}_{\varpi}(\mathrm{t},\wp) - \varrho_{\varpi}\bar{\xi}_{\varpi}(\mathrm{t},\wp),\ \varpi = 1,2,\ldots,n. \end{aligned} \tag{4}$$

We investigate the error system (4) under the following initial and boundary conditions:

$$\begin{aligned}
&\zeta_\varphi(\mathfrak{s},\wp) = \phi_\varphi(\mathfrak{s},\wp),\ \mathfrak{s}\in(-\infty,0],\ \wp\in\Omega,\\
&\bar{\xi}_\varpi(\mathfrak{s},\wp) = \tilde{\phi}_\varpi(\mathfrak{s},\wp),\ \mathfrak{s}\in(-\infty,0],\ \wp\in\Omega,\\
&\zeta_\varphi(\mathrm{t},\wp) = 0,\ \mathrm{t}\in\mathbb{R},\ \wp\in\partial\Omega,\\
&\bar{\xi}_\varpi(\mathrm{t},\wp) = 0,\ \mathrm{t}\in\mathbb{R},\ \wp\in\partial\Omega,\ \varphi=1,2,\dots,o,\ \varpi=1,2,\dots,n,
\end{aligned} \tag{5}$$

where ϕ_φ and $\tilde{\phi}_\varpi$ are continuous initial functions.

In our stability analysis, we need the following assumptions.

Assumption 1. *For ϑ_ϖ, $\bar{\vartheta}_\varpi \in \mathbb{R}$ and ζ_φ, $\bar{\zeta}_\varphi \in \mathbb{R}$, the activation functions f_ϖ and g_φ satisfy*

$$\left|\bigwedge_{\varpi=1}^{n} u_{\varphi\varpi} f_\varpi(\vartheta_\varpi) - \bigwedge_{\varpi=1}^{n} u_{\varphi\varpi} f_\varpi(\bar{\vartheta}_\varpi)\right| \le \sum_{\varpi=1}^{n} |u_{\varphi\varpi}|\left|f_\varpi(\vartheta_\varpi) - f_\varpi(\bar{\vartheta}_\varpi)\right|,\ \varpi = 1,2,\dots,n,$$
$$\left|\bigvee_{\varpi=1}^{n} v_{\varphi\varpi} f_\varpi(\vartheta_\varpi) - \bigvee_{\varpi=1}^{n} v_{\varphi\varpi} f_\varpi(\bar{\vartheta}_\varpi)\right| \le \sum_{\varpi=1}^{n} |v_{\varphi\varpi}|\left|f_\varpi(\vartheta_\varpi) - f_\varpi(\bar{\vartheta}_\varpi)\right|,\ \varpi = 1,2,\dots,n,$$
$$\left|\bigwedge_{\varphi=1}^{o} \tilde{u}_{\varpi\varphi} g_\varphi(\zeta_\varphi) - \bigwedge_{\varphi=1}^{o} \tilde{u}_{\varpi\varphi} g_\varphi(\bar{\zeta}_\varphi)\right| \le \sum_{\varpi=1}^{o} |\tilde{u}_{\varpi\varphi}|\left|g_\varphi(\zeta_\varphi) - g_\varphi(\bar{\zeta}_\varphi)\right|,\ \varphi = 1,2,\dots,o,$$
$$\left|\bigvee_{\varphi=1}^{o} \tilde{v}_{\varpi\varphi} g_\varphi(\zeta_\varphi) - \bigvee_{\varphi=1}^{o} \tilde{v}_{\varpi\varphi} g_\varphi(\bar{\zeta}_\varphi)\right| \le \sum_{\varphi=1}^{o} |\tilde{v}_{\varpi\varphi}|\left|g_\varphi(\zeta_\varphi) - g_\varphi(\bar{\zeta}_\varphi)\right|,\ \varphi = 1,2,\dots,o.$$

Assumption 2. *For any ϑ_ϖ, $\bar{\vartheta}_\varpi \in \mathbb{R}$ and ζ_φ, $\bar{\zeta}_\varphi \in \mathbb{R}$, there exists positive constants F_φ, F_ϖ, such that*

$$\begin{aligned}
&\left|f_\varpi(\vartheta_\varpi) - f_\varpi(\bar{\vartheta}_\varpi)\right| \le F_\varpi|\vartheta_\varpi - \bar{\vartheta}_\varpi|,\ \varpi = 1,2,\dots,n,\\
&\left|g_\varphi(\zeta_\varphi) - g_\varphi(\bar{\zeta}_\varphi)\right| \le G_\varphi|\zeta_\varphi - \bar{\zeta}_\varphi|,\ \varphi = 1,2,\dots,o.
\end{aligned}$$

Assumption 3. *The delay kernels $k_{\varphi\varpi}(\cdot)$ and $k_{\varpi\varphi}(\cdot)$ satisfy*

$$\int_0^\infty k_{\varphi\varpi}(s)ds \le 1,\ \int_0^\infty k_{\varpi\varphi}(s)ds \le 1$$

for $\varphi = 1,2,\dots,o$, $\varpi = 1,2,\dots,n$.

The next lemmas are also used.

Lemma 1 ([34]). *Let $p : [0,b] \times \Omega \to \mathbb{R}$ with $b > 0$ be a continuously differentiable function on t, $\mathrm{t} > 0$ for any $\wp \in \Omega$. Then, for any $\mathrm{t} \ge 0$, $\wp \in \Omega$*

$$\frac{1}{2}\frac{\partial^\lambda p^2(\mathrm{t},\wp)}{\partial \mathrm{t}^\lambda} \le p(\mathrm{t},\wp)\frac{\partial^\lambda p(\mathrm{t},\wp)}{\partial \mathrm{t}^\lambda}$$

for $0 < \lambda < 1$.

Lemma 2 ([34]). *For $0 < \beta < 1$, assume that the function $V(\mathrm{t})$ is continuous on $[0,\infty)$ satisfying*

$$D^\beta V(\mathrm{t}) \le \Upsilon V(\mathrm{t}),\ \Upsilon \in \mathbb{R}$$

whenever

$$V(\gamma + \xi) \le V(\gamma),\ -\infty < \xi \le 0.$$

Then,

$$V(t) \leq \max_{-\infty<\mathfrak{s}\leq 0} V(\mathfrak{s})E_\beta(\Upsilon t^\beta),\ t>0,$$

where E_β is the corresponding Mittag–Leffler function.

Lemma 3 ([42]). *Suppose that $V(t) \in \mathbb{R}$ is a continuous, differentiable, and non-negative function satisfying*

$$\begin{aligned} &D^\alpha V(t) \leq -bV(t) + cV(t-\tau),\ \ 0<\alpha<1, \\ &V(\gamma) = \varphi(\gamma) \geq 0. \quad \gamma \in [-\tau, 0]. \end{aligned}$$

If $b > \sqrt{2}c$ and $c > 0$, then for all $\varphi(\gamma) \geq 0$, $\tau > 0$, $\lim_{t\to+\infty} V(t) = 0$.

The assertion of Lemma 3 is true for $\tau = \infty$, too.

Lemma 4 (Fractional Barbalat's Lemma [43]). *If $\int_{t_0}^{t} \varsigma(\xi)d\xi$ includes a finite limit as $t \to +\infty$, and $D^\lambda \varsigma(t)$ is bounded, then $\varsigma(t) \to 0$ as $t \to \infty$, whenever $0 < \lambda < 1$.*

Lemma 5 ([44]). *Given any scalar $\epsilon > 0$, $x, y \in R^n$, and matrix A, then*

$$x^T Ay \leq \frac{1}{2\epsilon}x^T AA^T x + \frac{\epsilon}{2}y^T y.$$

Lemma 6 ([45]). *Let Ω be a cube $|x_k| < l_q$ $(k = 1, 2, \ldots, q)$, and let $v(x)$ be a real-valued function belonging to $C^1(\Omega)$ which vanishes on the boundary $\partial\Omega$ of Ω, i.e., $v(x)|_\Omega = 0$. Then,*

$$\int_\Omega v^2(x)dx \leq l_k^2 \int_\Omega \left|\frac{\partial v(x)}{\partial x_k}\right|^2 dx.$$

3. Global Asymptotic Stability via State Feedback Control

Definition 2. *The error system (4) is said to be globally asymptotically stable under the given controllers if*

$$\lim_{t\to\infty} (||\xi(t,\wp)||_1 + ||\bar{\xi}(t,\wp)||_2) = 0,$$

where $||.||_1$ and $||.||_2$ are the corresponding norms of $\xi(t,\wp) = (\xi_1(t,\wp), \xi_2(t,\wp), \ldots, \xi_0(t,\wp))^T \in \mathbb{R}^0$, and $\bar{\xi}(t,\wp) = (\bar{\xi}_1(t,\wp), \bar{\xi}_2(t,\wp), \ldots, \bar{\xi}_n(t,\wp))^T \in \mathbb{R}^n$, respectively.

Remark 1. *Since $\xi_\varphi(t,\wp) = \bar{\zeta}_\varphi(t,\wp) - \zeta_\varphi(t,\wp)$, $\varphi = 1, 2, \ldots, o$ and $\bar{\xi}_\varpi(t,\wp) = \bar{\Im}_\varpi(t,\wp) - \Im_\varpi(t,\wp)$, $\varpi = 1, 2, \ldots, n$, the global asymptotic stability of the error system (4) is equivalent to a global asymptotic synchronization of the nodes of system (2) onto those of system (1) under the appropriate controllers.*

Theorem 1. *Suppose that Assumptions 1–3 and the conditions of Lemma 6 hold, and* $\bar{M}_\varphi$, $\tilde{\bar{M}}_\varpi$ *are positive constants, such that* $\bar{M}_\varphi = \sum_{k=1}^{q} \frac{m_{\varphi k}}{l_k^2}$, $\tilde{\bar{M}}_\varpi = \sum_{k=1}^{q} \frac{\tilde{m}_{\varpi k}}{l_k^2}$. *The error system (4) is globally asymptotically stable, if there exist constants* $\rho > 0$ *and*

$$\mu_{\min}^{(1)} = \min_{1\le\varphi\le o}\Bigg\{2\bar{M}_\varphi + 2d_\varphi - \sum_{\varpi=1}^{n}|c_{\varphi\varpi}|F_\varpi\rho^{-1} - \sum_{\varpi=1}^{n}|a_{\varphi\varpi}|F_\varpi\rho^{-1}$$
$$- \sum_{\varpi=1}^{n}|u_{\varphi\varpi}|F_\varpi\rho^{-1} - \sum_{\varpi=1}^{n}|v_{\varphi\varpi}|F_\varpi\rho^{-1} + t_\varphi + \psi_\varphi - \sum_{\varpi=1}^{n}|c_{\varphi\varpi}|F_\varpi\rho\Bigg\} > 0,$$
$$\mu_{\min}^{(2)} = \min_{1\le\varpi\le n}\Bigg\{2\tilde{\bar{M}}_\varpi + 2\tilde{d}_\varpi - \sum_{\varphi=1}^{o}|\tilde{c}_{\varpi\varphi}|G_\varphi\rho^{-1} - \sum_{\varphi=1}^{o}|\tilde{a}_{\varpi\varphi}|G_\varphi\rho^{-1} - \sum_{\varphi=1}^{o}|\tilde{u}_{\varpi\varphi}|G_\varphi\rho^{-1}$$
$$- \sum_{\varphi=1}^{o}|\tilde{v}_{\varpi\varphi}|G_\varphi\rho^{-1} + \varpi_\varpi + \varrho_\varpi - \sum_{\varphi=1}^{o}|\tilde{c}_{\varpi\varphi}|G_\varphi\rho\Bigg\} > 0,$$
$$\Lambda_1^\mu = \max_{1\le\varphi\le o}\Bigg\{\sum_{\varpi=1}^{n}|\tilde{u}_{\varpi\varphi}|G_\varphi\rho + \sum_{\varpi=1}^{n}|\tilde{v}_{\varpi\varphi}|G_\varphi\rho + \sum_{\varpi=1}^{n}|\tilde{a}_{\varpi\varphi}|G_\varphi\rho\Bigg\} > 0,$$
$$\Lambda_2^\mu = \max_{1\le\varpi\le n}\Bigg\{\sum_{\varphi=1}^{o}|u_{\varphi\varpi}|F_\varpi\rho + \sum_{\varphi=1}^{o}|v_{\varphi\varpi}|F_\varpi\rho + \sum_{\varphi=1}^{o}|a_{\varphi\varpi}|F_\varpi\rho\Bigg\} > 0.$$

such that

$$\min\Big\{\mu_{\min}^{(1)}, \mu_{\min}^{(2)}\Big\} > \sqrt{2}\max\Big\{\Lambda_1^\mu, \Lambda_2^\mu\Big\}.$$

Proof. We define a Lyapunov function as

$$V(t) = \int_\Omega \sum_{\varphi=1}^{o} \frac{1}{2}\xi_\varphi^2(t,\wp)d\wp + \int_\Omega \sum_{\varpi=1}^{n} \frac{1}{2}\bar{\xi}_\varpi^2(t,\wp)d\wp. \tag{6}$$

Then, for the fractional derivative of V of order λ, we have

$$\begin{aligned}\frac{d^\lambda V(t)}{dt^\lambda} &= \frac{1}{2}\frac{d^\lambda}{dt^\lambda}\left(\int_\Omega \frac{1}{2}\sum_{\varphi=1}^{o}\xi_\varphi^2(t,\wp)d\wp + \int_\Omega \frac{1}{2}\sum_{\varpi=1}^{n}\bar{\xi}_\varpi^2(t,\wp)d\wp\right)\\ &= \frac{1}{2}\sum_{\varphi=1}^{o}\left[\frac{d^\lambda}{dt^\lambda}\left(\int_\Omega \xi_\varphi^2(t,\wp)d\wp\right)\right] + \frac{1}{2}\sum_{\varpi=1}^{n}\left[\frac{d^\lambda}{dt^\lambda}\left(\int_\Omega \bar{\xi}_\varpi^2(t,\wp)d\wp\right)\right].\end{aligned} \tag{7}$$

We have from Lemma 1 that

$$\frac{d^\lambda}{dt^\lambda}\left(\int_\Omega \xi_\varphi^2(t,\wp)d\wp\right) \le 2\int_\Omega \xi_\varphi(t,\wp)\frac{\partial^\lambda \xi_\varphi(t,\wp)}{\partial t^\lambda}d\wp,$$
$$\frac{d^\lambda}{dt^\lambda}\left(\int_\Omega \bar{\xi}_\varpi^2(t,\wp)d\wp\right) \le 2\int_\Omega \bar{\xi}_\varpi(t,\wp)\frac{\partial^\lambda \bar{\xi}_\varpi(t,\wp)}{\partial t^\lambda}d\wp.$$

Substituting the above inequalities in Equation (7), we obtain

$$
\begin{aligned}
D^{\lambda}V(t)) \leq & \sum_{\varphi=1}^{o}\int_{\Omega}\zeta_{\varphi}(\mathfrak{t},\wp)^{C}D^{\lambda}\zeta_{\varphi}(\mathfrak{t},\wp)d\wp+\sum_{\varpi=1}^{n}\int_{\Omega}\bar{\bar{\xi}}_{\varpi}(\mathfrak{t},\wp)^{C}D^{\lambda}\bar{\bar{\xi}}_{\varpi}(\mathfrak{t},\wp)d\wp \\
= & \sum_{\varphi=1}^{o}\int_{\Omega}\zeta_{\varphi}(\mathfrak{t},\wp)\Bigg(\sum_{k=1}^{q}\frac{\partial}{\partial\zeta_k}(m_{\varphi k}\frac{\partial\xi_{\varphi}(\mathfrak{t},\wp)}{\partial\wp_k})-d_{\varphi}\xi_{\varphi}(\mathfrak{t},\wp) \\
& +[\sum_{\varpi=1}^{n}c_{\varphi\varpi}f_{\varpi}(\bar{\Im}_{\varpi}(\mathfrak{t},\wp))-\sum_{\varpi=1}^{n}c_{\varphi\varpi}f_{\varpi}(\Im_{\varpi}(\mathfrak{t},\wp))] \\
& +[\sum_{\varpi=1}^{n}a_{\varphi\varpi}f_{\varpi}(\bar{\Im}_{\varpi}(\mathfrak{t}-\tau,\wp))-\sum_{\varpi=1}^{n}a_{\varphi\varpi}f_{\varpi}(\Im_{\varpi}(\mathfrak{t}-\tau,\wp))] \\
& +[\bigwedge_{\varpi=1}^{n}u_{\varphi\varpi}\int_0^{\infty}k_{\varphi\varpi}(s)f_{\varpi}(\bar{\Im}_{\varpi}(s-\tau,\wp))ds \\
& -\bigwedge_{\varpi=1}^{n}u_{\varphi\varpi}\int_0^{\infty}k_{\varphi\varpi}(s)f_{\varpi}(\Im_{\varpi}(s-\tau,\wp))ds] \\
& +[\bigvee_{\varpi=1}^{n}v_{\varphi\varpi}\int_0^{\infty}k_{\varphi\varpi}(s)f_{\varpi}(\bar{\Im}_{\varpi}(s-\tau,\wp))ds \\
& -\bigvee_{\varpi=1}^{n}v_{\varphi\varpi}\int_0^{\infty}k_{\varphi\varpi}(s)f_{\varpi}(\Im_{\varpi}(s-\tau,\wp))ds] \\
& -\mathfrak{t}_{\varphi}\xi_{\varphi}(\mathfrak{t},\wp)-\Psi_{\varphi}\xi_{\varphi}(\mathfrak{t},\wp)\Bigg)d\wp \\
& +\sum_{\varpi=1}^{n}\int_{\Omega}\bar{\bar{\xi}}_{\varpi}(\mathfrak{t},\wp)\Bigg(\sum_{k=1}^{q}\frac{\partial}{\partial\Im_k}(\tilde{m}_{\varpi k}\frac{\partial\bar{\bar{\xi}}_{\varpi}(\mathfrak{t},\wp)}{\partial\wp_k})-\tilde{d}_{\varpi}\bar{\bar{\xi}}_{\varpi}(\mathfrak{t},\wp) \\
& +[\sum_{\varphi=1}^{o}\tilde{c}_{\varpi\varphi}g_{\varphi}(\bar{\zeta}_{\varphi}(\mathfrak{t},\wp))-\sum_{\varphi=1}^{o}\tilde{c}_{\varpi\varphi}g_{\varphi}(\zeta_{\varphi}(\mathfrak{t},\wp))] \\
& +\Bigg[\sum_{\varphi=1}^{o}\tilde{a}_{\varpi\varphi}g_{\varphi}(\bar{\zeta}_{\varphi}(\mathfrak{t}-\tau,\wp))-\sum_{\varphi=1}^{o}\tilde{a}_{\varpi\varphi}g_{\varphi}(\zeta_{\varphi}(\mathfrak{t}-\tau,\wp))] \\
& +[\bigwedge_{\varphi=1}^{o}\tilde{u}_{\varpi\varphi}\int_0^{\infty}k_{\varpi\varphi}(s)g_{\varphi}(\bar{\zeta}_{\varphi}(s-\tau,\wp))ds \\
& -\bigwedge_{\varphi=1}^{o}\tilde{u}_{\varpi\varphi}\int_0^{\infty}k_{\varpi\varphi}(s)g_{\varphi}(\zeta_{\varphi}(s-\tau,\wp))ds] \\
& +[\bigvee_{\varphi=1}^{o}\tilde{v}_{\varpi\varphi}\int_0^{\infty}k_{\varpi\varphi}(s)g_{\varphi}(\bar{\zeta}_{\varphi}(s-\tau,\wp))ds \\
& -\bigvee_{\varphi=1}^{o}\tilde{v}_{\varpi\varphi}\int_0^{\infty}k_{\varpi\varphi}(s)g_{\varphi}(\zeta_{\varphi}(s-\tau,\wp))ds] \\
& -\varpi_{\varpi}\bar{\bar{\xi}}_{\varpi}(\mathfrak{t},\wp)-\varrho_{\varpi}\bar{\bar{\xi}}_{\varpi}(\mathfrak{t},\wp)\Bigg)d\wp.
\end{aligned}
$$

By Green's formula using the boundary conditions, we obtain

$$
\sum_{k=1}^{q}\int_{\Omega}\zeta_{\varphi}(\mathfrak{t},\wp)\frac{\partial}{\partial\wp_k}\left(m_{\varphi k}\frac{\partial\xi_{\varphi}(\mathfrak{t},\wp)}{\partial\wp_k}\right)d\wp=-\sum_{k=1}^{q}\int_{\Omega}m_{\varphi k}\left(\frac{\partial\xi_{\varphi}(\mathfrak{t},\wp)}{\partial\wp_k}\right)^2d\wp,
$$

$$\sum_{k=1}^{q}\int_{\Omega}\bar{\xi}_{\varpi}(\mathrm{t},\wp)\frac{\partial}{\partial\wp_k}\left(\tilde{m}_{\varpi k}\frac{\partial\bar{\xi}_{\varpi}(\mathrm{t},\wp)}{\partial\wp_k}\right)d\wp=-\sum_{k=1}^{q}\int_{\Omega}\tilde{m}_{\varpi k}\left(\frac{\partial\bar{\xi}_{\varpi}(\mathrm{t},\wp)}{\partial\wp_k}\right)^2 d\wp.$$

From the above identities and Lemma 6, we obtain

$$\begin{aligned}\sum_{k=1}^{q}\int_{\Omega}\xi_{\varphi}(\mathrm{t},\wp)\frac{\partial}{\partial\wp_k}\left(m_{\varphi k}\frac{\partial\xi_{\varphi}(\mathrm{t},\wp)}{\partial\wp_k}\right)d\wp&=-\sum_{k=1}^{q}\int_{\Omega}m_{\varphi k}\left(\frac{\partial\xi_{\varphi}(\mathrm{t},\wp)}{\partial\wp_k}\right)^2 d\wp\\&\leq-\sum_{k=1}^{q}\int_{\Omega}\frac{m_{\varphi k}}{l_k^2}\xi_{\varphi}^2(\mathrm{t},\wp)d\wp=-\bar{M}_{\varphi}\int_{\Omega}\xi_{\varphi}^2(\mathrm{t},\wp)d\wp.\end{aligned}$$

Similarly,

$$\begin{aligned}\sum_{k=1}^{q}\int_{\Omega}\bar{\xi}_{\varpi}(\mathrm{t},\wp)\frac{\partial}{\partial\wp_k}\left(\tilde{m}_{\varpi k}\frac{\partial\bar{\xi}_{\varpi}(\mathrm{t},\wp)}{\partial\wp_k}\right)d\wp&=-\sum_{k=1}^{q}\int_{\Omega}\tilde{m}_{\varpi k}\left(\frac{\partial\bar{\xi}_{\varpi}(\mathrm{t},\wp)}{\partial\wp_k}\right)^2 d\wp\\&\leq-\sum_{k=1}^{q}\int_{\Omega}\frac{\tilde{m}_{\varpi k}}{l_k^2}\bar{\xi}_{\varpi}^2(\mathrm{t},\wp)d\wp=-\tilde{\bar{M}}_{\varpi}\int_{\Omega}\bar{\xi}_{\varpi}^2(\mathrm{t},\wp)d\wp.\end{aligned}$$

Then, using Assumptions 1 and 2, we obtain

$$\begin{aligned}D^{\lambda}V(\mathrm{t})\leq\int_{\Omega}\Bigg\{&-\sum_{\varphi=1}^{o}\bar{M}_{\varphi}\xi_{\varphi}^2(\mathrm{t},\wp)-\sum_{\varphi=1}^{o}d_{\varphi}\xi_{\varphi}^2(\mathrm{t},\wp)+\sum_{\varphi=1}^{o}\sum_{\varpi=1}^{n}|c_{\varphi\varpi}|F_{\varpi}|\xi_{\varphi}(\mathrm{t},\wp)||\bar{\xi}_{\varpi}(\mathrm{t},\wp)|\\&+\sum_{\varphi=1}^{o}\sum_{\varpi=1}^{n}|a_{\varphi\varpi}|F_{\varpi}|\xi_{\varphi}(\mathrm{t},\wp)||\bar{\xi}_{\varpi}(\mathrm{t}-\tau,\wp)|\\&+\sum_{\varphi=1}^{o}\sum_{\varpi=1}^{n}|u_{\varphi\varpi}|\int_0^{\infty}k_{\varphi\varpi}(s)F_{\varpi}|\xi_{\varphi}(s,\wp)||\bar{\xi}_{\varpi}(s-\tau,\wp)|ds\\&+\sum_{\varphi=1}^{o}\sum_{\varpi=1}^{n}|v_{\varphi\varpi}|\int_0^{\infty}k_{\varphi\varpi}(s)F_{\varpi}|\xi_{\varphi}(s,\wp)||\bar{\xi}_{\varpi}(s-\tau,\wp)|ds-\sum_{\varphi=1}^{o}\mathrm{t}_{\varphi}\xi_{\varphi}^2(t,\wp)\\&-\sum_{\varphi=1}^{o}\Psi_{\varphi}\xi_{\varphi}^2(\mathrm{t},\wp)-\sum_{\varpi=1}^{n}\tilde{\bar{M}}_{\varpi}\bar{\xi}_{\varpi}^2(\mathrm{t},\wp)-\sum_{\varpi=1}^{n}\tilde{d}_{\varpi}\bar{\xi}_{\varpi}^2(\mathrm{t},\wp)\\&+\sum_{\varpi=1}^{n}\sum_{\varphi=1}^{o}|\tilde{c}_{\varpi\varphi}|G_{\varphi}|\bar{\xi}_{\varpi}(\mathrm{t},\wp)||\xi_{\varphi}(\mathrm{t},\wp)|\\&+\sum_{\varpi=1}^{n}\sum_{\varphi=1}^{o}|\tilde{a}_{\varpi\varphi}|G_{\varphi}|\bar{\xi}_{\varpi}(\mathrm{t},\wp)||\xi_{\varphi}(\mathrm{t}-\tau,\wp)|\\&+\sum_{\varpi=1}^{n}\sum_{\varphi=1}^{o}|\tilde{u}_{\varpi\varphi}|\int_0^{\infty}k_{\varpi\varphi}(s)G_{\varphi}\bar{\xi}_{\varpi}(s,\wp)||\xi_{\varphi}(s-\tau,\wp)|ds\\&+\sum_{\varpi=1}^{n}\sum_{\varphi=1}^{o}|\tilde{v}_{\varpi\varphi}|\int_0^{\infty}k_{\varpi\varphi}(s)G_{\varphi}\bar{\xi}_{\varpi}(s,\wp)|\xi_{\varphi}(s-\tau,\wp)|ds\\&-\sum_{\varphi=1}^{o}\varpi_{\varpi}\bar{\xi}_{\varphi}^2(\mathrm{t},\wp)-\sum_{\varphi=1}^{o}\varrho_{\varpi}\bar{\xi}_{\varphi}^2(\mathrm{t},\wp)\Bigg\}d\wp.\end{aligned}$$

Lemma 5 implies the existence of a constant $\rho>0$ such that

$$
\begin{aligned}
D^{\lambda}V(t) \leq \int_{\Omega}\Bigg\{ & -\sum_{\varphi=1}^{o}\bar{M}_{\varphi}\xi_{\varphi}^{2}(t,\wp)-\sum_{\varphi=1}^{o}d_{\varphi}\xi_{\varphi}^{2}(t,\wp)+\sum_{\varphi=1}^{o}\sum_{\varpi=1}^{n}|c_{\varphi\varpi}|F_{\varpi}[\frac{\rho^{-1}}{2}\xi_{\varphi}^{2}(t,\wp)+\frac{\rho}{2}\bar{\xi}_{\varpi}^{2}(t,\wp)] \\
& +\sum_{\varphi=1}^{o}\sum_{\varpi=1}^{n}|a_{\varphi\varpi}|F_{\varpi}[\frac{\rho^{-1}}{2}\xi_{\varphi}^{2}(t,\wp)+\frac{\rho}{2}\bar{\xi}_{\varpi}^{2}(t-\tau,\wp)] \\
& +\sum_{\varphi=1}^{o}\sum_{\varpi=1}^{n}|u_{\varphi\varpi}|\int_{0}^{\infty}k_{\varphi\varpi}(s)F_{\varpi}[\frac{\rho^{-1}}{2}\xi_{\varphi}^{2}(s,\wp)+\frac{\rho}{2}\bar{\xi}_{\varpi}^{2}(s-\tau,\wp)]ds \\
& +\sum_{\varphi=1}^{o}\sum_{\varpi=1}^{n}|v_{\varphi\varpi}|\int_{0}^{\infty}k_{\varphi\varpi}(s)F_{\varpi}[\frac{\rho^{-1}}{2}\xi_{\varphi}^{2}(s,\wp)+\frac{\rho}{2}\bar{\xi}_{\varpi}^{2}(s-\tau,\wp)]ds \\
& -\sum_{\varphi=1}^{o}t_{\varphi}\xi_{\varphi}^{2}(t,\wp)-\sum_{\varphi=1}^{o}\Psi_{\varphi}\xi_{\varphi}^{2}(t,\wp) \\
& -\sum_{\varpi=1}^{n}\bar{\tilde{M}}_{\varpi}\bar{\xi}_{\varpi}^{2}(t,\wp)-\sum_{\varpi=1}^{n}\tilde{d}_{\varpi}\bar{\xi}_{\varpi}^{2}(t,\wp)+\sum_{\varpi=1}^{n}\sum_{\varphi=1}^{o}|\tilde{c}_{\varpi\varphi}|G_{\varphi}[\frac{\rho^{-1}}{2}\bar{\xi}_{\varpi}^{2}(t,\wp)+\frac{\rho}{2}\xi_{\varphi}^{2}(t,\wp)] \\
& +\sum_{\varpi=1}^{n}\sum_{\varphi=1}^{o}|\tilde{a}_{\varpi\varphi}|G_{\varphi}[\frac{\rho^{-1}}{2}\bar{\xi}_{\varpi}^{2}(t,\wp)+\frac{\rho}{2}\xi_{\varphi}^{2}(t-\tau,\wp)] \\
& +\sum_{\varpi=1}^{n}\sum_{\varphi=1}^{o}|\tilde{u}_{\varpi\varphi}|\int_{0}^{\infty}k_{\varpi\varphi}(s)G_{\varphi}[\frac{\rho^{-1}}{2}\bar{\xi}_{\varpi}^{2}(s,\wp)+\frac{\rho}{2}\xi_{\varphi}^{2}(s-\tau,\wp)]ds \\
& +\sum_{\varpi=1}^{n}\sum_{\varphi=1}^{o}|\tilde{v}_{\varpi\varphi}|\int_{0}^{\infty}k_{\varpi\varphi}(s)G_{\varphi}[\frac{\rho^{-1}}{2}\bar{\xi}_{\varpi}^{2}(s,\wp)+\frac{\rho}{2}\xi_{\varphi}^{2}(s-\tau,\wp)]ds \\
& -\sum_{\varpi=1}^{n}\varpi_{\varpi}\bar{\xi}_{\varphi}^{2}(t,\wp)-\sum_{\varpi=1}^{n}\varrho_{\varpi}\bar{\xi}_{\varphi}^{2}(t,\wp)\Bigg\}.
\end{aligned}
$$

We apply Assumption 3 to obtain

$$
\begin{aligned}
D^{\lambda}V(t) \leq \int_{\Omega}\xi_{\varphi}^{2}(t,\wp)\Bigg\{ & -\sum_{\varphi=1}^{o}\tilde{M}_{\varphi}-\sum_{\varphi=1}^{o}d_{\varphi}+\sum_{\varphi=1}^{o}\sum_{\varpi=1}^{n}|c_{\varphi\varpi}|F_{\varpi}\frac{\rho^{-1}}{2}+\sum_{\varphi=1}^{o}\sum_{\varpi=1}^{n}|a_{\varphi\varpi}|F_{\varpi}\frac{\rho^{-1}}{2} \\
& +\sum_{\varphi=1}^{o}\sum_{\varpi=1}^{n}|u_{\varphi\varpi}|F_{\varpi}\frac{\rho^{-1}}{2}+\sum_{\varphi=1}^{o}\sum_{\varpi=1}^{n}|v_{\varphi\varpi}|F_{\varpi}\frac{\rho^{-1}}{2}-\sum_{\varphi=1}^{o}t_{\varphi}-\sum_{\varphi=1}^{o}\Psi_{\varphi}+\sum_{\varpi=1}^{n}\sum_{\varphi=1}^{o}|\tilde{c}_{\varpi\varphi}|G_{\varphi}\frac{\rho}{2}\Bigg\} \\
& +\max_{-\infty<\mathfrak{s}\leq 0}\xi_{\varphi}^{2}(\mathfrak{s},\wp)\Bigg\{\sum_{\varpi=1}^{n}\sum_{\varphi=1}^{o}|\tilde{a}_{\varpi\varphi}|G_{\varphi}\frac{\rho}{2}+\sum_{\varpi=1}^{n}\sum_{\varphi=1}^{o}|\tilde{v}_{\varpi\varphi}|G_{\varphi}\frac{\rho}{2}+\sum_{\varpi=1}^{n}\sum_{\varphi=1}^{o}|\tilde{u}_{\varpi\varphi}|G_{\varphi}\frac{\rho}{2}\Bigg\} \\
& +\bar{\xi}_{\varpi}^{2}(t,\wp)\Bigg\{-\sum_{\varpi=1}^{n}\bar{\tilde{M}}_{\varpi}-\sum_{\varpi=1}^{n}\tilde{d}_{\varpi}+\sum_{\varpi=1}^{n}\sum_{\varphi=1}^{o}|\tilde{c}_{\varpi\varphi}|G_{\varphi}\frac{\rho^{-1}}{2}+\sum_{\varpi=1}^{n}\sum_{\varphi=1}^{o}|\tilde{a}_{\varpi\varphi}|G_{\varphi}\frac{\rho^{-1}}{2} \\
& +\sum_{\varpi=1}^{n}\sum_{\varphi=1}^{o}|\tilde{u}_{\varpi\varphi}|G_{\varphi}\frac{\rho^{-1}}{2}+\sum_{\varpi=1}^{n}\sum_{\varphi=1}^{o}|\tilde{v}_{\varpi\varphi}|G_{\varphi}\frac{\rho^{-1}}{2}-\sum_{\varpi=1}^{n}\varpi_{\varpi}-\sum_{\varpi=1}^{n}\varrho_{\varpi} \\
& +\sum_{\varphi=1}^{o}\sum_{\varpi=1}^{n}|\tilde{c}_{\varphi\varpi}|G_{\varphi}\frac{\rho}{2}\Bigg\}+\max_{-\infty<\mathfrak{s}\leq 0}\bar{\xi}_{\varpi}^{2}(\mathfrak{s},\wp)\Bigg\{\sum_{\varphi=1}^{o}\sum_{\varpi=1}^{n}|u_{\varphi\varpi}|F_{\varphi}\frac{\rho}{2} \\
& +\sum_{\varphi=1}^{o}\sum_{\varpi=1}^{n}|v_{\varphi\varpi}|F_{\varphi}\frac{\rho}{2}+\sum_{\varphi=1}^{o}\sum_{\varpi=1}^{n}|a_{\varphi\varpi}|F_{\varphi}\frac{\rho}{2}\Bigg\}d\wp,
\end{aligned}
$$

or

$$D^{\lambda}V(\mathrm{t}) \leq \int_{\Omega}\Big\{-\mu_{\min}^{(1)}\sum_{\varphi=1}^{o}\xi_{\varphi}^{2}(\mathrm{t},\wp)-\mu_{\min}^{(2)}\sum_{\varpi=1}^{n}\bar{\xi}_{\varpi}^{2}(\mathrm{t},\wp)+\Omega_{\max}^{(1)}\sum_{\varphi=1}^{n}\max_{-\infty<\mathfrak{s}\leq 0}\xi_{\varphi}^{2}(\mathfrak{s},\wp)$$
$$+\Omega_{\max}^{(2)}\sum_{\varphi=1}^{n}\max_{-\infty<\mathfrak{s}\leq 0}\bar{\xi}_{\varpi}^{2}(\mathfrak{s},\wp)\Big\}d\wp \leq -\mu V(t)+\Lambda\max_{-\infty<\mathfrak{s}\leq 0}V(\mathfrak{s}),$$

where $\mu=\min\{\mu_{\min}^{(1)},\mu_{\min}^{(2)}\}$, and $\Lambda=\max\{\Lambda_{1}^{\mu},\Lambda_{2}^{\mu}\}$.

By Lemma 3, since $\mu>\sqrt{2}\Lambda$, we have $\lim_{\mathrm{t}\to\infty}V(\mathrm{t})=0$.

For $||\xi(\mathrm{t},\wp)||_{1}+||\bar{\xi}(\mathrm{t},\wp)||_{2}=V(\mathrm{t})$, we can conclude that system (4) is globally asymptotically stable. This means that the drive system (1) and the response system (2) are globally asymptotically synchronized via the state feedback controllers. This completes the proof of the theorem. □

Remark 2. *Different from all existent synchronization results for neural network models, we consider a class of more general structures which include Caputo type fractional derivatives, reaction–diffusion terms, discrete and distributed delays which allow us to divide all nodes in the network into different classes, a BAM two-layer connection, fuzzy logic, and hybrid feedback controllers. Thus, the proposed results in Theorem 1 generalize and complement numerous asymptotic synchronization results. For example, our results generalize the results in [16] to the BAM case considering Caputo's fractional differential operators. Moreover, the results established complement the results in [2] considering Caputo's fractional differential operators and hybrid feedback controllers.*

Remark 3. *The proposed global asymptotic synchronization criteria in Theorem 1 are in the forms of inequalities between the system parameters. This form allows applied researchers to easily apply the established results. The presence of the terms that include $|u_{\varphi\varpi}|$, $|v_{\varphi\varpi}|$, $|\tilde{u}_{\varpi\varphi}|$, and $|\tilde{v}_{\varpi\varphi}|$ in the conditions for $\mu_{\min}^{(1)}$, $\mu_{\min}^{(2)}$, Λ_{1}^{μ}, and Λ_{2}^{μ} reflects the role of the distributed delays with delay kernels which satisfy Assumption 3. Furthermore, the terms $t_{\varphi}+\psi_{\varphi}$ and $\varpi_{\varpi}+\varrho_{\varpi}$ reflect the design of the controllers.*

Remark 4. *Without feedback controllers, the error system (4) becomes*

$$\begin{aligned}
\frac{\partial^{\lambda}\xi_{\varphi}(\mathrm{t},\wp)}{\partial \mathrm{t}^{\lambda}} = & \sum_{k=1}^{q}\frac{\partial}{\partial\wp_{k}}\Big(m_{\varphi k}\frac{\partial\xi_{\varphi}(\mathrm{t},\wp)}{\partial\wp_{k}}\Big)-d_{\varphi}\xi_{\varphi}(\mathrm{t},\wp)\\
&+\Big[\sum_{\varpi=1}^{n}c_{\varphi\varpi}f_{\varpi}(\bar{\Im}_{\varpi}(\mathrm{t},\wp))-\sum_{\varpi=1}^{n}c_{\varphi\varpi}f_{\varpi}(\Im_{\varpi}(\mathrm{t},\wp))\Big]\\
&+\Big[\sum_{\varpi=1}^{n}a_{\varphi\varpi}f_{\varpi}(\bar{\Im}_{\varpi}(\mathrm{t}-\tau,\wp))-\sum_{\varpi=1}^{n}a_{\varphi\varpi}f_{\varpi}(\Im_{\varpi}(t-\tau,\wp))\Big]\\
&+\Big[\bigwedge_{\varpi=1}^{n}u_{\varphi\varpi}\int_{0}^{\infty}k_{\varphi\varpi}(s)f_{\varpi}(\bar{\Im}_{\varpi}(s-\tau,\wp))ds\\
&-\bigwedge_{\varpi=1}^{n}u_{\varphi\varpi}\int_{0}^{\infty}k_{\varphi\varpi}(s)f_{\varpi}(\Im_{\varpi}(s-\tau,\wp))ds\Big]\\
&+\Big[\bigvee_{\varpi=1}^{n}v_{\varphi\varpi}\int_{0}^{\infty}k_{\varphi\varpi}(s)f_{\varpi}(\bar{\Im}_{\varpi}(s-\tau,\wp))ds\\
&-\bigvee_{\varpi=1}^{n}v_{\varphi\varpi}\int_{0}^{\infty}k_{\varphi\varpi}(s)f_{\varpi}(\Im_{\varpi}(s-\tau,\wp))ds\Big],\varphi=1,2,\ldots,o,
\end{aligned}$$

$$\begin{aligned}\frac{\partial^{\lambda}\bar{\xi}_{\varpi}(t,\wp)}{\partial t^{\lambda}} &= \sum_{k=1}^{q}\frac{\partial}{\partial\wp_k}(\tilde{m}_{\varpi k}\frac{\partial\bar{\xi}_{\varpi}(t,\wp)}{\partial\wp_k}) - \tilde{d}_{\varpi}\bar{\xi}_{\varpi}(t,\wp) \\ &+ [\sum_{\varphi=1}^{o}\tilde{c}_{\varpi\varphi}g_{\varphi}(\bar{\zeta}_{\varphi}(t,\wp)) - \sum_{\varphi=1}^{o}\tilde{c}_{\varpi\varphi}g_{\varphi}(\zeta_{\varphi}(t,\wp))] \\ &+ [\sum_{\varphi=1}^{o}\tilde{a}_{\varpi\varphi}g_{\varphi}(\bar{\zeta}_{\varphi}(t-\tau,\wp)) - \sum_{\varphi=1}^{o}\tilde{a}_{\varpi\varphi}g_{\varphi}(\zeta_{\varphi}(t-\tau,\wp))] \\ &+ [\bigwedge_{\varphi=1}^{o}\tilde{u}_{\varpi\varphi}\int_0^{\infty}k_{\varpi\varphi}(s)g_{\varphi}(\bar{\zeta}_{\varphi}(s-\tau,\wp))ds \\ &- \bigwedge_{\varphi=1}^{o}\tilde{u}_{\varpi\varphi}\int_0^{\infty}k_{\varpi\varphi}(s)g_{\varphi}(\bar{\zeta}_{\varphi}(s-\tau,\wp))ds] \\ &+ [\bigvee_{\varphi=1}^{o}\tilde{v}_{\varpi\varphi}\int_0^{\infty}k_{\varpi\varphi}(s)g_{\varphi}(\bar{\zeta}_{\varphi}(s-\tau,\wp))ds \\ &- \bigvee_{\varphi=1}^{o}\tilde{v}_{\varpi\varphi}\int_0^{\infty}k_{\varpi\varphi}(s)g_{\varphi}(\zeta_{\varphi}(s-\tau,\wp))ds], \varpi = 1,2,\ldots,n. \end{aligned} \tag{8}$$

Theorem 2. *Suppose that Assumptions 1–3, $\tau < 1$, and conditions of Lemma 6 hold. The error system (8) is globally asymptotically stable, if there exist constants*

$$\begin{aligned}\Theta_1 &= \min_{1\le\varphi\le o}\left\{(\tilde{M}_{\varphi}+d_{\varphi}) - \sum_{\varpi=1}^{n}|\tilde{c}_{\varpi\varphi}|G_{\varphi}\right\} > 0, \\ \Theta_2 &= \min_{1\le\varphi\le o}\left\{(\tilde{\bar{M}}_{\varpi}+\tilde{d}_{\varpi}) - \sum_{\varphi=1}^{o}|c_{\varphi\varpi}|F_{\varpi}\right\} > 0, \\ \Lambda_1^{\theta} &= \left\{\sum_{\varpi=1}^{n}\sum_{\varphi=1}^{o}|\tilde{a}_{\varpi\varphi}|G_{\varphi} + \sum_{\varpi=1}^{n}\sum_{\varphi=1}^{o}|\tilde{u}_{\varpi\varphi}|G_{\varphi} + \sum_{\varpi=1}^{n}\sum_{\varphi=1}^{o}|\tilde{v}_{\varpi\varphi}|G_{\varphi}\right\} > 0, \\ \Lambda_2^{\theta} &= \left\{\sum_{\varphi=1}^{o}\sum_{\varpi=1}^{n}|a_{\varphi\varpi}|F_{\varpi} + \sum_{\varphi=1}^{o}\sum_{\varpi=1}^{n}|u_{\varpi\varphi}|F_{\varpi} + \sum_{\varphi=1}^{o}\sum_{\varpi=1}^{n}|v_{\varpi\varphi}|F_{\varpi}\right\} > 0,\end{aligned}$$

such that

$$\min\{\Theta_1,\Theta_2\} > \max\left\{\Lambda_1^{\theta},\Lambda_2^{\theta}\right\}.$$

Proof. We define a Lyapunov function as

$$\begin{aligned}V(t) &= \int_{\Omega}D^{-(1-\lambda)}\left[\sum_{\varphi=1}^{o}|\zeta_{\varphi}(t,\wp)| + \sum_{\varpi=1}^{n}|\bar{\xi}_{\varpi}(t,\wp)|\right]d\wp + \int_{\Omega}\sum_{\varphi=1}^{o}\int_{t-\tau}^{t}|\zeta_{\varphi}(s,\wp)|dsd\wp \\ &+ \int_{\Omega}\sum_{\varpi=1}^{n}\int_{t-\tau}^{t}|\bar{\xi}_{\varpi}(s,\wp)|dsd\wp.\end{aligned} \tag{9}$$

Taking the time derivative of (9), we obtain

$$\begin{aligned}\frac{dV(t)}{dt} &= \int_{\Omega}D^{\lambda}\left[\sum_{\varphi=1}^{o}|\zeta_{\varphi}(t,\wp)| + \sum_{\varpi=1}^{n}|\bar{\xi}_{\varpi}(t,\wp)|\right]d\wp + \int_{\Omega}\sum_{\varphi=1}^{o}|\zeta_{\varphi}(t,\wp)|d\wp - \int_{\Omega}\sum_{\varphi=1}^{o}|\zeta_{\varphi}(t-\tau,\wp)|d\wp \\ &+ \int_{\Omega}\sum_{\varpi=1}^{n}|\bar{\xi}_{\varpi}(t,\wp)|d\wp - \int_{\Omega}\sum_{\varpi=1}^{n}|\bar{\xi}_{\varpi}(t-\tau_1(t),\wp)|d\wp.\end{aligned}$$

The rest of the proof is similar to the proof of Theorem 1. Instead of Lemma 3, the fractional Barbalat's Lemma is used. □

4. Global Mittag–Leffler Synchronization

For fractional-order systems, the concept of Mittag–Leffler stability was introduced in [23]. This notion generalizes the exponential stability notion for integer-order systems and has been investigated intensively [23–29,34,44]. In this section, we establish criteria for the global Mittag–Leffler stability of the error system (8).

Definition 3. *The error system (8) is said to be globally Mittag–Leffler stable, if for any continuous initial functions ϕ, $(\phi_1, \phi_2, \dots, \phi_o)^T$ and $\tilde{\phi}$, $(\tilde{\phi}_1, \tilde{\phi}_2, \dots, \tilde{\phi}_n)^T$, there exist positive constants δ and q such that*

$$||\xi(t,\wp)||_1 + ||\bar{\xi}(t,\wp)||_2 \leq \left\{M(||\phi||^1_\infty + ||\tilde{\phi}||^2_\infty)E_\lambda(-\delta t^\lambda)\right\}^q$$

for $t \geq 0$, where E_λ is the corresponding Mittag–Leffler function, $||\phi||^1_\infty = \max_{\mathfrak{s}\in(-\infty,0]} ||\phi(\mathfrak{s})||_1$, $||\tilde{\phi}||^2_\infty = \max_{\mathfrak{s}\in(-\infty,0]} ||\tilde{\phi}(\mathfrak{s})||_2$, $M(0) = 0$, $M \geq 0$, and M is Lipschitz with respect to its argument.

The global Mittag–Lefler stability of the error system (8) is equivalent to the global Mittag–Leffler synchronization of the master and response systems.

Theorem 3. *Suppose that Assumptions 1–3 and the conditions of Lemma 6 hold. The error system (8) is globally Mittag–Leffler stable if there exist constants $\rho > 0$ and*

$$\begin{aligned}
\nu^{(1)}_{\min} = \min_{1\leq\varphi\leq o} \Bigg\{ & 2\tilde{M}_\varphi + 2d_\varphi - \sum_{\varpi=1}^{n} |c_{\varphi\varpi}|F_\varpi \rho^{-1} - \sum_{\varpi=1}^{n} |a_{\varphi\varpi}|F_\varpi \rho^{-1} \\
& - \sum_{\varpi=1}^{n} |u_{\varphi\varpi}|F_\varpi \rho^{-1} - \sum_{\varpi=1}^{n} |v_{\varphi\varpi}|F_\varpi \rho^{-1} - \sum_{\varpi=1}^{n} |c_{\varphi\varpi}|F_\varpi \rho \Bigg\} > 0, \\
\nu^{(2)}_{\min} = \min_{1\leq\varpi\leq n} \Bigg\{ & 2\tilde{\bar{M}}_\varpi + 2\tilde{d}_\varpi - \sum_{\varphi=1}^{o} |\tilde{c}_{\varpi\varphi}|G_\varphi \rho^{-1} - \sum_{\varphi=1}^{o} |\tilde{a}_{\varpi\varphi}|G_\varphi \rho^{-1} - \sum_{\varphi=1}^{o} |\tilde{u}_{\varpi\varphi}|G_\varphi \rho^{-1} \\
& - \sum_{\varphi=1}^{o} |\tilde{v}_{\varpi\varphi}|G_\varphi \rho^{-1} - \sum_{\varphi=1}^{o} |\tilde{c}_{\varpi\varphi}|G_\varphi \rho \Bigg\} > 0, \\
\Lambda^\nu_1 = \max_{1\leq\varphi\leq o} & \left\{ \sum_{\varpi=1}^{n} |\tilde{u}_{\varpi\varphi}|G_\varphi \rho + \sum_{\varpi=1}^{n} |\tilde{v}_{\varpi\varphi}|G_\varphi \rho + \sum_{\varpi=1}^{n} |\tilde{a}_{\varpi\varphi}|G_\varphi \rho \right\} > 0, \\
\Lambda^\nu_2 = \max_{1\leq\varpi\leq n} & \left\{ \sum_{\varphi=1}^{o} |u_{\varphi\varpi}|F_\varpi \rho + \sum_{\varphi=1}^{o} |v_{\varphi\varpi}|F_\varpi \rho + \sum_{\varphi=1}^{o} |a_{\varphi\varpi}|F_\varpi \rho \right\} > 0,
\end{aligned}$$

such that

$$\min\left\{\nu^{(1)}_{\min}, \nu^{(2)}_{\min}\right\} \geq \max\{\Lambda^\nu_1, \Lambda^\nu_2\}.$$

Proof. We define again a Lyapunov function as

$$V(t) = \int_\Omega \sum_{\varphi=1}^{o} \frac{1}{2}\bar{\xi}^2_\varphi(t,\wp)d\wp + \int_\Omega \sum_{\varpi=1}^{n} \frac{1}{2}\bar{\xi}^2_\varpi(t,\wp)d\wp. \tag{10}$$

Applying the same technique and steps as in the proof of Theorem 1, we obtain

$$D^\lambda V(t) \leq -\nu V(t) + \Lambda \max_{-\infty<\mathfrak{s}\leq 0} V(\mathfrak{s}),$$

where $\nu = \min\left\{\nu^{(1)}_{\min}, \nu^{(2)}_{\min}\right\}$ and $\Lambda = \max\left\{\Lambda^\mu_1, \Lambda^\mu_2\right\}$.

We apply the Razumikhin condition

$$V(\mathfrak{s}) \leq V(\mathrm{t}),\ -\infty < \mathfrak{s} \leq \mathrm{t} \tag{11}$$

to the above inequality to obtain

$$D^{\lambda}V(\mathrm{t}) \leq -(\nu - \Lambda)V(\mathrm{t}).$$

Since $\nu \geq \Lambda$, there exists a positive constant δ, such that

$$D^{\lambda}V(\mathrm{t}) \leq -\delta V(\mathrm{t}).$$

Then, by Lemma 2, we have

$$V(\mathrm{t}) \leq \max_{-\infty<\mathfrak{s}\leq 0} V(\mathfrak{s})E_{\lambda}(-\delta t^{\lambda}),\ \mathrm{t} > 0.$$

Therefore,

$$||\xi(\mathrm{t},\wp)||_1 + ||\bar{\xi}(\mathrm{t},\wp)||_2 \leq \Big(||\phi||_{\infty}^1 + ||\bar{\phi}||_{\infty}^2\Big)E_{\lambda}(-\delta t^{\lambda}),$$

i.e., according to Definition 3, the error system (8) is globally Mittag–Leffler stable, which means that the master and response systems are globally Mittag–Leffler synchronized. The proof is completed. □

Remark 5. *When the distributed delays and diffusion terms are not considered in model (1), the fractional-order fuzzy BAM neural network is denoted as follows:*

$$\begin{aligned}
\frac{\partial^{\lambda}\zeta_{\varphi}(\mathrm{t})}{\partial \mathrm{t}^{\lambda}} &= -d_{\varphi}\zeta_{\varphi}(\mathrm{t}) + \sum_{\varpi=1}^{n} c_{\varphi\varpi}f_{\varpi}(\Im_{\varpi}(\mathrm{t})) \\
&\quad + \sum_{\varpi=1}^{n} a_{\varphi\varpi}f_{\varpi}(\Im_{\varpi}(\mathrm{t}-\tau)) + I_{\varphi},\ \varphi = 1,2,\ldots,o, \\
\frac{\partial^{\lambda}\Im_{\varpi}(\mathrm{t})}{\partial \mathrm{t}^{\lambda}} &= -\tilde{d}_{\varpi}\Im_{\varpi}(\mathrm{t}) + \sum_{\varphi=1}^{o} \tilde{c}_{\varpi\varphi}g_{\varphi}(\zeta_{\varphi}(\mathrm{t})) \\
&\quad + \sum_{\varphi=1}^{o} \tilde{a}_{\varpi\varphi}g_{\varphi}(\zeta_{\varphi}(\mathrm{t}-\tau)) + J_{\varpi},\ \varpi = 1,2,\ldots,n.
\end{aligned} \tag{12}$$

Under the assumption that the activation functions f_{ϖ} and g_{φ} are bounded, the above neural network system (12) has an equilibrium point $(\zeta^*,\Im^*)^T$. Let $\check{\zeta}(\mathrm{t}) = \zeta(\mathrm{t}) - \zeta^*$, $\check{\Im}(\mathrm{t}) = \Im(\mathrm{t}) - \Im^*$. Then, we can apply the established results for system (4) to the following system

$$\begin{aligned}
\frac{\partial^{\lambda}\check{\zeta}_{\varphi}(\mathrm{t})}{\partial \mathrm{t}^{\lambda}} &= -d_{\varphi}\check{\zeta}_{\varphi}(\mathrm{t}) + \sum_{\varpi=1}^{n} c_{\varphi\varpi}f_{\varpi}(\check{\Im}_{\varpi}(\mathrm{t})) \\
&\quad + \sum_{\varpi=1}^{n} a_{\varphi\varpi}f_{\varpi}(\check{\Im}_{\varpi}(\mathrm{t}-\tau)),\ \varphi = 1,2,\ldots,o, \\
\frac{\partial^{\lambda}\check{\Im}_{\varpi}(\mathrm{t})}{\partial \mathrm{t}^{\lambda}} &= -\tilde{d}_{\varpi}\check{\Im}_{\varpi}(\mathrm{t}) + \sum_{\varphi=1}^{o} \tilde{c}_{\varpi\varphi}g_{\varphi}(\check{\zeta}_{\varphi}(\mathrm{t})) \\
&\quad + \sum_{\varphi=1}^{o} \tilde{a}_{\varpi\varphi}g_{\varphi}(\check{\zeta}_{\varphi}(\mathrm{t}-\tau)),\ \varpi = 1,2,\ldots,n.
\end{aligned} \tag{13}$$

Theorem 4. *Under Assumption 2, system (13) is globally Mittag–Leffler stable if the activation functions are bounded and $\delta = (\varpi_1^{\theta} - \varpi_2^{\theta}) > 0$, $\varpi_1^{\theta} = \min\{\varpi_1,\varpi_2\}$, $\varpi_2^{\theta} = \max\{\varpi_3,\varpi_4\}$,*

$\varpi_1 = \min_{1\le\varphi\le o}\{[d_\varphi - |\tilde{c}_{\varpi\varphi}|G_\varphi]\}$, $\varpi_2 = \min_{1\le\varphi\le o}\{[\tilde{d}_\varpi - |c_{\varphi\varpi}|F_\varpi|]\}$, $\varpi_3 = \min_{1\le\varphi\le o} \sum_{\varpi=1}^{n} |a_{\varphi\varpi}|F_\varpi$, $\varpi_4 = \max_{1\le\varpi\le n} \sum_{\varphi=1}^{o} |\tilde{a}_{\varpi\varphi}|G_\varphi$.

Proof. We define a Lyapunov function as

$$V(t,\hat{\zeta},\check{\Im}) = \sum_{\varphi=1}^{o} |\hat{\zeta}_\varphi(t)| + \sum_{\varpi=1}^{n} |\check{\Im}_\varpi(t)| \tag{14}$$

For the Caputo derivative along the trajectories of (13) and using Assumption 2, we have

$$\begin{aligned}
D^\lambda V(t,\hat{\zeta},\check{\Im}) &= D^\lambda\left[\sum_{\varphi=1}^{o} |\hat{\zeta}_\varphi(t)| + \sum_{\varpi=1}^{n} |\check{\Im}_\varpi(t)|\right] \\
&\le \left\{\sum_{\varphi=1}^{o}(-d_\varphi|\hat{\zeta}_\varphi(t)| + \sum_{\varpi=1}^{n} |c_{\varphi\varpi}|F_\varpi|\check{\Im}_\varpi(t)|\right. \\
&+ \sum_{\varpi=1}^{n} |a_{\varphi\varpi}|F_\varpi|\check{\Im}_\varpi(t-\tau)| + \sum_{\varpi=1}^{n}(-\tilde{d}_\varpi\check{\Im}_\varpi(t) + \sum_{\varphi=1}^{o} |\tilde{c}_{\varpi\varphi}|G_\varphi|\hat{\zeta}_\varphi(t)| \\
&\left.+ \sum_{\varphi=1}^{o} |\tilde{a}_{\varpi\varphi}|G_\varphi|\hat{\zeta}_\varphi(t-\tau|)\right\} \\
&= -\left\{\sum_{\varphi=1}^{o}[d_\varphi - |\tilde{c}_{\varpi\varphi}|G_\varphi]|\hat{\zeta}_\varphi(t)| - \sum_{\varpi=1}^{n}[\tilde{d}_\varpi - |c_{\varphi\varpi}|F_\varpi|]|\check{\Im}_\varpi(t)|\right. \\
&+ \sum_{\varphi=1}^{o}\sum_{\varpi=1}^{n} |a_{\varphi\varpi}|F_\varpi|\check{\Im}_\varpi(t-\tau)| + \sum_{\varphi=1}^{o} |\tilde{a}_{\varpi\varphi}|G_\varphi|\hat{\zeta}_\varphi(t-\tau)|)\}, \\
&= -\varpi_1\sum_{\varphi=1}^{o} |\hat{\zeta}_\varphi(t)| - \varpi_2\sum_{\varpi=1}^{n} |\check{\Im}_\varpi(t)| + \sum_{\varphi=1}^{o}\sum_{\varpi=1}^{n} \varpi_3|\hat{\zeta}_\varphi(t-\tau)| \\
&\left.+ \sum_{\varphi=1}^{o}\sum_{\varpi=1}^{n} \varpi_4|\check{\Im}_\varpi(t-\tau)|\right\} \\
&\le -\varpi_1^\theta V(t,\hat{\zeta}(t),\check{\Im}_\varpi(t)) + \varpi_2^\theta \sup_{t-\tau\le\mathfrak{s}\le t} V(\mathfrak{s},\hat{\zeta}(\mathfrak{s}),\check{\Im}(\mathfrak{s})).
\end{aligned} \tag{15}$$

We apply the Razumikhin condition,

$$\sup_{t-\tau\le\mathfrak{s}\le t} V(\mathfrak{s},\hat{\zeta}(\mathfrak{s}),\check{\Im}(\mathfrak{s})) \le V(t,\hat{\zeta}(t),\check{\Im}(t)), \tag{16}$$

to (15) and obtain

$$D^\lambda V(t,\hat{\zeta}(t),\check{\Im}(t)) \le -(\varpi_1^\theta - \varpi_2^\theta)V(t,\hat{\zeta}(t),\check{\Im}(t)). \tag{17}$$

We can choose a positive constant $\delta > 0$, such that

$$(\varpi_1^\theta - \varpi_2^\theta) \ge \delta \tag{18}$$

From (17) and (18), we obtain

$$D^\lambda V(t,\hat{\zeta}(t),\check{\Im}(t)) \le -\delta V(t,\hat{\zeta}(t),\check{\Im}(t)). \tag{19}$$

According to Lemma 2,

$$V(t,\hat{\zeta}(t),\check{\Im}(t)) \le \sup_{t-\tau\le\mathfrak{s}\le t} V(o,\hat{\zeta}(\mathfrak{s}),\check{\Im}(\mathfrak{s}))E_\lambda(-\delta t^\lambda). \tag{20}$$

For

$$V(t,\hat{\zeta}(t),\check{\Im}(t)) = ||\zeta(t)-\zeta^*||_1 + ||\Im(t)-\Im^*||_2,$$
$$= \sum_{\varphi=1}^{o} |\zeta_\varphi(t)-\zeta^*| + \sum_{\varpi=1}^{n} |\Im_\varpi(t)-\Im^*|,$$

we have from (20)

$$||\zeta(t)-\zeta^*||_1 + ||\Im(t)-\Im^*||_2 \leq \left(||\phi_\varphi-\zeta^*||_\tau^1 + ||\phi_\varpi-\Im^*||_\tau^2\right)E_\lambda(-\delta t^\lambda), \quad (21)$$

where ϕ_φ and $\tilde{\phi}_\varpi$ are the initial functions that correspond to system (12), and $||\phi||_\tau^1 = \max_{\mathfrak{s}\in-\tau,0]} ||\phi(\mathfrak{s})||_1$, $||\tilde{\phi}||_\tau^2 = \max_{\mathfrak{s}\in[-\tau,0]} ||\tilde{\phi}(\mathfrak{s})||_2$.

Therefore, system (13) is globally Mittag–Leffler stable, i.e., the equilibrium of system (12) is globally Mittag–Leffler stable. The proof is completed. □

Remark 6. *Notice that the results provided by Theorems 3 and 4 are particular cases of the results established in Theorem 1. In addition, it is seen that the Mittag–Leffler stability concept is a particular case of the asymptotic stability notion and generalizes the exponential stability in the fractional-order case.*

5. Numerical Examples

In this section, numerical examples are addressed to demonstrate the usefulness of the proposed results.

Example 1. *For $\varphi = \varpi = 2$, we consider the master system (1) and response system (2) of fuzzy BAM NNs with the following parameters: $\lambda = 0.97, \tau = 0.2$,*

$$D = \tilde{D} = \begin{bmatrix} 1.5 & 0 \\ 0 & 1.5 \end{bmatrix}, c_{\varphi\varpi} = \tilde{c}_{\varpi\varphi} = \begin{bmatrix} 0.2 & -0.1 \\ 0.1 & 0.2 \end{bmatrix}, a_{\varphi\varpi} = \tilde{a}_{\varpi\varphi} = \begin{bmatrix} -0.4 & 0.5 \\ 0.4 & -2.5 \end{bmatrix},$$
$$u_{\varphi\varpi} = \tilde{u}_{\varpi\varphi} = \begin{bmatrix} 0.5 & -0.5 \\ 0.6 & 0.8 \end{bmatrix}, P_{\varphi\varpi} = \tilde{P}_{\varpi\varphi} = \begin{bmatrix} -0.4 & -0.8 \\ 0.5 & 0.1 \end{bmatrix}, v_{\varphi\varpi} = \tilde{v}_{\varpi\varphi} = \begin{bmatrix} -0.5 & -0.1 \\ -0.2 & -0.5 \end{bmatrix},$$
$$Q_{\varphi\varpi} = \tilde{Q}_{\varpi\varphi} = \begin{bmatrix} -0.4 & 0.5 \\ 0.4 & -2.5 \end{bmatrix}, M_1 = M_2 = \begin{bmatrix} 0 & 0 \\ 0 & 0 \end{bmatrix}, I_\varphi = J_\varpi = \begin{bmatrix} -0.2\cos(t) \\ -0.2\sin(t) \end{bmatrix},$$
$$\tilde{M_1} = \tilde{M_2} = \begin{bmatrix} 0 & 0 \\ 0 & 0 \end{bmatrix}.$$

Consider the activation functions defined by

$$g_\varphi(\zeta_\varphi(t,\wp)) = |\zeta_\varphi(t,\wp)+2| - |\zeta_\varphi(t,\wp)-2|,$$

$$f_\varpi(\Im_\varpi(t,\wp)) = |\Im_\varpi(t,\wp)+2| - |\Im_\varpi(t,\wp)-2|,$$

which satisfy Assumption 2 for $F_\varpi = \frac{1}{2}$ and $G_\varphi = \frac{1}{2}$.

Although Assumptions 1–3 are satisfied, the numerical simulations demonstrated in Figure 1 show that the global asymptotic synchronization cannot be realized for systems (1) and (2), or the corresponding error system is not globally asymptotically stable in the absence of a control input.

Now, let us consider feedback controllers with $\mathfrak{t}_\varphi = 2.1$, $\Upsilon_\varphi = 1.1$, $\varpi_\varpi = 0$, $\varrho_\varpi = 2$, and let $\rho = 0.2$.

Substituting the above values in Theorem 1, we obtain

$$
\begin{aligned}
\mu_{\min}^{(1)} = \min_{1\le\varphi\le o}\Bigg\{ & 2\tilde{M}_{\varphi} + 2d_{\varphi} - \sum_{\varpi=1}^{n}|c_{\varphi\varpi}|F_{\varpi}\rho^{-1} - \sum_{\varpi=1}^{n}|a_{\varphi\varpi}|F_{\varpi}\rho^{-1} \\
& - \sum_{\varpi=1}^{n}|u_{\varphi\varpi}|F_{\varpi}\rho^{-1} - \sum_{\varpi=1}^{n}|v_{\varphi\varpi}|F_{\varpi}\rho^{-1} + t_{\varphi} + \psi_{\varphi} - \sum_{\varpi=1}^{n}|c_{\varphi\varpi}|F_{\varpi}\rho\Bigg\} = 1.22 > 0, \\
\mu_{\min}^{(2)} = \min_{1\le\varpi\le n}\Bigg\{ & 2\bar{\bar{\tilde{M}}}_{\varpi} + 2\tilde{d}_{\varpi} - \sum_{\varphi=1}^{o}|\tilde{c}_{\varpi\varphi}|G_{\varphi}\rho^{-1} - \sum_{\varphi=1}^{o}|\tilde{a}_{\varpi\varphi}|G_{\varphi}\rho^{-1} - \sum_{\varphi=1}^{o}|\tilde{u}_{\varpi\varphi}|G_{\varphi}\rho^{-1} \\
& - \sum_{\varphi=1}^{o}|\tilde{v}_{\varpi\varphi}|G_{\varphi}\rho^{-1} + \omega_{\varpi} + \varrho_{\varpi} - \sum_{\varphi=1}^{o}|\tilde{c}_{\varpi\varphi}|G_{\varphi}\rho\Bigg\} = 1.29 > 0, \\
\Lambda_1^{\mu} = \max_{1\le\varphi\le o} & \left\{\sum_{\varpi=1}^{n}|\tilde{u}_{\varpi\varphi}|G_{\varphi}\rho + \sum_{\varpi=1}^{n}|\tilde{v}_{\varpi\varphi}|G_{\varphi}\rho + \sum_{\varpi=1}^{n}|\tilde{a}_{\varpi\varphi}|G_{\varphi}\rho\right\} = 0.86 > 0, \\
\Lambda_2^{\mu} = \max_{1\le\varpi\le n} & \left\{\sum_{\varphi=1}^{o}|u_{\varphi\varpi}|F_{\varpi}\rho + \sum_{\varphi=1}^{o}|v_{\varphi\varpi}|F_{\varpi}\rho + \sum_{\varphi=1}^{o}|a_{\varphi\varpi}|F_{\varpi}\rho\right\} = 0.45 > 0.
\end{aligned}
$$

Hence, $\mu > \sqrt{2}\Lambda$, where $\mu = \min\left\{\mu_{\min}^{(1)}, \mu_{\min}^{(2)}\right\} = 1.22$ and $\Lambda = \max\left\{\Lambda_1^{\mu}, \Lambda_2^{\mu}\right\} = 0.86$, and by Theorem 1, systems (1) and (2) are globally asymptotically synchronized. This means that the corresponding error system is globally asymptotically stable via the controllers. The trajectories of the error system for $\lambda = 0.97$ are given in Figure 2.

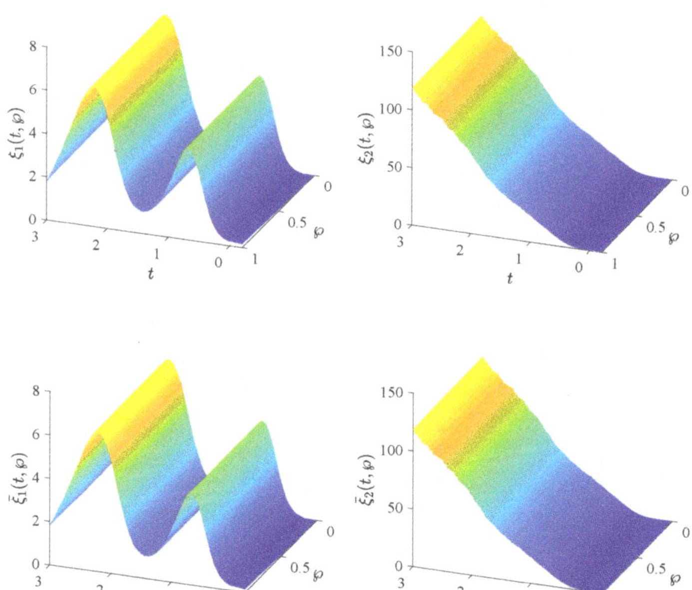

Figure 1. State trajectories of the error system corresponding to the fractional-order fuzzy BAM neural networks in Example 1 for $\lambda = 0.97$ without controllers.

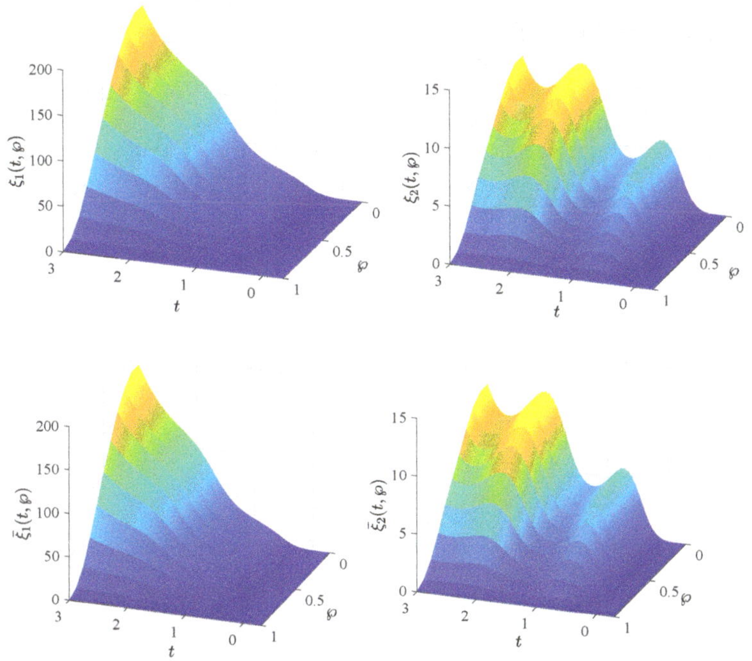

Figure 2. State trajectories of the error system corresponding to the fractional-order fuzzy BAM neural networks in Example 1 with fractional order $\lambda = 0.97$ with controllers.

Example 2. *In this example, consider the error system (8) for $\varphi = \varpi = 2$ and the following parameters: $\lambda = 0.95, \tau = 0.2$*

$$D = \tilde{D} = \begin{bmatrix} 1.5 & 0 \\ 0 & 1.5 \end{bmatrix}, c_{\varphi\varpi} = \tilde{c}_{\varpi\varphi} = \begin{bmatrix} 0.2 & -0.1 \\ 0.1 & 0.3 \end{bmatrix}, a_{\varphi\varpi} = \tilde{a}_{\varpi\varphi} = \begin{bmatrix} -0.2 & 0.6 \\ 0.5 & -3.5 \end{bmatrix},$$
$$u_{\varphi\varpi} = u_{\varpi\varphi} = \begin{bmatrix} 0.4 & -0.4 \\ 0.7 & 0.6 \end{bmatrix}, P_{\varphi\varpi} = \tilde{P}_{\varpi\varphi} = \begin{bmatrix} -0.3 & -0.7 \\ 0.4 & -2 \end{bmatrix}, v_{\varphi\varpi} = \tilde{v}_{\varpi\varphi} = \begin{bmatrix} -0.7 & -0.2 \\ -0.1 & -0.5 \end{bmatrix},$$
$$Q_{\varphi\varpi} = \tilde{Q}_{\varpi\varphi} = \begin{bmatrix} -0.3 & 0.4 \\ 0.3 & -2.6 \end{bmatrix}, M_1 = M_2 = 0, \tilde{M}_1 = \tilde{M}_2 = 0, I = \begin{bmatrix} -0.2\cos(t) \\ -0.2\sin(t) \end{bmatrix}.$$

Then, the following functions are defined

$$g_{\varphi}(\zeta_{\varphi}(t,\wp)) = |\zeta_{\varphi}(t,\wp) + 2| - |\zeta_{\varphi}(t,\wp) - 2|.$$

$$f_{\varpi}(\Im_{\varpi}(t,\wp)) = |\Im_{\varpi}(t,\wp) + 2| - |\Im_{\varpi}(t,\wp) - 2|,$$

Substituting the above values in Theorem 3, we obtain

$$\nu_{\min}^{(1)} = \min_{1\le\varphi\le o}\left\{2\tilde{M}_{\varphi} + 2d_{\varphi} - \sum_{\varpi=1}^{n}|c_{\varphi\varpi}|F_{\varpi}\rho^{-1} - \sum_{\varpi=1}^{n}|a_{\varphi\varpi}|F_{\varpi}\rho^{-1}\right.$$
$$\left. - \sum_{\varpi=1}^{n}|u_{\varphi\varpi}|F_{\varpi}\rho^{-1} - \sum_{\varpi=1}^{n}|v_{\varphi\varpi}|F_{\varpi}\rho^{-1} - \sum_{\varpi=1}^{n}|c_{\varphi\varpi}|F_{\varpi}\rho\right\} = 2.10 > 0,$$
$$\nu_{\min}^{(2)} = \min_{1\le\varpi\le n}\left\{2\tilde{\bar{M}}_{\varpi} + 2\tilde{d}_{\varpi} - \sum_{\varphi=1}^{o}|\tilde{c}_{\varpi\varphi}|G_{\varphi}\rho^{-1} - \sum_{\varphi=1}^{o}|\tilde{a}_{\varpi\varphi}|G_{\varphi}\rho^{-1} - \sum_{\varphi=1}^{o}|\tilde{u}_{\varpi\varphi}|G_{\varphi}\rho^{-1}\right.$$
$$\left. - \sum_{\varphi=1}^{o}|\tilde{v}_{\varpi\varphi}|G_{\varphi}\rho^{-1} - \sum_{\varphi=1}^{o}|\tilde{c}_{\varpi\varphi}|G_{\varphi}\rho\right\} = 2.10 > 0,$$
$$\Lambda_1^{\nu} = \max_{1\le\varphi\le o}\left\{\sum_{\varpi=1}^{n}|\tilde{u}_{\varpi\varphi}|G_{\varphi}\rho + \sum_{\varpi=1}^{n}|\tilde{v}_{\varpi\varphi}|G_{\varphi}\rho + \sum_{\varpi=1}^{n}|\tilde{a}_{\varpi\varphi}|G_{\varphi}\rho\right\} = 1.98 > 0,$$
$$\Lambda_2^{\nu} = \max_{1\le\varpi\le n}\left\{\sum_{\varphi=1}^{o}|u_{\varphi\varpi}|F_{\varpi}\rho + \sum_{\varphi=1}^{o}|v_{\varphi\varpi}|F_{\varpi}\rho + \sum_{\varphi=1}^{o}|a_{\varphi\varpi}|F_{\varpi}\rho\right\} = 0.87 > 0.$$

Hence, since $2.10 = \min\left\{\nu_{\min}^{(1)}, \nu_{\min}^{(2)}\right\} > \max\{\Lambda_1^{\nu}, \Lambda_2^{\nu}\} = 1.98$*, Theorem 3 implies that the error system (8) is globally Mittag–Leffler stable. The state trajectories for the given system parameters are shown in Figure 3.*

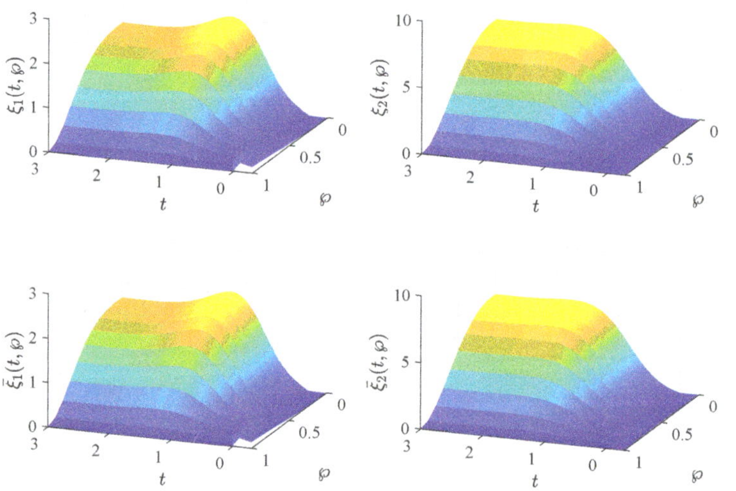

Figure 3. The state trajectories of the fractional-order fuzzy BAM neural network system (8) in Example 2.

Example 3. *In this Example, we consider a model of type (13) with* $\varphi = \varpi = 2$ *and* $\lambda = 0.9, \tau = 0.2$,

$$c_{\varphi\varpi} = \tilde{c}_{\varpi\varphi} = \begin{bmatrix} 0.6 & -0.3 \\ 0.3 & 0.7 \end{bmatrix},\ a_{\varphi\varpi} = \tilde{a}_{\varpi\varphi} = \begin{bmatrix} -0.2 & 0.4 \\ 0.4 & -1.2 \end{bmatrix},$$

and activation functions defined by

$$g_{\varphi}(\hat{\zeta}_{\varphi}(t)) = |\hat{\zeta}_{\varphi}(t) + 2| - |\hat{\zeta}_{\varphi}(t) - 2|,$$

$$f_{\varpi}(\check{\Im}_{\varpi}(t)) = |\check{\Im}_{\varpi}(t) + 2| - |\check{\Im}_{\varpi}(t) - 2|.$$

Substituting the above values in Theorem 3, we obtain $\varpi_1 = \min_{1 \le \varphi \le o}\{[d_{\varphi} - |\tilde{c}_{\varpi\varphi}|F_{\varphi}]\} = 2.87$, $\varpi_2 = \min_{1 \le \varphi \le o}\{[\tilde{d}_{\varpi} - |c_{\varphi\varpi}|F_{\varpi}|]\} = 1.78$, $\varpi_3 = \min_{1 \le \varphi \le o}[\sum_{\varpi=1}^{n} |a_{\varphi\varpi}|F_{\varpi}] = 0.87$, $\varpi_4 = \max_{1 \le \varpi \le n}[\sum_{\varphi=1}^{o} |\tilde{a}_{\varpi\varphi}|F_{\varphi}] = 0.87$.

By utilizing Theorem 4, we are able to ascertain that system (13) is globally Mittag–Leffler stable. The stable behavior of the states is shown in Figure 4.

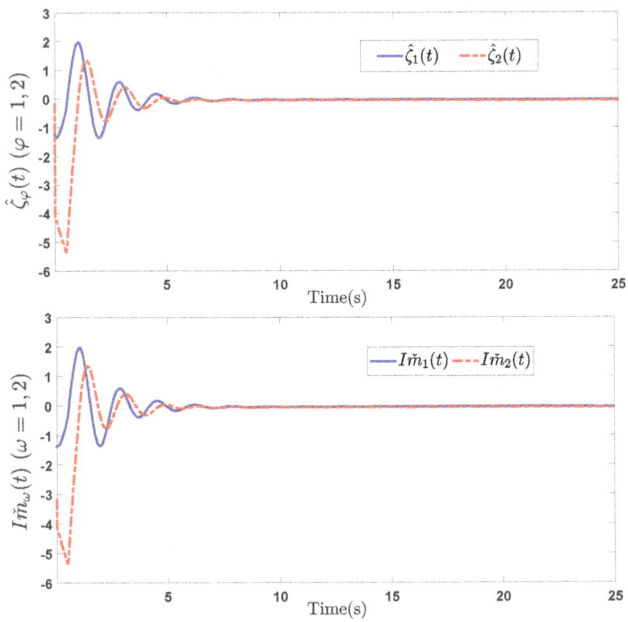

Figure 4. The state trajectories of the fractional-order BAM neural network system in Example 3.

Remark 7. *The parameters, initial values, software, and computer configurations used in establishing numerical simulations were as follows:*

Example 1: $N = 2000$; $d = [0.5; 0.5]$; $D_1 = diag(d)$; $f_1 = 2$; $f_2 = 2$; $g_1 = 1$; $g_2 = 1$; $dis = 1$; $ti = 3$; $a = 0.2$; $b = 0.1$; $\tau = 0.3$; $tstep = 0.01$; $dstep = 0.1$; $\tau no = \tau/tstep$; $tno = ti/tstep$; $dno = dis/dstep$; $N1 = 10$; $T1 = zeros(1, N1)$; $delta2 = zeros(1, N1)$; $T1(1) = \tau no$; $\beta = \min(F1)/\max(F)N = 2000$.

Example 2: $f_1 = 2$; $f_2 = 2$; $g_1 = 1$; $g_2 = 1$; $Dis = 1$; $ti = 3$; $a = 0.2$; $b = 0.1$; $\tau = 0.3$; $tstep = 0.01$; $dstep = 0.1$; $\tau no = \tau/tstep$; $tno = ti/tstep$; $dno = dis/dstep$; $N1 = 10$; $T1 = zeros(1, N1)$; $delta_2 = zeros(1, N1)$; $T1(1) = \tau no$; *for* $k = 2 : N1$; $T1(k) = \tau no + 30 * (k-1) + (-1)^k * (rem((k-1), 10))$; *for* $k = 1 : N1 - 1$ $delta(k) = T1(k) + round(0.6 * (T1(k+1) - T1(k)))$; $delta(N1) = T1(N1) + 20$.

Example 3: $et = 25$; $h = 0.02$; $t = -st : h : et$; $N_0 = floor(st/h)$; $N_1 = et/h$; $n = N_0 + N_1$; $q1 = 0.95$; $q2 = 0.95$; $q3 = 0.95$; $q4 = 0.95$

System configuration: Window 10 and Matlab 2017A software.

6. Conclusions

In this paper, we considered a reaction–diffusion fractional-order fuzzy BAM neural network with discrete and distributed delays. The global asymptotic stability and global asymptotic synchronization behaviors were investigated using novel hybrid feedback controllers. In addition, sufficient conditions ensuring the globally Mittag–Leffler stability of such systems were derived based on the inequality technique and an analysis method for the controller was also developed. The criteria were in the form of algebraic inequalities and were convenient for applications. The established global asymptotic synchronization results also reflected the presence of distributed delays and the design of the proposed controllers. Numerical examples were given to verify the effectiveness of the main results.

The obtained results advance the related state of the art by considering a more general structure which allows one to divide all nodes in the network into different classes and includes a BAM two-layer connection, fuzzy logic, and hybrid feedback controllers. The applied technique can be extended to systems under impulsive perturbations which can also be used as a control mechanism. Considering real case studies, such as proportional–integral–derivative controllers, variable-order fractional derivatives are also subjects for future development of the topic.

Author Contributions: Conceptualization, M.S.A., G.S., I.S., T.F.I., A.A.D. and F.M.O.B.; methodology, M.S.A., G.S., I.S., T.F.I., A.A.D. and F.M.O.B.; formal analysis, M.S.A., G.S., I.S., T.F.I., A.A.D. and F.M.O.B.; investigation, M.S.A., G.S., I.S., T.F.I., A.A.D. and F.M.O.B.; writing—original draft preparation, M.S.A. and I.S. All authors have read and agreed to the published version of the manuscript.

Funding: This research is founded through a project under grant number RGP.2/141/44.

Data Availability Statement: Not applicable.

Acknowledgments: The authors extend their appreciation to the Deanship of Scientific Research at King Khalid University for funding this work through large groups (project under grant number RGP.2/141/44).

Conflicts of Interest: The authors declare no conflict of interest.

References

1. Syed Ali, M.; Hymavathi, M.; Saroha, S.; Krishna Moorthy, R. Global asymptotic stability of neutral type fractional-order memristor-based neural networks with leakage term, discrete and distributed delays. *Math. Methods Appl. Sci.* **2021**, *44*, 5953–5973. [CrossRef]
2. Syed Ali, M.; Hymavathi, M.; Rajchakit, G.; Saroha, S.; Palanisamy, L.; Hammachukiattikul, P. Synchronization of fractional order fuzzy BAM neural networks with time varying delays and reaction diffusion terms. *IEEE Access* **2020**, *8*, 186551–186571.
3. Baleanu, D.; Diethelm, K.; Scalas, E.; Trujillo, J.J. *Fractional Calculus: Models and Numerical Methods*, 1st ed.; World Scientific: Singapore, 2012; ISBN 978-981-4355-20-9.
4. Bao, H.; Park, J.H.; Cao, J. Non-fragile state estimation for fractional-order delayed memristive BAM neural networks. *Neural Netw.* **2019**, *119*, 190–199. [CrossRef]
5. Bohner, M.; Jonnalagadda, J.M. Discrete fractional cobweb models. *Chaos Solit. Fract.* **2022**, *162*, 112451. [CrossRef]
6. Magin, R. *Fractional Calculus in Bioengineering*, 1st ed.; Begell House: Redding, CA, USA, 2006; ISBN 978-1567002157.
7. Podlubny, I. *Fractional Differential Equations*, 1st ed.; Academic Press: San Diego, CA, USA, 1999; ISBN 558840-2.
8. Singh, H.; Srivastava, H.M.; Nieto, J.J. (Eds.) *Handbook of Fractional Calculus for Engineering and Science*, 1st ed.; CRC Press, Taylor and Francis Group: Boca Raton, USA, 2022; ISBN 9781003263517.
9. Wang, Z.; Huang, X.; Shi, G. Analysis of nonlinear dynamics and chaos in a fractional order financial system with time delay. *Comput. Math. Appl.* **2011**, *62*, 1531–1539. [CrossRef]
10. Wang, L.; Song, Q.; Liu, Y.; Zhao, Z.; Alsaadi, F. Finite-time stability analysis of fractional order complex-valued memristor-based neural networks with both leakage and time-varying delays. *Neurocomputing* **2017**, *245*, 86–101. [CrossRef]
11. Zhang, L.; Yang, Y.; Wang, F. Synchronization analysis of fractional-order neural networks with time-varying delays via discontinuous neuron activations. *Neurocomputing* **2017**, *275*, 40–49. [CrossRef]
12. Abdurahman, A.; Jiang, H.; Teng, Z. Finite-time synchronization for fuzzy cellular neural networks with time-varying delays. *Fuzzy Sets Syst.* **2016**, *297*, 96–111. [CrossRef]
13. Li, X.; Rakkiyappan, R.; Balasubramaniam, P. Existence and global stability analysis of equilibrium of fuzzy cellular neural networks with time delay in the leakage term under impulsive perturbations. *J. Franklin Inst.* **2011**, *348*, 135–155. [CrossRef]

14. Kumar, A.; Das, S.; Yadav, V.K.; Jinde Cao, J.; Huang, C. Synchronizations of fuzzy cellular neural networks with proportional time-delay. *AIMS Math.* **2021**, *6*, 10620–10641. [CrossRef]
15. Du, F.; Lu, J.G. Finite-time stability of fractional-order fuzzy cellular neural networks with time delays. *Fuzzy Sets Syst.* **2022**, *438*, 107–120. [CrossRef]
16. Singh, A.; Rai, J.N. Stability of fractional order fuzzy cellular neural networks with distributed delays via hybrid feedback controllers. *Neural Process. Lett.* **2021**, *53*, 1469–1499. [CrossRef]
17. Kosko, B. Adpative bidirecctional associative memoreis. *Appl. Opt.* **1987**, *26*, 4947–4960. [CrossRef] [PubMed]
18. Huang, C.; Wang, J.; Chen, X.; Cao, J. Bifurcations in a fractional-order BAM neural network with four different delays. *Neural Netw.* **2021**, *141*, 344–354. [CrossRef] [PubMed]
19. Syed Ali, M.; Hymavathi, M.; Kauser, S.A.; Boonsatit, N.; Hammachukiattikul, P.; Rajchakit, G. Synchronization of fractional order uncertain BAM competitive neural networks. *Fractal Fract.* **2022**, *6*, 14. [CrossRef]
20. Li, Y.; Wang, C. Existence and global exponential stability of equilibrium for discrete-time fuzzy BAM neural networks with variable delays and impulses. *Fuzzy Sets Syst.* **2013**, *217*, 62–79. [CrossRef]
21. Zhang, Y.; Li, Z.; Jiang, W.; Liu, W. The stability of anti-periodic solutions for fractional-order inertial BAM neural networks with time-delays. *AIMS Math.* **2023**, *8*, 6176–6190. [CrossRef]
22. Zhu, Q.; Li, X.; Yang, X. Exponential stability for stochastic reaction–diffusion BAM neural networks with time-varying and distributed delays. *Appl. Math. Comput.* **2011**, *217*, 6078–6091. [CrossRef]
23. Li, Y.; Chen, Y.Q.; Podlubny, I. Stability of fractional-order nonlinear dynamic systems: Lyapunov direct method and generalized Mittag–Leffler stability. *Comput. Math. Appl.* **2010**, *24*, 1429–1468. [CrossRef]
24. Liu, S.; Li, X.Y.; Jiang, W.; Zhou, X.F. Mittag–Leffler stability of nonlinear fractional neutral singular systems. *Commun. Nonlinear Sci. Numer. Simul.* **2012**, *17*, 3961–3966. [CrossRef]
25. Stamov, T.; Stamova, I. Design of impulsive controllers and impulsive control strategy for the Mittag–Leffler stability behavior of fractional gene regulatory networks. *Neurocomputing* **2021**, *424*, 54–62. [CrossRef]
26. Wu, A.; Liu, L.; Huang, T.; Zeng, Z. Mittag–Leffler stability of fractional-order neural networks in the presence of generalized piecewise constant arguments. *Neural Netw.* **2017**, *85*, 118–127. [CrossRef] [PubMed]
27. Wu, A.; Zeng, Z. Global Mittag–Leffler stabilization of fractional-order memristive neural networks. *IEEE Trans. Neural Netw. Learn. Syst.* **2015**, *28*, 206–217. [CrossRef] [PubMed]
28. Xiao, J.; Zhong, S.; Li, Y.; Xu, F. Finite-time Mittag–Leffler synchronization of fractional-order memristive BAM neural networks with time delays. *Neurocomputing* **2017**, *219*, 431–439. [CrossRef]
29. Yan, H.; Qiao, Y.; Duan, L.; Zhang, L. Global Mittag–Leffler stabilization of fractional-order BAM neural networks with linear state feedback controllers. *Math. Probl. Eng.* **2020**, *2020*, 6398208. [CrossRef]
30. Li, X.; Caraballo, T.; Rakkiyappan, R.; Han, X. On the stability of impulsive functional differential equations with infinite delays. *Math. Methods Appl. Sci.* **2015**, *38*, 3130–3140. [CrossRef]
31. Song, Q.; Wang, Z. Neural networks with discrete and distributed time-varying delays: A general stability analysis. *Neural Netw.* **2008**, *37*, 1538–1547. [CrossRef]
32. Syed Ali, M.; Saravanan, S. Robust finite-time H_∞ control for a class of uncertain switched neural networks of neutral-type with distributed time varying delays. *Neurocomputing* **2016**, *177*, 454–468.
33. Zhang, G.; Zeng, Z.; Hu, J. New results on global exponential dissipativity analysis of memristive inertial neural networks with distributed time-varying delays. *Neural Netw.* **2018**, *97*, 183–191. [CrossRef]
34. Stamova, I.; Stamov, G. Mittag–Leffler synchronization of fractional neural networks with time-varying delays and reaction-diffusion terms using impulsive and linear controllers. *Neural Netw.* **2017**, *96*, 22–32. [CrossRef]
35. Li, R.; Cao, J.; Alsaedi, A.; Alsaadi, F. Exponential and fixed-time synchronization of Cohen–Grossberg neural networks with time-varying delays and reaction-diffusion terms. *Appl. Math. Comput.* **2017**, *313*, 37–51. [CrossRef]
36. Wang, C.; Zhang, H.; Stamova, I.; Cao, J. Global synchronization for BAM delayed reaction-diffusion neural networks with fractional partial differential operator. *J. Franklin Inst.* **2023**, *360*, 635–656. [CrossRef]
37. Wang, L.; Zhou, Q. Global exponential stability of BAM neural networks with time-varying delays and reaction-diffusion terms. *Phys. Lett. A* **2007**, *371*, 83–89.
38. Wei, T.; Li, X.; Stojanovic, V. Input-to-state stability of impulsive reaction–diffusion neural networks with infinite distributed delays. *Nonlinear Dyn.* **2021**, *103*, 1733–1755. [CrossRef]
39. Wu, X.; Liu, S.; Wang, Y. Stability analysis of Riemann–Liouville fractional-order neural networks with reaction-diffusion terms and mixed time-varying delays. *Neurocomputing* **2021**, *431*, 169–178. [CrossRef]
40. Antsaklis, P.J. Special issue on hybrid systems: theory and applications-a brief introduction to the theory and applications of hybrid systems. *Proc. IEEE* **2000**, *88*, 879–887. [CrossRef]
41. Diethelm, K.; Ford, N.J. Analysis of fractional differential equations. *J. Math. Anal. Appl.* **2002**, *265*, 229–248. [CrossRef]
42. Liang, S.; Wu, R.; Chen, L. Comparision principles and stability of nonlinear fractional-order cellular neural networks with multiple time delays. *Neurocomputing* **2015**, *168*, 618–625. [CrossRef]
43. Kuang, J.C. *Applied Inequalities*, 3rd ed.; Shandong Science and Technology Press: Jinan, China, 2004; ISBN 9787533136185. (In Chinese)

44. Wu, H.; Zhang, X.; Xue, S.; Wang, L.; Wang, Y. LMI conditions to global Mittag-Leffler stability of fractional-order neural networks with impulses. *Neurocomputing* **2016**, *193*, 148–154. [CrossRef]
45. Lu, J.G. Global exponential stability and periodicity of reaction-diffusion delayed recurrent neural networks with Dirichlet boundary conditions. *Chaos Solitons Fract.* **2008**, *35*, 116–125. [CrossRef]

Disclaimer/Publisher's Note: The statements, opinions and data contained in all publications are solely those of the individual author(s) and contributor(s) and not of MDPI and/or the editor(s). MDPI and/or the editor(s) disclaim responsibility for any injury to people or property resulting from any ideas, methods, instructions or products referred to in the content.

mathematics

MDPI

Article

An Accurate Metaheuristic Mountain Gazelle Optimizer for Parameter Estimation of Single- and Double-Diode Photovoltaic Cell Models

Rabeh Abbassi [1,2,3,*], Salem Saidi [2,4], Shabana Urooj [5,*], Bilal Naji Alhasnawi [6], Mohamad A. Alawad [7] and Manoharan Premkumar [8]

1 Department of Electrical Engineering, College of Engineering, University of Ha'il, Ha'il City 81451, Saudi Arabia
2 LaTICE Laboratory, Higher National Engineering School of Tunis (ENSIT), University of Tunis, 5 Avenue Taha Hussein, P.O. Box 56, Tunis 1008, Tunisia; salem.saidi@enstab.ucar.tn
3 Institute of Applied Sciences and Technology of Kasserine (ISSATKas), University of Kairouan, P.O. Box 471, Kasserine 1200, Tunisia
4 National School of Advanced Sciences and Technologies of Borj Cédria (ENSTAB), University of Carthage, P.O. Box 122, Hammam-Chott 1164, Tunisia
5 Department of Electrical Engineering, College of Engineering, Princess Nourah bint Abdulrahman University, P.O. Box 84428, Riyadh 11671, Saudi Arabia
6 Department of Electricity Techniques, Al-Samawah Technical Institute, Al-Furat Al-Awsat Technical University, Kufa 66001, Iraq; bilalnaji11@yahoo.com
7 Department of Electrical Engineering, Imam Mohammad Ibn Saud Islamic University, Riyadh 11564, Saudi Arabia; maawaad@imamu.edu.sa
8 Department of Electrical and Electronics Engineering, Dayananda Sagar College of Engineering, Bengaluru 560078, Karnataka, India; drpremkumar-eee@dayanandasagar.edu
* Correspondence: r.abbassi@uoh.edu.sa (R.A.); smurooj@pnu.edu.sa (S.U.)

Abstract: Accurate parameter estimation is crucial and challenging for the design and modeling of PV cells/modules. However, the high degree of non-linearity of the typical I–V characteristic further complicates this task. Consequently, significant research interest has been generated in recent years. Currently, this trend has been marked by a noteworthy acceleration, mainly due to the rise of swarm intelligence and the rapid progress of computer technology. This paper proposes a developed Mountain Gazelle Optimizer (MGO) to generate the best values of the unknown parameters of PV generation units. The MGO mimics the social life and hierarchy of mountain gazelles in the wild. The MGO was compared with well-recognized recent algorithms, which were the Grey Wolf Optimizer (GWO), the Squirrel Search Algorithm (SSA), the Differential Evolution (DE) algorithm, the Bat–Artificial Bee Colony Optimizer (BABCO), the Bat Algorithm (BA), Multiswarm Spiral Leader Particle Swarm Optimization (M-SLPSO), the Guaranteed Convergence Particle Swarm Optimization algorithm (GCPSO), Triple-Phase Teaching–Learning-Based Optimization (TPTLBO), the Criss-Cross-based Nelder–Mead simplex Gradient-Based Optimizer (CCNMGBO), the quasi-Opposition-Based Learning Whale Optimization Algorithm (OBLWOA), and the Fractional Chaotic Ensemble Particle Swarm Optimizer (FC-EPSO). The experimental findings and statistical studies proved that the MGO outperformed the competing techniques in identifying the parameters of the Single-Diode Model (SDM) and the Double-Diode Model (DDM) PV models of Photowatt-PWP201 (polycrystalline) and STM6-40/36 (monocrystalline). The RMSEs of the MGO on the SDM and the DDM of Photowatt-PWP201 and STM6-40/36 were 2.042717×10^{-3}, 1.387641×10^{-3}, 1.719946×10^{-3}, and 1.686104×10^{-3}, respectively. Overall, the identified results highlighted that the MGO-based approach featured a fast processing time and steady convergence while retaining a high level of accuracy in the achieved solution.

Keywords: metaheuristic algorithm; parameter identification; photovoltaic cells; single-diode; double-diode; mathematical models; mountain gazelle optimization

MSC: 68T20; 90C26

1. Introduction

1.1. Motivation

The last few decades have been marked by a continuous increase in global energy needs due to demographic, industrial, and agricultural development. On the other hand, fossil fuels, causing greenhouse gas emissions and an increase in air pollution, such as coal, oil, and natural gas are experiencing dangerous exhaustion [1]. Faced with this and under the Kyoto Protocol, energy production is a critical challenge for the coming years, whether it is for developed countries to meet their needs or for developing countries to carry out their development.

In this context, several efforts have been made to discover other reliable, profitable, and renewable sources of energy [2–4]. However, due to the intrinsic volatile nature of Hybrid Renewable Energy Systems (HRESs), the evaluation of the reliability aspect of such systems to withstand unpredicted events in loaded power systems was investigated in [5]. To overcome the lack of a comparative assessment of multi-objective optimization sizing for HRESs equipped with hybrid energy storage, a comparative multi-objective framework was proposed in [6].

Among these sources are the following: solar energy coming directly from the Sun is not polluting, has no greenhouse gas emissions, is not dangerous for future generations, and is, therefore, inimitable as long as it radiates [7]. The solar Photovoltaic (PV) industry is the most-promising and powerful source of renewable energy. Photovoltaic energy comes from the direct transformation of part of the solar radiation into electrical energy. This energy conversion takes place through a PV cell exposed to light based on a physical phenomenon called the photovoltaic effect, which was discovered by the French physicist Antoine César Becquerel in 1839 [8]. Since then, several scientific pieces of research (important attempts) have led to the beginning of the actual use of PV cells to reach maturity in the last few years.

Currently, the expansion of the solar energy market is mainly due to the rising competitiveness associated with growing electricity demand, as well as the growing awareness of the potential of solar PV worldwide [9]. China is at the top of the world in terms of solar energy production. In 2022 alone, China installed 87.41 GW of new solar power (60.3% more than in 2021) to reach a cumulative capacity of 392.61 GW [10].

By the crucial importance of the use of solar energy, several aspects related to PV systems have attracted the attention of researchers and industrialists, namely the design of PV cells [11–13], maximum power point tracking [14], fault diagnosis [15,16], modeling and control [17], and the extraction of the parameters of the PV cells/panels [18]. In this paper, we are interested in extracting the main characteristic parameters of the Single-Diode Model (SDM) and the Double-Diode Model (DDM) of a solar cell. This choice of one- and two-exponential models is justified by their great importance and reputation for studying the behavior of solar cells.

1.2. Literature Review

Commonly, two famous extraction techniques are deployed: (1) the analytical [19–23] and (2) numerical ones [18,24,25]. The analytical approach is less complicated, but its accuracy is inextricably linked to the specification of some key points of the I–V curve. The accuracy of such an analytical extraction technique depends strongly on the proposed optimizer [18]. As a matter of fact, if the computed parameters are incorrectly specified, the errors can have very significant adverse effects on the PV system performance assessment [25]. Alternatively, the numerical extraction approach rests upon certain mathematical algorithms, which enables more accuracy since it allows fitting all the I–V curves. Although it is more beneficial, in terms of precision, its fitting requires more-sophisticated computation. Also, it is very important to point out that the initial values of the parameters to be estimated should be adequately selected to avoid the non-convergence of the algorithm [26].

Currently, metaheuristic algorithms seen a substantial history to achieve the optimal solution in fine-tuning machine learning algorithms and solving continuous optimization problems [27,28]. They have gained great popularity in different application domains such as smart grid applications [29–31], Green Building Energy-Optimization Systems (GBEOSs) [32], Electric Vehicles (EVs) [33–35], the Internet of Things (IoT) [36–39], the military domain [40–42], structural health monitoring applications [43,44], Resilient Cyber–Physical Systems (RCPSs) [45,46], robotics [47,48], etc. With the growth of solar energy systems and their various design and control aspects seen as complex problems, where metaheuristics are the best candidates for addressing them, PV cell parameter identification is becoming a wide research discipline, which involves artificial intelligence and bio-inspired optimization algorithms. In this context, many new trends have been proposed to offer the possibility of enhanced task performance, high reliability, and decreased complexity and time computation over analytical, numerical, and hybrid algorithms [24, 49]. In [50], the Genetic Algorithm (GA) method was the first proposed. The Particle Swarm Optimization (PSO) method was also presented in [51]. Nevertheless, the found results showed relatively high error percentages and premature convergence problems, respectively. For this, many enhanced versions of the PSO technique have been proposed like [52,53] and [54]. Alternatively, many other methods such as ABC-TRR [55], TLABC [56], and MABC [57] are intended to avoid the above problems in extracting PV cell parameters. Since the performance of all these algorithms is highly dependent on many factors like proper tuning, this makes it extremely difficult to obtain better results.

1.3. Drawbacks and Gaps in the Literature

Different optimization problems suffer from the issue of premature convergence [58,59]. To address this problem, it is mandatory that key parameter settings be well-tuned to avoid premature convergence by ensuring a balance of exploration and exploitation [60]. The best-known enhancements proposed in recently published works, especially those focusing on swarm intelligence, have been centered on the following aspects: swarm size [61], initial population [62,63], inertia weight [64], acceleration coefficients [65,66], and many others [67–69]. Although such efforts have achieved great success in dealing with low-dimensional problems [70,71], it is still a big challenge for recent approaches to address the multi-dimensionality present in the case of large-scale optimization problems.

Keeping in mind the critical trade-off between exploitation and exploration and the effect on the performance of evolutionary optimization algorithms, the achievement of the desired performance of such an algorithm relies on different levels of exploration–exploitation trade-offs at various stages of evolution. In the literature, this issue has been marked as the main drawback of the recent metaheuristics since exploration and exploitation are considered to be two complementary activities that contribute to the exploration of the search space [72]. Exploration is the process by which the search algorithm explores as much of the search space as possible, in order to escape as much as it can from converging on local optima. Exploitation, on the other hand, is the development of well-targeted approaches to find the best solutions [73]. In this way, the exploitation activity can be seen as an optimized result derived from the exploration activity, and the process of finding additional solutions continues to converge on the most-optimal ones.

To guarantee a trade-off between exploration and exploitation, various techniques have been envisaged by metaheuristic approaches, depending on their parameters and design. Indeed, the objective of avoiding premature convergence and stagnation states can be achieved by selection, replacement, or diversity operators, which ensure the diversity of solutions in the search population or memory [74]. Furthermore, the alternation of the intensification and diversification phases enables profitable exploitation of solutions considered to be the best, as well as the exploration of new search regions [75]. The alternation between the two phases is very useful, as the first guarantees improved solution quality through local search, crossover, or hill climbing, while the second is responsible for generating new solutions due to mutation, perturbation, or restart phenomena [72].

To dynamically adjust the level of exploration and exploitation of the metaheuristic optimizer, another solution relies on the adaptation of its components or parameters according to the feedback of the search process. This solution is known as adaptive control [76].

1.4. Contribution

Improving the performance of metaheuristic algorithms remains a vital topic for complex engineering optimization problems. The ensurance of a trade-off between the exploration and exploitation is crucial to high-performance achievement. In this paper, the exploitation and exploration phases of the suggested optimizer were performed using the mountain gazelle optimizer [77], exploiting four mechanisms acting in parallel.

In summary, the main contributions of this work are as follows:

- To use the new MGO-based approach to tackle, for the first time, the problem of the PV cell/module key parameters' identification.
- To apply and experimentally validate the proposed approach to accurately approximate both the single-diode model and the double-diode model and extract their five and seven unknown parameters, respectively.
- To conduct a thorough comparison of the performance of the MGO-based approach with that of the well-established optimization algorithms of the BABCO [78], BA [78], M-SLPSO [79], GCPSO [80], TPTLBO [81], CCNMGBO [82], OBLWOA [82], FC-EPSO [83], DE [84], GWO [85], and SSA [86].
- The experimentation on two commercialized PV panels (Photowatt-PWP201, and STM6-40/36) to confirm the accuracy, stability, and convergence speed of the proposed approach.

The remainder of this paper is structured as follows. The modeling of the two different models of PV cells is presented in Section 2. The problem formulation is proposed in Section 3. The proposed MGO-based extraction method is suggested in Section 4. The executed experiments and the found results, as well as the empirical comparison with new well-known approaches are investigated in Section 5. Section 6 concludes the paper and reveals future works.

2. Different PV Cell Types' Modeling

2.1. Single Diode Model

According to the equivalent electric circuit of the SDM PV cell model [18], Kirchhoff's Current Law (KCL) can be described by Equation (1):

$$I = I_{ph} - I_{d1} - I_{sh} \tag{1}$$

where I_{ph} (A) is the photocurrent generated in the Standard Test Conditions (STCs), I_{d1} (A) is the diode D_1 current, and I_{sh} (A) is the current flowing through the shunt resistor R_{sh} (Ω). Based on Shockley diode modeling, I_{d1} is expressed by Equation (2):

$$I_{d1} = I_{sd}\left(e^{\left(\frac{V+R_sI}{\eta V_t}\right)} - 1\right) \tag{2}$$

In Equation (2), I_{sd} (A) refers to the diode dark saturation current, R_s (Ω) is the series resistor, and V_t (V) is the junction thermal voltage at STCs.

$$V_t = \frac{k_B T_i}{q} \tag{3}$$

where η is the diode ideality factor referring to the measurement of the degree to which the diode complies with the ideal diode equation, ranging from 1–2, k_B ($1.3806503 \times 10^{-23}$ J/K), is the Boltzmann constant, T_i (K) is the operating temperature of the PV cell, and q ($1.60217646 \times 10^{-19}$ C) is the elementary charge.

The last term of Equation (4) evaluates the current flowing through R_{sh} as described in:

$$I_{sh} = \frac{V + IR_s}{R_{sh}} \tag{4}$$

Based on the previous assumptions, Equation (1) is rewritten as follows:

$$I = I_{ph} - I_{sd}\left[e^{\left(\frac{V+IR_s}{\eta V_t}\right)} - 1\right] - \frac{V + IR_s}{R_{sh}} \tag{5}$$

The main objective of the PV cell/module model's key parameters' identification can be achieved through optimization algorithms in order to mimic the real performance of such system. The evolved parameters are: η, R_{sh}, R_s, I_{ph}, and I_{sd}.

2.2. Double-Diode Model

To describe the double-diode model's properties, certain assumptions have to be considered in presenting a simplified version for research applications with regard to the PVSs. The equation depicting the equivalent circuit diagram of the DDM model is, thus, given by Equation (6):

$$I = I_{ph} - I_{d1} - I_{d2} - I_{sh} \tag{6}$$

Herein, the two diodes currents are given by Equation (7) and Equation (8), respectively:

$$I_{d1} = I_{sd1}\left(e^{\left(\frac{V+R_sI}{\eta_1 V_{t1}}\right)} - 1\right) \tag{7}$$

$$I_{d2} = I_{sd2}\left(e^{\left(\frac{V+R_sI}{\eta_2 V_{t2}}\right)} - 1\right) \tag{8}$$

Keeping in mind that V_{t1} and V_{t2} are expressed similarly as in Equation (3) and I_{sh} as in Equation (4), the PV cell output current is obtained by Equation (9):

$$I = I_{ph} - I_{sd1}\left[e^{\left(\frac{V+IR_s}{\eta_1 V_{t1}}\right)} - 1\right] - I_{sd2}\left[e^{\left(\frac{V+IR_s}{\eta_2 V_{t2}}\right)} - 1\right] - \frac{V + IR_s}{R_{sh}} \tag{9}$$

η_1 and η_2 are the first and second diodes' ideality factors, respectively.

Taking into account all the previous equations, the main parameters of the DDM to be identified are: I_{ph}, I_{sd1}, I_{sd2}, R_s, R_{sh}, η_1, and η_2. Likewise, these seven parameters will be estimated by an optimization technique with high precision and robustness.

As the module contains N_s cells, the output voltage and resistance of the module are adjusted according to specific rules:

$$\begin{cases} V' = N_s \cdot V \\ R_s' = N_s \cdot R_s \\ R_{sh}' = N_s \cdot R_{sh} \end{cases} \tag{10}$$

3. Problem Formulation

In the problem of PV module parameter estimation, the main objective is to minimize the difference between the measured and simulated current data. The difference is usually quantified by a multitude of errors such as the Root-Mean-Squared Error (RMSE), the RMSE Deviation (RMSD), the Normalized RMSD (NRMSD), the Mean Absolute Error (MAE), the MAE in Power (MAEP), the Mean Bias Error (MBE), the Mean-Squared Error (MSE), the

Sum of Squares Error (SSE), the value of the Residual Error of the Fitness Function (REFF), etc. In this paper, the objective function is expressed as follows:

$$RMSE(x) = \sqrt{\frac{1}{N}\sum_{i=1}^{n}(f_k(V', I, x))^2} \tag{11}$$

N represents the number of experimental data. Accordingly, (12) represents the SDM of the PV module:

$$\begin{cases} f_k(V', I, x_{sdm}) = I_{ph} - I_{sd}\left(e^{\left(\frac{V'+R_s' I}{\eta V_t}\right)} - 1\right) - \frac{V + R_s' I}{R_{sh}'} \\ x_{sdm} = \left\{I_{ph}, I_{sd}, R_s', R_{sh}', \eta\right\} \end{cases} \tag{12}$$

In a similar form, the representation of the DDM is as follows:

$$\begin{cases} f_k(V', I, x_{ddm}) = I_{ph} - I_{sd1}\left(e^{\left(\frac{V'+R_s' I}{\eta_1 N_s V_{t1}}\right)} - 1\right) - I_{sd2}\left(e^{\left(\frac{V'+R_s' I}{\eta_2 N_s V_{t2}}\right)} - 1\right) - \frac{V' + R_s' I}{R_{sh}'} \\ x_{ddm} = \left\{I_{ph}, I_{sd1}, I_{sd2}, R_s', R_{sh}', \eta_1, \eta_2\right\} \end{cases} \tag{13}$$

The values of I and V' are the current and the voltage vectors measured experimentally from the PV modules. Thus, the parameters' estimation is a process that minimizes the objective function $RMSE(x)$ by adjusting the model parameters' vector x within the range of a given bound.

In this paper, the variation of the climatic conditions was taken into account according to Equations (14)–(19).

$$I_{ph,i} = \frac{G_i}{G_{STC}}(I_{ph} + \alpha_{I_{sc}}(T_i - T_{STC})) \tag{14}$$

$$E_{gap,i} = E_{gap,STC}.(1 - 0.0002677.(T_i - T_{STC})) \tag{15}$$

$$I_{sd,i} = I_{sd}.(\frac{T_i}{T_{STC}})^3 \cdot e^{(\frac{E_{gap}}{k.T_{STC}} - \frac{E_{gap}}{k.T_i})} \tag{16}$$

$$\eta_i = \eta.\frac{T_i}{T_{STC}} \tag{17}$$

$$R_{s,i} = R_s \tag{18}$$

$$R_{sh,i} = R_{sh}.\frac{G_i}{G_{STC}} \tag{19}$$

where G_i and G_{STC} are, respectively, the current irradiance and that under STCs. T_{STC} is the module temperature under STCs. $\alpha_{I_{sc}}$ is the temperature coefficient. $E_{gap,i}$ and $E_{gap,STC}$ are the gap band and that under STCs.

4. Proposed MGO-Based Extraction Method

In order to understand the general concept of the MGO, it is mandatory to bring forward its basic idea by introducing the following.

4.1. MGO's Inspiration

The mountain gazelle is a type of gazelle that lives in low densities and is distributed in large areas of the Arabian Peninsula and its surroundings, especially where Robinia trees are grown. The mountain gazelle lives in three groups: the first includes mothers of offspring; the second includes young males; the third includes the single males' herd [87]. Although this type of animal lives in remote areas, fighting between certain components of the herd is an important feature of their coexistence. In fact, horn struggles between neighboring immature males over the environment when they reach adulthood are even more intense than those over female possession. In terms of foraging for food, the mountain gazelle's tremendous ability to run at speeds of up to 80 km per hour is a very important property that enables it to migrate distances of 120 km to graze in areas where food is abundant.

4.2. MGO Mathematical Modeling

The formulation of the MGO mathematical model is based on the simulation of the fundamental characteristics of the life of mountain gazelles and, more precisely, of their social and grouping behaviors, along with all the factors that rule the communication between their herds, reproduction, grazing, etc. [77]. One of the most-important assets of this algorithm is that the optimization processes are mainly based on more than one factor. Indeed, four factors are involved in such a dynamic process: maternity herds, solitary, bachelor male herds, territorialmales, and migration to grazing areas to search for food.

Depending on the nature of the members of the male bachelor group, who are still in the youth stage and unable to impose their dominance over the females and then carry out the reproduction process, the research population in the MGO algorithm is selected as one-third of the total population, which helps to reduce the cost compared to other options for mathematical modeling [88].

During the optimization process within the MGO, the overall best solution is identified as the adult male gazelle in the herd territory. Nevertheless, each member (Gi gazelle) can join the herd of single males, the maternity her, or solitary territorial males. On the other hand, the birth of a deer can also take place.

However, the mechanism of the MGO algorithm admits the opportunity of other solutions represented primarily by gazelles in the maternity herds. The selection is formulated so that the total population retains the stronger gazelles considered high-quality solutions and eliminates the sick and/or aged gazelles, which have a much weaker cost.

4.3. Territorial Solitary Males

Mountain gazelles live in herds that include both males, young, and females. By adulthood, the young male mountain gazelles have the strength they need to establish their dominance and continue their life cycle. At this point, newly adult males occupy a remote solitary territory. During courtship or mating season, fierce battles take place between the males, who jostle each other using their horns, as the adults try to protect their territories while the young fight for a spot in these areas, as well as for the possession of females [77]. The territory of the adult male can be established by Equation (20).

$$TSM = male_G - |(ri_1 \times BH - ri_2 \times X(t)) \times F| \times Cof_r \tag{20}$$

Herein, $male_G$ refers to the best global solution representing the position vector of the adult male. ri_1 and ri_2 are random integers, which can be taken as 1 or 2. BH is the coefficient vector of the young male herd. It can be approximated by:

$$BH = X_{ra} \times \lfloor r_1 \rfloor + M_{pr} \times \lceil r_2 \rceil, ra = \left\{ \left\lceil \frac{N}{3} \right\rceil \dots N \right\} \tag{21}$$

with

$$ra = \left\{ \left\lceil \frac{N}{3} \right\rceil \dots N \right\} \tag{22}$$

X_{ra} is a random solution in the interval of ra, which represents a young male. r_1 and r_2 are values chosen randomly between 0 and 1. M_{pr} is considered as the average number of randomly selected search agents $\left\lceil \frac{N}{3} \right\rceil$, and N is the total number of herd gazelles.

In Equation (20), F is evaluated according to Equation (23).

$$F = N_1(D) \times \exp\left(2 - Iter \times \left(\frac{2}{MaxIter}\right)\right) \tag{23}$$

According to the problem dimensions, N_1 is a random number originating from the standard distribution [77]. $Iter$ and $MaxIter$ are the ongoing iterations' number and the total iterations' number, respectively.

Furthermore, in each iteration, the coefficient vector Cof_r initially randomly selected is updated in order to increase the search capability, as formulated in Equation (24).

$$Cof_i = \begin{cases} (a+1) + r_3, \\ a \times N_2(D), \\ r_4(D), \\ N_3(D) \times N_4(D)^2 \times \cos((r_4 \times 2) \times N_3(D)) \end{cases} \tag{24}$$

The numbers $rand$, r_3, and r_4 are randomly chosen in the interval [0, 1]. Also, the numbers N_2, N_3, and N_4 are randomly fixed according to the normal range and the problem dimensions [88]. The parameter a is expressed by:

$$a = -1 + Iter \times \left(\frac{-1}{MaxIter}\right) \tag{25}$$

4.4. Maternity Herds

As in the life cycle of all animals, maternity herds are the most-important members, which ensure the continuity of the herd's life by giving birth to new strong male gazelles. Male gazelles contribute significantly to the delivery of new gazelles and young males attempting to acquire female gazelles according to Equation (26).

$$MH = \left(BH + Cof_{1,r}\right) + (ri_3 \times male_G - ri_4 \times X_{\text{rand}}) \times Cof_{1,r} \tag{26}$$

Consider Equation (21), evaluating the young males' impact factor vector BH; the selection of the coefficient vectors $Cof_{2,r}$ and $Cof_{3,r}$ is perform at random according to Equation (24). $male_G$ is the adult male considered as the global solution for the present repetition, while the vector position of a randomly chosen gazelle is rand. Otherwise, ri_3 and ri_4 are random integers of 1 or 2.

4.5. Bachelor Male Herds

Usually and according to the living conditions, the mountain deer lives for about 8 years. The breeding process begins at the age of 18 months for males and 12 months for females. The onset of winter is the typical period for the breeding season. According to zoology and sociobiology, mountain gazelles reproduce, like many mammals, by the practice of male reproduction with several females in what is known as polygamy. Most often, the female gives birth once a year, usually in April or May. While males seek to attract females and compete to mate with them, females choose selectively among available males in the herd. In this context, male dominance becomes a significant factor in the determination of mating relationships. As they mature, young male gazelles begin to gain dominance over new territories and defend them vigorously, as well as attempt to mate with females. In this critical phase, violent behavior increases between the two male groups to achieve these ends, according to Equation (27).

$$BMH = (X(t) - D) + (ri_5 \times male_G - ri_6 \times BH) \times Cof_r \tag{27}$$

Through each iteration, $X(t)$ defines the position of the gazelle vector. As defined previously, ri_5 and ri_6 are selected at random to be 1 or 2, and $male_G$ is the best solution.

In addition, Cof_r is a randomly selected coefficient vector. D is established according to Equation (28) [88].

$$D = (|X(t)| + |male_G|) \times (2 \times r_6 - 1) \tag{28}$$

Here, r_6 is a number chosen randomly in the interval [0, 1].

4.6. Migration to Search for Food

Mountain deer sleep most of the night and are awake most of the day, as they are active especially in the early morning and sunset. In addition to being very territorial within groups of three to eight individuals, these deer are herbivores that graze and feed on grass, leaves, or small shrubs. Usually, deer groups travel long distances to graze and search for food, taking advantage of their agile stature and their great speed in running, sprinting, and jumping. Among the important characteristics imposed by the environment in which they live, mountain deer can withstand long periods without drinking water, as they suffice with fresh herbs, dew drops, young shoots, and low-hanging tree branches, especially when their range includes the acacia tree. The mathematical formulation of the mountain gazelles' behavior is as follows (Equation (29)):

$$MSF = (ub - lb) \times r_7 + lb \tag{29}$$

Here, ub is the upper limit of the treated optimization problem, while ul is the lower limit. r_7 is a random integer ranging in the [0, 1] interval.

Assuming that each generation is equal to a repetition, the production of new generations of mountain gazelles is ensured by the application of the four mechanisms described above. The addition of a new era to the total population is also considered to classify all mountain gazelles at the end of each era. Since the male adult gazelle that dominates the territory is considered the best gazelle, the classification is performed in increasing order according to the quality of the solutions. Indeed, weak or old gazelles are eliminated from the population, and only those considered to cost less and more promising are kept.

4.7. Pseudocode of the Proposed MGO Algorithm

The application of the MGO algorithm to identify the investigated PV cell/modules model parameters is summarized in Algorithm 1.

Algorithm 1: Pseudocode of the proposed MGO.

```
Input: The measured I–V data, the population size N, and the maximum number of iterations MaxIter
Output: The best solutions and the fitness value in the search space
Initialize MGO parameters;
Create a random population X_i (i = 1,2,...,N)
Calculate the fitness levels of the gazelles
while Stopping criterion is not satisfied do
    for each gazelle (X_i) do
        Load the measured I–V data
        Compute the TSM by employing Equation (20)
        Compute the MH by employing Equation (26)
        Compute thee BMH according to Equation (27)
        Compute thee MSF by employing Equation (29)
        Compute the fitness values of the TSM, MH, BMH, and MSF, then add them to the habitat
    Sort the entire population in ascending order
    Update the best gazelle
    Save the N best gazelles in the Max number of the population
```

5. Executed Experiments and Results

In this section, the MGO algorithm was used to extract the parameters of the two well-known commercial photovoltaic panels Photowatt-PWP201 and STM6-40/36. The two chosen photovoltaic panels represent the most-popular types, as monocrystalline and polycrystalline, respectively. These panels were experimented with by adopting both the SDM and DDM models. Each of these modules consists of a series of 36 connected cells. The configurations of the lower (L_B) and upper (U_B) terminals for the Photowatt-PWP201 (polycrystalline) and STM6-40/36 (monocrystalline) modules are displayed in the Table 1 [82]. The I–V experimental data used to identify the parameters of the electrical model of the Photowatt-PWP201 module were obtained under an irradiance of 1000 W/m^2 and a cell temperature of 45 °C [78,82]. In addition, to estimate the parameters of the electrical model of the STM6-40/36 module, real experimental data are provided for an irradiance of 1000 W/m^2 and a photovoltaic temperature of 51 °C [78,82].

Table 1. Parameter range of the investigated PV modules.

Parameters	Photowatt -PWP201		STP6-40/36	
	L_b	U_b	L_b	U_b
I_{ph}	0	2	0	2
I_{sd}, I_{sd1}, I_{sd2}	0	50	0	50
R_{sh}	0	2	0	0.36
R_s	0	2000	0	1000
η, η_1, η_2	1	50	1	60

The parameters of the MGO algorithm for extracting the PV model parameters (Photowatt-PWP201 and STM6-40/36) were as follows: $N = 30$ and $MaxIter = 100$. This metaheuristic MGO algorithm was compared with three other optimization methods implemented under the same conditions: Grey Wolf Optimizer (GWO), Squirrel Search Algorithm (SSA), and Differential Evolution (DE) algorithm. It is important to emphasize that all methods were tested assuming the same configuration, i.e., a number of agents of 30 and a maximum number of iterations of 100. This configuration was kept unchanged to ensure a fair comparison between the different approaches. The results obtained from the proposed approach (MGO) and the other three algorithms are presented in terms of the mean, median, minimum, maximum, and standard deviation, based on 30 runs for each algorithm. These criteria enabled us to assess the MGO's performance in terms of accuracy, stability, and efficiency in extracting PV panel's key parameters.

In keeping with the aim of ensuring a fair and thorough comparison of the performance of the MGO method, this comparative study also included other methods reported in the literature including the Bat–Artificial Bee Colony Optimizer (BABCO) [78], the Bat Algorithm [78], Multiswarm Spiral Leader Particle Swarm Optimization (M-SLPSO) [79], the Guaranteed Convergence Particle Swarm Optimization algorithm (GCPSO) [80], Triple-Phase Teaching–Learning-Based Optimization (TPTLBO) [81], the Criss-Cross-based Nelder–Mead simplex Gradient-Based Optimizer (CCNMGBO) [82], the quasi-Opposition-Based Learning Whale Optimization Algorithm (OBLWOA) [82], and the Fractional Chaotic Ensemble Particle Swarm Optimizer (FC-EPSO) [83]. These tests were carried out on a PC Laptop whose specifications were as follows: AMD Ryzen 7 3750H with Radeon Vega Mobile Gfx 2.30 GHz, 16 GB RAM, Windows 11, and 64 bit.

The results of identifying the parameters driving the mathematical model of the Photowatt-PWP201 polycrystalline PV module for the SDM and DDM models are tabulated in Table 2. According to these results, the MGO method performed best for the SDM, with an RMSE of 2.042717×10^{-3}, closely followed by the BABCO (2.046524×10^{-3}), M-SLPSO (2.046535×10^{-3}), and SSA (2.423290×10^{-3}) in descending order. For the DDM-based model, the best RMSE value (1.387641×10^{-3}) was also obtained by the MGO.

Based on the same investigations, the results of the parameter estimation for the STM6-40/36 monocrystalline PV module are presented in Table 3, for both the SDM and the DDM. Indeed, the results obtained with the one-diode-based model showed that the MGO method yielded the best RMSE value (1.719946×10^{-3}), followed by the BABCO (1.721921×10^{-3}), SSA (1.723619×10^{-3}), and finally, TPTLOBO (1.729800×10^{-3}). For the two-diode-based model, the best RMSE value (1.686104×10^{-3}) was achieved through the MGO approach, followed by the BABCO (1.686275×10^{-3}) and GCPSO (1.688361×10^{-3}).

As part of our comparative study of the performance of the different algorithms previously specified, each algorithm was run for 30 executions, and the descriptive statistics of the results achieved were collected for each test case about the SDM and the DDM. For each of these test cases, the following information is provided: the Mean of the best results (Mean), the Best result (Best), the Worst result (Worst), and the Standard deviation (Std.). The findings of these two tests are summarized in Tables 4 and 5. From the data presented in these two tables, it can be concluded that extremely satisfactory results were achieved by the MGO algorithm for both test cases. Overall, the MGO's performance clearly outperformed that of the other competitive algorithms for the two investigated models.

Once the parameters of the various PV module models have been identified, it is necessary to calculate the output current corresponding to each measured voltage value. The estimated current values were compared with the measured current values to obtain the Individual Absolute Error (IAE) for each measurement. Figures 1 and 2 illustrate the results obtained by the MGO method, where the IAE is presented as a function of the measured voltage. These plots demonstrate that the IAE, when using the Photowatt-PWP201 module, did not exceed 4.00×10^{-3} for the SDM and 3.50×10^{-3} for the DDM (Figure 1a,b). For the STM6-40/36 module, it is clear that the IAE value remained below 6.00×10^{-3} with both the SDM and the DDM (Figure 2a,b).

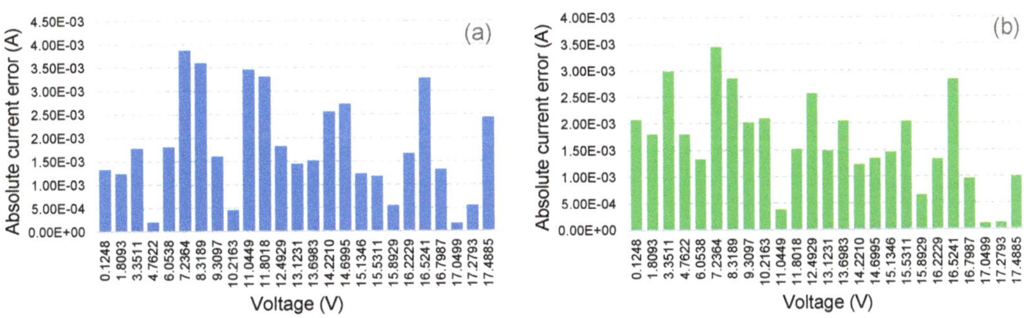

Figure 1. Current Individual Absolute Error (IAE) obtained by the MGO for the Photowatt-PWP-201 module: (**a**) using the SDM; (**b**) using the DDM.

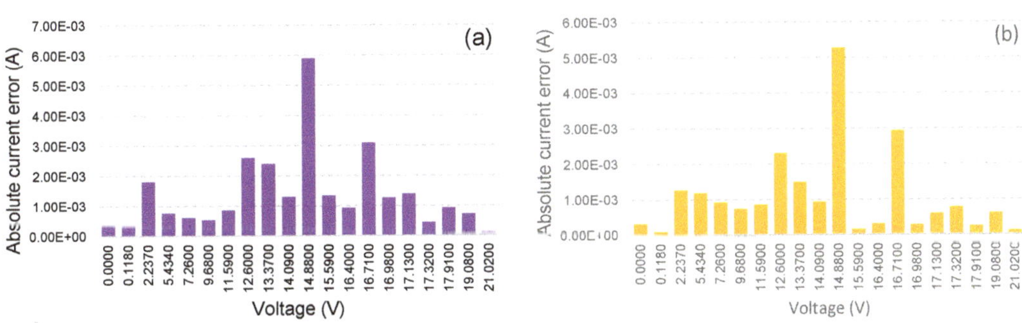

Figure 2. Current Individual Absolute Error (IAE) obtained by the MGO for the STM6-40/36 module: (**a**) using the SDM; (**b**) using the DDM.

Table 2. Comparison of the results produced by various algorithms when applied to the Photowatt-PWP201 module model.

Model	Algorithms	Parameters								RMSE × E^{-3}
		I_{ph} (A)	I_{sd} (μA)	I_{sd1} (μA)	R_s (Ω)	R_{sh} (Ω)	η	η_1	η_2	
SDM	BABCO [78]	1.032382	2.512893	-	1.239289	744.712668	47.422839	-	-	2.046524
	BA [78]	1.044856	37.14342	-	1.318087	1495.40620	60.819912	-	-	9.771899
	M-SLPSO [79]	1.032382	2.512927	-	1.239287	744.715807	01.317305	-	-	2.046535
	TPTLBO [81]	1.030500	3.482300	-	1.201300	981.982200	48.642800	-	-	2.425100
	CCNMGBO [82]	1.030514	3.48×10^{-6}	-	1.201271	981.981900	48.642830	-	-	2.425074
	OBLWOA [82]	1.030514	3.48×10^{-6}	-	1.201271	981.984500	48.642840	-	-	2.425074
	DE	1.030515	3.443584	-	1.202534	976.587000	48.599900	-	-	2.854231
	GWO	1.028367	4.9185403	-	1.158806	1544.30824	50.000000	-	-	2.714233
	SSA	1.029777	3.529950	-	1.200619	1062.66958	48.693308	-	-	2.423290
	MGO	**1.030231**	**3.604135**	**-**	**1.198040**	**1033.45081**	**48.774295**	**-**	-	**2.042717**
DDM	BABCO [78]	1.034753	0.132561	0.312026	1.999999	591.476886	-	47.821141	42.201067	1.397480
	BA [78]	0.591915	32.63274	45.26637	0.141905	1706.06090	-	37.685352	2.455933	9.635400
	M-SLPSO [79]	1.032382	2.512910	1.00×10^{-6}	1.239288	744.713773	-	1.317304	2.499659	2.046535
	CCNMGBO [82]	1.030514	2.67×10^{-6}	3.48×10^{-6}	1.20127	981.998700	-	49.301220	48.642860	2.425000
	OBLWOA [82]	1.030514	2.17×10^{-6}	3.48×10^{-6}	1.201271	981.983200	-	49.9817404	48.642830	2.427000
	DE	1.029337	2.425199	1.1064803	1.206851	1113.0658	-	49.585175	47.312278	2.879032
	GWO	1.027243	4.787116	32.994732	1.166377	1901.8138	-	50.0000	44.840739	2.736613
	SSA	1.030626	3.311942	4.928627	1.207096	953.657	-	48.45034	36.9958	2.430466
	MGO	**1.030179**	**3.258267**	**35.384629**	**1.1979727**	**1039.3818**	-	**48.868761**	**48.080506**	**1.387641**

Table 3. Comparison of the results produced by various algorithms when applied to the STM6-40/36 module model.

Model	Algorithms	Parameters								RMSE × E^{-3}
		I_{ph} (A)	I_{sd} (μA)	I_{sd1} (μA)	R_s (Ω)	R_{sh} (Ω)	η	η_1	η_2	
SDM	BABCO [78]	1.663903	2.048509	-	0.004267	15.93149	1.520463	-	-	1.721921
	GCPSO [80]	1.663904	1.738656	-	0.153855	573.1486	1.520302	-	-	1.729814
	TPTLOBO [81]	1.663900	1.738700	-	0.004300	15.92830	1.520300	-	-	1.729800
	DE	1.661559	5.682411	-	0.001573	785.9564	59.84265	-	-	2.891765
	GWO	1.663878	5.848076	-	0.003536	791.0496	52.56819	-	-	3.646006
	SSA	1.663668	1.908620	-	0.143125	590.8344	55.10250	-	-	1.723619
	MGO	**1.663931**	**1.722884**	**-**	**0.154881**	**571.6459**	**54.69487**	**-**	-	**1.719946**
DDM	BABCO [78]	1.663963	0.241206	6.596730	0.296972	621.1424226	-	1.363856	1.917464	1.686275
	BA [78]	1.497952	13.006836	47.796001	0.067902	929.420389	-	17.920435	3.956525	3.716638
	GCPSO [80]	1.663948	3.0995227	2.50×10^{-4}	0.295269	617.024493	-	1.636433	0.972892	1.688361
	DE	1.674689	4.774236	45.00142	0.09731012	530.006	-	59.84157	56.85469	2.819434
	GWO	1.661477	5.693952	5.023007	0.0225408	999.3609	-	60.00000	54.7395	3.591568
	SSA	1.660818	4.362375	1.246851	0.07989438	983.4837	-	59.73068	59.10384	1.759782
	MGO	**1.664853**	**1.577101**	**0.390000**	**0.1657537**	**548.3743**	-	**57.39241**	**51.57719**	**1.686104**

Table 4. RMSE statistical analysis of the Photowatt-PWP201 module for the SDM and the DDM.

Model	Algorithms	RMSE			
		Min	*Max*	*Mean*	*STD*
SDM	BABCO [78]	2.046524×10^{-3}	2.046424×10^{-3}	2.046524×10^{-3}	9.434855×10^{-18}
	BA [78]	9.771899×10^{-3}	1.718934×10^{-1}	3.859675×10^{-2}.	4.450036×10^{-2}
	M-SLPSO [79]	2.046535×10^{-3}	2.046535×10^{-3}	2.046535×10^{-3}	3.527834×10^{-11}
	TPTLBO [81]	2.425100×10^{-3}	2.425100×10^{-3}	2.425100×10^{-3}	1.200000×10^{-17}
	DE	2.854231×10^{-3}	9.453298×10^{-3}	4.909067×10^{-3}	1.809489×10^{-3}
	GWO	2.714233×10^{-3}	2.752705×10^{-1}	4.983853×10^{-2}	9.312518×10^{-2}
	SSA	2.432902×10^{-3}	2.742507×10^{-1}	4.272723×10^{-2}	8.299818×10^{-2}
	MGO	$\mathbf{2.042717 \times 10^{-3}}$	$\mathbf{2.0558335 \times 10^{-3}}$	$\mathbf{2.045717 \times 10^{-3}}$	$\mathbf{1.650466 \times 10^{-3}}$
DDM	BABCO [78]	1.397480×10^{-3}	1.397488×10^{-3}	1.397481×10^{-3}	2.907850×10^{-9}
	BA [78]	9.635465×10^{-3}	4.404159×10^{-1}	2.362236×10^{-1}	1.850432×10^{-1}
	M-SLPSO [79]	2.046535×10^{-3}	2.051405×10^{-3}	2.046600×10^{-3}	5.093012×10^{-7}
	ED	2.879032×10^{-3}	2.463344×10^{-2}	9.559961×10^{-3}	5.874627×10^{-3}
	GWO	2.736613×10^{-3}	9.989661×10^{-2}	1.287483×10^{-2}	2.133245×10^{-2}
	SSA	2.430466×10^{-3}	2.742507×10^{-1}	7.527784×10^{-2}	1.088360×10^{-1}
	MGO	$\mathbf{1.387641 \times 10^{-3}}$	$\mathbf{1.397421 \times 10^{-3}}$	$\mathbf{1.3902611 \times 10^{-3}}$	$\mathbf{2.992436 \times 10^{-9}}$

Table 5. RMSE statistical analysis of the STM6-40/36 module for the SDM and the DDM.

Model	Algorithms	RMSE			
		Min	*Max*	*Mean*	*STD*
SDM	BABCO [78]	1.721921×10^{-3}	1.721921×10^{-3}	1.721921×10^{-3}	1.637363×10^{-17}
	BA [78]	4.316935×10^{-2}	3.589394×10^{-1}	2.805906×10^{-1}	1.214878×10^{-1}
	TPTLOBO [81]	1.729800×10^{-3}	1.729800×10^{-3}	1.728800×10^{-3}	4.960000×10^{-18}
	DE	2.891765×10^{-3}	4.961929×10^{-3}	3.406166×10^{-3}	3.888576×10^{-4}
	GWO	3.646006×10^{-3}	2.404023×10^{-2}	9.813445×10^{-3}	5.675926×10^{-3}
	SSA	1.743619×10^{-3}	3.107574×10^{-1}	1.367193×10^{-2}	5.612953×10^{-1}
	MGO	$\mathbf{1.719946 \times 10^{-3}}$	$\mathbf{1.729499 \times 10^{-3}}$	$\mathbf{1.718746 \times 10^{-3}}$	$\mathbf{7.535025 \times 10^{-17}}$
DDM	BABCO [78]	1.686275×10^{-3}	1.698849×10^{-3}	1.6912799×10^{-3}	3.481031×10^{-6}
	BA [78]	3.716638×10^{-2}	3.536434×10^{-1}	$1.847427E \times 10^{-1}$	1.390727×10^{-1}
	FC-EPSO1 [83]	1.772100×10^{-3}	-	-	3.071900×10^{-10}
	DE	2.819434×10^{-3}	7.931632×10^{-3}	4.289150×10^{-3}	1.061135×10^{-3}
	GWO	3.591568×10^{-3}	2.317158×10^{-2}	1.179205×10^{-2}	6.004844×10^{-3}
	SSA	1.759782×10^{-3}	3.107574×10^{-1}	1.836926×10^{-2}	5.674788×10^{-2}
	MGO	$\mathbf{1.686104 \times 10^{-3}}$	$\mathbf{1.781279 \times 10^{-3}}$	$\mathbf{1.69973 \times 10^{-3}}$	$\mathbf{4.873634 \times 10^{-17}}$

Figures 3 and 4 show the values of the objective function obtained by the different optimization algorithms investigated during the parameter estimation process for the two PV modules (Photowatt-PWP201 and STM6-40/36) for both the mathematical SDM and DDM.

The results presented in these figures revealed that the MGO stood out for its high convergence speed right from the first iterations (around 40 iterations). Moreover, its accuracy was better than that of the other methods. These results proved that the MGO-based approach is a particularly effective alternative for solving the problems in question. This performance was due to the ability of the proposed MGO to avoid convergence to local solutions. In addition, the GWO, SSA, and DE algorithms showed a low convergence speed, particularly for the first iterations.

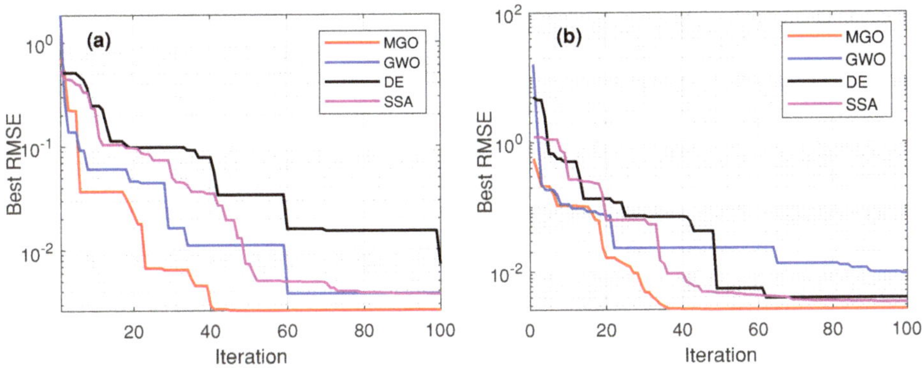

Figure 3. Comparative study of the MGO and other well-known optimization techniques in terms of the convergence characteristics for the Photowatt-PWP-201 module: (**a**) using the SDM; (**b**) using the DDM.

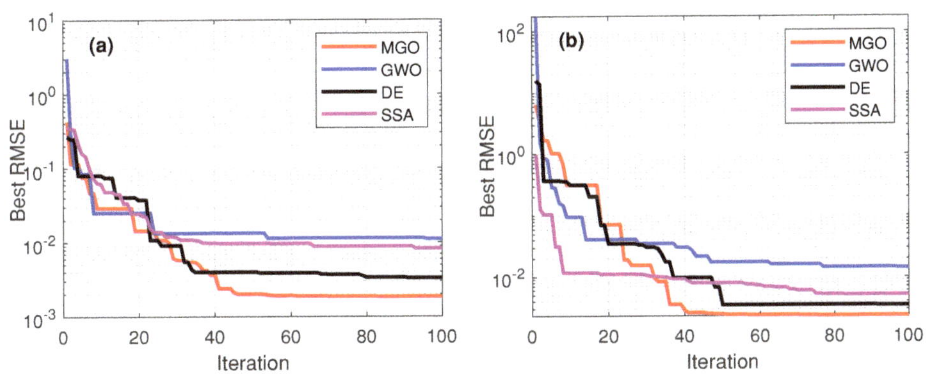

Figure 4. Comparative study of the MGO and other well-known optimization techniques in terms of the convergence characteristics for the STM6-40/36 module: (**a**) using the SDM; (**b**) using the DDM.

After obtaining the electrical parameters of the two equivalent models (SDM and DDM) of the experimented PV panels, the I–V and P–V characteristics of the two PV modules, Photowatt-PWP-201 and TM6-40/36, estimated by the proposed MGO algorithm for the SDM and the DDM are plotted.

In fact, the five key parameters of the SDM and the seven ones of the DDM PV module obtained by implementing the MGO algorithm were used to calculate the generated currents in accordance with Equations (5) and (9), respectively. As a result, the I–V and P–V characteristics were easily obtained. Accordingly, Figures 5–8 show such plots highlighting clearly that the estimated characteristics (I–V and P–V) were in good agreement with the experimental data points, thereby proving the effectiveness of the MGO compared to the other algorithms.

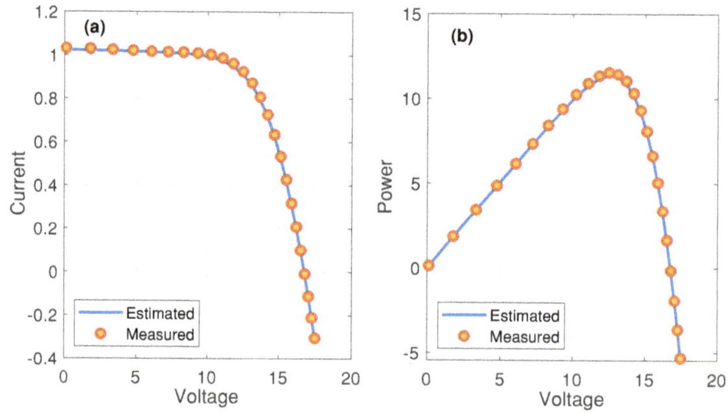

Figure 5. Comparison of measured data and simulated data obtained by the MGO of the Photowatt-PWP201 module for the SDM: (**a**) I–V curve. (**b**) P–V curve.

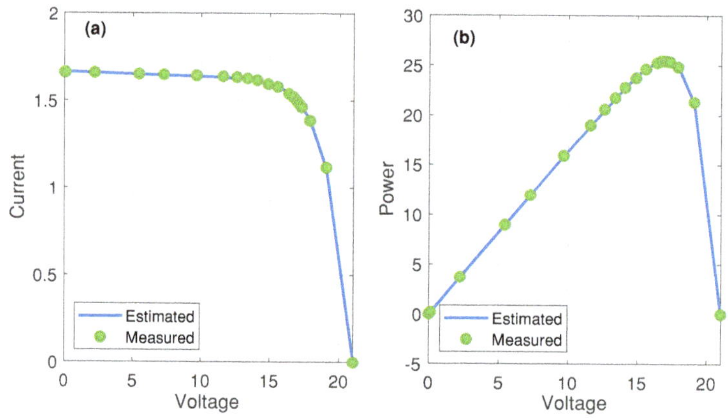

Figure 6. Comparison of measured data and simulated data obtained by the MGO of the STM6-40/36 module for the SDM: (**a**) I–V curve. (**b**) P–V curve.

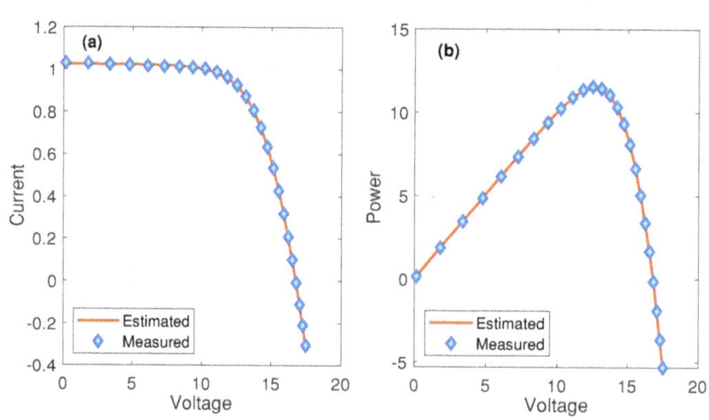

Figure 7. Comparison of measured data and simulated data obtained by the MGO of the Photowatt-PWP201 module for the DDM: (**a**) I–V curve. (**b**) P–V curve.

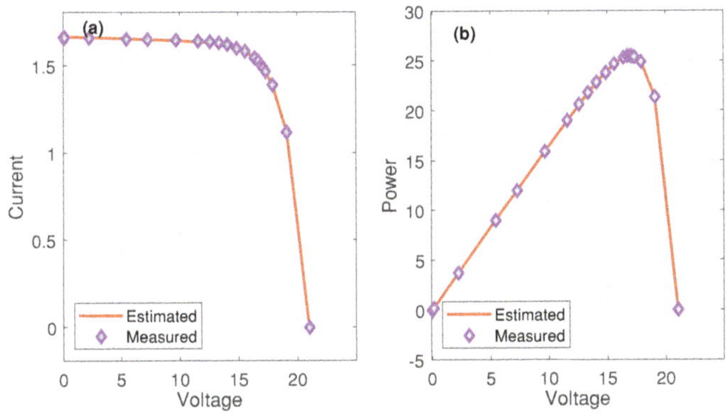

Figure 8. Comparison of measured data and simulated data obtained by the MGO of the STM6-40/36 module for the DDM: (**a**) I–V curve. (**b**) P–V curve.

6. Conclusions and Future Works

This investigation presented a new application of a Mountain Gazelle Optimizer-based approach (MGO) for identifying the key parameters of the photovoltaic Single-Diode Model (SDM) and Double-Diode Model (DDM) of technologies widely used in the literature: monocrystalline STM6-40/36 and polycrystalline Photowatt-PWP20 photovoltaic panels. The performance of the suggested MGO was assessed by many statistical indicators such as the standard deviation, Max RMSE, mean RMSE, Min RMSE, IAE, and the I–V, and P–V characteristics. The results of the experiment showed that the MGO-based method achieved superior performance and produced a competitive end result compared with other well-cited algorithms. Hence, the MGO can be a feasible alternative for parameter estimation of complex PV cell models. The experimental validation of the parameter estimation of the tested PV modules used data extracted from the I–V and P–V characteristics. For all models examined, the suggested MGO outperformed all the selected state-of-the-art optimizers by achieving the best performance in terms of accuracy, stability, and statistical data and the lowest RMSE over 30 independent runs. More concretely, the extensive experiments on the MGO showed that it outperformed the GWO algorithm by 47.17% and 46.94% on the SDM and DDM of the STM6-40/36 module, respectively. As future prospects, the MGO will be investigated to deal with many other complex optimization problems such as the maximum power point tracking issue in photovoltaic- and wind-energy-conversion systems and economic dispatch in modern power systems and smart grids.

Author Contributions: Conceptualization, R.A., S.S. and S.U.; methodology, R.A., S.S., S.U., B.N.A. and M.P.; software, R.A. and S.S.; validation, R.A., S.S. and S.U.; formal analysis, R.A., S.S. and S.U.; investigation, R.A. and S.U.; resources, S.U. and M.A.A.; data curation, R.A. and S.S.; writing—original draft preparation, R.A., S.S., S.U., B.N.A., M.A.A. and M.P.; writing—review and editing, R.A., S.S., B.N.A., M.P. and M.A.A.; visualization, R.A. and S.U.; supervision, R.A. and S.U.; funding acquisition, S.U. All authors have read and agreed to the published version of the manuscript.

Funding: This research was funded by Princess Nourah bint Abdulrahman University Researchers Supporting Project Number PNURSP2023R79, Princess Nourah bint Abdulrahman University, Riyadh, Saudi Arabia.

Institutional Review Board Statement: Not applicable.

Informed Consent Statement: Not applicable.

Data Availability Statement: Not applicable.

Acknowledgments: Princess Nourah bint Abdulrahman University Researchers Supporting Project Number PNURSP2023R79, Princess Nourah bint Abdulrahman University, Riyadh, Saudi Arabia.

Conflicts of Interest: The authors declare no conflict of interest.

Abbreviations

The following abbreviations are used in this manuscript:

PEMFC	Proton Exchange Membrane Fuel Cell
DO	Dandelion Optimizer
GWO	Grey Wolf Optimizer
GBO	Gradient-Based Optimizer
HHO	Harris Hawks Optimizer
IAEO	Improved Artificial Ecosystem Optimizer
VSDE	Vortex Search Differential Evolution
ABCDESC	Artificial Bee Colony Differential Evolution Shuffled Complex
HR	Hail Region
CO_2	Carbon dioxide
CO	Carbon monoxide
H_2O	Water molecule
H_2	Hydrogen gas
O_2	Dioxygen gas
RE	Renewable Energy
KSA	Kingdom of Saudi Arabia
UNWTO	World Tourism Organization
COVID-19	Coronavirus Disease
EV	Electric Vehicle
ZEV	Zero-Emission Vehicle
AC	Alternating Current
GTO	Gorilla Troops Optimizer
MGTO	Modified GTO
HBO	Honey Badger Optimizer
SSE	Sum of Squared Errors
BO	Bonobo Optimizer
QOBO	Quasi-Oppositional Bonobo Optimizer
EBES	Enhanced Bald Eagle Search
DA	Dandelion Algorithm
ELM	Extreme Learning Machine
NNA	Neural Network Algorithm
ELMD	Dandelion algorithm with ELM

References

1. Łukasiewicz, K.; Pietrzak, P.; Kraciuk, J.; Kacperska, E.; Cieciora, M. Sustainable Energy Development—A Systematic Literature Review. *Energies* **2022**, *15*, 8284. [CrossRef]
2. Alturki, M.; Abbassi, R.; Albaker, A.; Jerbi, H. A New Hybrid Synchronization PLL Scheme for Interconnecting Renewable Energy Sources to an Abnormal Electric Grid. *Mathematics* **2022**, *10*, 1101. [CrossRef]
3. Sidea, D.O.; Tudose, A.M.; Picioroaga, I.I.; Bulac, C. Two-Stage Optimal Active-Reactive Power Coordination for Microgrids with High Renewable Sources Penetration and Electrical Vehicles Based on Improved Sine–Cosine Algorithm. *Mathematics* **2023**, *11*, 45. [CrossRef]
4. Zhao, L.; Jerbi, H.; Abbassi, R.; Liu, B.; Latifi, M.; Nakamura, H. Sizing renewable energy systems with energy storage systems based microgrids for cost minimization using hybrid shuffled frog-leaping and pattern search algorithm. *Sustain. Cities Soc.* **2021**, *73*, 103124. [CrossRef]
5. Rasool, M.H.; Perwez, U.; Qadir, Z.; Hassan Ali, S.H. Scenario-based techno-reliability optimization of an off-grid hybrid renewable energy system: A multi-city study framework. *Sustain. Energy Technol. Assess.* **2022**, *53*, 102411. [CrossRef]
6. Rasool, M.H.; Taylan, O.; Perwez, U.; Batunlu, C. Comparative assessment of multi-objective optimization of hybrid energy storage system considering grid balancing. *Renew. Energy* **2023**, *216*, 119107. [CrossRef]
7. Abbassi, R.; Hammami, M.; Chebbi, S. Improvement of the integration of a grid-connected wind-photovoltaic hybrid system. In Proceedings of the International Conference on Electrical Engineering and Software Applications, Hammamet, Tunisia, 17–19 March 2013.

8. Gorjian, S.; Shukla, A. (Eds.) *Photovoltaic Solar Energy Conversion: Technologies, Applications and Environmental Impacts*; Elsevier Science: Amsterdam, The Netherlands, 2020; Volume 15, p. 8284.
9. Sara, O.P.; Paulo, R.S.; Francisco T.P. Assessment of the potential of combining wave and solar energy resources to power supply worldwide offshore oil and gas platforms. *Energy Convers. Manag.* **2020**, *223*, 113299.
10. Available online: https://www.pv-magazine.com/2023/01/18/china-added-87-41-gw-of-solar-in-2022 (accessed on 3 April 2023).
11. Okai, V.; Chahul, H.F.; Shikler, R. Enhancement of Power Conversion Efficiency of Non-Fullerene Organic Solar Cells Using Green Synthesized Au–Ag Nanoparticles. *Polymers* **2023**, *15*, 1482. [CrossRef]
12. Ye, X.; Tao, Z.; Huifeng, Y.; Jingwen, W.; Pengqing, B.; Jianhui, H. Design of ultranarrow-bandgap acceptors for efficient organic photovoltaic cells and highly sensitive organic photodetectors. *J. Energy Chem.* **2022**, *72*, 388–394.
13. Zheng, Z.; Shao, Y.; Ding, C.; Li, M.; Lu, W. Rational design of ZL003-based organic dyes for highly efficient dye-sensitized solar cells: Influence of alkynyl group and π-spacers on photovoltaic performance. *J. Mol. Struct.* **2022**, *1269*, 133728. [CrossRef]
14. Shaolei, G.; Rabeh, A.; Houssem, J.; Alireza, R.; Kengo, S. Efficient maximum power point tracking for a photovoltaic using hybrid shuffled frog-leaping and pattern search algorithm under changing environmental conditions. *J. Clean. Prod.* **2021**, *297*, 126573.
15. Boubaker, S.; Kamel, S.; Ghazouani, N.; Mellit, A. Assessment of Machine and Deep Learning Approaches for Fault Diagnosis in Photovoltaic Systems Using Infrared Thermography. *Remote Sens.* **2023**, *15*, 1686. [CrossRef]
16. Liu, Y.; Ding, K.; Zhang, J.; Lin, Y.; Yang, Z.; Chen, X.; Li, Y.; Chen, X. Intelligent fault diagnosis of photovoltaic array based on variable predictive models and I–V curves. *Sol. Energy* **2022**, *237*, 340–351. [CrossRef]
17. Syed, H.J.; Puviarasi, R.; Chilambarasan, M.; Sarita, S.S.; Raviteja, S.; Vipin, S.; Madhavarao, S.; Sudhakar, M.; Mohanavel, V. An approach to the utilization of grid integration to analyze the performance and quality of solar photovoltaic model. *Energy Rep.* **2022**, *8*, 1029–1044.
18. Rabeh, A.; Abdelkader, A.; Mohamed, J.; Souad, C. Identification of unknown parameters of solar cell models: A comprehensive overview of available approaches. *Renew. Sustain. Energy Rev.* **2018**, *90*, 453–474.
19. Elkholy, A.; Abou El-Ela, A.A. Optimal parameters estimation and modelling of photovoltaic modules using analytical method. *Heliyon* **2019**, *5*, e02137. [CrossRef]
20. Martin, Ć.; Shady, H.E.; Ahmed, F.Z. On the root mean square error (RMSE) calculation for parameter estimation of photovoltaic models: A novel exact analytical solution based on Lambert W function. *Energy Convers. Manag.* **2020**, *210*, 112716.
21. Firoz, K.; Amir, A.A.; Fahad, A.A. Critical analysis of the limitations and validity of the assumptions with the analytical methods commonly used to determine the photovoltaic cell parameters. *Renew. Sustain. Energy Rev.* **2021**, *140*, 110753.
22. Ma, J.; Hong, D.; Wang, K.; Bi, Z.; Zhu, X.; Zhang, J. Analytical modeling and parameter estimation of photovoltaic strings under partial shading conditions. *Sol. Energy Mater. Sol. Cells* **2022**, *235*, 111494. [CrossRef]
23. Dris, B.H.; Mustapha, E.; El Hanafi, A.; Driss, S.; Souad, L.; Jamal, C.; Ahmed, I.; Rabya, A.; Daoudi, E.; Sergey, O. A novel hybrid numerical with analytical approach for parameter extraction of photovoltaic modules. *Energy Convers. Manag. X* **2022**, *14*, 100219.
24. Rabeh, A.; Boudjemline, A.; Abdelkader, A.; Torchani, A.; Gasmi, H.; Guesmi, T. A Numerical-Analytical Hybrid Approach for the Identification of SDM Solar Cell Unknown Parameters. *Eng. Technol. Appl. Sci. Res.* **2018**, *8*, 2907–2913.
25. Kawtar, T.; Noureddine, M.; Askar, S.S.; Mohamed, A. Numerical procedure for accurate simulation of photovoltaic modules performance based on the identification of the single-diode model parameters. *Energy Rep.* **2023**, *9*, 5532–5544.
26. Chen, X.; Ding, K.; Yang, H.; Chen, X.; Zhang, J.; Jiang, M.; Gao, R.; Liu, Z. Research on real-time identification method of model parameters for the photovoltaic array. *Appl. Energy* **2023**, *342*, 121157. [CrossRef]
27. Abbassi, R.; Saidi, S.; Abbassi, A.; Jerbi, H.; Kchaou, M.; Alhasnawi, B.N. Accurate Key Parameters Estimation of PEMFCs' Models Based on Dandelion Optimization Algorithm. *Mathematics* **2023**, *11*, 1298. [CrossRef]
28. Abdelfattah, E.; Mustapha, E.; El Hanafi, A.; Dris, B.H.; Souad, L.; Driss, S.; Imade, C.; Ismail, A. Dandelion Optimizer algorithm-based method for accurate photovoltaic model parameter identification. *Energy Convers. Manag. X* **2023**, *19*, 100405.
29. Papadimitrakis, M.; Giamarelos, N.; Stogiannos, M.; Zois, E.N.; Livanos, N.A.-I.; Alexandridis A. Metaheuristic search in smart grid: A review with emphasis on planning, scheduling and power flow optimization applications. *Renew. Sustain. Energy Rev.* **2023**, *145*, 111072. [CrossRef]
30. Koteswara, R.D.; Seshu, K.R.; Phani, R.L.; Singh, A.R. Enhancement of loadability and voltage stability in grid-connected microgrid network. *J. Clean. Prod.* **2023**, *374*, 133881.
31. Wu, Q.; Xue, F.; Lu, S.; Jiang, L.; Huang, T.; Wang, X.; Sang, Y. Integrated network partitioning and DERs allocation for planning of Virtual Microgrids. *Electr. Power Syst. Res.* **2023**, *216*, 109024. [CrossRef]
32. Qiong, W.; Gang, C.; Mohammad, K.; Banar, F.I.; Shima, R. Multi-objective optimization of IoT-based green building energy system using binary metaheuristic algorithms. *J. Build. Eng.* **2023**, *68*, 106031.
33. Leite, G.M.C.; Marcelino, C.G.; Pedreira, C.E.; Jiménez-Fernández, S.; Salcedo-Sanz, S. Evaluating the risk of uncertainty in smart grids with electric vehicles using an evolutionary swarm-intelligent algorithm. *J. Clean. Prod.* **2023**, *401*, 136775. [CrossRef]
34. Hubert, M.S.; Dirk, U.S. Metaheuristic for the integrated electric vehicle and crew scheduling problem. *Appl. Energy* **2023**, *339*, 120915.
35. Mohd, B.; Fareed, A.; Rizwan, M. Techno- economic assessment of grid and renewable powered electric vehicle charging stations in India using a modified metaheuristic technique. *Energy Convers. Manag.* **2023**, *284*, 116995.
36. Mohamed, A.K.; Sihem, S.; Okba, K.; Abdelhak, M.; Seyedali, M. Deep learning and metaheuristics application in internet of things: A literature review. *Microprocess. Microsyst.* **2023**, *98*, 104792.

37. Ali, S.; Tania, T.; Ali, G. Towards developing a machine learning-metaheuristic-enhanced energy-sensitive routing framework for the internet of things. *Microprocess. Microsyst.* **2023**, *96*, 104747.
38. Agostino, F. Metaheuristic algorithm for anomaly detection in Internet of Things leveraging on a neural-driven multiagent system. *Knowl.-Based Syst.* **2021**, *228*, 107241.
39. Banghua, W.; Xuebin, L.; Wameed, D.S.; Ebrahim, G.D. Optimal deploying IoT services on the fog computing: A metaheuristic-based multi-objective approach. *J. King Saud Univ.-Comput. Inf. Sci.* **2022**, *34 Pt B*, 10010–10027.
40. Ayyarao, T.S.L.V.; Ramakrishna, N.S.S.; Elavarasan, R.M.; Polumahanthi, N.; Rambabu, M.; Saini, G.; Khan, B.; Alatas, B. War Strategy Optimization Algorithm: A New Effective Metaheuristic Algorithm for Global Optimization. *IEEE Access* **2022**, *10*, 25073–25105. [CrossRef]
41. Lin, C.J.; Prasetyo, Y.T. A metaheuristic-based approach to optimizing color design for military camouflage using particle swarm optimization. *Color Res. Appl.* **2019**, *44*, 740–748. [CrossRef]
42. Ismail, M.A.; Hasan, H.T.; Sondoss, E. A military fleet mix problem for high-valued defense assets: A simulation-based optimization approach. *Expert Syst. Appl.* **2023**, *213*, 118964.
43. Naman S.B.; Abhishek, D.P.; Jegadeeshwaran, R.; Sujit, S.P.; Kaushal, A.K.; Rohan, S.G. Application of metaheuristic optimization based support vector machine for milling cutter health monitoring. *Intell. Syst. Appl.* **2023**, *18*, 200196.
44. Mohamed, O.M.; Zineb, Z.; Abdellah, N.; Seifeddine, C.; Nouzha, L.; Mohamed, E. Optimal sensor placement methodology of triaxial accelerometers using combined metaheuristic algorithms for structural health monitoring applications. *Structures* **2023**, *51*, 1959–1971.
45. Malik, M.I.; Ibrahim, A.; Hannay, P.; Sikos, L.F. Developing Resilient Cyber-Physical Systems: A Review of State-of-the-Art Malware Detection Approaches, Gaps, and Future Directions. *Computers* **2023**, *12*, 79. [CrossRef]
46. Hadeel, A.; Mohammed, A.; Jaber, S.A.; Fahd, N.A.; Anwer, M.H.; Abu Sarwar, Z.; Azza, E.O.; Amani, A.A. Chaotic marine predators optimization based task scheduling scheme for resource limited cyber-physical systems. *Comput. Electr. Eng.* **2023**, *106*, 108597.
47. Xu, Y.; Li, Q.; Xu, X.; Yang, J.; Chen, Y. Research Progress of Nature-Inspired Metaheuristic Algorithms in Mobile Robot Path Planning. *Electronics* **2023**, *12*, 3263. [CrossRef]
48. Soyeon, P.; Jongwoo, K.; Jieun, P.; Jessica, B.K.; Gunwoo, N. Design of patterns in tubular robots using DNN-metaheuristics optimization. *Int. J. Mech. Sci.* **2023**, *251*, 108352.
49. Kumar, M.; Kumar, A. An efficient parameters extraction technique of photovoltaic models for performance assessment. *Sol. Energy* **2017**, *158*, 192–206. [CrossRef]
50. Dizqah, A.M.; Maheri, A.; Busawon, K. An accurate method for the pv model identification based on a genetic algorithm and the interior-point method. *Renew. Energy* **2014**, *72*, 212–222. [CrossRef]
51. Khanna, V.; Das, B.K.; Bisht, D.; Vandana; Singh, P.K. A three diode model for industrial solar cells and estimation of solar cell parameters using pso algorithm. *Renew. Energy* **2015**, *78*, 105–113. [CrossRef]
52. Jordehi, A.R. Time varying acceleration coefficients particle swarm optimisation (tvacpso): A new optimisation algorithm for estimating parameters of pv cells and modules. *Energy Convers. Manag.* **2016**, *129*, 262–274. [CrossRef]
53. Nunes, H.G.G.; Pombo, J.A.N.; Mariano, S.J.P.S.; Calado, M.R.A.; Felippe de Souza, J.A.M. A new high performance method for determining the parameters of pv cells and modules based on guaranteed convergence particle swarm optimization. *Appl. Energy* **2018**, *211*, 774–791. [CrossRef]
54. Jordehi, A.R. Enhanced leader particle swarm optimisation (elpso): An efficient algorithm for parameter estimation of photovoltaic (pv) cells and modules. *Sol. Energy* **2018**, *159*, 78–87. [CrossRef]
55. Wu, L.; Chen, Z.; Long, C.; Cheng, S.; Lin, P.; Chen, Y.; Chen, H. Parameter extraction of photovoltaic models from measured I-V characteristics curves using a hybrid trust region reflective algorithm. *Appl. Energy* **2018**, *232*, 36–53. [CrossRef]
56. Chen, X.; Xu, B.; Mei, C.; Ding, Y.; Li, K. Teaching–learning–based artificial bee colony for solar photovoltaic parameter estimation. *Appl. Energy* **2018**, *212*, 1578–1588. [CrossRef]
57. Jamadi, B.M.; Merrikh-Bayat, F. Very accurate parameter estimation of single- and double-diode solar cell models using a modified artificial bee colony algorithm. *Int. J. Energy Environ. Eng.* **2016**, *7*, 13–25. [CrossRef]
58. Li, D.; Guo, W.; Lerch, A.; Li, Y.; Wang, L.; Wu, Q. An Adaptive Particle Swarm Optimizer with Decoupled Exploration and Exploitation for Large Scale Optimization. *Swarm Evol. Comput.* **2021**, *60*, 100789. [CrossRef]
59. Premkumar, M.; Shankar, N.; Sowmya, R.; Jangir, P.; Kumar, C.; Abualigah, L.; Derebew, B. A reliable optimization framework for parameter identification of single-diode solar photovoltaic model using weighted velocity-guided grey wolf optimization algorithm and Lambert-W function. *IET Renew. Power Gener.* **2023**, *17*, 2711–2732. [CrossRef]
60. Irudayaraj, A.X.R.; Wahab, N.I.A.; Veerasamy, V.; Premkumar, M.; Radzi, M.A.M.; Sulaiman, N.B.; Haes Alhelou, H. Decentralized frequency control of restructured energy system using hybrid intelligent algorithm and non-linear fractional order proportional integral derivative controller. *IET Renew. Power Gener.* **2023**, *17*, 2009–2037. [CrossRef]
61. Premkumar, M.; Sowmya, R.; Ramakrishnan, C.; Pradeep, J.; Essam, H.H.; Sanchari, D.; Nallapaneni, M.K. An efficient and reliable scheduling algorithm for unit commitment scheme in microgrid systems using enhanced mixed integer particle swarm optimizer considering uncertainties. *Energy Rep.* **2023**, *9*, 1029–1053. [CrossRef]
62. Chen, W.-C.; Tai, Y.-C.; Wang, M.-W.; Tsai, H.-C. Parameter optimization of etching process for a LGP stamper. *Neural Comput. Appl.* **2013**, *23*, 1539–1550. [CrossRef]

63. Chen, W.-C.; Kurniawan, D. Process parameters optimization for multiple quality characteristics in plastic injection molding using Taguchi method, BPNN, GA, and hybrid PSO-GA. *Int. J. Precis. Eng. Manuf.* **2014**, *15*, 1583–1593. [CrossRef]
64. Li, M.; Chen, H.; Shi, X.; Liu, S.; Zhang, M.; Lu, S. A multi-information fusion riple variables with iterationinertia weight PSO algorithm and its application. *Appl. Soft Comput.* **2019**, *84*, 105677. [CrossRef]
65. Ji, K.; Zhao, P.; Zhou, X.; Chen, Y.; Dong, Z.; Zheng, J.; Fu, J.; Zhou, H. Uniform Initialization in Response Space for PSO and its Applications. *Appl. Math. Comput.* **2022**, *431*, 127351. [CrossRef]
66. Rezaee, A.J.; Jasni, J. Parameter selection in particle swarm optimisation: A survey. *J. Exp. Theor. Artif. Intell.* **2013**, *25*, 527–542. [CrossRef]
67. Chen, Y.; Li, L.; Xiao, J.; Yang, Y.; Liang, J.; Li, T. Particle swarm optimizer with crossover operation. *Eng. Appl. Artif. Intell.* **2018**, *70*, 159–169. [CrossRef]
68. Liu, W.; Wang, Z.; Liu, X.; Zeng, N.; Bell, D. A novel particle swarm optimization approach for patient clustering from emergency departments. *IEEE Trans. Evol. Comput.* **2013**, *23*, 718–724. [CrossRef]
69. Li, J.; Zhang, J.Q.; Jiang, C.J.; Zhou, M.C. Composite particle swarm optimizer with historical memory for function optimization. *IEEE Trans. Cybern.* **2017**, *45*, 2350–2363. [CrossRef]
70. Sibalija, T.V. Particle swarm optimisation in designing parameters of manufacturing processes: A review. *Appl. Soft Comput.* **2019**, *84*, 105743. [CrossRef]
71. Sengupta, S.; Basak, S.; Peters, R.A. Particle swarm optimization: A survey of historical and recent developments with hybridization perspectives. *J. Mach. Learn. Knowl. Extract.* **2019**, *1*, 157–191. [CrossRef]
72. Anthony, T.; Anthony, S.M.; Ashok, K. Exploration in neo-Hebbian reinforcement learning: Computational approaches to the exploration–exploitation balance with bio-inspired neural networks. *Neural Netw.* **2022**, *151*, 16–33.
73. Nikhil, A.; Siba, S.M. Switching from exploration to exploitation in gravitational search algorithm based on diversity with Chaos. *Inf. Sci.* **2023**, *635*, 298–327.
74. Wang, P.; Xue, B.; Liang, J.; Zhang, M. Feature Selection Using Diversity-Based Multi-objective Binary Differential Evolution. *Inf. Sci.* **2023**, *626*, 586–606. [CrossRef]
75. Atefeh, R.K.; Fatemeh, G.J.; Iman, S.; Mostafa, H.K. Utilizing hybrid metaheuristic approach to design an agricultural closed-loop supply chain network. *Expert Syst. Appl.* **2023**, *217*, 119504.
76. Souhail, D.; Alaeddine, Z. Adaptive iterated stochastic metaheuristic to optimize holes drilling path in manufacturing industry: The Adaptive-Dhouib-Matrix-3 (A-DM3). *Eng. Appl. Artif. Intell.* **2023**, *120*, 105898.
77. Benyamin, A.; Farhad, S.G.; Nima, K.; Seyedali, M. Mountain Gazelle Optimizer: A new Nature-inspired Metaheuristic Algorithm for Global Optimization Problems. *Adv. Eng. Softw.* **2022**, *174*, 103282.
78. Aoufi, B.; Hachana, O.; Sid, M.A.; Giuseppe, M.T. Precise and fast parameter identification of monocrystalline, polycrystalline, and mono-facial photovoltaic modules using a new Bat Artificial Bee Colony optimizer. *J. Comput. Electron.* **2022**, 21, 491–512. [CrossRef]
79. Nunes, H.G.G.; Silva, P.N.C.; Pombo, J.A.N.; Mariano, S.J.P.S.; Calado, M.R.A. Multiswarm spiral leader particle swarm optimisation algorithm for PV parameter identification. *Energy Convers. Manag.* **2020**, *225*, 113388. [CrossRef]
80. Nunes, H.G.G.; Pombo, J.A.N.; Mariano, S.J.P.S.; Calado, M.R.A. Suitable mathematical model for the electrical characterization of different photovoltaic technologies: Experimental validation. *Energy Convers. Manag.* **2021**, *231*, 113820. [CrossRef]
81. Liao, Z.; Chen, Z.; Li, S. Parameters Extraction of Photovoltaic Models Using Triple-Phase Teaching-Learning-Based Optimization. *IEEE Access* **2020**, *8*, 69937–69952. [CrossRef]
82. Wang, D.; Sun, X.; Kang, H.; Shen, Y.; Chen, Q. Heterogeneous differential evolution algorithm for parameter estimation of solar photovoltaic models. *Energy Rep.* **2022**, *8*, 15249–15285. [CrossRef]
83. Yousri, D.; Thanikanti, S.B.; Allam, D.; Ramachandaramurthy, V.K.; Eteiba, M.B. Fractional chaotic ensemble particle swarm optimizer for identifying the single, double, and three diode photovoltaic models' parameters. *Energy* **2020**, *195*, 116979. [CrossRef]
84. Manoharan, P.; Chandrasekaran, K.; Thankkapan, D.; Somasundaram; David, T.S.J.; Pradeep, J.; Hassan, H.A. A reliable optimization framework using ensembled successive history adaptive differential evolutionary algorithm for optimal power flow problems. *IET Gener. Transm. Distrib.* **2023**, *17*, 1333–1357.
85. Mirjalili, S.; Mirjalili, S.M.; Lewis, A. grey wolf optimizer. *Adv. Eng. Softw.* **2014**, *69*, 46–61. [CrossRef]
86. Mohit, J.; Vijander, S.; Asha, R. A novel nature-inspired algorithm for optimization: Squirrel search algorithm. *Swarm Evol. Comput.* **2019**, *44*, 148–175.
87. Palestine Mountain Gazelle Officially an Endangered Species. Available online: https://www.newarab.com/news/palestine-mountain-gazelle-officially-endangered-species (accessed on 16 June 2023).
88. Chandrasekaran, K.; Thaveedhu, A.S.R.; Manoharan, P.; Vijayarajan, P. Optimal estimation of parameters of the three-diode commercial solar photovoltaic model using an improved Berndt-Hall-Hall-Hausman method hybridized with an augmented mountain gazelle optimizer. *Environ. Sci. Pollut. Res.* **2023**, *30*, 57683–57706. [CrossRef]

Disclaimer/Publisher's Note: The statements, opinions and data contained in all publications are solely those of the individual author(s) and contributor(s) and not of MDPI and/or the editor(s). MDPI and/or the editor(s) disclaim responsibility for any injury to people or property resulting from any ideas, methods, instructions or products referred to in the content.

mathematics

MDPI

Article

Analysis of Meshfree Galerkin Methods Based on Moving Least Squares and Local Maximum-Entropy Approximation Schemes

Hongtao Yang [1], Hao Wang [2] and Bo Li [1,*]

[1] College of Engineering, Peking University, Beijing 100187, China; marcoyoung14@pku.edu.cn
[2] School of Mechanical Engineering, Purdue University, 585 Purdue Mall, West Lafayette, IN 47907, USA; wang5336@purdue.edu
* Correspondence: bo.li@pku.edu.cn

Abstract: Over the last two decades, meshfree Galerkin methods have become increasingly popular in solid and fluid mechanics applications. A variety of these methods have been developed, each incorporating unique meshfree approximation schemes to enhance their performance. In this study, we examine the application of the Moving Least Squares and Local Maximum-Entropy (LME) approximations within the framework of Optimal Transportation Meshfree for solving Galerkin boundary-value problems. We focus on how the choice of basis order and the non-negativity, as well as the weak Kronecker-delta properties of shape functions, influence the performance of numerical solutions. Through comparative numerical experiments, we evaluate the efficiency, accuracy, and capabilities of these two approximation schemes. The decision to use one method over the other often hinges on factors like computational efficiency and resource management, underscoring the importance of carefully considering the specific attributes of the data and the intrinsic nature of the problem being addressed.

Keywords: meshfree methods; local maximum entropy; moving least squares; boundary value problems

MSC: 65M60

1. Introduction

Over the past few decades, conventional grid-based numerical methods have been well-developed and successfully applied to a wide variety of boundary value problems in engineering and applied science. Despite their numerical advantages and great success, grid-dependent methods face inherent difficulties in various aspects when employed to solve large-deformation problems. In response to these challenges, a myriad of meshfree methods have emerged as powerful numerical techniques. These methods aim to mitigate certain issues by constructing the approximation of unknowns based on scattered points without relying on fixed mesh connectivity. Related reviews of meshfree methods may be found in [1–3].

Notable examples of meshfree methods encompass Smoothed Particle Hydrodynamics (SPH) [4–6], Element-Free Galerkin (EFG) [7,8], Reproducing Kernel Particle Method (RKPM) [9], Material Point Method (MPM) [10,11], Natural Element Method (NEM) [12–14] and Optimal Transportation Meshfree (OTM) [15,16]. Despite their diversity, meshfree methods can be categorized based on the approximation schemes employed to construct compactly supported shape functions. The spectrum of meshfree approximation schemes include geometry-based approximation, such as natural neighbour interpolation, kernel estimates, as well as optimization-based schemes including moving least squares and maximum-entropy approximation.

The concept of kernel estimates (KE), introduced in [4,5], forms the basis for SPH. The kernel function used in this process serves the same role as the test function in Galerkin methods. Despite the zeroth-order completeness of SPH's continuous form and the high-order consistency of most kernel functions, discrete SPH struggles to reproduce constant fields on irregular node sets. As a result, numerous improvements have been made to fulfill the completeness, such as Johnson-Beissel correction [17], Randles-Libersky correction [18], Krongauz-Belytschko correction [19], Monaghan's symmetrization on derivative approximation [20], etc. However, the SPH shape functions are still non-interpolant and do not verify the Kronecker-delta property. Under these circumstances, the imposition of Dirichlet boundary conditions proves to be more challenging in meshfree methods compared to the finite element method.

Moving Least Squares (MLS) serves as a method for attaining high-accuracy approximations based on specified nodes within a domain, initially proposed by Lancaster and Salkauskas [21] for curve and surface fitting. After its successful application in solid mechanics, notably in the Diffuse Element Method (DEM) introduced by Nayroles et al. [22], MLS has been integrated into various meshfree techniques, including SPH [23], RKPM [24] and the Immersed Boundary Method (IBM) [25]. MLS typically employs a polynomial basis to meet consistency conditions: any consistency order can be reached provided the order of the polynomial basis is high enough. Nevertheless, the utilization of a high-order polynomial basis introduces potential challenges, such as the negativity of shape functions. In addition, similarly to SPH, MLS lacks satisfaction of the Kronecker-delta property along boundaries. The efficient imposition of essential boundary conditions in Galerkin-based meshfree methods remains a challenge.

The approximation scheme used in NEM, where elements are defined based on the natural connectivity of nodes, is referred to as natural neighbour (NN) interpolation. It constructs interpolants based on the natural neighbour coordinates, drawing from foundational works by Sibson [26,27] and Belikov [28,29]. Following the application of NEM to elliptic boundary value problems in solid mechanics by Sukumar [13], Chinesta et al. further extended NEM to structural and process simulations [30]. While NEM demonstrates remarkable completeness and accuracy, as validated by Sukumar [31], it does entail a substantial computational cost, particularly for Sibson interpolation. An analysis, made by Alfaro et al. [32], showed that Sibson interpolation demands computational efforts several orders of magnitude greater than traditional piecewise polynomial interpolation in finite elements. However, in the realm of nonlinear computations, where frequent Newton-Raphson iterations are essential, the relative cost of calculating the interpolants becomes less prominent in comparison to the computational load associated with updating the tangent stiffness matrix.

More recently, there has been a growing interest in maximum-entropy (max-ent) approximation schemes within the category of meshfree particle methods. In Sukumar's original work [33], max-ent approximation is applied to polygonally-shaped simplices in order to circumvent the challenges associated with full matrices. Successive research on the robustness, efficiency, and versatility of the max-ent approximation scheme include but are not limited to the convergence analysis [34], the automatic adaptation of support size [35], and higher-order consistency max-ent schemes [36].

Leveraging the principles of the maximum-entropy and delaunay triangulation, Arroyo and Ortiz [37] proposed the Local Maximum-Entropy (LME) approximation scheme as a statistical inference problem, incorporating the positivity and consistency requirements as constraints. This scheme bears similarities with those obtained from MLS, but possesses the weak Kronecker-delta property at the boundary, which allows the direct imposition of essential boundary conditions. Hence, the LME approximation has demonstrated its accuracy and stability in dealing with problems involving large deformation and phase transition when employed as shape functions. Additionally, the LME approximation is incorporated in constructing the surrogate models for structural reliability analysis, offering an accurate and robust approach for highly nonlinear problems [38,39].

By integrating optimal transportation theory with the LME approximation scheme, Li and Ortiz [15,16] developed the Optimal Transportation Meshfree method. The optimal transportation theory establishes a robust theoretical foundation for the explicit time integration algorithm, ensuring momentum conservation and symplecticity in time discretization. For spatial discretization, the OTM method employs the material point sampling method, where the computational domain is described by two sets of points, i.e., nodes and material points. Nodes store kinematic information, and material points preserve mechanical information and serve as integration points. The connection between nodes and material points are constructed dynamically, and LME approximation is introduced as the shape functions. In this way, the OTM method overcomes the challenges in SPH, including tensile instability issues and imposing Dirichlet boundary conditions. These advantageous features effectively make OTM well-suited for simulating complex mechanical problems such as hyper-velocity impact [40], dynamic crack initiation and propagation [41,42], and thermo-fluid-solid interactions [43,44]. Readers of interest can refer to [15,16] for more theoretical details.

Although numerous meshfree methods were initially introduced with a specific approximation scheme, they are able to adapt and utilize various types of shape functions to approximate unknowns as long as the chosen kernel maintains the essential characteristics required for the method. Sukumar [45] has presented an overview of the comparisons and links between different meshfree approximation schemes, with emphasis on the construction of shape functions. However, limited attention has been given to evaluating the performance of distinct schemes within the same meshfree Galerkin method. This paper addresses this gap by selecting the Moving Least Squares and Local Maximum-Entropy approximation schemes for nodal interpolation within the framework of the OTM method. The efficiency, accuracy, and capability of these two approximation schemes are studied by comparing their solutions to the given boundary value problems.

The outline of this paper is as follows. A comprehensive overview of the construction of the LME and MLS approximates are described in Section 2. In Section 2.3, a blending algorithm for MLS to enforce essential boundary conditions is outlined. Section 3 is dedicated to presenting verification tests aimed at comparing the limitations and key advantages of both methods, and we close with a few concluding remarks in Section 4.

2. Materials and Methods

2.1. Local Maximum Entropy Approximation

In this section, we present a brief review of the construction of Local Maximum-Entropy approximation scheme. LME represents a compromise between shape function locality [46] and global entropy [47] in the sense of Pareto optimality. Elements of the pareto set provide a smooth transition between finite element interpolants and meshfree approximants.

Consider a finite set of N distinct nodes in d dimensions, $X = \{\mathbf{x}_a, a = 1, \cdots, N\}$, with nodal coordinates $\mathbf{x}_a \in \mathbb{R}^d$. The domain bounded by the convex hull of X is denoted as $\Omega \subset \mathbb{R}^d$. Shape functions of a fixed point $\mathbf{x}$ over the convex domain Ω are defined for every node $\mathbf{x}_a$ as the solution of a convex constrained optimization problem:

$$\begin{aligned}
\text{(LME) For fixed } \mathbf{x} \in \Omega, \text{ minimize} \quad & f_\beta(\mathbf{x}, \mathbf{N}) \equiv \beta \sum_{a=1}^{n} N_a ||\mathbf{x} - \mathbf{x_a}||^2 + \sum_{a=1}^{n} N_a \log N_a, \\
\text{subject to} \quad & N_a(\mathbf{x}) \geq 0, \ a = 1, \ldots, N, \\
& \sum N_a(\mathbf{x}) = 1, \\
& \sum N_a(\mathbf{x}) \mathbf{x}_a = \mathbf{x},
\end{aligned} \tag{1}$$

where $\mathbf{N} = (N_1, \cdots, N_N)^T$ is the vector of shape functions, and $\beta \in (0, +\infty)$ is Pareto optimal, which takes global max-ent ($\beta \to 0$) and local delaunay ($\beta \to \infty$) schemes as limiting cases. The zeroth- and first-order consistency guarantees the reproduction of affine functions by the approximation scheme and the three mathematical constraints together ensure that the solutions are non-negative and consistent under h-refinement. It is noteworthy that the local max-ent approximation can be extended to higher orders of consistency [36], but they are not covered here due to their increasingly intricate formulation.

It is proved in [37] that LME has a unique solution if and only if $\mathbf{x} \in \Omega$. In principle, the problem is solved by the conventional Lagrange multipliers method as below.

By using shifted nodal coordinates $\mathbf{y}_a = \mathbf{x}_a - \mathbf{x}$ and using the zeroth-order consistency constraint, it is possible to rewrite the first-order consistency condition as

$$\sum_{a=1}^{N} N_a(\mathbf{x}_a - \mathbf{x}) \equiv \sum_{a=1}^{N} N_a \mathbf{y}_a = 0. \tag{2}$$

This choice is more efficient and stable in numerical computations than the conditions appear in LME. By introducing the Lagrange multipliers $\boldsymbol{\lambda} \in \mathbb{R}^d$ and $\mu \in \mathbb{R}$, the Lagrangian $\mathcal{L} : \mathbb{R}^N \times \mathbb{R} \times \mathbb{R}^d \mapsto \mathbb{R}$ takes the form:

$$\mathcal{L}(\mathbf{N}, \mu, \boldsymbol{\lambda}) = f_\beta(\mathbf{N}) + \mu\left(\sum_{a=1}^{N} N_a(\mathbf{x}) - 1\right) + \boldsymbol{\lambda} \cdot \sum_{a=1}^{N} N_a \mathbf{y}_a, \tag{3}$$

where the fixed variable $\mathbf{x}$ is omitted in cost function $f_\beta(\mathbf{N})$ for notional simplicity. Now the Lagrange multipliers are ready to be determined by standard duality analysis, which also provide a practical way for the calculation of shape functions.

It is convenient to verify that LME satisfies Slater's condition, in which case strong duality holds. By the KKT (Karush-Kuhn-Tucker) conditions, there exist Lagrange multipliers $\boldsymbol{\lambda}^*$ and μ^* such that $\{\mathbf{N}^*, \mu^*, \boldsymbol{\lambda}^*\}$ is a saddle point of the Lagrangian $\mathcal{L}$:

$$\frac{\partial \mathcal{L}}{\partial N_a}(\mathbf{N}^*, \mu^*, \boldsymbol{\lambda}^*) = 0, \tag{4}$$

$$\sum N_a^*(\mathbf{x}) = 1, \tag{5}$$

$$\sum N_a^*(\mathbf{x}) \mathbf{x}_a = \mathbf{x}, \tag{6}$$

for $\mathbf{x} \in \operatorname{relint}(\Omega)$, where $\mathbf{N}^*$ is the solution to the original problem. From Equation (3), together with conditions (5) and (6), the explicit expression for Equation (4) can be written as

$$\beta||\mathbf{x} - \mathbf{x}_a||^2 + \log N_a^* + 1 + \mu^* + \boldsymbol{\lambda}^* \cdot (\mathbf{x}_a - \mathbf{x}) = 0 \quad a = 1, \ldots, N, \tag{7}$$

whence we obtain the solution of (LME) as

$$N_a^*(\mathbf{x}) = \frac{Z_a(\mathbf{x}, \boldsymbol{\lambda}^*)}{\exp(\mu^* + 1)}, \tag{8}$$

where

$$Z_a(\mathbf{x}, \boldsymbol{\lambda}) = \exp[-\beta||\mathbf{x} - \mathbf{x}_a||^2 + \boldsymbol{\lambda} \cdot (\mathbf{x} - \mathbf{x}_a)], \tag{9}$$

and $Z(\mathbf{x}, \boldsymbol{\lambda}) = \sum_{a=1}^{N} Z_a(\mathbf{x}, \boldsymbol{\lambda})$ is known as the partition function in statistical mechanics.

The Lagrange dual function of the primal problem (1) is given by

$$g(\mu, \boldsymbol{\lambda}) = \inf_{N_a \in \mathbb{R}^+} \mathcal{L}(\mathbf{N}, \mu, \boldsymbol{\lambda}) = -\mu - \exp(-\mu - 1) Z(\mathbf{x}, \boldsymbol{\lambda}), \tag{10}$$

and the dual problem is

$$\max_{\mu \in \mathbb{R}, \boldsymbol{\lambda} \in \mathbb{R}^d} g(\mu, \boldsymbol{\lambda}), \tag{11}$$

whose solutions are the above optimal Lagrange parameters $\boldsymbol{\lambda}^*$ and μ^*. We can simplify the dual function by maximizing over the dual variable μ analytically. For fixed $\boldsymbol{\lambda}$, the objective function is maximized when the derivative with respect to μ equals zero, which gives

$$\mu^* + 1 = \log Z(\mathbf{x}, \boldsymbol{\lambda}). \tag{12}$$

Substituting this optimal value of μ^* back into the dual problem gives the reduced form

$$\min_{\boldsymbol{\lambda} \in \mathbb{R}^d} \log Z(\mathbf{x}, \boldsymbol{\lambda}), \tag{13}$$

which is an unconstrained geometric program (in a convex form) finally to be solved. The function $F(\boldsymbol{\lambda}) \equiv \log Z(\mathbf{x}, \boldsymbol{\lambda})$ for fixed $\mathbf{x}$ is also introduced as a potential function for determining the Lagrange parameter $\boldsymbol{\lambda}$. In our program, it was solved efficiently and robustly by a combination of the Newton-Raphson algorithm and Nelder-Mead simplex algorithm [48].

Note again that the parameter $\beta \in \mathbb{R}^+$ is used to ponder the locality term against the entropy term in the local maximum entropy approximation. In practice, dimensionless parameter γ is used. It is related to β by

$$\gamma = \beta h^2, \tag{14}$$

where h is a local characteristic length of the considered node set X. Hence, the shape functions (8) become

$$N_a(\mathbf{x}) = \frac{1}{Z(\mathbf{x}, \boldsymbol{\lambda}^*)} \exp\left[-\frac{\gamma}{h^2} ||\mathbf{x} - \mathbf{x}_a||^2 + \boldsymbol{\lambda}^* \cdot (\mathbf{x} - \mathbf{x}_a)\right]. \tag{15}$$

Moreover, to obtain a better convergence, the term $\boldsymbol{\lambda}^* \cdot (\mathbf{x} - \mathbf{x}_a)$ is scaled depending on the node density. Figure 1 represents LME shape functions for a one-dimensional node set containing five uniformly distributed nodes with different values of γ. As γ tends to 0, the LME scheme transitions into the global max-ent scheme, yielding non-zero shape functions over the entire domain. With an increase in γ, local influence becomes dominant, making shape functions more compactly supported. At $\gamma = 5$, these shape functions are almost identical to the linear interpolation used in Finite Elements. No matter how γ changes, the non-negativity of shape functions holds, and the weak Kronecker-delta property at the boundary is consistently satisfied.

It is straightforward to apply this theory to an irregular node set with spatially non-uniform γ regardless of the dimension.

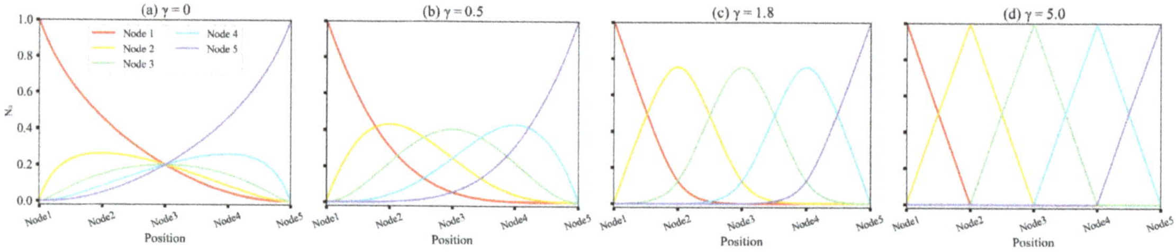

Figure 1. LME shape functions for five uniformly distributed nodes in one dimension with various γ: (**a**) $\gamma = 0$ (global entropy), (**b**) $\gamma = 0.5$, (**c**) $\gamma = 1.8$, (**d**) $\gamma = 5.0$ (local linear interpolation).

The computation of the spatial derivatives of LME shape functions presents challenges, particularly due to the involvement of derivatives of the Lagrange multiplier $\boldsymbol{\lambda}^*(\mathbf{x})$. The general computation procedure with non-uniform $\beta(\mathbf{x})$ and the explicit form of the derivatives with respect to $\mathbf{x}$ are elucidated in the Appendix A of [37]. They are formulated as

$$\nabla N_a = -N_a \mathbf{J}^{*-1} \cdot (\mathbf{x} - \mathbf{x}_a) + N_a K_a \nabla \beta, \tag{16}$$

where

$$K_a = \left[\sum_b N_b ||\mathbf{x} - \mathbf{x}_b||^2 (\mathbf{x} - \mathbf{x}_b) \right] \cdot \mathbf{J}^{*-1} \cdot (\mathbf{x} - \mathbf{x}_a) - ||\mathbf{x} - \mathbf{x}_a||^2 + U(\mathbf{x}, \mathbf{N}), \tag{17}$$

$$\mathbf{J}^* \equiv \partial_\lambda \partial_\lambda \log Z(\mathbf{x}, \boldsymbol{\lambda}^*), \tag{18}$$

$$U(\mathbf{x}, \mathbf{N}) \equiv \sum_b N_b ||\mathbf{x} - \mathbf{x}_b||^2. \tag{19}$$

2.2. Moving Least Squares Approximation

In this section, MLS shape functions are constructed for computing an approximation function $u^h(\mathbf{x})$ of the real solution $u(\mathbf{x})$, while knowing the actual value $u_a \equiv u(\mathbf{x}_a)$ at the nodes $\mathbf{x}_a$. To do so, a local standard least squares is conducted at the computing point $\bar{\mathbf{x}}$ based on minimizing the sum of the squares of the residuals $[u_L^h(\mathbf{x}_a, \bar{\mathbf{x}}) - u_a]^2$ obtained from each node a. While the computing point dynamically moves, the local approximation expression $u_L^h(\mathbf{x}_a, \bar{\mathbf{x}})$ undergoes modifications, leading to oscillations in the curve.

Subsequently, the idea of compact support domain is being considered. This is performed by the use of a predefined weight function $w_a(\mathbf{x}) \equiv w(\mathbf{x} - \mathbf{x}_a)$ combined with a parameter *support radius* ρ_a for each node a. The most basic one is a constant weight function taking 1 within the support domain and 0 outside. While it meets the essential criterion for a weight function to be non-negative and exhibit a monotonically decreasing behavior as the distance $||\mathbf{x} - \mathbf{x}_a||$ increases, it may not be the optimal choice since it fails to reflect the greater significance of contributions from closer nodes. From this perspective, the Gaussian weight function and the cubic spline weight function are the most practical choices, with the latter being more efficient due to the lower computational cost compared to the former, which involves the calculation of an exponential.

The Gaussian weight function, as manifested in LME, has been selected as the weight function for MLS. Similar to the partition function in Equation (15), the Gaussian weight function used in MLS is defined as

$$w_a(\mathbf{x}) = \exp\left[-\frac{\gamma_a}{h_a^2} ||\mathbf{x} - \mathbf{x}_a||^2 \right], \tag{20}$$

where γ_a and h_a have same meanings as in Equation (14) but are limited to node a. The support domain is directly determined by ρ_a, starting from the node and truncated at the periphery of the Gaussian weight function, measured by a parameter *tol* as

$$\rho_a = \sqrt{\frac{-\log tol}{\gamma}} h, \tag{21}$$

from which γ can be deduced if the size of the support domain is given.

The concept of *simplex* is used to stand for the radius of the support domain. As depicted in Figure 2, the 1-simplex, 3-simplices, and 5-simplices support domains correspond to values of ρ_a being h, $3h$, and $5h$, and so forth. Generally, the value of *tol* is often chosen as 10^{-3}, in which case γ would become 6.9, 0.77 and 0.28 for 1-simplex, 3-simplices, and 5-simplices.

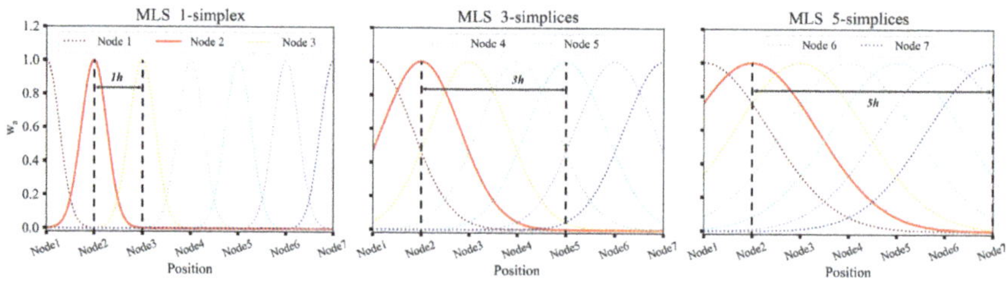

Figure 2. Representatives of support domain under the Gaussian weight function: $\gamma = 6.9$ (1-simplex); $\gamma = 0.77$ (3-simplices); $\gamma = 0.28$ (5-simplices). The truncated tolerance is taken as 10^{-3}.

Let $\bar{\Omega}(\bar{\mathbf{x}})$ be the intersection of support domains of nodes whose weight function are nonzero at $\bar{\mathbf{x}}$. Record these nodes which have overlapping influences on $\bar{\mathbf{x}}$ and label them from 1 to N. Therefore, the weighted least squares functional, also named as the cost function, at a material point $\bar{\mathbf{x}}$, can be written as

$$\begin{aligned} J &= \frac{1}{2}\sum_{a=1}^{N} w_a(\bar{\mathbf{x}})\left[u_L^h(\mathbf{x}_a,\bar{\mathbf{x}}) - u_a\right]^2 \\ &= \frac{1}{2}\sum_{a=1}^{N} w_a(\bar{\mathbf{x}})\left[\mathbf{p}^T(\mathbf{x}_a)\mathbf{g}(\bar{\mathbf{x}}) - u_a\right]^2. \end{aligned} \tag{22}$$

As seen in the above equation, $u_L^h(\mathbf{x},\bar{\mathbf{x}})$ has been resolved into the dot product of a basis function vector $\mathbf{p}(\mathbf{x})$ and a coefficient vector $\mathbf{g}(\bar{\mathbf{x}})$ as

$$\begin{aligned} u_L^h(\mathbf{x},\bar{\mathbf{x}}) &= g_1(\bar{\mathbf{x}})p_1(\mathbf{x}) + g_2(\bar{\mathbf{x}})p_2(\mathbf{x}) + \cdots + g_k(\bar{\mathbf{x}})p_k(\mathbf{x}) \\ &= \sum_{i=1}^{k} g_i(\bar{\mathbf{x}})p_i(\mathbf{x}) = \mathbf{p}^T(\mathbf{x})\mathbf{g}(\bar{\mathbf{x}}). \end{aligned} \tag{23}$$

Note that $\mathbf{p}$ can be any basis functions conserving the properties of independence, including polynomial and trigonometric functions. Generally, it would be set as a complete polynomial of order m here out of simpleness. For instance, if $m = 3$, $\mathbf{p}$ is a cubic polynomial in 1D such that $\mathbf{p} = \left[1\; x\; x^2\; x^3\right]^T$. For the same order in 2D, $\mathbf{p} = \left[1\; x\; y\; x^2\; xy\; y^2\; x^3\; x^2y\; xy^2\; y^3\right]^T$. And for $m = 2$ in 3D, $\mathbf{p} = \left[1\; x\; y\; z\; x^2\; xy\; xz\; y^2\; yz\; z^2\right]^T$. Let k be the number of terms in a complete polynomial basis. It depends on the order m and the dimension, and it can be calculated by the expression listed in Table 1.

Table 1. Calculation of the number of terms in a complete polynomial basis of order m.

Dimension	k
1D	$m+1$
2D	$(m+1)(m+2)/2$
3D	$(m+1)(m+2)(m+3)/6$

$\mathbf{g}(\bar{\mathbf{x}})$ signifies that these coefficients are varying with $\bar{\mathbf{x}}$ and the curve is fitted within the local context. These coefficients are obtained by solving Equation (22).

The functional J can also be written in matrix form as

$$J = \frac{1}{2}(\mathbf{Pg} - \mathbf{u})^T\mathbf{W}(\mathbf{Pg} - \mathbf{u}), \tag{24}$$

where $\mathbf{u}$ is a vector of nodal values

$$\mathbf{u} = \left[u_1 \quad u_2 \quad \cdots \quad u_N\right]^T, \tag{25}$$

$\mathbf{P}$ is formed by $\mathbf{p}^T(\mathbf{x}_a)$ as rows

$$\mathbf{P} = \begin{bmatrix} p_1(\mathbf{x}_1) & p_2(\mathbf{x}_1) & \cdots & p_k(\mathbf{x}_1) \\ \vdots & \ddots & & \vdots \\ \vdots & & \ddots & \vdots \\ p_1(\mathbf{x}_N) & p_2(\mathbf{x}_N) & \cdots & p_k(\mathbf{x}_N) \end{bmatrix}_{N\times k}, \tag{26}$$

and $\mathbf{W}$ is a diagonal N by N matrix such that

$$\mathbf{W} = \begin{bmatrix} w_1(\mathbf{x}) & & & 0 \\ & w_2(\mathbf{x}) & & \\ & & \ddots & \\ 0 & & & w_N(\mathbf{x}) \end{bmatrix}_{N\times N}. \tag{27}$$

To minimize J in (24) with respect to $\mathbf{g}(\bar{\mathbf{x}})$, $\partial J/\partial \mathbf{g} = \mathbf{0}$ leads to

$$\mathbf{P}^T\mathbf{W}\mathbf{P}\mathbf{g} = \mathbf{P}^T\mathbf{W}\mathbf{u}. \tag{28}$$

Now, let $\mathbf{A} = \mathbf{P}^T\mathbf{W}\mathbf{P}$ be the moment matrix and $\mathbf{B} = \mathbf{P}^T\mathbf{W}$. Note that $\mathbf{A}$ is k by k and $\mathbf{B}$ is k by N. $\mathbf{g}$ can be now solved by

$$\mathbf{g} = \mathbf{A}^{-1}\mathbf{B}\mathbf{u}, \tag{29}$$

when $\mathbf{A}$ is non-singular. And the local approximation function $u_L^h(\mathbf{x}, \bar{\mathbf{x}})$ is then given by:

$$u_L^h(\mathbf{x}, \bar{\mathbf{x}}) = \mathbf{p}^T(\mathbf{x})\mathbf{g}(\bar{\mathbf{x}}) = \mathbf{p}^T(\mathbf{x})\mathbf{A}^{-1}(\bar{\mathbf{x}})\mathbf{B}(\bar{\mathbf{x}})\mathbf{u}. \tag{30}$$

Obviously, it is important to discuss how to derive the global MLS approximation function $u^h(\mathbf{x})$ from the local approximation function $u_L^h(\mathbf{x}, \bar{\mathbf{x}})$. Firstly, an interpolated value $u_L^h(\bar{\mathbf{x}}, \bar{\mathbf{x}})$ at $\bar{\mathbf{x}}$ can be obtained from the local approximation, abbreviated as $u_L^h(\bar{\mathbf{x}})$. Numerically, the global MLS approximation is composed of the set of all the evaluations of the local approximation at $\mathbf{x} = \bar{\mathbf{x}}$, i.e.,

$$u^h(\mathbf{x}) = \mathbf{p}^T(\mathbf{x})\mathbf{A}^{-1}(\mathbf{x})\mathbf{B}(\mathbf{x})\mathbf{u}. \tag{31}$$

Rewrite it as a form of shape functions,

$$u^h(\mathbf{x}) = \mathbf{N}(\mathbf{x})\mathbf{u} = \sum_{a=1}^{N} N_a(\mathbf{x})u_a, \tag{32}$$

where N_a is the shape function regarding node $\mathbf{x}_a$, and is defined by:

$$N_a(\mathbf{x}) = \mathbf{p}^T\mathbf{A}^{-1}\mathbf{B}_a, \tag{33}$$

where the subscript a represents the a-th column of matrix $\mathbf{B}$.

Figure 3 shows 1D MLS shape functions for different orders and support sizes. Generally, larger the support domain, the wider the shape functions. When the first-order polynomial basis is used, the shape functions closely resemble those obtained through the LME scheme. But discrepancies arise at two crucial points. Firstly, the non-negativity is broken, as observed in the fourth image with a support domain radius of 4-simplices, where curves dip below zero near the boundary. This issue intensifies with higher-order polynomial bases. Secondly, these shape functions do not satisfy the Kronecker-delta property at the boundaries of Ω_{MLS}, especially with an increased support domain radius. This will arouse difficulties in imposing essential boundary conditions. Excellently, MLS is able to achieve shape functions of high continuity and compatibility by choosing low-order polynomial bases with proper weight functions since the approximation would inherit the continuity of the weight function.

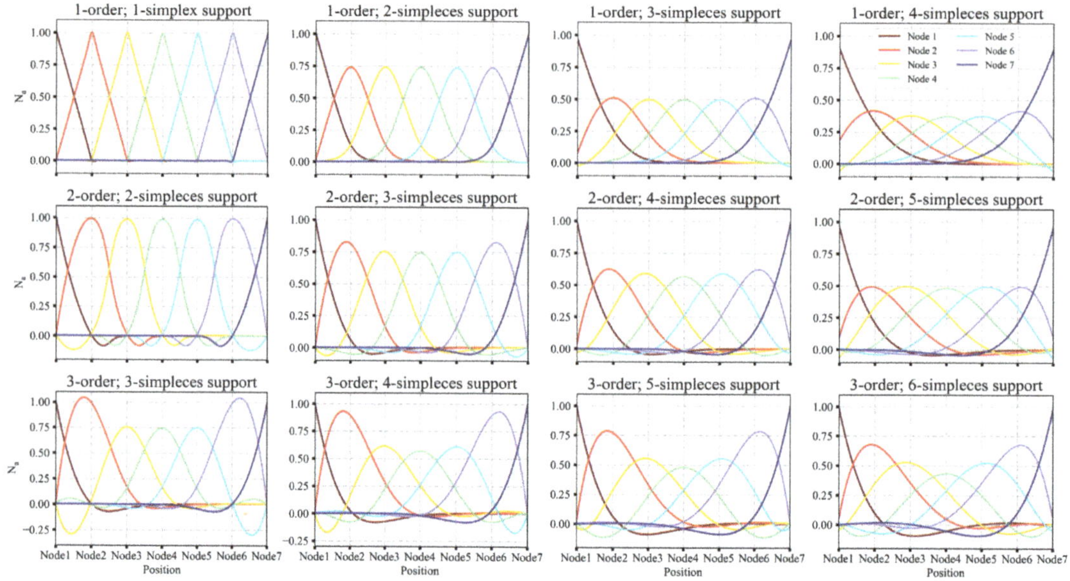

Figure 3. MLS shape functions for different polynomial orders and support sizes in one dimension. The order of polynomial bases ranges from 1 to 3 in rows, and the radius of the support domain ranges from 1-simplex to 6-simplices in columns.

Now, an effective way to compute the derivatives proposed by Belytschko [49] is detailed. Let us define $\mathbf{p}^T(\mathbf{x})\mathbf{A}^{-1}(\mathbf{x})$ as $\boldsymbol{\alpha}^T(\mathbf{x})$. Since $\mathbf{A}$ is symmetric, this equation can also be written as

$$\mathbf{A}\boldsymbol{\alpha} = \mathbf{p}, \tag{34}$$

where $\mathbf{A} = \mathbf{P}^T\mathbf{W}\mathbf{P}$ is the moment matrix defined in the previous section and $\boldsymbol{\alpha}$ a k by 1 vector. Therefore, $\boldsymbol{\alpha}$ can be easily determined by inversing $\mathbf{A}$:

$$\boldsymbol{\alpha} = \mathbf{A}^{-1}\mathbf{p}. \tag{35}$$

Differentiate (34) with respect to $\mathbf{x}$ (denoted by the subscript ", $\mathbf{x}$"):

$$\mathbf{A}_{,\mathbf{x}}\boldsymbol{\alpha} + \mathbf{A}\boldsymbol{\alpha}_{,\mathbf{x}} = \mathbf{p}_{,\mathbf{x}}. \tag{36}$$

Since $\boldsymbol{\alpha}$, $\mathbf{A}$, $\mathbf{A}^{-1}$ are known and $\mathbf{p}_{,\mathbf{x}}$ can be easily found, $\boldsymbol{\alpha}_{,\mathbf{x}}$ is computed as

$$\boldsymbol{\alpha}_{,\mathbf{x}} = \mathbf{A}^{-1}(\mathbf{p}_{,\mathbf{x}} - \mathbf{A}_{,\mathbf{x}}\boldsymbol{\alpha}). \tag{37}$$

The derivatives of shape functions are then given by

$$N_{a,\mathbf{x}} = \boldsymbol{\alpha}_{,\mathbf{x}}^T\mathbf{B}_a + \boldsymbol{\alpha}^T\mathbf{B}_{a,\mathbf{x}}. \tag{38}$$

2.3. Blending Algorithm for MLS

In order to enforce essential boundary conditions through the MLS approximation, Fernandez-Mendez and Huerta [50,51] introduced a blending algorithm, facilitating the coupling of a meshfree approximation with the classic Finite Element (FE) method. This section outlines the procedure for integrating the MLS approximation with FE interpolation.

We are going to build modified MLS shape functions. Let us consider a domain $\Omega = \Omega_{FEM} \cup \Omega_{MLS}$. Ω_{FEM} and Ω_{MLS} represent areas where the FE basis is complete and MLS shape functions are defined, respectively. The region Ω_{MIX}, contained in Ω_{MLS}, denotes the layer of elements where the MLS shape functions should be modified to meet the consistency condition due to incomplete FE bases. From now on, $\hat{N}_a$ will denote the modified MLS shape functions and $N_a^{MIX} = \hat{N}_a + N_a^{FEM}$ will represent the final shape functions in the mixed domain. Examples of the discretized domain in 1D and 2D, where the coupling of FEM and MLS interpolation is applied, are shown in Figures 4 and 5.

Figure 4. Discretized domain in one dimension. Finite element active nodes ○, MLS particles × and support of the incomplete base of FE shape functions Ω_{MIX} (- -).

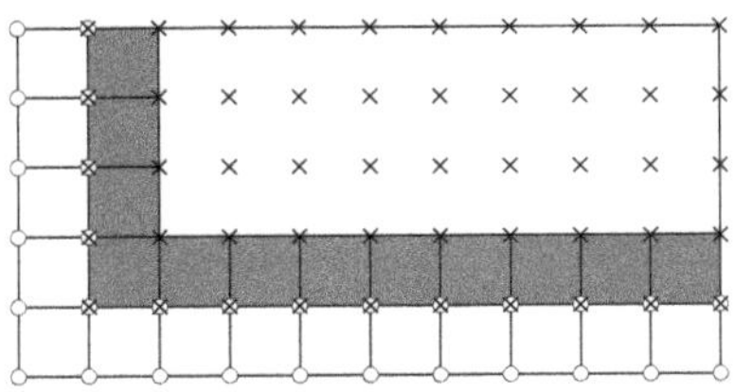

Figure 5. Discretized domain in two dimension. Finite element active nodes ○, MLS particles × and support of the incomplete base of FE shape functions Ω_{MIX} (in gray).

As shown, there are many hybrid nodes which belong to both Ω_{FEM} and Ω_{MLS}. Now let us consider a material point $\mathbf{x}$ in the mixed domain. The objective is to ensure that the new shape functions in the mixed domain satisfy the consistency conditions. Here, two considerations are involved: firstly, the FEM shape functions must remain unchanged, and secondly, the MLS shape functions need to be adjusted to uphold consistency. It is crucial to emphasize that the consistency order is determined by the lowest consistency order verified by the FE shape functions and MLS shape functions separately. For example, if the FE shape functions are linear, then the consistency order of the mixed shape functions will be limited to one.

In order to retain the integrity of the FEM shape functions within the mixed domain, the modified MLS shape functions $\hat{N}_a$ must be set to zero at the mixed nodes to satisfy the consistency equations, which at $\mathbf{x}$ are:

$$\sum_a \hat{N}_a(\mathbf{x})\mathbf{p}(\mathbf{x}_a) + \sum_b N_b^{FEM}(\mathbf{x})\mathbf{p}(\mathbf{x}_b) = \mathbf{p}(\mathbf{x}), \tag{39}$$

where $\mathbf{p}$ is the basis function vector.

Introduce an unknown vector $\mathbf{c}(\mathbf{x}) \equiv [c_1\, c_2\, \ldots\, c_k]^T$ to determine $\hat{N}_a(\mathbf{x})$:

$$\hat{N}_a(\mathbf{x}) = \mathbf{c}^T(\mathbf{x})\mathbf{p}(\mathbf{x}_a)w_a(\mathbf{x}), \tag{40}$$

and Equation (39) thus becomes

$$\mathbf{p}(\mathbf{x}) = \sum_a \mathbf{c}^T(\mathbf{x})\mathbf{p}(\mathbf{x}_a)w_a(\mathbf{x})\mathbf{p}(\mathbf{x}_a) + \sum_b N_b^{FEM}(\mathbf{x})\mathbf{p}(\mathbf{x}_b). \tag{41}$$

Reiterate the definition of the moment matrix $\mathbf{A} = \mathbf{P}^T\mathbf{W}\mathbf{P}$, resulting in

$$\mathbf{A}\mathbf{c} = \mathbf{p}(\mathbf{x}) - \sum_b N_b^{FEM}(\mathbf{x})\mathbf{p}(\mathbf{x}_b), \tag{42}$$

where **c** can be solved as

$$\mathbf{c} = \mathbf{A}^{-1}\left(\mathbf{p}(\mathbf{x}) - \sum_b N_b^{FEM}(\mathbf{x})\mathbf{p}(\mathbf{x}_b)\right). \tag{43}$$

Therefore, we can reuse $\mathbf{B} = \mathbf{P}^T\mathbf{W}$ and rewrite the modified MLS shape functions as following:

$$\hat{N}_a(\mathbf{x}) = \mathbf{A}^{-1}(\mathbf{x})\left(\mathbf{p}(\mathbf{x}) - \sum_b N_b^{FEM}(\mathbf{x})\mathbf{p}(\mathbf{x}_b)\right)\mathbf{B}_a(\mathbf{x}). \tag{44}$$

Finally, the general shape functions N_a are defined over Ω as

$$\forall \mathbf{x} \in \Omega,\ N_a(\mathbf{x}) = \begin{cases} N_a^{FEM}(\mathbf{x}) & \text{if } \mathbf{x} \in \Omega_{FEM} \\ N_a^{FEM}(\mathbf{x}) + \hat{N}_a(\mathbf{x}) & \text{if } \mathbf{x} \in \Omega_{MIX} \\ N_a^{MLS}(\mathbf{x}) & \text{if } \mathbf{x} \in \Omega_{MLS} \setminus \Omega_{MIX} \end{cases}, \tag{45}$$

and the derivatives can be calculated directly from Equation (45):

$$\forall \mathbf{x} \in \Omega,\ N_{a,\mathbf{x}}(\mathbf{x}) = \begin{cases} N_{a,\mathbf{x}}^{FEM}(\mathbf{x}) & \text{if } \mathbf{x} \in \Omega_{FEM} \\ N_{a,\mathbf{x}}^{FEM}(\mathbf{x}) + \hat{N}_{a,\mathbf{x}}(\mathbf{x}) & \text{if } \mathbf{x} \in \Omega_{MIX} \\ N_{a,\mathbf{x}}^{MLS}(\mathbf{x}) & \text{if } \mathbf{x} \in \Omega_{MLS} \setminus \Omega_{MIX} \end{cases}, \tag{46}$$

where the gradient $\hat{N}_{a,\mathbf{x}}$ is obtained by direct derivation of Equation (44):

$$\begin{aligned} \hat{N}_{a,\mathbf{x}}(\mathbf{x}) =& \mathbf{A}_{,\mathbf{x}}^{-1}(\mathbf{x})\left(\mathbf{p}(\mathbf{x}) - \sum_b N_b^{FEM}(\mathbf{x})\mathbf{p}(\mathbf{x}_b)\right)\mathbf{B}_a(\mathbf{x}) \\ &+ \mathbf{A}^{-1}(\mathbf{x})\left(\mathbf{p}_{,\mathbf{x}}(\mathbf{x}) - \sum_b N_{b,\mathbf{x}}^{FEM}(\mathbf{x})\mathbf{p}(\mathbf{x}_b)\right)\mathbf{B}_a(\mathbf{x}) \\ &+ \mathbf{A}^{-1}(\mathbf{x})\left(\mathbf{p}(\mathbf{x}) - \sum_b N_b^{FEM}(\mathbf{x})\mathbf{p}(\mathbf{x}_b)\right)\mathbf{B}_{a,\mathbf{x}}(\mathbf{x}). \end{aligned} \tag{47}$$

Figure 6 shows the mixed shape functions for the one-dimensional case presented in Figure 4.

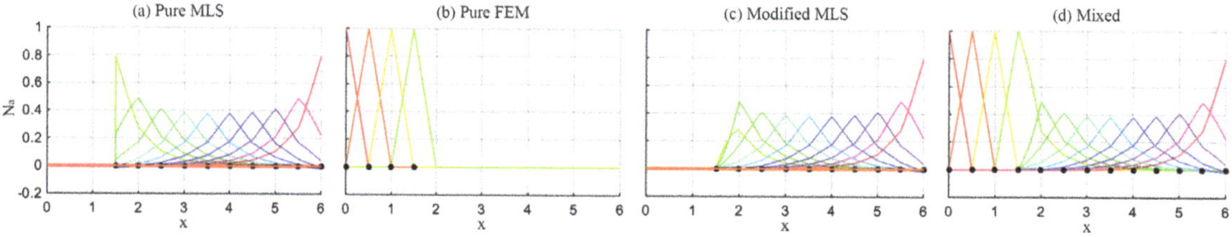

Figure 6. Details of the mixed shape functions from the blending algorithm for a one−dimensional example: (**a**) Pure MLS shape functions in the MLS region; (**b**) Pure FEM shape functions in the FEM region; (**c**) Modified MLS shape functions in the MLS region; (**d**) Mixed shape functions in the whole computational region.

3. Numerical Examples

This section aims to compare the capabilities of LME and MLS approximants within the framework of OTM, focusing on the accuracy and the convergence rate of the numerical solutions. The OTM method utilizes two sets of points: nodal points and material points. Nodal points, containing position information, describe the deformation of a structure, while material points represent the continuum and carry all physical information. Numerical integration is performed based on material points, akin to the MPM [10,52].

To position the material points, a mesh generated by an arbitrary third-party software is employed. After discretizing the computational domain into a list of elements, the material points are created and distributed at positions such as Gauss points through a loop over all the elements. It is crucial to note that the mesh and elements are only used for material point creation, and once this is accomplished, they are no longer needed or used. Only the nodes and the material points are conserved for subsequent computations.

The original MLS approximation scheme, introduced by Belytschko, lacks the Kronecker-delta property at the boundary, making the imposition of essential boundary conditions less straightforward compared to OTM equipped with the LME scheme. In the subsequent thermal examples, a modified MLS, detailed in Section 2.3, is adopted to enforce prescribed values along the boundaries. The numerical errors introduced by essential boundary conditions may be neglected, allowing us to focus on comparing the shape function performance based on their positivity properties. This modification is implemented exclusively at the interpolation level through the blending algorithm, proving to be an efficient, robust, and versatile technique applicable to various meshfree codes, including OTM or EFG. Unlike the original MLS, the modified version ensures both numerical stability and a uniform order of consistency, leading to convergence across the computational domain.

3.1. LME and MLS Shape Functions in 1D

A comparison between the LME and MLS shape functions in one dimension is presented in Figure 7. The dimensionless length has been normalized to the unit and discretized into seven regular nodes. The connection between LME and MLS is established through the dimensionless parameter γ used in Equations (15) and (20) based on the Gaussian weight function. Due to the inherent symmetry of the node set, the two types of shape functions are placed in the same image in a comparative scenario, distinguished by different line styles. LME shape functions are drawn in solid lines at Node1 to Node4, while MLS shape functions are drawn in dashdot lines at Node4 to Node7.

As shown in Figure 7a,b, shape functions for LME and the first-order MLS of the same node almost have no difference within a local context, where the radius of the support domain is smaller than 2-simplices. When the support domain expands, MLS shape functions are likely to take negative values away from the nodal center and fail to satisfy the Kronecker-delta property at the boundary of the domain, as illustrated in Figure 7c,d. The presence of negative shape functions may induce unphysical deformations or responses in the engineering applications, given that physical quantities like temperatures and currents inherently cannot be negative. This can lead to inaccuracies in the predictions of the analysis and make it difficult for iterative solvers to converge.

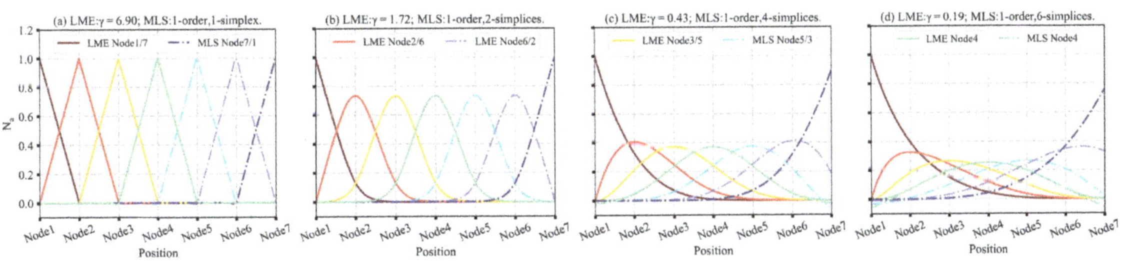

Figure 7. LME and MLS shape functions for a one-dimensional seven-node uniformly distributed node set. The solid line represents LME shape functions for Node1 to Node4, while the dashdot line represents MLS shape functions for Node4 to Node7. Each image encapsulates a distinct γ corresponding to a specific support domain in the first-order MLS: **(a)** $\gamma = 6.90$ to 1-simplex; **(b)** $\gamma = 1.72$ to 2-simplices; **(c)** $\gamma = 0.43$ to 4-simplices; **(d)** $\gamma = 0.19$ to 6-simplices.

Moreover, in the case of a small radius ρ_a, the utilization of high-order polynomial bases in MLS renders the least squares minimization problem ill-posed due to an insufficient number of nodes within the support domain. The usual solution requires the expansion of the influence domain for each material point to eliminate the singularity of the moment matrix **A**. Additionally, Joldes [53] proposed a robust modified MLS method that maintains the support domain size while addressing the singularity issue by augmenting the error functional (24) with additional constraints.

3.2. Approximation of Sine Function in 1D

By using a uniform distribution of 10 nodes within $[0, 8]$, the approximations of a non-polynomial function $u(x) = \sin x$ under LME and MLS for different values of γ and ρ_a are shown in Figure 8. The approximation accuracy is determined by the L_2-*norm*:

$$||e^h||_2^2 = ||u - u^h||_2^2 = \int_0^8 \left(u(x) - u^h(x)\right)^2 dx, \tag{48}$$

where e^h represents the error between the approximated value u^h and the exact value u. The definite integral is estimated by the trapezoid rule of 2000 sub-intervals for numerical integration.

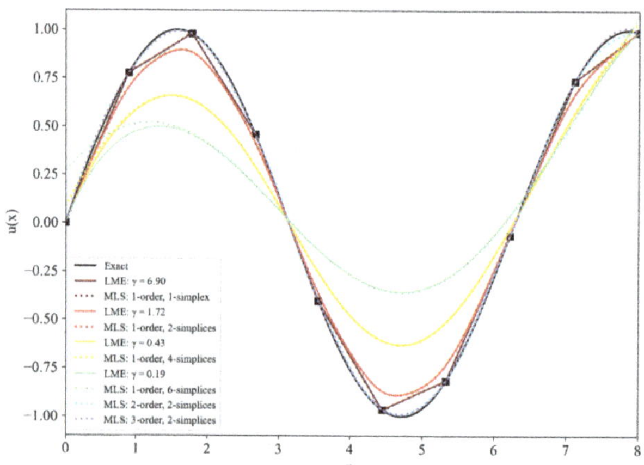

Figure 8. Approximations of the sine function for LME and MLS under different conditions. The black solid line represents the exact solution. The colored solid lines represent the LME approximations, γ being 6.90, 1.72, 0.43 and 0.19. The colored dashdot lines represent the MLS approximations, whose order ranges from 1 to 3.

The outcomes are depicted in Figure 8 and quantified in Table 2. The findings reveal that the approximation accuracy of LME closely aligns with that of the classical first-order MLS when they share similar support domain sizes. Notably, the approximation error diminishes with a reduction in the support domain size. As the support domain size contracts to 1-simplex, both approximations coincide with the linear interpolation used in finite elements. The failure of MLS to satisfy the Kronecker-delta property is confirmed at $x = 0$ and $x = 8$, as observed in the yellow and green dashed lines.

Furthermore, Figure 8 clearly shows the advantage of using higher-order polynomial basis functions. The higher-order MLS has better approximation properties, leading to better solution accuracy as compared to the first-order MLS and LME, albeit at the expense of increased computational effort.

Table 2. Error of approximations of the sine function for LME and MLS under different conditions.

Approximation	$\|u - u^h\|_2^2$	Approximation	$\|u - u^h\|_2^2$
MLS: 1-order, ρ_a = 1-simplex	0.0203	LME: $\gamma = 6.90$	0.0205
MLS: 1-order, ρ_a = 2-simplices	0.0448	LME: $\gamma = 1.72$	0.0451
MLS: 1-order, ρ_a = 3-simplices	0.1742	LME: $\gamma = 0.77$	0.1744
MLS: 1-order, ρ_a = 4-simplices	0.4094	LME: $\gamma = 0.43$	0.4171
MLS: 1-order, ρ_a = 5-simplices	0.7210	LME: $\gamma = 0.28$	0.7226
MLS: 1-order, ρ_a = 6-simplices	1.0615	LME: $\gamma = 0.19$	1.0918
MLS: 2-order, ρ_a = 2-simplices	0.0015		
MLS: 3-order, ρ_a = 2-simplices	0.0006		

3.3. Thermal Problem with Dirichlet Boundary Conditions

In the following two examples, the modified MLS is utilized to impose essential boundary conditions. Once the influence of boundary conditions on the performance of approximation schemes is eliminated, the focus will shift to highlighting the effectiveness of non-negative shape functions.

Here, we consider thermal conduction through a plate whose size is 1 by 1. This Laplace problem is described in the mathematical form (49):

$$\Delta u = 0 \text{ in } \Omega = [0,1]^2, \tag{49a}$$

$$u(0,y) = u(1,y) = u(x,0) = 300, \tag{49b}$$

$$u(x,1) = x(1-x) * 2000 + 300, \tag{49c}$$

of which the exact solution is given by

$$u(x,y) = \frac{4}{\pi^3} \sum_{i=0}^{\infty} \frac{1-(-1)^i}{i^3 \sinh(i\pi)} \sin(i\pi x)\sinh(i\pi y) * 2000 + 300. \tag{50}$$

A representative of the initial mesh of regular nodes is shown in Figure 9, where the neighborhood of each material point is composed of all the nodes within the second ring around it. The result obtained from the LME approximation is given by Figure 10. The LME approximants satisfy a weak Kronecker-delta property at the boundary of the convex hull of the nodes, which facilitates the imposition of essential boundary conditions. In the case of the MLS approximants, the blending algorithm described in the Section 2.3 is used for proper imposition of essential boundary conditions.

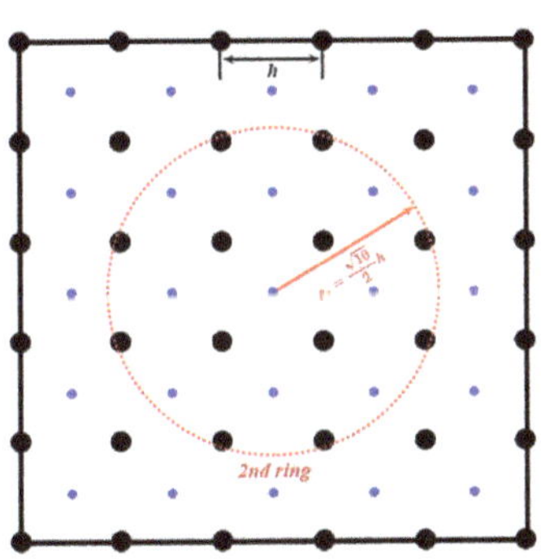

Figure 9. A representative of the investigated regular set of nodes. Black solid line represents the boundary, the black solid circle represents the element node, and the smaller blue circle represents the material point. The second ring region, whose radius ρ_a is $\frac{\sqrt{10}}{2}h$, is denoted by the red dotted curve.

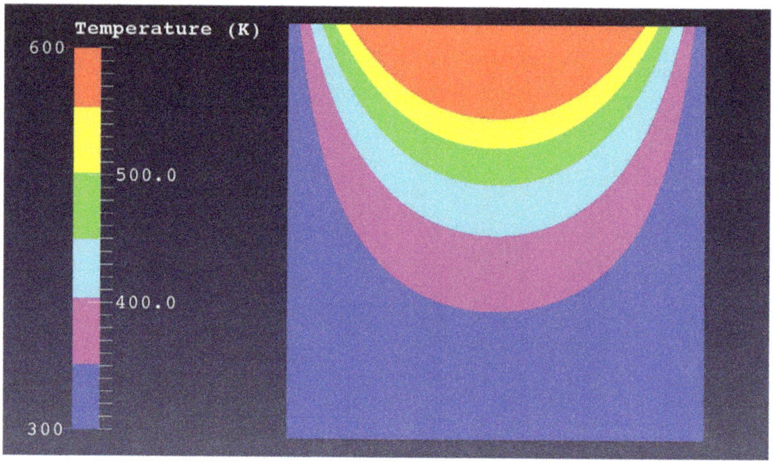

Figure 10. Equilibrium state of the two-dimensional Laplace problem obtained from the LME approximation. The temperature of the upper bound is set as a parabola while the other three sides are set as fixed values.

Figure 11 compares the computed solutions using different approximation schemes with the analytical solution (50) by the L_2-*norm*. The total number of nodes, which are used to fit the convergence rate, varies from 100 to 10,000 in maximum. It shows that both Finite Element Analysis (FEA) and LME analysis have a convergence order of 2 whereas the modified MLS approximation has a smaller convergence order and accuracy.

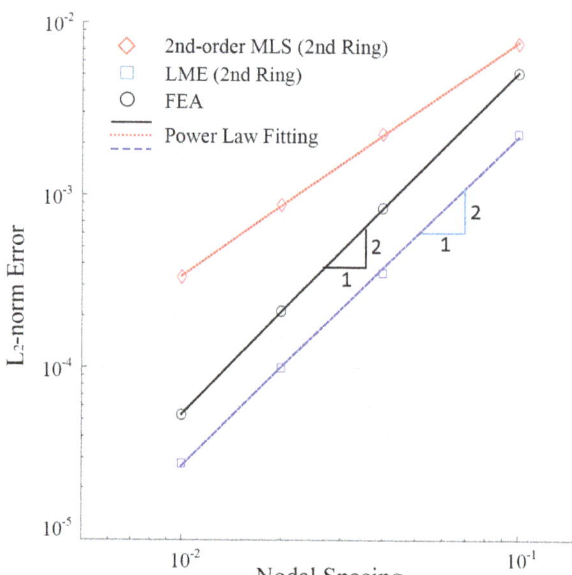

Figure 11. Convergence rate of the Laplace problem for different approximation schemes. The blue dashed line represents a power law fitting result fitted by blue square scatters, which are calculated using the LME approximation scheme at various nodal spacings. The black and red lines represent the corresponding results obtained through FEA and MLS, respectively.

3.4. Thermal Problem with Heat Sources

This example further validates the significance of the non-negativity of shape functions. In this numerical case, localised heat sources are considered in a heat conduction problem and we present the convergence in L_2-*norm* of the FE interpolants, LME approximants and MLS approximants in the Galerkin solution of the Poisson boundary-value problem defined by

$$-\Delta u = s(x,y) \text{ in } \Omega = [0,1]^2, \tag{51a}$$

$$u = \bar{u} \text{ on } \partial\Omega, \tag{51b}$$

where the exact solution of this problem is given by

$$u(x,y) = \sum_{i=1}^{4} A_i e^{-\beta\left[(x-x_i)^2+(y-y_i)^2\right]}. \tag{52}$$

The coefficients that appear in the exact solution are provided in Table 3.

Table 3. Coefficients to calculate the exact solution to the Poisson problem.

i	A_i	β_i	x_i	y_i
1	10	180	0.51	0.52
2	50	450	0.31	0.34
3	100	800	0.73	0.71
4	50	1000	0.28	0.72

The mesh used in this example is same as that illustrated in Figure 9. The equilibrium state obtained from the simulation using the LME approximation is shown in Figure 12.

The total number of nodes to fit the convergence rate varies from 100 to 10,000. As seen in Figure 13, the LME approximation gives both the best accuracy and convergence rate but it is worth noticing that the MLS approximation gives better results in this example than FEA.

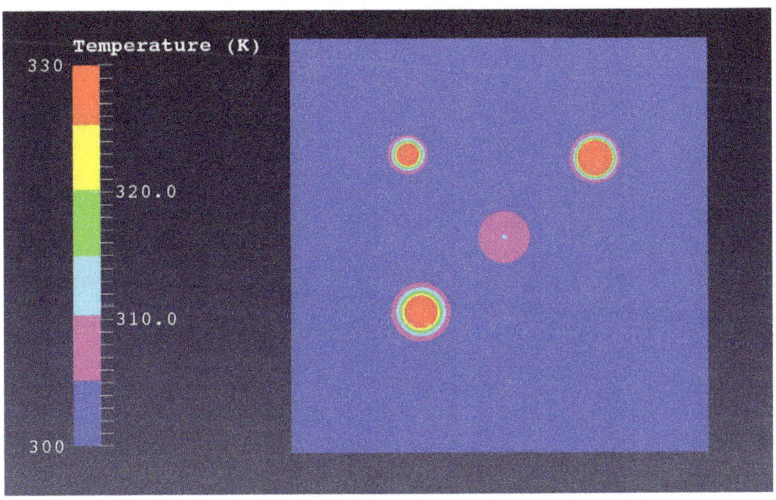

Figure 12. Equilibrium state of the two-dimensional Poisson problem obtained from the LME approximation. The temperature along the four sides is prescribed as a fixed value and four heat sources are distributed within the domain.

As observed in the preceding two examples, the accuracy of the solution is closely linked to the characteristics of the shape functions in numerous numerical methods. Positive shape functions are more likely to be compatible with certain physical fields. Specifically, in the realm of heat conduction analysis, the incorporation of positive temperature shape functions ensures that the physical constraints are satisfied and makes the numerical solution more physically meaningful.

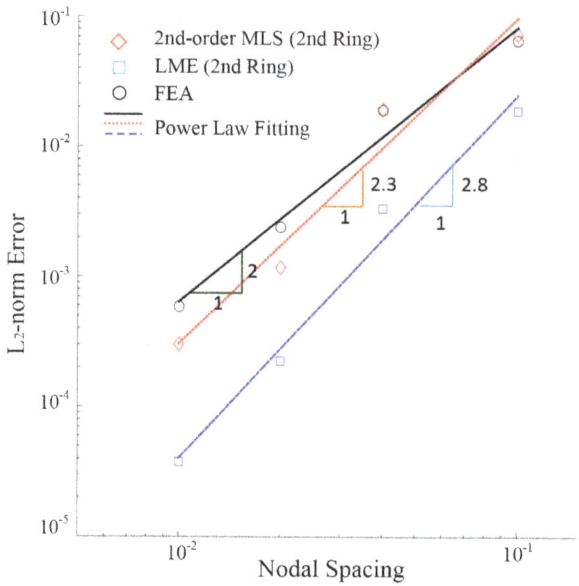

Figure 13. Convergence rate of the Poisson problem for different approximation schemes. The blue dashed line represents a power law fitting result fitted by blue square scatters, which are calculated using the LME approximation scheme at various nodal spacings. The black and red lines represent the corresponding results obtained through FEA and MLS, respectively.

4. Conclusions

This paper presents a thorough examination of two prominent approximation techniques, specifically, the Local Maximum-Entropy and Moving Least Squares methods, within the context of Optimal Transportation Meshfree, a Galerkin-based meshfree approach. Four numerical experiments were undertaken to elucidate the comparisons and interrelations between these schemes. These experiments involved an analysis of their shape function characteristics, assessing their capabilities in approximating non-polynomial functions and performance in numerical simulations.

Our studies highlight the significance of maintaining the positivity of shape functions and their weak Kronecker-delta property at the boundary for ensuring the stability, accuracy, and physical interpretability of numerical solutions across diverse applications. It facilitates a convenient implementation of the essential boundary conditions commonly encountered in thermal-mechanical problems. Furthermore, when solving heat transfer equations using the OTM method, we observed that the accuracy and convergence rate are superior when employing the LME shape functions compared to MLS approximation.

Our results indicate that the classical LME performs comparably to first-order MLS using the Gaussian weight function in a regular node set. However, as the consistency order is raised, both methods demonstrate enhanced accuracy. The straightforward extension of MLS to higher orders makes it a preferred option when striving for highly accurate results. However, in the case of irregular nodal distribution, modifications [53–55] to MLS become necessary to enable the use of high-order basis functions without expanding the support domain.

In general, when conducting a comparative analysis of the Local Maximum-Entropy and Moving Least Squares approximation schemes, it becomes evident that both methods exhibit significant utility within the OTM framework for solving engineering problems. The selection between these approaches may hinge on factors such as computational efficiency and the type of differential equations. Consequently, it is crucial to meticulously assess the distinctive attributes of the data and the underlying nature of the problem before making a decision.

Author Contributions: Conceptualization, methodology and formal analysis made by H.Y. and B.L.; original draft preparation, review and editing by H.Y. and H.W.; supervision, project administration, and funding acquisition, B.L. All authors have read and agreed to the published version of the manuscript.

Funding: This research was supported by the National Natural Science Foundation of China (Grant No. 12372205).

Data Availability Statement: No new data were created or analyzed in this study. Data sharing is not applicable to this article.

Acknowledgments: The authors are grateful for the comprehensive discussions with N. Sukumar at University of California, Davis. Additionally, we acknowledge the generous funding support of the National Natural Science Foundation of China under Grant No.12372205 for this study.

Conflicts of Interest: The authors declare no conflict of interest.

References

1. Belytschko, T.; Krongauz, Y.; Organ, D.; Fleming, M.; Krysl, P. Meshless methods: An overview and recent developments. *Comput. Methods Appl. Mech. Eng.* **1996**, *139*, 3–47. [CrossRef]
2. Liu, G. An overview on meshfree methods: For computational solid mechanics. *Int. J. Comput. Methods* **2016**, *13*, 1630001. [CrossRef]
3. Chen, J.S.; Hillman, M.; Chi, S.W. Meshfree methods: Progress made after 20 years. *J. Eng. Mech.* **2017**, *143*, 04017001. [CrossRef]
4. Lucy, L.B. A numerical approach to the testing of the fission hypothesis. *Astron. J.* **1977**, *82*, 1013–1024. [CrossRef]
5. Gingold, R.A.; Monaghan, J.J. Smoothed particle hydrodynamics: Theory and application to non-spherical stars. *Mon. Not. R. Astron. Soc.* **1977**, *181*, 375–389. [CrossRef]
6. Liu, G.R.; Liu, M.B. *Smoothed Particle Hydrodynamics: A Meshfree Particle Method*; World Scientific: Singapore, 2003.
7. Belytschko, T.; Lu, Y.Y.; Gu, L. Element-free Galerkin methods. *Int. J. Numer. Methods Eng.* **1994**, *37*, 229–256. [CrossRef]
8. Dolbow, J.; Belytschko, T. An introduction to programming the meshless Element F reeGalerkin method. *Arch. Comput. Methods Eng.* **1998**, *5*, 207–241. [CrossRef]
9. Liu, W.K.; Jun, S.; Zhang, Y.F. Reproducing kernel particle methods. *Int. J. Numer. Methods Fluids* **1995**, *20*, 1081–1106. [CrossRef]
10. Sulsky, D.; Chen, Z.; Schreyer, H.L. A particle method for history-dependent materials. *Comput. Methods Appl. Mech. Eng.* **1994**, *118*, 179–196. [CrossRef]
11. Zhang, X.; Chen, Z.; Liu, Y. *The Material Point Method: A Continuum-Based Particle Method for Extreme Loading Cases*; Academic Press: Cambridge, MA, USA, 2016.
12. Braun, J.; Sambridge, M. A numerical method for solving partial differential equations on highly irregular evolving grids. *Nature* **1995**, *376*, 655–660. [CrossRef]
13. Sukumar, N.; Moran, B.; Belytschko, T. The natural element method in solid mechanics. *Int. J. Numer. Methods Eng.* **1998**, *43*, 839–887. [CrossRef]
14. Sukumar, N.; Moran, B.; Yu Semenov, A.; Belikov, V. Natural neighbour Galerkin methods. *Int. J. Numer. Methods Eng.* **2001**, *50*, 1–27. [CrossRef]
15. Li, B.; Habbal, F.; Ortiz, M. Optimal transportation meshfree approximation schemes for fluid and plastic flows. *Int. J. Numer. Methods Eng.* **2010**, *83*, 1541–1579. [CrossRef]
16. Wang, H.; Liao, H.; Fan, Z.; Fan, J.; Stainier, L.; Li, X.; Li, B. The Hot Optimal Transportation Meshfree (HOTM) method for materials under extreme dynamic thermomechanical conditions. *Comput. Methods Appl. Mech. Eng.* **2020**, *364*, 112958. [CrossRef]
17. Johnson, G.R.; Beissel, S.R. Normalized smoothing functions for SPH impact computations. *Int. J. Numer. Methods Eng.* **1996**, *39*, 2725–2741. [CrossRef]
18. Randles, P.; Libersky, L. Smoothed particle hydrodynamics: Some recent improvements and applications. *Comput. Methods Appl. Mech. Eng.* **1996**, *139*, 375–408. [CrossRef]
19. Belytschko, T.; Krongauz, Y.; Dolbow, J.; Gerlach, C. On the completeness of meshfree particle methods. *Int. J. Numer. Methods Eng.* **1998**, *43*, 785–819. [CrossRef]

20. Monaghan, J.J. Smoothed particle hydrodynamics. *Rep. Prog. Phys.* **2005**, *68*, 1703. [CrossRef]
21. Lancaster, P.; Salkauskas, K. Surfaces generated by moving least squares methods. *Math. Comput.* **1981**, *37*, 141–158. [CrossRef]
22. Nayroles, B.; Touzot, G.; Villon, P. Generalizing the finite element method: Diffuse approximation and diffuse elements. *Comput. Mech.* **1992**, *10*, 307–318. [CrossRef]
23. Ghoneim, A.Y. A smoothed particle hydrodynamics-phase field method with radial basis functions and moving least squares for meshfree simulation of dendritic solidification. *Appl. Math. Model.* **2020**, *77*, 1704–1741. [CrossRef]
24. Salehi, R.; Dehghan, M. A generalized moving least square reproducing kernel method. *J. Comput. Appl. Math.* **2013**, *249*, 120–132. [CrossRef]
25. Spandan, V.; Lohse, D.; de Tullio, M.D.; Verzicco, R. A fast moving least squares approximation with adaptive Lagrangian mesh refinement for large scale immersed boundary simulations. *J. Comput. Phys.* **2018**, *375*, 228–239. [CrossRef]
26. Sibson, R. A vector identity for the Dirichlet tessellation. In *Mathematical Proceedings of the Cambridge Philosophical Society*; Cambridge University Press: Cambridge, UK, 1980; Volume 87, pp. 151–155.
27. Sibson, R. A brief description of natural neighbour interpolation. In *Interpreting Multivariate Data*; John Wiley & Sons: New York, NY, USA, 1981; pp. 21–36.
28. Belikov, V.; Ivanov, V.; Kontorovich, V.; Korytnik, S.; Semenov, A.Y. The non-Sibsonian interpolation: A new method of interpolation of the values of a function on an arbitrary set of points. *Comput. Math. Math. Phys.* **1997**, *37*, 9–15.
29. Belikov, V.V.; Semenov, A.Y. Non-Sibsonian interpolation on arbitrary system of points in Euclidean space and adaptive isolines generation. *Appl. Numer. Math.* **2000**, *32*, 371–387. [CrossRef]
30. Chinesta, F.; Cescotto, S.; Cueto, E.; Lorong, P. *Natural Element Method for the Simulation of Structures and Processes*; John Wiley & Sons: Hoboken, NJ, USA, 2013.
31. Sukumar, N.; Moran, B. C^1 natural neighbor interpolant for partial differential equations. *Numer. Methods Partial. Differ. Equ.* **1999**, *15*, 417–447. [CrossRef]
32. Alfaro, I.; Bel, D.; Cueto, E.; Doblare, M.; Chinesta, F. Three-dimensional simulation of aluminium extrusion by the α-shape based natural element method. *Comput. Methods Appl. Mech. Eng.* **2006**, *195*, 4269–4286. [CrossRef]
33. Sukumar, N. Construction of polygonal interpolants: A maximum entropy approach. *Int. J. Numer. Methods Eng.* **2004**, *61*, 2159–2181. [CrossRef]
34. Bompadre, A.; Schmidt, B.; Ortiz, M. Convergence analysis of meshfree approximation schemes. *SIAM J. Numer. Anal.* **2012**, *50*, 1344–1366. [CrossRef]
35. Rosolen, A.; Millán, D.; Arroyo, M. On the optimum support size in meshfree methods: A variational adaptivity approach with maximum-entropy approximants. *Int. J. Numer. Methods Eng.* **2010**, *82*, 868–895. [CrossRef]
36. González, D.; Cueto, E.; Doblaré, M. A higher order method based on local maximum entropy approximation. *Int. J. Numer. Methods Eng.* **2010**, *83*, 741–764. [CrossRef]
37. Arroyo, M.; Ortiz, M. Local maximum-entropy approximation schemes: A seamless bridge between finite elements and meshfree methods. *Int. J. Numer. Methods Eng.* **2006**, *65*, 2167–2202. [CrossRef]
38. Fan, J.; Liao, H.; Wang, H.; Hu, J.; Chen, Z.; Lu, J.; Li, B. Local maximum-entropy based surrogate model and its application to structural reliability analysis. *Struct. Multidiscip. Optim.* **2018**, *57*, 373–392. [CrossRef]
39. Fan, J.; Yuan, Q.; Jing, F.; Xu, H.; Wang, H.; Meng, Q. Adaptive local maximum-entropy surrogate model and its application to turbine disk reliability analysis. *Aerospace* **2022**, *9*, 353. [CrossRef]
40. Jiang, H.; Wang, H.; Scott, V.; Li, B. Numerical analysis of oblique hypervelocity impact damage to space structural materials by ice particles in cryogenic environment. *Acta Astronaut.* **2022**, *195*, 392–404. [CrossRef]
41. Fan, Z.; Liao, H.; Jiang, H.; Wang, H.; Li, B. A dynamic adaptive eigenfracture method for failure in brittle materials. *Eng. Fract. Mech.* **2021**, *244*, 107540. [CrossRef]
42. Navas, P.; Rena, C.Y.; Li, B.; Ruiz, G. Modeling the dynamic fracture in concrete: An eigensoftening meshfree approach. *Int. J. Impact Eng.* **2018**, *113*, 9–20. [CrossRef]
43. Wang, H.; Li, X.; Phipps, M.; Li, B. Numerical and experimental study of hot pressing technique for resin-based friction composites. *Compos. Part A Appl. Sci. Manuf.* **2022**, *153*, 106737. [CrossRef]
44. Huang, Z.; Wang, H.; Chen, L.; Gomez, H.; Li, B.; Cao, C. A meshfree phase-field model for simulating the sintering process of metallic particles for printed electronics. *Eng. Comput.* **2023**, 1–17. [CrossRef]
45. Sukumar, N.; Wright, R. Overview and construction of meshfree basis functions: From moving least squares to entropy approximants. *Int. J. Numer. Methods Eng.* **2007**, *70*, 181–205. [CrossRef]
46. Rajan, V. Optimality of the Delaunay triangulation in $\mathbb{R}^d$. *Discret. Comput. Geom.* **1994**, *12*, 189–202. [CrossRef]
47. Shannon, C.E. A mathematical theory of communication. *ACM SIGMOBILE Mob. Comput. Commun. Rev.* **2001**, *5*, 3–55. [CrossRef]
48. Nelder, J.A.; Mead, R. A simplex method for function minimization. *Comput. J.* **1965**, *7*, 308–313. [CrossRef]
49. Belytschko, T.; Krongauz, Y.; Fleming, M.; Organ, D.; Liu, W.K.S. Smoothing and accelerated computations in the element free Galerkin method. *J. Comput. Appl. Math.* **1996**, *74*, 111–126. [CrossRef]
50. Huerta, A.; Fernández-Méndez, S. Enrichment and coupling of the finite element and meshless methods. *Int. J. Numer. Methods Eng.* **2000**, *48*, 1615–1636. [CrossRef]
51. Fernández-Méndez, S.; Huerta, A. Imposing essential boundary conditions in mesh-free methods. *Comput. Methods Appl. Mech. Eng.* **2004**, *193*, 1257–1275. [CrossRef]

52. Sulsky, D.; Zhou, S.J.; Schreyer, H.L. Application of a particle-in-cell method to solid mechanics. *Comput. Phys. Commun.* **1995**, *87*, 236–252. [CrossRef]
53. Joldes, G.R.; Chowdhury, H.A.; Wittek, A.; Doyle, B.; Miller, K. Modified moving least squares with polynomial bases for scattered data approximation. *Appl. Math. Comput.* **2015**, *266*, 893–902. [CrossRef]
54. Tey, W.Y.; Che Sidik, N.A.; Asako, Y.; Muhieldeen, M.W.; Afshar, O. Moving least squares method and its improvement: A concise review. *J. Appl. Comput. Mech.* **2021**, *7*, 883–889.
55. Matinfar, M.; Pourabd, M. Modified moving least squares method for two-dimensional linear and nonlinear systems of integral equations. *Comput. Appl. Math.* **2018**, *37*, 5857–5875. [CrossRef]

Disclaimer/Publisher's Note: The statements, opinions and data contained in all publications are solely those of the individual author(s) and contributor(s) and not of MDPI and/or the editor(s). MDPI and/or the editor(s) disclaim responsibility for any injury to people or property resulting from any ideas, methods, instructions or products referred to in the content.

MDPI AG
Grosspeteranlage 5
4052 Basel
Switzerland
Tel.: +41 61 683 77 34

Mathematics Editorial Office
E-mail: mathematics@mdpi.com
www.mdpi.com/journal/mathematics

Disclaimer/Publisher's Note: The title and front matter of this reprint are at the discretion of the Guest Editors. The publisher is not responsible for their content or any associated concerns. The statements, opinions and data contained in all individual articles are solely those of the individual Editors and contributors and not of MDPI. MDPI disclaims responsibility for any injury to people or property resulting from any ideas, methods, instructions or products referred to in the content.

www.ingramcontent.com/pod-product-compliance
Lightning Source LLC
Chambersburg PA
CBHW041950260926
51850CB00019B/2306
* 9 7 8 3 7 2 5 8 4 7 0 5 1 *